STATE OF THE
WORLD
1987

Other Norton/Worldwatch Books

Lester R. Brown et al.
State of the World — 1984
State of the World — 1985
State of the World — 1986

STATE OF THE WORLD
1987

A Worldwatch Institute Report on Progress Toward a Sustainable Society

PROJECT DIRECTOR
Lester R. Brown

ASSOCIATE PROJECT DIRECTOR
Edward C. Wolf

EDITOR
Linda Starke

SENIOR RESEARCHERS
Lester R. Brown
William U. Chandler
Christopher Flavin
Cynthia Pollock
Sandra Postel
Edward C. Wolf

RESEARCHER
Jodi Jacobson

W·W·NORTON & COMPANY

NEW YORK   LONDON

Published simultaneously in Canada by Penguin Books Canada Ltd., 2801 John Street,
Markham, Ontario L3R 1B4.
Printed in the United States of America.

The text of this book is composed in Baskerville, with
display type set in Caslon. Composition and
manufacturing by The Haddon Craftsmen, Inc.

ISBN 0-393-02399-0

ISBN 0-393-30389-6 (PBK)

W. W. Norton & Company, Inc., 500 Fifth Avenue, New York, N.Y. 10110
W. W. Norton & Company Ltd., 37 Great Russell Street, London WC1B 3NU

2 3 4 5 6 7 8 9 0

Acknowledgments

State of the World 1987, like its predecessors, could not be published without the help of a great many people beyond the authors of the report.

We have been fortunate since the inception of the *State of the World* series to have the sustained support and enthusiasm of William Dietel, President of the Rockefeller Brothers Fund. RBF and the Winthrop Rockefeller Trust, which along with David Rockefeller provided start-up funding for *State of the World*, have maintained their commitment to the project. Beginning this year, the George Gund Foundation is also providing support for *State of the World*.

The 1987 volume draws on Institute work supported by the Edna McConnell Clark, Geraldine R. Dodge, William and Flora Hewlett, W. Alton Jones, Andrew W. Mellon, Edward John Noble, and Jessie Smith Noyes Foundations and by the United Nations Fund for Population Activities.

Timely production of *State of the World* is largely due to the efforts of two people at W.W. Norton & Company: Iva Ashner and Andy Marasia. Iva handles the administrative responsibilities, while Andy manages the production of the book from the time he receives our word processing disks. Their commitment to the project ensures both speedy production and a delightful Norton/Worldwatch working relationship.

Among the most important contributions made to *State of the World* are the comments of outside reviewers who help the authors shape and refine their ideas. This year that capable group included Douglas Barnes, József Bognár, Robert Civiak, Paul Clark, Dieter Deumling, Chris Dodge, Andrea Fella, James Fish, Howard Geller, John H. Gibbons, Nora Goldstein, Nigel Green, Holly L. Gwin, Carl Haub, Maureen Hinkle, Don Hinrichsen, Bruce Horwith, Gábor Hoványi, Judith Jacobsen, William Kellogg, Peter Knight, Justin Lancaster, István Láng, William Liebhardt, Gene Likens, Ben Livingston, James MacKenzie, Thomas Merrick, Alan Miller, Charles Movit, Lorie Parker, Jerry Powell, Paul Rankin, Robert Rodale, Ralph Rotty, Mark Silberman, Joseph Speidel, John Stuyt, Ed Sulzberger, Ken Tull, Arthur Vander, Stephen Viederman, Garth Youngberg, and David Zoellner. Errors that remain are, of course, the responsibility of the authors.

Linda Starke edited and coordinated production of this fourth edition of *State of the World*, as she has the previous three. Authors are indebted to Linda for her sure editorial judgment, sound stylistic and aesthetic sense, and unbending enforcement of a tight production schedule. This year, as last, the index that enhances the book's value as a reference was compiled by Bart Brown.

Capable research assistance, which strengthens all the work of the Institute, is particularly important in the production of *State of the World*. The authors are grateful to Angela Coyle (Chapter 10), Gretchen Daily (Chapter 9), and Alan

Durning (Chapters 4 and 8) for their reliable and insightful assistance. Jodi Jacobson, coauthor of Chapter 3, made substantive contributions to Chapters 1, 2, and 7 as well.

Our greatest debt is to the other members of the Worldwatch Institute staff, full partners in all facets of the *State of the World* project. Reah Janise Battenfield, Jodi Johnson, and Susan Norris typed chapter drafts and oversaw the book's demanding gestation. Cynthia Bainton and Jodi Johnson coordinated sales of Worldwatch Papers and *State of the World* that exceeded all previous records. Robin Bell, new Director of Communications, managed the outreach and marketing of *State of the World* while editing seven Worldwatch Papers in the course of the year. Brian Brown again split his time between maintaining the flow of papers and magazines in the office and competing as a member of the U.S. Kayak Team. Our gratitude, too, goes to Pamela Berkeley and Colleen Bickman, who left the Institute for other pursuits this year, and to Claver Bickman and Linda Doherty, who pitched in when we needed extra hands.

Above all, we thank Worldwatch Vice President Blondeen Gravely, whose skillful administration eases the burden on researchers and support staff alike. The guidance provided by the Institute's Board of Directors, chaired by Orville Freeman, likewise reinforces our commitment to raise awareness about the challenges that face humanity.

Lester R. Brown and Edward C. Wolf

Contents

Tables and Figures

LIST OF TABLES

LIST OF FIGURES

Foreword

When we decided, with the encouragement of the Rockefeller Brothers Fund, to launch the *State of the World* reports, beginning with 1984, we expected there would be a strong demand. We did not anticipate the rate at which the demand would grow. Using virtually any indicator—sales, translations, orders from policymakers, or course adoptions on college campuses—interest in *State of the World* expands each year.

The first printing of *State of the World 1984* totaled 16,000 copies. By year's end it had gone through five printings for a total of 27,000 copies. For *State of the World 1987,* the first printing will be 50,000 copies.

State of the World now appears in most of the world's major languages. In addition to English, it is published in Spanish, Arabic, Chinese, and Japanese. It also appears in several less widely spoken languages, including Indonesian, Polish, Romanian, and Thai. We estimate that the worldwide market in all languages is now in excess of 200,000 copies.

State of the World 1986 is used as a textbook in nearly 200 U.S. colleges and universities. As in 1985, the University of Wisconsin campus at Madison still leads the way, with five separate courses having adopted the book. The University of California at Berkeley uses the text in four courses and several other institutions, including Harvard, use *State of the World* in three different courses.

Worldwide media interest in *State of the World* has also risen with each annual volume. Without this extensive print and electronic media coverage, it would be virtually impossible to reach a worldwide audience. Whether through an article in *The People's Daily* (China) or an appearance on the *Today Show,* all media coverage of *State of the World* raises public awareness of both the long-standing and the newly emergent environmental issues that now confront the entire world.

Last year, we reported that we had been approached by the producers of NOVA to collaborate on a 10-part television series based on *State of the World.* Most of the $6 million for this project has now been raised, and the British Broadcasting Corporation and television film production units in India and Australia will be joining NOVA in the production of the series. NHK, the national network in Japan, has also indicated a strong interest.

We are excited by this major initiative not only because it adds a new dimension to our global public educational effort in its own right, but also because the film and print versions of *State of the World* will reinforce each other throughout the world. For educators, a telecourse and instructional guide are being developed with the support of the Carnegie Corporation and the Hitachi Foundation. Another promising complement to the television series is the preparation of a *Citizen's Guide to a Sustainable Society* by the Global Tomorrow Coalition, a Washington-based organization of some 70 public interest groups, from the Audubon Society to Zero Population Growth.

Occasionally a news reporter, an editorial writer, or a columnist will write a piece on *State of the World* that strikes a responsive chord, measurably raising public awareness. When Hugh Sidey devoted his February 24th *Time* magazine column, "The Presidency," to a comparison of President Reagan's State of the Union address and our *State of the World* report, such a chord was struck. Sidey concluded that *State of the World* was "arguably a more accurate and provocative picture of the globe than the one sketched by the President." For the following week, our phones rang on average once every six minutes as *Time* readers called to order the report.

Sometimes the information in *State of the World* contributes directly to shaping policy. In other cases, the contribution is more indirect. An annual two-day retreat of the senior staff at the World Bank held in November 1985 was devoted to sustainable development and addressed by the project director of *State of the World.* And in April 1986, the African Development Bank invited the authors of last year's chapter on "Reversing Africa's Decline" to lead a seminar for directors and senior staff in Abidjan on the links between the environment and the economy. No policy decisions were made at either the November retreat or the April seminar. But key decision makers in the field of international development discussed what was sustainable and what was not, considering sustainability along with the financial concerns that have traditionally dominated development policymaking.

For the world to respond to global challenges such as soil erosion, species extinction, or human-induced climate change, we must cross what Harvard University professor Harvey Brooks terms a "perceptual threshold." Enough people must perceive the threat for a cogent response to emerge. Information is the key to crossing such thresholds. Once public concern is aroused, it becomes possible and indeed necessary for politicians to act.

One such threshold was crossed when Congress passed the Food Security Act in December 1985. After two comprehensive USDA soil surveys and several studies by environmental groups indicated erosion severe enough to undermine U.S. agriculture, farm groups joined national environmental organizations to demand action. Congress voted overwhelmingly to establish a conservation reserve designed to convert 45 million acres of the most highly erodible cropland into grassland or woodland.

The information that underpins change may come in more dramatic form. For societies weighing the pros and cons of nuclear power, the accident at Chernobyl in April 1986 confirmed the consequences of a core-damaging power plant accident. European countries exposed to the radiation from Chernobyl were soon reexamining the future of their nuclear power programs. Although statistical models of the risks and consequences of a nuclear accident had long been available, the magnitude of the Chernobyl accident prompted actions that even widely publicized studies had never inspired.

State of the World is intended to help societies cross perceptual thresholds *before*, rather than after, such disruptive events occur. The task of the series, in part, is to highlight the risks that confront societies, and to indicate the most promising avenues for preemptive policies and actions. Soil conservation, energy efficiency, materials recycling, and population stabilization—a few of the themes emphasized here—can broaden the options open to societies and enhance the prospects of the next generation.

As in the past, we welcome ideas and suggestions. Insightful comments from readers often help us cross the perceptual thresholds that we hope keep *State of the World* fresh and useful.

        Lester R. Brown
          Project Director

        Edward C. Wolf
          Associate Project Director

        Worldwatch Institute
        1776 Massachusetts Ave., N.W.
        Washington, D.C. 20036

December 1986

STATE OF THE
WORLD
1987

1

Thresholds of Change

Lester R. Brown and Sandra Postel

Daily news events remind us that our relationship with the earth and its natural systems is changing, often in ways we do not understand. In May 1985, a British research team reported finding a sharp decline in the level of atmospheric ozone over Antarctica. Verified by other scientists, the discovery of this unanticipated "hole" in the earth's protective shield of ozone sent waves of concern throughout the international scientific community. A thinning ozone layer would allow more of the sun's ultraviolet radiation to reach the earth, causing more skin cancers, impairing human immune systems, and retarding crop growth.[1]

In late July 1986, a team of scientists studying the effect of rising atmospheric levels of carbon dioxide (CO_2) and other "greenhouse gases" published evidence that the predicted global warming has begun. Meteorologists at the University of East Anglia in the United Kingdom constructed a comprehensive global temperature series for the last 134 years. Their conclusion: "The data show a long time scale warming trend, with the three warmest years being 1980, 1981 and

Units of measurement are metric unless common usage dictates otherwise.

1983, and five of nine warmest years in the entire 134-year record occurring after 1978." Three months later, a U.S. Geological Survey team reported that the frozen earth beneath the Arctic tundra in Alaska had warmed 4–7 degrees Fahrenheit (2.2–3.9 degrees Celsius) over the last century, providing further evidence that a CO_2-induced warming was under way.[2]

Sometime in mid-1986, world population reached 5 billion. Yet no celebrations were held in recognition of this demographic milestone. Indeed, many who reflected on it were left with a profound sense of unease about the mounting pressures on the earth's forests, soils, and other natural systems. With 3 billion young people entering their reproductive years over the next generation, these pressures are certain to intensify.[3]

In October 1986, the U.S. National Academy of Sciences and the Smithsonian Institution convened a National Forum on Biodiversity in Washington, D.C. Addressed by nearly 100 prominent biologists, the conference sounded a clear note of urgency about the multiplying threats to species survival. Scientists warned of a forthcoming wave of mass extinction—one that would approach the magnitude of that which wiped out the dinosaurs and half of all other extant species some 65 million years ago. There is one important difference: Whereas the earlier cataclysm was of natural origin, the one now unfolding is driven by human activities.[4]

These changes in atmospheric chemistry, global temperature, and the abundance of living species reflect the crossing of key thresholds in natural systems, crossings that may impair the earth's capacity to sustain an ever-growing human population. A frustrating paradox is emerging. Efforts to improve living standards are themselves beginning to threaten the health of the global economy. The very notion of progress begs for redefinition in light of the intolerable consequences unfolding as a result of its pursuit.

Many thresholds have been breached inadvertently from advances in technology and growth in human numbers. Corporations manufacturing the family of chemicals known as chlorofluorocarbons, for example, surely did not intend for these compounds to deplete the ozone layer. Their goal was to produce efficient refrigerants, a practical propellant for aerosol spray cans, and a chemical agent used to make foam products. Nonetheless, the accumulation of chlorofluorocarbons in the atmosphere threatens to subject all forms of life to damaging doses of ultraviolet radiation, a threat that will take on new urgency if scientists determine that these compounds play a role in the periodic depletion of the ozone layer over Antarctica.

By the same token, radiation falling across Europe during April and May of 1986 was not the result of a planned nuclear attack. It was released accidentally on April 26 from Chernobyl 4, a nuclear reactor in the Soviet Union. While the production of electricity to power the Soviet economy is clearly a valid objective, it nonetheless resulted in unprecedented fallout of long lasting radioactive materials in many parts of Europe. The tragic mishap at Chernobyl may have pushed nuclear power beyond some previously undefined threshold of social acceptability. In the aftermath of the world's first major nuclear disaster, many nations are scaling back plans for nuclear power development. (See Chapter 4.)[5]

Other trends of the mid-eighties also call into question the viability of our path toward economic progress. World agriculture is producing surpluses, but for the wrong reasons. (See Chapter 7.) A portion of today's surplus is being produced only by diminishing the agricultural resource base—for example, by plowing highly erodible land and overdrafting underground water supplies. The extent of unsustainable land use in the United States was recognized when Congress voted in December 1985 to convert 45 million acres (18 million hectares) of highly erodible cropland to grassland or woodland. The Food Security Act of 1985 aims to shift one eighth of U.S. cropland to alternative, sustainable uses before erosion turns it into wasteland.[6]

Burgeoning populations in many urban areas are overtaxing local water sources, fuel supplies, and waste disposal capacities, crossing natural thresholds and translating directly into economic costs. Resource demands in numerous cities already exceed the limits of local supplies, whether it be water in Tucson and Mexico City, or firewood in Hyderabad. (See Chapter 3.) Especially in Third World areas experiencing unprecedented rates of urbanization, these imbalances will frustrate efforts to improve living standards.

A sustainable society satisfies its needs without diminishing the prospects of the next generation. By many measures, contemporary society fails to meet this criterion. Questions of ecological sustainability are arising on every continent. The scale of human activities has begun to threaten the habitability of the earth itself. Nothing short of fundamental adjustments in population and energy policies will stave off the host of costly changes now unfolding, changes that could overwhelm our long-standing efforts to improve the human condition.

ENERGY, ENVIRONMENT, AND THE ECONOMY

When this century began, scarcely one life span ago, world population numbered 1.6 billion. Assuming an average per capita income of $400 per year (1986 dollars), the gross world product was $640 billion, just slightly more than France's 1986 national product of $550 billion. (See Table 1–1.) Over the next half-century, world population grew by nearly a billion, bringing the total to 2.5 billion. Modest progress in raising per capita income brought the gross world product to roughly $3 trillion in 1950.

Though impressive by historical standards, this growth was dwarfed by what followed. Between 1950 and 1986, human numbers doubled to 5 billion, expanding as much during these 36 years as during the preceding few million. Per capita income also roughly doubled, pushing the gross world product over $13 trillion. Within a generation, the global output of goods and services quadrupled. A variety of technological advances aided this expansion, but none compare with the growth in fossil fuel use. Between 1950 and 1986, world fossil fuel consumption also increased fourfold, paralleling the growth in the global economy.

Resource constraints on global economic expansion emerged from time to time throughout the century. But a combination of advancing technology and cheap energy repeatedly pushed them back. As opportunities for adding new cropland diminished, for example, energy was widely substituted for land in boosting food production. After midcentury, relatively little new land was brought under the plow in most regions, yet global crop output expanded even faster than before. World agriculture

Table 1-1. World Population, Economic Output, and Fossil Fuel Consumption, 1900–86

	Population	Gross World Product	Fossil Fuel Consumption
	(billions)	(trillion 1980 dollars)	(billion tons of coal equivalent)
1900	1.6	0.6	1
1950	2.5	2.9	3
1986	5.0	13.1	12

SOURCE: Population statistics from United Nations; gross world product in 1900, authors' estimate, and in 1950 from Herbert R. Block, *The Planetary Product in 1980: A Creative Pause?* (Washington, D.C.: U.S. Department of State, 1981), with updates from International Monetary Fund; fossil fuels consumption in 1900 from M. King Hubbert, "Energy Resources," in *Resources and Man* (Washington, D.C.: National Academy of Sciences, 1969); for remaining years, Worldwatch estimates based on data from American Petroleum Institute and U.S. Department of Energy.

made a smooth transition from expanding cropland area to raising yields, and even picked up the pace of food production in doing so.

Economic growth became the central goal of governments everywhere. Regardless of ideology or stage of development, all sought similar ends—an expansion of their economies and improvements in living standards. Though the gains achieved were far from equally distributed, the world as a whole experienced remarkable economic progress.

Economic activity could be approaching a level where further growth in gross world product costs more than it is worth.

While the global economy has expanded continuously, the natural systems that support it unfortunately have not. Economist Herman Daly suggests that "as the economy grows beyond its present physical scale, it may increase costs faster than benefits and initiate an era of uneconomic growth which impoverishes rather than enriches." In essence, Daly points to an economic threshold with profound implications. As currently pursued, economic activity could be approaching a level where further growth in the gross world product costs more than it is worth.[7]

The burning of fossil fuels literally fueled industrial expansion throughout the century and remains at the heart of many Third World development plans. Yet the buildup of atmospheric carbon dioxide attributable to that energy path threatens to make the earth far warmer than at any time in human history. The cost to farmers of adjusting to new temperature and rainfall regimes could deprive agriculture of the investment capital needed to expand output. (See Chapter 9.) And the costs of protecting populations in low-lying areas from a rise in sea level could divert vast amounts of capital away from other development goals.

The earth's forest cover is diminishing, most dramatically in the Third World as a result of land clearing, firewood gathering, and logging, but also in central Europe as a result of air pollution and acid deposition. Besides the direct losses forest damage causes to forest industries, serious environmental consequences are emerging, including increased rainfall runoff, accelerated soil erosion, and diminished water quality. Only time will reveal the complete tally of ecological costs, since the forest damage continues to spread.[8]

World food production increased an impressive two-and-a-half times between 1950 and 1986, but this too has its costs. Four fifths of this increase resulted from more intensive use of land, but between 1950 and 1976, the year growth in the cropland area ended, some 130 million hectares of grainland were added. Though small compared with growth in the demand for food, this addition exceeded that of earlier, equivalent periods when cropland expansion accounted for virtually all growth in output. In the headlong rush to meet the demand for food, many countries overexpanded their cropland base. Farmers plowed land that was steeply sloping, and hence vulnerable to water erosion, or so arid that it was easily eroded by wind. Besides contributing to price-depressing surpluses, such unsustainable production cannot be supported indefinitely. Several countries are already reducing the amount of land planted to crops.[9]

The negative side effects of this century's twentyfold expansion of economic activity are now becoming inescapable. Whether through spreading forest damage, a changing climate, or eroding soils, the pursuit of short-term economic growth at the environment's expense will exact a price. As the natural systems that underpin economies deteriorate, actions that make good sense environmentally will begin to converge with those that make good sense economically. But that convergence may not occur before irreversible changes have unfolded.

CROSSING NATURAL THRESHOLDS

Sometimes a natural threshold can be defined fairly precisely, and the consequences of breaching that threshold known with a reasonable degree of certainty. If wood harvesting exceeds annual forest growth, for example, the volume of standing timber will diminish, and it will do so at a rate directly tied to how much the sustainable yield has been exceeded. Similarly, in a fishery, if the annual fish catch exceeds the rate of replacement, the stock of fish will gradually dwindle.

With many of the natural systems now at risk, however, thresholds are not well defined, systemic responses to threshold crossings are not well understood, and the consequences of those crossings are largely incalculable. Moreover, threshold effects are now appearing in systems of continental and global scale.

The onset of forest damage in the early eighties took West German scientists and foresters by surprise, despite the nation's long tradition of meticulous forest management. In 1982, rough estimates placed the damage at 8 percent of the nation's trees. Just one year later, a thorough survey showed that 34 percent of the trees were yellowing and losing foliage. And by the summer of 1984 the share of unhealthy trees had climbed to 50 percent. Something inadvertently had tipped the balance within forest systems, triggering widespread decline.[10]

Scientists believe that pollutants from the burning of fossil fuels are behind the spreading forest damage in central and northern Europe, which now covers more than 19 million hectares. (See Chapter 9.) But the precise mechanisms at work are surrounded with uncertainty. Curiously, the destruction unfolded during a period when the use of fossil fuels had more or less leveled off in many countries, including West Germany. The long-term, cumulative effects of chemical stress apparently have overwhelmed the trees' levels of tolerance, making them less able to cope with natural stresses such as extreme cold, wind, insects, or drought.[11]

New light recently was shed on thresholds of acidification when scientists at the Freshwater Institute in Manitoba, Canada, reported their findings from purposefully acidifying a small lake in northwestern Ontario. Over an eight-year period, they increased the lake's acidity from a pH of 6.8 to 5.0 and documented how the ecosystem changed along the way. At pH 5.9, for example, the population of one shrimp species declined dramatically, fathead minnow failed to reproduce, and one species of crustacean disappeared altogether. When the pH fell below 5.4, no species of fish was able to reproduce. At that level of acidity, the lake would become devoid of fish within a decade. Many lakes and streams in Scandinavia and eastern North America are believed to have acidified in such a way. Many more remain vulnerable as acid rain persists.[12]

Scientists also have documented acidification thresholds in soils, the crossing of which may irreversibly damage terrestrial ecosystems. The chemistry of soils is determined largely by natural acid and chemical inputs and the rate of rock and mineral weathering, which releases elements that neutralize acidity. In some cases, soils cannot buffer all of the acidity added by fossil fuel pollutants, and, as a result, their chemistry markedly changes. The level of acidity increases, vital nutrients are leached out, and sometimes elements toxic to plants—such as aluminum—are released. Severe soil acidification has already occurred in heavily polluted industrial regions, including extensive areas of Eastern Europe that now resemble a wasteland. In parts of southwestern Sweden, soil acidity has increased tenfold over the last 60 years. If acid rain continues unabated, susceptible soils will acidify further; once severely degraded, they may take decades, if not centuries, to recover.[13]

While temperate-zone forests are being pushed beyond a threshold of pollution tolerance, those in the tropics are being driven below a critical moisture threshold. Conventional wisdom holds that tropical rain forests are typically too wet to burn naturally, but in late 1982 and early 1983 some seven forest fires spread through Indonesia's East Kalimantan province and Malaysia's Sabah province, both on the island of Borneo. They consumed 3.5 million hectares of tropical rain forest, an area almost the size of Taiwan and equal to nearly half the average annual loss of moist tropical forests from all causes.[14]

Satellite data show that some 16 percent of India's forest cover was lost between 1973 and 1981.

The forest that ignited in Kalimantan and Sabah had been degraded and destabilized by land clearing for resettlement programs, slash-and-burn farming, and commercial logging. The severe El Niño drought of 1982 and 1983 tipped the balance by reducing soil moisture to a level below that needed to protect the forest from fire. U.S. scientists studying the fires concluded that they "were ecological events of major proportions that have profoundly affected the human, plant and animal communities of a tropical ecosystem already subjected to numerous pressures."[15]

Far away, in the Ivory Coast, some 450,000 hectares of forest were destroyed by fire during the 1983 drought, apparently linked to similar human pressures. And in neighboring Ghana, fires during the same drought destroyed not only an extensive stand of forest, but also 10 percent of the country's cacao plantations. With pressures building on rain forests throughout the tropics, the moisture level below which they become more vulnerable to fire is likely to be crossed in an ever-widening area.[16]

In agriculture, an important threshold is crossed when the rate of soil erosion exceeds that of new soil formation. Over long stretches of geologic history, soil material accumulated faster than wind and water washed it away, yielding the thin mantle of rich topsoil on which the world's food is produced. In recent decades, the intensification of farming practices and the extension of agriculture into marginal areas have pushed the rate of topsoil loss beyond that of new soil formation on an estimated one third of the world's cropland.[17]

The world is now uncomfortably close to what may be the most economically costly threshold crossing of all. For at least a century, the annual release of carbon to the atmosphere from human activities—mainly fossil fuel combustion and deforestation—has exceeded the uptake of carbon by terrestrial vegetation and the oceans. As a result, carbon dioxide has been building up in the atmosphere. Analyses of air trapped in

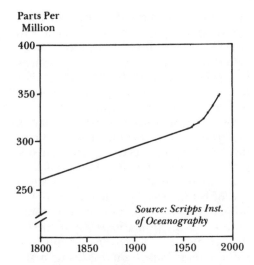

Parts Per
Million

Figure 1-1. Atmospheric Levels of Carbon Dioxide, 1800-1986

Source: Scripps Inst.
of Oceanography

glaciers indicate that the atmospheric carbon dioxide level in 1860 was about 260 parts per million (ppm). Today CO_2 measures 346 ppm, a 30-percent increase. Just since 1958, when scientists began routinely monitoring CO_2, the concentration has risen 9 percent. (See Figure 1–1.)[18]

Climate modelers warn that if the CO_2 concentration approaches double preindustrial levels, a dramatic change in climate will result. By pushing the release of CO_2 into the atmosphere above the rate at which it could be assimilated by natural systems, we have crossed one threshold. But we can still avoid crossing a second threshold: the level of atmospheric CO_2 that will cause an unprecedented and irreversible change in climate.[19]

Complex interactions between vegetation, soils, and water supplies are also being altered as human demands overwhelm the regenerative capacities of local biological systems. In India, for example, the demands of 785 million people for food and fuelwood and the grazing and browsing demands of 260 million cattle and 120 million goats and sheep are steadily reducing vegetative cover. Satellite data show that some 16 percent of India's forest cover was lost between 1973 and 1981. With less vegetation to protect soils and help retain rainfall, land degradation and desertification are spreading.[20]

As the human population continues to grow, the earth's biological systems are becoming less able to adequately support it. An increasing share of the earth's net primary productivity (the total amount of solar energy fixed biologically through photosynthesis minus the amount of energy respired by plants) is being spent on meeting human demands. Stanford University biologist Peter M. Vitousek and his colleagues estimate that nearly 40 percent of the potential net primary productivity on land is now used directly or indirectly by human populations—mostly for food production but also for fiber, lumber, and fuel—or is lost as a result of human activities. The portion remaining to sustain all other species, and to maintain the integrity of natural systems, gets smaller and smaller as the size and demands of the human population mount. Deprived of needed energy, natural support systems could begin to deteriorate on a large scale.[21]

Identifying environmental thresholds and pinpointing when they will be crossed are not easy tasks. To have predicted the onset of pollution-induced forest damage, for example, would have required detailed knowledge of how trees respond to various levels of pollution and of how natural stresses and pollutants jointly affect trees, as well as a finely tuned monitoring system for tracking forest health. Such extensive data and depth of understanding simply do not exist yet for most natural systems.

This inability to recognize thresholds and predict when they will be breached makes efforts to relieve resource imbalances and environmental stresses all the more crucial. In the tropics, for instance, 10 trees are being cut for every 1 planted. The ratio is 29 to 1 in Africa. Apart from the gradual loss of fuelwood and wood product supplies, is the integrity of larger systems at stake? Will, for example, losses of forest cover over a broad area affect regional hydrologic cycles? Will extensive deforestation in the Amazon impair the capacity of that tropical system to recycle rainfall inland, setting in motion a self-reinforcing process that will dry out the Amazonian region? Some evidence suggests that this may already be happening, but whether a threshold will be breached—leading to irreversible changes in the climate and vegetation of the Amazon—is unknown.[22]

OIL DEPLETION AND FOOD PRODUCTION

At mid-century, world agriculture crossed a major threshold in its efforts to feed a global population that had reached 2.5 billion. As population growth accelerated and the expansion of cropland slowed, farmers were forced for the first time to rely primarily on raising land productivity. The crossing of this population/cropland threshold started a rise in the oil intensity of world food production that has continued to date.

Notwithstanding pockets of modernized farms, the world's farmers were still largely self-sufficient in energy in 1950, relying on livestock wastes for fertilizer and draft animals for tillage power. Since then, however, the agricultural use of energy has multiplied sevenfold. (See Chapter 7.) Between 1950 and 1985, the farm tractor fleet quadrupled, world irrigated area tripled, and fertilizer use increased ninefold. Coal is used to fabricate the steel in tractors and natural gas is widely used to synthesize nitrogen fertilizer, but it is oil that provides most of the energy for modern farming.[23]

Given agriculture's heavy reliance on oil, trends in oil production and prices directly affect efforts to expand food output. Agriculture's share of total world oil use remains small, so an absolute shortage of oil for food production is not an immediate concern. But the economics of food production are greatly shaped by the price of oil. Moreover, in contrast to some other important oil-using activities, such as electricity generation, agriculture does not appear to be reducing its reliance on oil, which makes it more vulnerable to future price increases.

The worldwide production of oil and grain have moved in opposite directions since 1978. (See Figure 1–2.) Both moved steadily upward from 1950 to 1978, but then oil production turned downward while that of grain continued

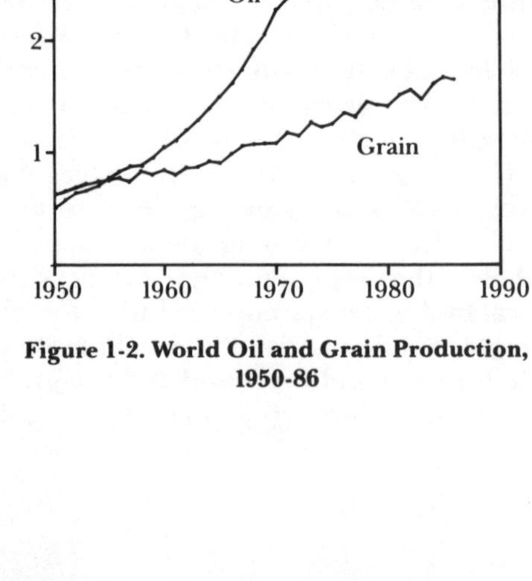

Billion Tons

Sources: U.S. Dept. of Agriculture and Amer. Petroleum Inst.

Figure 1-2. World Oil and Grain Production, 1950-86

to go up. More importantly, the demand for grain is projected to continue to rise until at least the middle of the next century, yet oil production is projected to decline over this period. Efforts to boost crop output by using more energy-intensive inputs will make agriculture more dependent on oil at a time when oil supplies are diminishing.[24]

The best available indicator of the energy intensity of food production is the amount of energy used to produce a ton of grain. Between 1950 and 1985, this more than doubled, rising from the equivalent of 0.44 barrels of oil to more than 1 barrel. (See Table 1–2.) The oil equivalent of energy used in farming in 1985 totaled 1.9 billion barrels, less than one tenth the world's petroleum output of 21 billion barrels.[25]

The increase in the price of oil and in energy prices generally during the seventies raised the cost of inputs on which farmers now depend so heavily to raise production—fuel for tractors and irrigation pumps, fertilizer, and pesticides. After the oil price hikes, agriculture's

use of energy-intensive inputs continued to increase, but at a slower rate. Notwithstanding the drop during 1986, oil prices inevitably will rise, and in the process they will pull all energy prices broadly upward. Higher energy prices will make it more difficult to restore the economic gains needed in the Third World to boost per capita purchasing power among the poorly fed. And they will, of course, further raise the costs of agricultural inputs.

As the twenty-first century approaches, two issues are of paramount concern in the oil/food relationship. One is the increase in competition among different oil-using sectors of the economy as total petroleum production diminishes. The second is the location of oil reserves.

By 1986, nearly half of all oil discovered had already been consumed. In North America, which produces nearly one fourth of the world's grain, four fifths of all the oil discovered to date has already been burned. Current proven U.S. reserves in the United States total

Table 1-2. World Agricultural Energy Use and Grain Production, 1950–85

Year	Energy Use in Agriculture	Grain Production	Energy Used to Produce a Ton of Grain
	(million barrels of oil equivalent)	(million metric tons)	(barrels of oil equivalent)
1950	276	624	0.44
1960	545	841	0.65
1970	970	1,093	0.89
1980	1,609	1,423	1.13
1985	1,903	1,667	1.14

SOURCE: Worldwatch Institute estimates based on U.S. Department of Agriculture data; David Pimentel, *Energy Utilization in Agriculture;* Gordon Sloggett, *Energy in U.S. Agriculture;* W.R. Rangeley, "Irrigation and Drainage in the World" and "Irrigation—Current Trends and A Future Perspective."

36 billion barrels, enough to supply U.S. needs for less than eight years at current rates of use. (See Table 1–3.) Without the jump of one fifth in oil imports in 1986, the U.S. economy would be facing some difficult adjustments.[26]

Third World countries with rapidly rising food demands, small oil reserves, and financial constraints on expanding oil imports could be in for some traumatic times. The Indian subcontinent, with a billion people to feed now and another billion projected to be added before population growth stops, has less than 1 percent of the world's oil reserves. China is in somewhat better shape with little population growth projected, yet it also has a billion people, and just 3 percent of the world's current oil reserves.

The Middle East, with reserves of 398 billion barrels, lies at the other end of the spectrum. It has 56 percent of global

Table 1-3. World Oil Reserves by Region, 1985

	Current Oil Reserves	Share of Total Oil Reserves[1]
	(billion barrels)	(percent)
North America	43	6
Latin America	84	12
Western Europe	26	4
Africa	56	8
Middle East	398	56
Soviet Union	61	9
China	18	3
Indian Subcontinent	4	1
Rest of World	18	3
Total	708	100

[1]Total does not equal 100 due to rounding.
SOURCE: British Petroleum Company, *BP Statistical Review of World Energy* (London: 1986).

oil reserves but only 4 percent of the world's people. Moreover, the Middle East's share of global reserves is rising, since reserves outside the region are being depleted more rapidly. Despite the difficulties the members of the Organization of Petroleum Exporting Countries have had in agreeing on a production strategy, the growing Middle East control of the world's oil is setting the stage for price rises in the not too distant future. With petroleum reserves concentrated in one region and with food production becoming more oil-dependent, food security and access to oil are becoming closely entwined.

Agriculture cannot expand indefinitely its use of petroleum over the next several decades if oil production is declining. Ever expanding oil-based agriculture simply is not sustainable, and this underlines the need for food production technologies that are less energy-intensive. (See Chapter 8.) In addition, the prospect of higher energy prices suggests that the real cost of producing food is likely to rise. If it does, the affluent of the world will adjust by boosting the share of their incomes used to purchase food. But for those on the lower rungs of the global economic ladder, the only adjustments possible may be cuts in consumption of the sort seen in Africa since 1970 and in Latin America since 1981.

THE COSTS OF CROSSING NATURAL LIMITS

Natural thresholds are not merely of scientific interest; the consequences of crossing them can directly affect economies and people's livelihoods. Deforestation is driving up firewood prices in scores of Third World countries. Exces-

Table 1-4. India: Index of Real Prices for Food and Fuelwood in 41 Urban Centers, 1960–84

	1960	1977	1980	1984
Food	100	106	102	102
Fuelwood	100	116	140	165

SOURCE: B. Bowonder et al., *Deforestation and Fuelwood Use in Urban Centres* (Hyderabad, India: Centre for Energy, Environment, and Technology and National Remote Sensing Agency, 1985).

sive soil erosion is contributing to reductions in per capita food production in many more. The economic costs of some approaching thresholds, such as CO_2-induced climate change, are only beginning to be assessed. Unfortunately, a lack of integrated research makes it difficult to detect linkages between the economy and its environmental underpinnings. As a result, many of the economic consequences of environmental deterioration are only realized after the fact.

In many developing countries, firewood is as vital to local economies as oil is to the global economy. The depletion of forests in some areas has pushed fuelwood prices up almost as fast as those for petroleum-based kerosene. Between 1972–75 and 1980–82, the forested areas within 100 kilometers of India's 41 largest cities collectively diminished by a third. (See Chapter 3.) Fuelwood prices in these cities, which increased quite slowly from 1960 to 1977, rose some 42 percent in real terms between 1977 and 1984. Food prices, by comparison, remained remarkably stable. (See Table 1–4.)

Rising firewood prices directly diminish prospects for improved livelihoods among the poor, who are forced to spend more of their small incomes on cooking fuel. In extreme cases, fuelwood scarcity reduces some families to one hot meal a day. Unfortunately, given the continuing rapid depletion of India's woodlands, the rise in fuelwood prices is likely to continue and perhaps even accelerate.

Dozens of developing countries are feeling the economic effects of deforestation. Many that were once exporters of forest products have become importers as their woodlands have diminished while their demand for wood products has climbed. Deforestation has worsened flooding and the silting of reservoirs in some areas. In India, damages from flooding below disrupted Himalayan watersheds averaged $250 million annually during the early eighties. Some Central American nations have had to ration electricity because siltation reduced the reservoir capacities at hydroelectric facilities.[27]

The excessive erosion of soils—which, like forests, are a renewable resource if properly managed—imposes numerous economic costs. In four countries that contain roughly a quarter of Africa's population—Mozambique, Nigeria, Sudan, and Tanzania—crop yields in the mid-eighties were lower than in the early fifties, in part because of heavy topsoil losses. (See Table 1–5.) The extension of agriculture onto marginal land may also have contributed to this decline in

Table 1-5. Grain Yields Per Hectare in Four African Countries With Declining Yields, 1950–52 to 1983–85

	Average Yields		
Country	1950–52	1983–85	Change
	(kilograms)		(percent)
Nigeria	760	714	− 6
Mozambique	620	545	−12
Tanzania	1,271	1,091	−14
Sudan	780	479	−38

SOURCE: U.S. Department of Agriculture, *World Indices of Food and Agricultural Production 1950-85* (unpublished printout) (Washington, D.C.: 1986).

cropland productivity, which among the four countries averaged some 17 percent over three decades. In agrarian economies, declining crop yields often translate into falling incomes and living standards.

Ironically, fossil fuel combustion—quite literally the engine behind this century's remarkable industrial expansion—could well have some of the costliest economic consequences of all. Each year power plants, automobiles, home furnaces, and other technologies that burn fossil fuels release 5 billion tons of carbon into the atmosphere, a global rate of one ton per person. Coal and oil combustion release about as much sulfur and nitrogen oxides as are released from all natural sources combined. In many industrial countries, pollutants from fossil fuels annually cause billions of dollars of damage to forests, crops, fisheries, building materials, and human health.[28]

In Switzerland, officials are concerned about increased risk of landslides as dying trees are removed in Alpine regions.

Forest damage, which in Europe now covers an area the size of Austria and East Germany combined, could impose the heaviest medium-term economic losses. Dead and dying trees are being salvaged and dumped on wood markets; in the short run, lumber and pulp prices may drop. At some point in the future, when trees cut prematurely would otherwise have been harvested, a period of shortages and rising wood prices could occur. Along with these market disruptions, foresters undoubtedly will face increasing forest management costs. Researchers in Berlin estimate that the West German forest industry could

suffer losses averaging $1 billion annually through the middle of the next century.[29]

Some of the economic consequences of forest damage are felt outside the industry itself. In Switzerland, for example, where 36 percent of all forests now show signs of damage, officials are concerned about the increased risk of landslides as dying trees are removed in the Alpine regions. Wintertime avalanches will become more commonplace in some mountainous Swiss villages, forcing villagers to evacuate. The use of roads and ski trails will also become riskier, threatening the tourist industry that underpins the economy in some of Switzerland's alpine cantons.[30]

Worldwide, the costs of adjusting to a greenhouse-gas induced warming of the earth may loom the largest. Agriculture, a highly climate-dependent sector, will face numerous adjustments. (See Chapter 9.) The existing pattern of world crop production evolved in response to particular climatic regimes that have been more or less stable over the last few centuries. The global warming will bring not only higher temperatures, but also changes in rainfall patterns. As a result, areas that do not now need irrigation and drainage systems may require them to sustain crop production. Water supplies could diminish in some regions, forcing farmers to take land out of irrigated production. Altogether, investments totaling hundreds of billions of dollars may be needed in the agricultural sector to maintain global food security.

One of the most feared consequences of the projected global warming is the rise in sea level that will result from both thermal expansion of the oceans and the melting of glaciers and polar ice caps. During this century, the ocean has been rising at just over one millimeter per year, or one centimeter per decade. A 1-degree Celsius increase in ocean temperature would raise sea level an estimated 60 centimeters, or roughly two feet.[31]

Calculating the effect of the warming on the earth's ice sheets is more complicated. Scientists agree that the warming will be more pronounced at the poles. If the earth as a whole warms by 2–4 degrees Celsius, as is predicted with a doubling of preindustrial CO_2 levels, polar temperatures are likely to rise 6–8 degrees. Current estimates suggest that the rise in ocean levels from such a warming would be on the order of one meter. With greater temperature increases, sea level would of course rise further.[32]

Coastal areas are obviously most at risk from rising seas. Many major cities are close to sea level, including Shanghai, London, and New York. Low-lying, densely populated regions of Asia, including parts of Bangladesh and Indonesia and the deltas of the Indus, Mekong, and Chang Jiang (Yangtze) rivers, would be especially threatened.

Faced with increased risks of flooding and inundation, governments would have to decide whether to abandon such low-lying regions, evacuating populations to higher elevations, or to build dikes much as the Dutch have done to reclaim land from the Zuider Zee. The costs of protecting the rice-growing plains and deltas of Asia and the densely populated coastal regions found throughout the world are incalculable. One 2.4-kilometer dike completed by the Dutch in the Scheldt river delta in 1986 to minimize the risk of flooding from severe storms cost $2.4 billion. For some poor countries, such as Bangladesh, the costs of coping with a rising ocean level combined with the agricultural adjustments needed to adapt to climate change could deprive the nation of the investment capital needed to improve living standards.[33]

LESSONS FROM THE PAST

Contemporary societies are not the first to cross important thresholds of natural and social stability. Today we study the archaeological sites of civilizations that for various reasons could not sustain themselves. In some cases, military invaders may have destroyed the social and cultural fabric of the conquered people. In others, however, the decline seems to have spawned internally, with an insidious deterioration of environmental support systems playing a central role.

Several thousand years ago, the Mesopotamian civilization thrived in a fertile plain between the Tigris and Euphrates rivers. Supported by an impressive system of irrigated agriculture, Mesopotamian society became a seedbed of discovery, and is today credited with developing writing, the wheel, and domesticated cereals. Sometime around 2400 B.C., however, the productivity of its agricultural land began to decline. Lack of underground drainage for irrigated land had caused the water table to rise near the surface, a situation that often occurs in irrigated areas today. In dry climates, evaporation of this water leaves the soil surface covered with a layer of salt that greatly reduces crop productivity.[34]

This process occurs gradually, and its significance may have escaped the Mesopotamian agriculturalists. Records indicate that yields of barley, which accounted for 84 percent of the society's cereals production, declined 65 percent over several hundred years. Salinization forced the Mesopotamians to completely abandon production of wheat.[35]

Archaeological evidence suggests that political weaknesses, civil strife, and warfare eventually caused the collapse of Mesopotamian civilization. But the decline of sociopolitical structures may have partially been triggered by the decline of the food-producing system. As researchers Thorkild Jacobsen and Robert Adams wrote in 1958: "Probably there is no historical event of this magnitude for which a single explanation is adequate, but that growing soil salinity played an important part in the breakup of Sumerian civilization seems beyond question."[36]

Some centuries later, in the New World, a major center of Mayan civilization arose in the highlands and coastal areas of Guatemala, El Salvador, and southern Mexico. Over many centuries, the Mayans developed a sophisticated administrative and social structure, techniques for terracing hillsides and draining swamps to cultivate maize, and rich cultural traditions.[37]

The decline of Mayan sociopolitical structures may have partially been triggered by the decline of the food-producing system.

At its zenith, Mayan society supported a population estimated at 5 million, over half the size of Guatemala's population today. Then around 750 A.D. the so-called Classic Maya civilization, which encompassed more than 100 individual centers, began to decline. Within less than two centuries, the population fell to one tenth its previous level and this advanced New World culture essentially disintegrated.[38]

Uncovering the exact causes of such a dramatic decline from the physical ruins is a monumental task, one that has so far eluded archaeologists. But many have come to believe that the burgeoning Mayan population may have outgrown its agricultural resource base, and that the resulting food shortages and social pressures unraveled the social and political order.

New insights into this theory emerged recently through the work of anthropologist John W.G. Lowe. He developed a model that mathematically describes Mayan society—including variables such as population growth, per capita productivity, and the distribution of labor—and then introduced various stress factors to simulate how the Mayan society would respond. Lowe describes his findings as "a tale of two thresholds."[39]

The first threshold defines a critical degree of food shortage at the local level below which his simulated Mayan system recovers and returns to normal conditions, but above which it destabilizes and collapses. The second describes a point at which the frequency of local collapse brings the whole Mayan system into an unstable state. Lowe's simulation further suggests that some external pressure could then drive this weakened society to collapse within a relatively short period of time. The overall pattern of the simulated decline apparently is consistent with what the limited archaeological record suggests actually happened.

In the modern world, the aura of high technology, sophisticated industrial processes, and a century of unprecedented economic growth might easily lead us to think that we are immune from the kinds of stresses the Mayans faced. Yet a Mayan pondering that flourishing society from its pinnacle in the early eighth century would probably never have believed it could deteriorate so rapidly.

A large-scale nuclear war poses the most obvious threat of total destruction today. Yet successful prevention of nuclear war by no means assures the persistence of modern societies. Historical accounts of societal decline portray complex syndromes of stress, often unrecognizable in their early stages, to which some regions and perhaps the world as a whole are becoming increasingly susceptible.

Population pressures and environmental stresses are mounting in many parts of the Third World. Per capita grain production in Africa has fallen by roughly one fifth since 1970, and in Latin America, by 8 percent in just the last five years. In agrarian societies, declining per capita food production inevitably translates into declining per capita income. Both Africa and Latin America are projected to end this decade with lower income per person than they began it with.[40]

Northern Africa, especially, is experiencing clear symptoms of decline today. Deterioration of its agricultural resources—its soils, forests, and water supplies—compounds stresses stemming from rapid population growth, unsound economic policies, and warfare. Per capita food production is diminishing and societal tensions are rising. Over the last three years, Egypt, Morocco, the Sudan, and Tunisia have each experienced riots or demonstrations connected with increases in food prices. It is difficult to believe that some 2,000 years ago, northern Africa's fertile fields made it the granary of the expanding Roman Empire. Today, vast deserts cover the region, and fully half of its grain supplies are imported.[41]

For the world as a whole, destabilizing stresses could arise from the global economy's pervasive dependence on oil. Hints of that vulnerability emerged with the oil price increases of the seventies, which in many countries triggered rampant inflation, declining rates of economic growth, and rising unemployment. Whether oil-dependent nations successfully adjust to a reconcentration of oil production in the Middle East, and to the inevitable decline in total production, will strongly influence prospects for economic growth and social stability.

Lessons from the past can help sketch the broad outlines of societal decline, but they offer little guidance as to which of the many stresses evident today may ultimately prove destabilizing. At the very least, we know that diminishing forests and soils, a changing climate, acid pollution, and dwindling oil supplies will impose real economic costs, if not on our generation, then on that of our children or grandchildren. At worst, a constellation of such stresses, especially if accompanied by military tensions, ultimately could drive some nations or regions beyond critical thresholds of stability.

OUR NEW RESPONSIBILITY

As we near the end of the twentieth century, we are entering uncharted territory. Localized changes in natural systems are now being overlaid with continental and global shifts, some of which may be irreversible. Everyday human activities—driving automobiles, generating electricity, and producing food—may collectively cause changes of geological proportions within a matter of decades.

A 1986 report from the Earth Systems Science Committee of the U.S. National Aeronautics and Space Administration begins: "We, the peoples of the world, face a new responsibility for our global future. Through our economic and technological activity we are now contributing to significant global changes on the earth within the span of a few human generations. We have become part of the Earth System and one of the forces for Earth change." The scientists actively monitoring changes in natural systems are among the first to recognize the new responsibility that we have brought upon ourselves.[42]

A human population of 5 billion, expanding at 83 million per year, has combined with the power of industrial technologies to create unprecedented momentum toward human-induced environmental change. We have inadvertently set in motion grand ecological experiments involving the entire earth without yet having the means to systematically monitor the results.[43]

The ozone depletion and pollution-induced forest damage described in this chapter are relatively recent discoveries. Yet the activities believed to have brought about these threats—the release of chlorofluorocarbons and fossil fuel pollutants—have been under way for decades. Taken further by surprise, industrial societies may trap themselves into costly and dubious tasks of planetary maintenance—perhaps seeding clouds in attempts to trigger rainfall where it has diminished with climatic change, or seeking means of protection from increased exposure to ultraviolet radiation, or liming vast areas of land sterilized by acidification.

The existence of thresholds beyond which change occurs rapidly and unpredictably creates an urgent need for early warning systems and mechanisms for averting disastrous effects. Despite impressive progress, the scientific groundwork has yet to be laid for monitoring the pulse of the earth's life-support systems. Meanwhile, the pace of change quickens.

We have crossed many natural thresholds in a short period of time. No one knows how the affected natural systems will respond, much less how changes in natural systems will in turn affect economic and political systems. We can be reasonably certain that deforestation will disrupt hydrologic cycles and that ozone depletion will induce more skin cancer. But beyond these first-order effects, scientists can provide little detail.

Any system pushed out of equilibrium behaves in unpredictable ways. Small external pressures may be sufficient to cause dramatic changes. Stresses may become self-reinforcing, rapidly increasing the system's instability.

Economic systems, with which we are perhaps more familiar, display some of these features. If a heavily indebted developing country reaches a point where it can no longer pay all the interest on its debt, the unpaid interest is added to the principal. The principal grows, further raising the interest. After a point, without debt forgiveness or other outside intervention, the debt grows out of control, and the system moves toward bankruptcy. Mexico is perhaps the most prominent of many developing countries now on this path.

Never have so many systems vital to the earth's habitability been out of equilibrium simultaneously. New environmental problems also span time periods and geographic areas that stretch beyond the authority of existing political and social institutions. No single nation can stabilize the earth's climate, protect the ozone layer, preserve the planet's mantle of forests and soils, or reverse the acidification of lakes and streams. Only a sustained, international commitment will suffice. The final report of the World Commission on Environment and Development that was established by the U.N. General Assembly, scheduled for release in the spring of 1987, could help launch such a commitment.[44]

Matters of the global environment now warrant the kind of high-level attention and concern that the global economy receives. World leaders historically have cooperated to preserve economic stability, even to the point of completely overhauling the international monetary system at the 1944 conference in Bretton Woods. Summit meetings are held periodically to attempt to iron out international economic problems. Policymakers carefully track economic indicators to determine when adjustments—national or international—are required.

Similar efforts are needed to delineate the bounds of environmental stability, along with mechanisms for making prompt adjustments when these bounds draw near.

With so many natural systems becoming unstable within such a short period of time, discontinuous, surprising, and rapid changes may become common-place. Resulting economic and political pressures could overwhelm the capacity of governments and individuals to adjust adequately. Societies faced with multiplying, self-generated stresses have two options: Initiate the needed reforms in population, energy, agricultural, and economic policies, or risk deterioration and decline.

2

Analyzing the Demographic Trap

Lester R. Brown

In 1945, the eminent demographer Frank Notestein outlined a theory of demographic change based on the effect of economic and social progress on population growth. His theory, known as the demographic transition, classified all societies into one of three stages. Drawing heavily on the European experience, it has provided the conceptual framework for demographic research ever since.[1]

During the first stage of the demographic transition, which characterizes premodern societies, both birth and death rates are high and population grows slowly, if at all. In the second stage, living conditions improve as public health measures, including mass immunizations, are introduced and food production expands. Birth rates remain high, but death rates fall and population grows rapidly. The third stage follows when economic and social gains, combined with lower infant mortality rates, reduce the desire

An expanded version of this chapter appeared as Worldwatch Paper 74, *Our Demographically Divided World.*

for large families. As in the first stage, birth rates and death rates are in equilibrium, but at a much lower level.

This remarkably useful conceptualization has been widely used by demographers to explain differential rates of growth and to project national and global populations. But as we approach the end of the twentieth century, a gap has emerged in the analysis. The theorists did not say what happens when developing countries get trapped in the second stage, unable to achieve the economic and social gains that are counted upon to reduce births. Nor does the theory explain what happens when second-stage population growth rates of 3 percent per year—which means a twentyfold increase per century—continue indefinitely and begin to overwhelm local life-support systems.

Once incomes begin to rise and birth rates begin declining, the process feeds on itself and countries can quickly move to the equilibrium of the demographic transition's third stage. Unfortunately, these self-reinforcing trends also hold for the forces that lead to ecological deterioration and economic decline: Once populations expand to the point where their demands begin to exceed the sustainable yield of local forests, grasslands, croplands, or aquifers, they begin directly or indirectly to consume the resource base itself. Forests and grasslands disappear, soils erode, land productivity declines, water tables fall, or wells go dry. This in turn reduces food production and incomes, triggering a downward spiral.

A DEMOGRAPHICALLY DIVIDED WORLD

Close to a generation ago, countries were conveniently classified as developed or developing based strictly on economic criteria. Roughly one fifth of the world was classified as developed and four fifths as developing. Whether living standards are improving or deteriorating may be a more useful indicator than the differences in living standards among countries. By this measure, polarized population growth rates are driving roughly half the world toward a better future and half toward ecological deterioration and economic decline.

As the nineties approach, new demographic criteria are needed. The world is dividing largely into countries where population growth is slow or nonexistent and where living conditions are improving, and those where population growth is rapid and living conditions are deteriorating or in imminent danger of doing so. In the second group are countries now in or entering their fourth decade of rapid population growth. Not only have they failed to complete the demographic transition, but the deteriorating relationship between people and

ecological support systems is lowering living standards in many of these countries, making it difficult for them to do so.

The risk in some countries is that death rates will begin to rise in response to declining living standards, pushing countries back into the first stage. In 1963, Frank Notestein pointed out that "such a rise in mortality would demonstrate the bankruptcy of all our [development] efforts." For a number of countries, that specter of bankruptcy is growing uncomfortably close.[2]

Grouping geographic regions according to the rate of population growth shows five of them, containing 2.3 billion people, in the slow growth category. (See Table 2–1.) Bracketed by Western Europe, which is on the verge of reaching zero population growth, and by populous East Asia, which grows 1.0 percent annually, this group has a collective growth rate of 0.8 percent per year. In these societies, rising living standards and low fertility rates reinforce each other.

A demographically divided world is likely to become more deeply divided along economic lines as well.

The other five geographic regions are in the rapid growth group, which contains 2.6 billion people—just over half the world's total. This group is growing at 2.5 percent per year, three times as fast as the slowly expanding half. In actual numbers, the slow growth half adds 19 million people each year while the rapid growth group adds 64 million, more than three times as many. For many countries in this latter group, rapid population growth and falling incomes are now reinforcing each other. Many others, such as India and Zaire, are

Table 2-1. World Population Growth by Geographic Region, 1986

Region	Population	Population Growth Rate	Annual Increment
	(million)	(percent)	(million)
Slow Growth Regions			
Western Europe	381	0.2	0.8
North America	267	0.7	1.9
E. Eur. and Soviet Union	392	0.8	3.1
Australia and New Zeal.	19	0.8	0.1
East Asia[1]	1,263	1.0	12.6
Total	2,322	0.8	18.6
Rapid Growth Regions			
Southeast Asia[2]	414	2.2	9.1
Latin America	419	2.3	9.6
Indian Subcontinent	1,027	2.4	24.6
Middle East	178	2.8	5.0
Africa	583	2.8	16.3
Total[3]	2,621	2.5	65.5

[1]Principally China and Japan. [2]Principally Burma, Indonesia, the Philippines, Thailand, and Vietnam. [3]Numbers may not add up to totals due to rounding.
SOURCE: Population Reference Bureau, *1986 World Population Data Sheet* (Washington, D.C.: 1986).

still registering increases in per capita incomes, but they risk a reversal in this trend if they do not slow population growth soon.[3]

These numbers signal just how demographically divided the world has become. The demographic middle ground has almost disappeared. All regions are either growing slowly—at 1 percent per year or less—or rapidly—at 2.2 percent or more. Although a few specific countries in the rapid growth regions are approaching or have reached the third stage of the demographic transition, such as Argentina, Cuba, and Uruguay in Latin America, their populations are not large enough to markedly influence regional trends.

Southeast Asia, home to some 414 million people, is probably the best candidate for joining the slow growth group in the foreseeable future. Two countries in this region, Thailand and Indonesia, have good family planning programs and rapidly falling fertility. They may well follow China into the small family category. By contrast, the Philippines and Vietnam, with high birth rates and falling living standards, are unlikely to make the breakthrough to low fertility in the near future.

Long-term population projections dramatize the diverging prospects for countries in the slow and rapid growth categories. (See Table 2–2.) The population of the United Kingdom, for example, is expected to level off at 59 million, just 5 percent above the current level. West Germany's population is expected to stabilize at 52 million, some 15 percent below the current population. For the United States, population growth is expected to halt at 289 million, roughly one fifth larger than in 1986.

Table 2-2. Projected Population Size at Stabilization, Selected Countries

Country	Population in 1986	Annual Rate of Population Growth	Size of Population at Stabilization	Change from 1986
	(million)	(percent)	(million)	(percent)
Slow Growth Countries				
China	1,050	1.0	1,571	+ 50
Soviet Union	280	0.9	377	+ 35
United States	241	0.7	289	+ 20
Japan	121	0.7	128	+ 6
United Kingdom	56	0.2	59	+ 5
West Germany	61	−0.2	52	− 15
Rapid Growth Countries				
Kenya	20	4.2	111	+455
Nigeria	105	3.0	532	+406
Ethiopia	42	2.1	204	+386
Iran	47	2.9	166	+253
Pakistan	102	2.8	330	+223
Bangladesh	104	2.7	310	+198
Egypt	46	2.6	126	+174
Mexico	82	2.6	199	+143
Turkey	48	2.5	109	+127
Indonesia	168	2.1	368	+119
India	785	2.3	1,700	+116
Brazil	143	2.3	298	+108

SOURCE: World Bank, *World Development Report 1985* (New York: Oxford University Press, 1985).

In stark contrast, Nigeria's population, now just over 100 million, is projected to reach 532 million before it stops growing toward the middle of the next century. If this were to happen, Nigeria would then have within its borders nearly as many people as in all of Africa today, a sobering picture to say the least. Kenya's population is projected to more than quintuple before stabilizing, as is Ethiopia's, where a combination of soil erosion and ill-conceived agricultural policies have already led to widespread starvation. Needless to say, these projections are unrealistic for the simple reason that life-support systems will begin to collapse long before the additional numbers materialize.

Population projections for those Third World countries where life-support systems are already disintegrating can only be described as projections of disaster. India's population is expected to more than double, reaching 1.7 billion and making it the world's most populous country, surpassing China, around 2010. During the same period Mexico's population of 82 million is projected to reach 199 million, just over four fifths that of the United States today.

These wide variations in projected population growth suggest that a demographically divided world is likely to become more deeply divided along economic lines as well. Unless this relationship between rapidly multiplying populations and their life-support systems can be stabilized, development policies, however imaginative, are likely to fail.

CARRYING CAPACITY STRESSES

The concept of carrying capacity has long been used by biologists, but until recently was rarely considered by economists. It focuses on interactions between a population, its activities, and the surrounding environment, and it highlights natural thresholds that might otherwise remain obscure. In its simplest form, the concept helps in understanding individual biological systems such as forests or fisheries. But it also can be applied to an entire ecosystem or even a country.

Knowledgeable biologists can calculate rather precisely the carrying capacity of a particular system. A natural grassland can indefinitely support a set number of cattle or a somewhat larger number of sheep. A fishery will meet the protein needs for a certain number of people, and the forests surrounding a village will supply the firewood for only so large a population.

If the numbers depending on these forms of biological support become excessive, the systems will slowly be destroyed: When herds grow too large, livestock decimate grazing lands. When the fish catch exceeds a fishery's capacity to replace itself, stocks dwindle and the fishery eventually collapses. Where forest cutting exceeds regrowth, the forest cover diminishes.

This concept can also be applied to such basic resources as land and water. In 1982, the U.N. Food and Agriculture Organization in collaboration with the International Institute for Applied Systems Analysis published a study analyzing the population-sustaining capacity of land in 117 developing countries. Calculations were made of land productivity assuming three levels of agricultural inputs: low, moderate, and high.[4]

The study concluded that at the low level of agricultural inputs, by the year 2000 some 65 countries—with 1.1 billion people—would not be able to provide even the minimum level of nutrition. Their populations would overshoot the numbers who could be sustained by 440 million, implying a heavy dependence on imported food, widespread starvation, or, more likely, both.[5]

With the full range of modern agricultural inputs, the number of countries unable to feed their people at minimal levels dropped dramatically—to 19, with a total population of 104 million. Yet the high cost of these inputs coupled with the recent growth of external indebtedness indicate that many of these countries will not be able to afford much beyond the low level of inputs.[6]

Unfortunately, even these numbers understate the problems facing developing countries. No effort was made in this study to determine whether the investment needed for the various input levels would be available—only how their use would affect the land's carrying capacity if they were available.

As in any set of projections, the assumptions here strongly influence the results. The first assumption was that all possible land that could be cultivated would indeed be brought into production; this included, for example, a sevenfold expansion in Latin American cropland, which would entail plowing vast portions of the Amazon. And no cropland was expected to be lost to degradation, an assumption that developments in Ethiopia and elsewhere have already invalidated. Second, it was assumed that no land capable of producing food for human consumption would be used to support livestock. Third, no allowance was made for green vegetables or non-food crops, such as cotton, tea, and coffee.

On the demand side, it was assumed that only the minimum nutritional standards would be satisfied and that all food would be evenly distributed. Perhaps the most important drawback of this study was that the projections went only to the year 2000, failing to consider the inevitable further declines in cropland per person as population growth continues.

A more recent, more detailed study by the World Bank of seven West African countries analyzed the carrying capacity of various ecological zones as delineated by rainfall. Directed by Jean Gorse, a French agronomist, the study gauged carrying capacity in terms of fuelwood and food supplies, the latter including the livestock products from grasslands as well as crop output. (See Table 2–3.) In the two northernmost zones, where rainfall is lowest, sustainable agricultural and fuelwood yields are already being matched or exceeded. In all countries and all zones, forests have less capacity than croplands and grazing lands to support people sustainably.

The actual population for the seven countries in 1980 was 31 million—already well beyond the 21 million who could be sustainably supplied with fuelwood. The result, of course, is rapid deforestation. The region's rural population of 27 million was still below the 36 million who could be sustained agriculturally, but today's population growth rates ensure that this carrying capacity will also soon be exceeded.[7]

In some situations, carrying capacity can be raised through the investment of capital and technology; in others it can-

Table 2-3. Measures of Sustainability in Seven African Countries, by Ecological Zones, 1980[1]

Zone	Food			Fuelwood		
	Agriculturally Sustainable Population	Actual Rural Population	Food Disparity	Fuelwood Sustainable Population	Actual Total Population	Fuel Disparity
	(million)					
Sahelo-Saharan	1.0	1.8	−0.8	0.1	1.8	−1.7
Sahelian	3.9	3.9	0.0	0.3	4.0	−3.7
Sahelo-Sudanian	8.7	11.1	−2.4	6.0	13.1	−7.1
Sudanian	8.9	6.6	2.3	7.4	8.1	−0.7
Sudano-Guinean	13.8	3.6	10.2	7.1	4.0	3.1
Total	36.3	27.0	9.3	20.9	31.0	−10.1

[1]Burkina Faso, Chad, Gambia, Mali, Mauritania, Niger, and Senegal. The five ecological zones are delineated by amounts of rainfall.
SOURCE: World Bank, *Desertification in the Sahelian and Sudanian Zones of West Africa* (Washington, D.C.: 1985).

not. With cropland, investment in modern inputs can raise dramatically its population carrying capacity. But no practical and profitable means exist to raise the yield of oceanic fisheries. The same is true for the carrying capacity of rangeland, although in some countries, notably New Zealand, an abundance of rainfall makes it worthwhile to apply chemical fertilizer.

One of the principal conclusions of the West African study was that no significant increase in carrying capacity was possible without a technological breakthough. Even though technologies exist, their use in these countries is not profitable. The World Bank team concluded that the "available intensive production techniques [that would increase the carrying capacity] have not proven sufficiently remunerative for wide adoption despite the pressure on land." As a result, the team notes that "desertification has set in and crop yields are falling in many areas."[8]

Unfortunately, the various support systems cannot readily be separated: Excessive pressures tend to spread from one to another. Once the demand for fuelwood exceeds the sustainable yield of local forests, it not only reduces tree cover but also leads to soil erosion and land degradation. When grasslands deteriorate to where they can no longer support cattle, livestock herders often take to lopping foliage from trees, thus putting even more pressure on remaining tree cover. Both contribute to a loss of protective vegetation, without which both wind and water erosion of soil accelerate, leading to desertification—a sustained decline in the biological productivity of land.

A decline in the diversity of plant and animal communities marks the onset of desertification. This in turn leads to a reduction of soil organic matter, a decline in soil structure, and a loss of water retention capacity. It also lowers soil fertility, reduced further by increasing wind and water erosion. Typically the end result is desert: a skeletal shell of soil consisting almost entirely of sand and lacking in the fine particles and organic matter that make soil productive.

Uncontrolled population growth in subsistence economies is degrading the resource base throughout Africa.

As this process continues, it reduces local water supplies, which further lowers carrying capacity. Although water was not included in the Bank's assessment of West Africa, its scarcity is partially a by-product of exceeding the sustainable thresholds of forests and grasslands. With lower water retention and percolation, water tables begin to fall, and as vegetation is lost, its role in cycling water inland is diminished.

Although this discussion focuses on seven West African countries, this same basic process driven by the same forces —namely, uncontrolled population growth in subsistence economies—is degrading the resource base throughout Africa. Breaches of carrying capacity thresholds are also commonplace in the Indian subcontinent, Central America, the Andean countries, and Brazil. For example, ecologists James Nations and H. Jeffrey Leonard describe deforestation and soil erosion in Central America as being of "crisis proportions." They write that "the region's renewable resources are being depleted . . . the long-term consequences will be severe: declines in income and per capita food production; financial losses; and the sacrifice of future economic opportunities."[9]

In countries where rates of population growth remain high, a three-stage "ecological transition" emerges that is almost the reverse of the demographic transition in that its end result is disastrous. In the first stage, expanding human demands are well within the sustainable yield of the biological support system. In the second, they are in excess of the sustainable yield but still expanding as the biological resource itself is being consumed. And in the final stage, human consumption is forcibly reduced as the biological system collapses.[10]

As human needs and numbers multiplied over the last generation, more countries moved into the second stage of the ecological transition. Carrying capacity thresholds were commonly breached, often reducing food and fuel self-sufficiency, raising external debt, and lowering living standards. Understanding these trends in international development requires a mastery of ecology as well as economics. National governments and the international development community have been slow to take carrying capacity into account when formulating economic and population policies.

DIVERGING FOOD AND INCOME TRENDS

Throughout the third quarter of this century, a rising global economic tide was raising incomes everywhere. Between 1950 and 1973, when the world economy expanded at a robust 5 percent per year, incomes were rising in virtually all countries, regardless of their economic system or stage of development.[11]

Since 1973, the global economy has expanded at less than 3 percent per year; the decline is more dramatic in per capita terms, falling from just over 3 percent to scarcely 1 percent. By far the most influential reason for this development was the 1973 oil price hike, reinforced by the 1979 price rise.[12]

Part and parcel of this global economic slowdown was the loss of momentum in agriculture. Even as oil prices were rising, soil erosion and desertification were beginning to take a toll on agriculture. Grain production, expanding at over 3 percent per year before 1973, has increased at only 2.3 percent annually since then. Growth in per capita grain output for the world as a whole since 1973 has been a negligible 0.4 percent per year. If China is excluded, it is almost nonexistent.[13]

When oil prices climbed, political leaders of developing countries were under pressure to keep their economies expanding rapidly so as to maintain per capita gains, and many borrowed heavily to do so. This effort succeeded briefly, but soaring interest rates combined with the slowdown in the global economy to leave many countries heavily indebted and unable to make even their interest payments.

As a result, much of the Third World now devotes the lion's share of export earnings to paying interest on external debts. In extreme cases, such as the Sudan, 80 percent of export earnings are required to service debt. (See Table 2–4.) With the weakening of oil prices in early 1986, Mexico's debt rose to $102 billion. With Mexico unable to make all the payments, international lenders began adding the unpaid interest to the outstanding debt.[14]

When the United Nations proclaimed the seventies the Decade of Development, it was scarcely conceivable that half a dozen countries would experience declines in per capita grain production greater than 20 percent over the following 15 years. (See Table 2–5.) In three countries—Angola, Haiti, and Iraq—it has fallen by half. Rapid population growth, agricultural mismanagement,

Table 2-4. Selected Debtor Countries Where Interest Payments on External Debt Exceed 20 Percent of Export Earnings, 1985

Country	Total External Debt	Share of Export Earnings to Pay Interest[1]
	(billion dollars)	(percent)
Sudan	7	80[2]
Argentina	48	50
Egypt	34	50[2]
Bolivia	4	42
Chile	21	41
Brazil	105	38
Mexico	97	33
Peru	15	29
Philippines	26	27
Ecuador	9	27

[1]Percentages are higher if payments of principal are included. [2]Export earnings data from 1984. SOURCES: Morgan Guaranty Trust Company, New York, private communication, November 9, 1986; Sudan data from U.S. Department of Agriculture, Economic Research Service, *Agricultural Outlook,* Washington, D.C., October 1985.

Table 2-5. Rapid Population Growth Countries With Declining Per Capita Grain Production, 1970–72 to 1985

Country	Rate of Population Growth- 1986	Grain Production Per Person	
		Annual Change	Total Change
		(percent)	
Kenya	4.2	− 1.7	− 19.0
Rwanda	3.8	− 0.3	− 4.0
Uganda	3.4	− 1.6	− 19.0
Iraq	3.3	− 5.7	− 54.0
Zambia	3.3	− 2.2	− 25.0
Malawi	3.2	− 1.4	− 17.0
Liberia	3.1	− 0.4	− 5.0
Nigeria	3.0	− 0.5	− 7.0
Iran	2.9	− 0.5	− 7.0
Mali	2.8	− 0.4	− 5.0
Egypt	2.6	− 1.5	− 18.0
Mexico	2.6	− 0.3	− 4.3
Angola	2.5	− 5.4	− 52.0
Peru	2.5	− 2.1	− 24.0
Mozam- bique	2.5	− 5.0	− 49.0
Haiti	2.3	− 5.1	− 50.0
Nepal	2.3	− 0.1	− 2.0
Ethiopia	2.1	− 0.9	− 11.0

SOURCES: Population data from Population Reference Bureau, *World Population Data Sheet 1986* (Washington, D.C.: 1986); grain production data from U.S. Department of Agriculture, Economic Research Service, *World Indices of Agricultural and Food Production 1950–85* (unpublished printout) (Washington, D.C.: 1986)

environmental degradation, and war or civil unrest have contributed in varying measures to these declines. All too often, the adverse effects of ecological deterioration are abetted by food price policies that favor the cities and starve the countryside of capital needed for investment.

A comparison of trends in Western Europe, the region with the slowest population growth, and Africa, with the fastest, illustrates graphically how different population growth rates are driving grain production trends in opposite directions. In 1950, Western Europe produced somewhat more grain per capita than Africa (234 kilograms to 157 kilograms), but not a great deal more by international standards. (See Figure 2–1.)

Africa's per capita output edged upward to a peak of 174 kilograms in the midsixties, and then began to decline.[15]

By 1985, Western Europe produced 501 kilograms per person and Africa only 150. Total grain production over the 35-year span increased in Western Europe by 164 percent and in Africa by 129 percent. The big difference between the two continents was in population,

Kilograms

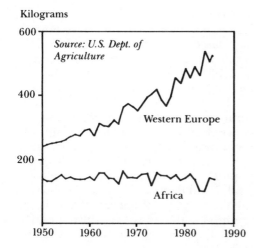

Figure 2-1. Per Capita Grain Production in Western Europe and Africa, 1950-86

which increased in Europe by perhaps one fifth at the same time that it easily doubled in Africa.[16]

Closely paralleling these diverging trends are those in per capita income. The patterns in some of the world's more populous countries illustrate the divergence that is becoming the hallmark of this decade. (See Table 2–6.) While Mexico's income fell by some 7 percent between 1980 and 1986, that of China increased 58 percent. Per capita income in Nigeria has fallen by nearly a third thus far during the eighties, while South Korea's has increased by that amount. Most of the major countries in Africa and all of the major Latin American ones—Argentina, Brazil, and Mexico—have experienced income declines during this decade.

During the seventies, Africa became the first region to experience a decade-long decline in per capita income during peacetime since the Great Depression. All indications are that during the eighties, the situation in Africa will worsen further. In addition, it is likely to be joined by Latin America, where regional incomes in 1986 were down nearly one

Table 2-6. Changes in Population and Per Capita Income, Major Countries, 1980–86

Country	Rate of Population Growth	Cumulative Change in Per Capita Income, 1980–86
	(percent)	
Rising Incomes		
China	1.0	+58
South Korea	1.6	+34
Japan	0.7	+21
India	2.1	+14
West Germany	−0.2	+10
United States	0.7	+10
United Kingdom	0.2	+12
France	0.4	+ 3
Declining Incomes		
Nigeria	3.0	−28
Argentina	1.6	−21
Philippines	2.5	−16
Peru	2.5	−11
Kenya	4.2	− 8
Mexico	2.6	− 7
Sudan	2.9	− 7
Brazil	2.3	− 6

SOURCES: Population growth rates from Population Reference Bureau, *1986 World Population Data Sheet* (Washington, D.C.: 1986); changes in per capita income for 1979-84 from B. Blazic-Metzner, and for 1985 from David Cieslikowski, Economic Analysis and Projections Department, World Bank, Washington, D.C., private communications, July 25 and October 22, 1986.

tenth from 1980. Barring a miracle, Latin America, like Africa, appears likely to end the decade with a lower per capita income.[17]

Will the forces that have slowed economic growth during the seventies and eighties and reversed the historical rise in per capita income in two regions lead to similar results elsewhere? This could happen on the Indian subcontinent, which now has over 1 billion people, if population growth there is not slowed soon. Bangladesh, India, Nepal, and Pakistan all have population growth rates well in excess of 2 percent per year. And the subcontinent is beset with serious environmental stresses.

As Table 2–6 indicates, many of the countries with rapid population growth have declining incomes, whereas almost all those with minimal or zero population growth are experiencing income rises. But this is not a simple cause-and-effect relationship. Among other things, countries that cannot manage their population growth may not be able to manage their economies very well either. Where energy is no longer cheap and abundant and where the natural resource base is deteriorating, countries with rapid population growth are finding it difficult to raise incomes. Thus, differential population growth rates are not the sole cause of rising or falling per capita incomes, but they often exercise a decisive influence.

GROWING RURAL LANDLESSNESS

In many ways, the most fundamental shift in the population/resource relationship during the demographic transition's middle stage occurs between people and land. Throughout most of human history, the gradual increase in human numbers was accompanied by a slow expansion of the cropland area. As populations grew, forests were cleared for farming. As land pressures built in Europe, the landless migrated to the New World.

By the mid-twentieth century, the amount of new land suitable for cropping was diminished just when population growth was accelerating. Cropland area continued to grow, but not nearly as fast as population. In the more densely populated parts of the Third World, the result was growing rural landlessness—lack of access to land either through ownership or tenancy.

Though fueled by population growth, rural landlessness is exacerbated by the concentration of landownership. In Latin America, the most extreme case, it is not uncommon for 5 percent of the populace to own four fifths of the farmland. Land distribution is at the heart of the civil war in El Salvador, and is undoubtedly the most sensitive political issue that the government of Brazil faces.[18]

The largest landless populations are concentrated in South Asia, principally on the Indian subcontinent. East Asia today has the largest population of any geographic region, but it has benefited from the early postwar land reforms undertaken in China, Japan, and South Korea. In China, although all land is owned by the state, farmers have access to it through long-term leases.[19]

Although the degree of landlessness varies among Bangladesh, India, and Pakistan, there are broad similarities. A World Bank study reports that the three countries now have over 30 million landless rural households, consisting of families who neither own nor lease land. Assuming an average of only 6 people per household, the subcontinent's landless rural population is nearly as large as the total U.S. population. In addition, 22 percent of the cultivated holdings are smaller than 0.4 hectares, not enough to support a family, even when intensively farmed. Another group of farmers has between 0.4 and 1.0 hectares, not usually enough to provide an adequate standard of living. A third group, farm families who cultivate between 1.0 and 2.0 hectares of land, accounts for some 21 percent of all cultivated holdings in South Asia.[20]

The 30 million landless rural households, plus the near-landless ones (with less than 0.4 hectares), now represent close to 40 percent of all rural households in South Asia. These people depend heavily on seasonal agricultural employment for their livelihoods, and increasingly on new jobs in the agricultural service industries that are springing up as farming modernizes.

Unfortunately, not nearly enough work exists to employ fully the swelling ranks of the landless and near-landless. As a result, many live at the edge of subsistence. And all indications are that the growth of landlessness in South Asia will continue. In India alone, the number of landless rural households is projected to reach 44 million by the end of the century. (See Table 2–7.)

For Africa, landlessness is a relatively new phenomenon, but one that is growing. Land hunger can be seen in the conflicts among people who are migrating from eroded, worn-out fields in search of new areas. It can also be seen in the movement of farmers into wildlife reserves—not because they wish to destroy the habitat, but because the struggle to survive on this famine-ridden continent takes precedence over all other considerations.

Table 2-7. India: Landless Rural Households, 1961 and 1981, With Projections to 2000

Year	Landless Households
	(million)
1961	15
1981	26
2000	44

SOURCE: Radha Singha, *Landlessness: A Growing Problem* (Rome: U.N. Food and Agriculture Organization, 1984).

Where landownership is heavily concentrated, the growth in landlessness can be curbed or even reversed by initiating land reform. In some countries, the base of landownership can also be broadened through resettlement. Unfortunately, Brazil and Indonesia, the two countries that have invested heavily in resettlement in virgin tropical forests, have done so at great ecological cost. Another way to check the growth in landlessness is to slow population growth through effective family planning. Resettlement (where feasible) and land reform can reduce landlessness in the short run, but in the long run only population stabilization will work.[21]

In India alone, the number of landless rural households is projected to reach 44 million by the end of the century.

The rural landless invariably have far higher levels of malnutrition, lower levels of education, and lower life expectancies than others in society. In Bangladesh, for example, those in rural households who own no land or less than 0.2 hectares consume on average 1,924 calories a day. Those who own 1.2 hectares or more consume 2,375 calories per day, 23 percent more. The difference in protein intake is even greater—28 percent on average. To be landless in an agrarian society is thus to be severely disadvantaged in the struggle for survival.[22]

In societies such as Bangladesh, where existing holdings, already divided and subdivided, cannot be divided further, population growth translates into the landlessness that feeds unemployment and worsens income distribution. It is the source of migrants who inhabit the shantytowns surrounding Third World cities and cross national borders in search of work. This landless class, often outside the mainstream of development and bereft of hope, is also a potential source of unrest.

POPULATION GROWTH AND CONFLICT

The relationship between population growth and social conflict has been largely ignored by the social science research community, lost in the gap between demography and political science. Nazli Choucri of the Massachusetts Institute of Technology, a pioneer in research in this area, notes a continued lack of awareness about it within the research community. Howard Wiarda and Iêda Siquiera Wiarda of the University of Massachusetts point out that policymakers also largely neglect this relationship in the formulation of both population and national security policies.[23]

Difficult though they may be to measure, numerous linkages exist between population growth and conflict, both within and among societies. Conflict arises when growing populations compete for a static or shrinking resource base. Inequitable distribution of resources—whether of income, land, or water—complicates the relationship. Increased competition and conflict fray the social fabric that helps to maintain social harmony.

One reason for the dearth of research on how population growth affects social stability is the complexity of the relationship. To begin with, several fields of knowledge are involved—economics and ecology as well as demography and political science. In addition, the relationship between trends in these fields is not a simple matter of cause and effect,

but rather of interaction. Any meaningful analysis must take into account a continuous interaction between demographic, economic, environmental, and social or political trends.

The analytical challenge is intimidating, but the issue is a serious one, and an effort must be made. In an analysis of the turmoil in Central America, political analyst Sergio Diaz-Briquets argues that rapid population growth "has added pressure to labor markets already saturated with unemployed and underemployed persons; it increases pressure on the land area, it taxes governments' ability to provide needed social services." Further, it indirectly "plants seeds of discord by continuously increasing the ranks of unemployed youth and creating stiffer competition among those trying to improve their lot in life, particularly in ossified social systems."[24]

When a society's population growth accelerates sharply, the age structure is increasingly dominated by young people. For example, in dozens of developing countries 40 percent of the population is now under the age of 15.

This shift can itself be a source of instability. When young people become so numerous, they are likely to achieve a much higher profile in society. Changing age structures also put pressure on social institutions. Educational systems are inundated with new students, initially for elementary schools and then for colleges. In parts of the Third World, the tidal wave of youngsters has overwhelmed the schools, making a mockery of compulsory education.

Economic stresses also generate political conflict. As indicated earlier, the difference between a stationary population and a rapidly growing one can spell the difference between societies that are raising their living standards and those that are suffering a sustained decline. A 2-percent rate of economic growth in West Germany or Denmark, which have no population growth, will bring steady progress. But in Kenya or Peru, where population growth is rapid, it leads to a steady decline in living standards and growing social unrest.

For many developing countries, the global economic slowdown has come just as record numbers of young people are entering the job market. The specter of growing numbers of restless unemployed youngsters in the streets does not convey an image of social tranquility. Foreign affairs columnist Georgie Anne Geyer notes, "Given what is coming—unemployed youths roaming the streets in countries where half the population often is under 18 years of age, with no prospect of job formation, hungry, and looking to irregular leaders to lead them in new and as yet unpredictable movements—there is little question that even more political explosions are on the immediate horizon."[25]

When deteriorating environmental support systems can no longer support local populations, conflicts can arise as people are forced to migrate in search of a livelihood. Often these "ecological refugees" cross national borders, a process now widespread within Africa. It is perhaps most noticeable in the movement of nomadic pastoralists being forced southward as a result of desertification. All too often these nomads, with their herds and flocks, come into conflict with farmers in the regions they are trying to enter.[26]

Intensified competition for renewable resources such as water can be seen along the Nile River, where the countries that depend on its flow—Egypt, the Sudan, and Ethiopia—all have rapidly growing populations. The competing claims on the Nile could generate conflict as water use grows and as the allocation of its waters becomes literally a matter of life or death. In a world where industrial and agricultural expansions are keyed to additional water, the alloca-tion of river flows among countries could become a contentious political issue.

One of the most neglected social is-sues relating to population growth is the contribution of crowding to human con-flict. The scientific literature in this field is weak. Most research has been done on animals. The Wiardas observe that these studies "show a close relationship be-tween crowding and violence, but the re-lationship is usually indirect . . . crowd-ing does provide a set of conditions, a context in which tension, violence, and various forms of aberrant behavior are more likely to occur." With human populations, the effects of crowding are not easily separated from those of pov-erty, with which it is usually closely as-sociated. Within societies, crowding and competition for jobs and land may exac-erbate long-standing religious, tribal, re-gional, or ethnic differences.[27]

In parts of the Third World, the tidal wave of youngsters has over-whelmed the schools.

Mexico and Egypt, two culturally con-trasting countries that are beginning to feel the effects of rapid population growth, illustrate the stresses faced in varying degrees throughout the Third World. Mexico's family planning pro-gram of the past decade has been right-fully praised for its role in reducing birth rates. Yet, because the problem of rapid growth was recognized too late, the country's population is still growing 2.6 percent annually. Mexico, home to 82 million, adds 2.1 million people each year. Over the remainder of this century, some 15 million youngsters will enter the job market—roughly 1 million annu-ally. The nation needs more new jobs than ever before, but the economy is staggering under an external debt of $102 billion. A broad-based deterioration of land resources and a scarcity of irrigation water are raising the dependence on imported food in the country where the Green Revolution began.[28]

The basic ingredients for internal political conflict and civil strife are in place. An economic slowdown induced by rising external debt, rising numbers of unemployed youth, and a highly skewed income distribution seem certain to breed social tensions and rising unrest. The wealthiest 10 percent of Mexicans receive 41 percent of total income; the poorest one fifth, less than 3 percent. Real wages have declined at least a fifth during the eighties. Fiscal stringencies have forced the elimination of subsidies on tortillas, the corn meal food staple, at precisely the time when wages were falling, thus weakening the social safety net.[29]

Unemployment is rising. Mexican political scientist Jorge Castaneda believes that Mexican youth who do not find jobs have three options: attempt to migrate to the United States, spend their time idle on the streets, or rise up in revolution. Exposure to the benefits of higher living standards, both through contact with migrants to the United States and through television, gives today's youth higher expectations than their parents had.[30]

Castaneda believes that because of the difficulty in creating enough jobs, average Mexicans may be poorer at the end of the century than they are today. The only way to offset the adverse social effects on the poor is to redistribute wealth. But this is exceedingly difficult, particularly when so much capital is fleeing the country. In looking toward the end of the century, Castaneda believes that Mexico will either be more just and more democratic or "it will be on the verge of splitting asunder—if it has not broken apart already."[31]

Egypt, whose 50 million people make it the most populous Arab country, is also suffering from a generation of rapid population growth. Adding 1.2 million per year, it is in a deepening economic crisis that is generating political unrest. As recently as 1970, Egypt was largely self-sufficient in grain production; in 1986, imports supplied over half the grain consumed. (See Figure 2–2.) More seriously, continuing population growth will further raise the need for imported food, since Egypt's crop yields are already high by international standards and urban encroachment on the narrow strip of farmland along the Nile is slowly shrinking the cropland area.[32]

The economic crisis in Egypt has been in the making for years, but it has been held at bay by a decade of rising oil exports, remittances of workers from abroad, capital investment from oil-rich neighbors, and growing tourism. The mid-eighties decline in oil prices has reduced both petroleum export revenues and worker remittances from abroad, while the terrorist threat has cut the flow of tourists.

Egypt, like Mexico, is burdened by external debt. At the end of 1985, this

Figure 2-2. Grain Self-Sufficiency in Egypt, 1960-86

totaled $34 billion, more than $9 billion of which was for weapons imports, largely from the United States. In 1985, the servicing of nonmilitary debt required some 32 percent of foreign-exchange earnings; in 1986, it took close to half.[33]

One of the most politically sensitive issues in Egypt today is the food subsidy and the growing economic pressures to reduce it. An attempt do this in 1977 led to widespread rioting and forced President Anwar Sadat to rescind the cut. In March 1986, thousands of police conscripts rioted, burning 4 hotels and 28 nightclubs in a resort area. They were protesting their low wages and a rumored one-year extension in their duty tours. This incident, which caused millions of dollars worth of damage, is an indication of how close social dissatisfaction in Egypt is to the flash point.[34]

For Egypt, efforts to reduce the burgeoning bread subsidy may bring its unfolding demographic and economic crisis into sharp focus. Although the International Monetary Fund and other lenders are pressing the Egyptian government to reduce this subsidy, which is contributing heavily to its fiscal deficits and external debt, many doubt that it will be politically able to do so. The average Egyptian does not understand the rising external debt, but does understand rising bread prices. Ironically, if Egypt cannot reduce its external debt, it may not be able to buy the needed wheat. The resulting shortage of bread would make the subsidy meaningless.

Mexico and Egypt have much in common: They export oil, have failed to substantially check population growth, have an external debt that is becoming unmanageable, have enormous numbers of new job applicants, and are forced by external debt and fiscal stringencies to reduce basic consumer subsidies. Except for their oil exports, they share these characteristics with dozens of other Third World countries. And like many others, Mexico and Egypt face the possibility that recent declines in living standards will continue.

The average Egyptian does not understand the rising external debt, but does understand rising bread prices.

Developments within Central America over the past generation illustrate how population growth can contribute to conflict. Following World War II, Central American economies diversified and grew rapidly. Per capita income nearly doubled. Then during the seventies, a number of trends converged to undermine economic progress.[35]

Even before the first oil price shock, deforestation and soil erosion had been accelerating, slowly undermining Central America's agricultural foundation. In effect, population growth began to overwhelm the ecosystems, the educational systems, and the employment-creating capacities of national economies. In some countries, the economic slowdown was aggravated by the inequitable distribution of land and, hence, of income. In Nicaragua, it led to revolution. In El Salvador, where incomes of the richest one fifth of the population are 33 times those of the poorest one fifth, social tensions eventually burst into civil war.[36]

Unfortunately, the conditions giving birth to the tragic recent history of bloodshed in Central America are not unique. In addition to Mexico and Egypt, scores of developing countries are faced with politically destabilizing economic crises. Mounting stresses may cause fragile political institutions to give way, leading to an age of disorder.

THE DEMOGRAPHIC TRAP

For many Third World countries, the demographic trap is becoming the grim alternative to completing the demographic transition. If countries are in the middle of the transition for too long, rapid population growth and the associated ecological and economic deterioration may prevent them from reaching the equilibrium of the final stage. The only long-term alternative then becomes a return to the equilibrium of the first stage—with high birth and death rates. Such a regression is already evident in Africa, where famine has raised death rates twice since 1970.

Most of the Third World entered the second stage of the demographic transition around mid-century. As recently as the forties, world population was growing at scarcely 1 percent per year. At that time, North America and Africa were growing at the same rate, both slightly faster than the world average. Suddenly, as a result of falling Third World death rates, world population growth accelerated sharply in the fifties—approaching 2 percent, where it has since remained.

A typical developing country has thus been in the middle stage of the demographic transition for close to four decades. This high-fertility, low-mortality stage cannot continue for long. After a few decades, countries should have put together a combination of economic policies and family planning programs that reduce birth rates and sustain gains in living standards. If they fail to do so, continuing rapid population growth eventually overwhelms natural support systems, and environmental deterioration starts to reduce per capita food production and income.

Most societies do not know when they are crossing the various biological thresholds that eventually lead to economic decline. Few notice when the top-

soil loss begins to exceed new soil formation. Similarly, when firewood harvesting first begins to exceed the sustainable yield, the effects are scarcely visible because the excessive harvesting is so small. But over time it increases and eventually, as population expands and the forested area dwindles, it begins to feed vigorously on itself. By the time the loss of tree cover becomes widely evident, the population growth that is driving the deforestation has so much momentum that the decline becomes difficult to arrest.

One of the first economic indications that pressure on the land is becoming excessive is declining grain production per person. In earlier agricultural societies, population increases were simply matched by those in cultivated area. Grain output per person was stable. When population growth is rapid and there is no new land to plow, expanding the use of modern inputs fast enough to offset the effects of land degradation and to raise land productivity in tandem with population growth is not easy. It thus comes as no surprise that per capita grain production is declining in some 40 developing countries.[37]

When this happens in an agrarian society, it is usually only a matter of time until it translates into a decline in per capita income, and into the need for food imports. Rising food imports contribute to growing external debt. If external debt rises fast enough, it will eventually cross a debt-servicing threshold, beyond which the debtor country can no longer pay all the interest. At this point, lenders insist that the unpaid interest be added to the principal, expanding the debt further. Dozens of other developing countries have either crossed the debt-servicing threshold or are in danger of doing so.[38]

The demographic trap is not easily recognized because it involves the interaction of population, environmental, and economic trends, which are monitored by various offices in different governmental ministries. And observers frequently fail to distinguish between triggering events, such as drought, and underlying instability in the population-environment relationship.

The inability to cope with these developments can make political leaders, even capable ones, appear incompetent. Economic stresses begin to generate social stresses. Ethnic and tribal tensions are exacerbated and governments become preoccupied with instability. More and more of their time and energy is required merely to stay in power. Dozens of countries in Africa, Latin America, the Middle East, and South Asia are already enmeshed in this demographic trap.

National governments in the modern era have little experience with a long-term, sustained decline in living standards. Thus countries find themselves caught in a downward spiral with little warning. Figuring out how to arrest the deterioration once it is under way may dwarf in difficulty the other challenges facing governments.

But they are probably not the first to be caught unawares. Archaeologists who have studied the long-term evolution of the Mayan civilization, centered in the Guatemalan lowlands, report that its population increased rather steadily for some 17 centuries before its abrupt collapse in the ninth century. They calculate that the Mayan population was doubling once every 408 years. Kenya's is doubling every 18 years.[39]

Lacking a grounding in ecology and an understanding of carrying capacity, all too many economic planners and population policymakers have failed to distinguish between the need to slow population growth and the need to halt it. If societal demands are far below the sustainable yield of natural systems, then slowing population growth is sufficient. But when they have passed these thresholds, the failure to halt population growth leads to a deterioration of support systems.

Countries find themselves caught in a downward spiral with little warning.

Governments are moving into uncharted territory in the population/environment/resources relationship. Most developing countries cannot remain much longer in the middle stage of the demographic transition. Either they must forge ahead with all the energies at their disposal, perhaps even on an emergency basis, to slow and halt population growth. Or they will slide into the demographic trap. For the first time, governments are faced with the monumental task of trying to reduce birth rates as living conditions deteriorate, a challenge that may require some new approaches along the lines discussed in Chapter 11. If they fail, economic deterioration could eventually lead to social disintegration of the sort that undermined earlier civilizations when population demands became unsustainable.

3

Assessing the Future of Urbanization

Lester R. Brown and Jodi Jacobson

Aside from the growth of world population itself, urbanization is the dominant demographic trend of the late twentieth century. The number of people living in cities increased from 600 million in 1950 to over 2 billion in 1986. If this growth continues unabated, more than half of humanity will reside in urban areas shortly after the turn of the century.[1]

Cities are a relatively recent innovation, lagging by several millennia the emergence of agriculture some 12,000 years ago. The first permanent human settlements evolved after traditionally nomadic Middle Eastern peoples began to cultivate crops. Successive agricultural advances, such as the harnessing of draft animals and the development of irrigation, enabled farmers to produce enough food to support nascent villages and towns. Diversification of trade and the production of a wider array of goods encouraged greater numbers to settle in what later became cities.[2]

Although large cities arose from time to time, including second-century Rome and Chang'an (Xian), the imperial capital of the Chinese T'ang dynasty, historically the world's population has been overwhelmingly rural. Widespread urbanization is largely a twentieth-century phenomenon: As recently as 1900, fewer than 14 percent of the world's people lived in cities.[3]

The Industrial Revolution, which began in nineteenth-century Britain, fostered the development of large, modern cities. Coal replaced firewood as the dominant energy source in Europe and fueled the growth of early industrial cities. It was later supplanted by oil, which has underwritten the massive urbanization of this century, providing fuel for transportation and the consolidation of industrial processes. Petroleum also enabled cities to lengthen their supply lines and draw basic resources, such as food and raw materials, from anywhere in the world.

Accelerated urbanization has spurred the concentration of political power within Third World cities, leading to policies that favor urban over rural areas. Subsidies and overvalued exchange rates often make food and other basic goods cheaper in the city, discouraging agricultural investment and pulling people into urban areas. Indeed, many cities have been enriched only by impoverishing their hinterlands.

Cheap oil and economic policies favoring cities together led to a phenomenal surge in urban growth. But the signs of urban stress now apparent throughout the world are calling into question the continuing expansion of cities, particularly the larger ones. Mounting external debts are forcing national governments to scale back investments in urban areas and to reorder economic priorities. The transition that is slowly getting under way from fossil fuels to renewable energy sources—hydropower, biomass, and solar collectors, to name a few—will further redefine the optimal balance between urban and rural populations.

THE GROWTH AND ROLE OF CITIES

Neolithic villages began giving way to the first cities about 5,000 years ago on the deltas of the Nile, Tigris, and Euphrates rivers. Not long after, flourishing urban centers throughout the Middle East became seedbeds of culture and commerce. Advances in science and the arts seem to have depended on the dynamics of a "human implosion" as the relative density of ancient cities speeded the exchange of ideas and innovations. Urban historian Lewis Mumford has noted that the maturation of cities in Greece resulted in a "collective life more highly energized, more heightened in its capacity for esthetic expression and rational evaluation" than ever before.[4]

The number and size of cities increased sporadically over the past two millennia in an incremental ebb and flow that paralleled the growth in human population. In the nineteenth century, however, the Industrial Revolution catalyzed rapid urban growth: The first countries to industrialize were also the first to urbanize. For example, fewer than one fourth of the British lived in cities in 1800, on the eve of the Industrial Revolution; a century later, two thirds of the population lived in cities.[5]

Historical developments provide only a foreshadowing of the dominant demographic and economic role that urban centers play today. Urbanization has accelerated over the past several decades. By 1987, some 43 percent of the world's people were living in cities.[6]

Urbanization has three demographic components: migration, natural increase (the excess of births over deaths), and reclassification of rural areas to cities. Migration is most important in the early stages of urbanization, such as in Africa, while natural increase now dominates city growth in parts of Asia and throughout Latin America. At the current growth rate of 2.5 percent yearly—half again as fast as total population—the number of people living in cities throughout the world will double in the next 28 years. Nearly nine tenths of this growth will occur in the Third World, where the annual urban growth rate is 3.5 percent—more than triple that of the industrial world.[7]

Latin America, with 65 percent of its people in urban areas, is the site of some of the world's largest cities: Mexico City and São Paulo contain 18 million and 14 million people, respectively. Latin America's population is growing 2.3 percent a year, but its urban population is increasing by 2.9 percent per year. By the turn of the century, 466 million Latin Americans are expected to be living in cities, representing over three fourths of the region's total population. (See Table 3–1).[8]

Table 3-1. Urban Share of Total Population, Selected Regions, 1950 and 1986, With Projections to 2000

Region	1950	1986	2000
	(percent)		
North America	64	74	78
Europe	56	73	79
Soviet Union	39	71	74
East Asia	43	70	79
Latin America	41	65	77
Oceania	61	65	73
China	12	32	40
Africa	15	30	42
South Asia	15	24	35
World	29	43	48

SOURCE: For 1986 data, Population Reference Bureau, *1986 World Population Data Sheet* (Washington, D.C.: 1986); for 1950 and 2000, Carl Haub, Population Reference Bureau, Washington, D.C., personal communication, August 28, 1986.

In Africa, the least urbanized developing region, urban population is growing 5 percent yearly as millions of Africans fleeing rural poverty and environmental degradation migrate to urban areas. Today 175 million Africans live in cities —30 percent of the continent's total. If current projections materialize, this number will reach 368 million in 2000, a tenfold increase since 1950.[9]

Most East Asian countries—Japan, Taiwan, North and South Korea—are predominantly urban. China sharply diverges from this pattern, with scarcely 32 percent of its population in cities. This is due in part to the strict regulations on internal migration that prevailed prior to 1978, and in part to the growing relative prosperity of the countryside. Yet, urbanization rates in China have stepped up recently as the government encourages the development of towns and small cities to reduce rural population pressures.[10]

South Asia presents a mixed picture.

Although most countries of the region have relatively small proportions of their populations in cities, urbanization seems to be accelerating. India is predominantly rural, with only 24 percent of its 765 million people in cities. Yet large cities such as Bombay, Calcutta, Delhi, and Madras are still growing, and rural migration to other metropolitan areas is rising. Similarly, the urban share of population in Indonesia, the Philippines, Thailand, and Vietnam ranges from 18 to 39 percent. Urban growth rates in these countries range from 2.4 percent annually in Vietnam to 4.8 percent in Indonesia, indicating rapid urbanization.[11]

Cities of more than 5 million can now be found on every continent. By 2000, three out of the five cities with populations of 15 million or more will be in the Third World—Mexico City, São Paulo, and Calcutta. Asia will contain 15 of the world's 35 largest cities. In Africa, only Cairo is now in the 5 million category, but by the end of the century, the continent is projected to have at least eight such centers.[12]

Recent urbanization trends in the Third World are without precedent. Between 1800 and 1910, Greater London's population grew almost sevenfold, from 1.1 million to 7.3 million, an increase now achieved within a generation in many Third World cities. Likewise, it took Paris more than a century to expand from 547,000 to about 3 million, a growth matched by many Third World cities just since World War II. Moreover, the population sizes to which today's high urban growth rates are adding are dramatically larger than those in the past.[13]

As Third World cities reach astounding proportions, they are outgrowing the administrative capacity of local governments. Many are struggling to provide the most basic of services. In Alexandria, Egypt, a sewage system built earlier this century for 1 million people now serves 4 million. Lack of investment capital to upgrade waste treatment and drainage systems has left parts of the city literally awash in raw sewage.[14]

The majority of people in large African cities—Lagos, Nairobi, Kinshasa, Addis Ababa, and Lusaka, among others—lack piped water and sanitation. A 1979 survey found that 75 percent of families in Lagos lived in single-room dwellings. Seventy-eight percent of the households shared kitchen facilities with another family, while only 13 percent had running water. If the urban growth forecast for Africa materializes, living standards will undoubtedly deteriorate further.[15]

The Germans call it "Weltstädte": Literally translated as world cities, it is an apt description of the changing urban role in the world economy. Most governments in the Third World have encouraged large-city growth to link domestic and international economies. As a result, one city, usually the capital, often dominates a country, controlling the trade between urban areas and both rural and international markets. The large share of national populations in these primary cities reinforces their concentrated wealth, power, and status. As the U.N. Fund for Population Activities notes, Manila and Bangkok have more in common with Tokyo and Washington than with their rural hinterlands.[16]

The growth of cities in industrial nations was an integral part of national economic development. Today's rapid growth of large cities, on the other hand, often works against widespread gains. National development strategies based solely on the economic success of one or a few urban areas lack the diversity and stability of more broadly based efforts. The negative effects of such approaches can currently be seen throughout the developing world. *Wall Street Journal* reporter Jonathan Kandell observes that

"the cost of supporting Mexico City may be exceeding its contribution in goods and services; the nation's economic locomotive is becoming a financial drain."[17]

By 2000, three out of the five cities with populations of 15 million or more will be in the Third World.

In 1983 an estimated 44 percent of Mexico's gross domestic product, 52 percent of its industrial product, and 54 percent of its services were concentrated within metropolitan Mexico City. Similarly, more than 60 percent of Philippine manufacturing establishments in 1979 were located in Greater Manila. Comparable statistics could be cited for Jakarta, Khartoum, Lagos, and a host of others.[18]

World Bank economist Andrew Hamer, reviewing the impact of urban economic concentration on Brazil's development, found that in 1975 São Paulo had less than 10 percent of the country's population but accounted for 44 percent of the electricity consumption, 39 percent of the telephones, and well over half the industrial output and employment. He concluded that "São Paulo has been the beneficiary of preferential public sector treatment for most of the last century . . . [while] large segments of the population and even larger segments of the national territory were subject to 'benign neglect'."[19]

This neglect is evident in the increasingly disparate standards of living within cities, and between urban and rural dwellers. In Lima and La Paz, for instance, the tin-and-tarpaper shacks of the urban poor are found in the shadow of tall, modern office buildings. Mexico City has gained notoriety for the large number of people living in makeshift burrows in a hillside garbage dump.

Scenes like these are repeated in shanty-towns and illegal settlements ringing cities throughout the Third World.

Sharp income stratifications result in part from too many people chasing too few jobs. In metropolitan Manila, 16 percent of the labor force is unemployed and 43 percent is underemployed. Low incomes and high land costs leave a growing number of families unable to buy or rent homes—even ones subsidized by the government. The Philippine government estimates that at least two thirds of all new housing being constructed within the city is "illegal and uncontrolled."[20]

The gap between groups within cities is also widening with people's efforts to feed themselves. Food purchases dominate expenditures by the urban poor. When food prices rise sharply, as they did in the 1972–76 period, the urban poor suffer disproportionately. For one thing, the energy invested in food transport and the multiple transaction costs along the way ensure that food prices are higher.[21]

In the past, most governments heavily subsidized food staples and other goods to encourage urban development while keeping wage costs down. Now, these same governments walk a tightrope between the constraints of ballooning budget deficits and the demands of urban residents accustomed to low-cost goods.

Egypt, once a food exporter, now meets 60 percent of its daily food needs with imports, bound primarily for urban markets. The government, which has barely recovered from the last spate of bread riots, is politically unable to reduce its $2-billion food subsidy but economically unable to sustain it. Ironically, urban-bias subsidies such as these helped create sharp divisions between urban and rural life-styles, and continue to draw people to the cities.[22]

Past urban development has been the product of agricultural success. By con-trast, today's trends in part reflect agricultural failure. Large-scale migrations from rural areas are a symptom of the severe imbalance that characterizes national economic strategies and the sheer weight of population growth pushing down rural incomes. High rates of rural population growth, heavily skewed land distribution, poor income prospects, and low or nonexistent levels of government investment in agriculture all combine to make even urban slums look more appealing than agrarian life.

URBAN ENERGY NEEDS

Recent urbanization has been closely tied to the use of fossil fuels. Coal, used to run the steam engines that powered both factories and rail transport, gave birth to industrial society and the early industrial cities. It dominated the fossil fuel age until a few decades ago, but it is oil that has made massive urbanization possible. As world petroleum production turned sharply upward after mid-century, the national and international transportation systems on which cities depend grew by leaps and bounds.

Although urbanization has largely come to a halt in industrial countries, it is proceeding rapidly in the Third World, where energy consumption is rising as a result. Whereas rural communities rely primarily on local supplies of food, water, and, to a lesser degree, fuel, cities import these commodities, often over long distances. Likewise, rural areas can absorb their wastes locally, whereas cities use energy to collect garbage and treat sewage. Urban dwellers in the Third World thus require more energy than their rural counterparts to achieve the same living standard.

Supplying cities with water requires energy expenditures that are unnecessary in villages. Water needs of large cities often exceed local supplies, forcing municipalities to import water from great distances. Household supplies, drawn from surface water sources, require physical and chemical purification, another energy-consuming process.

The energy required to satisfy food needs also increases in urban settings. Not only is the supply line longer for cities, frequently extending across national borders, but food shipped long distances needs more processing and packaging. Fruits, vegetables, and livestock products often require refrigerated transport if they are to be edible when they reach a city. Of the total energy used in the food system of the United States, a highly urbanized society, one third is used in the production of food, one third in transporting, processing, and distributing it, and one third in preparing it.[23]

Both the quantity and nature of urban fuel needs vary with the level of development. In Third World cities, for example, cooking dominates energy use. In industrial countries, by contrast, the transportation system consumes far more energy. Australian ecologist Kenneth Newcombe analyzed energy use in Hong Kong, a city of commerce and light industry, for each of the four sectors: domestic, commercial, industrial, and transport. (See Table 3–2.) The domestic sector accounted for only 18 percent of energy use; the industrial sector required slightly more than the transport sector.

Although such detailed data are not readily available for most cities, urban energy consumption patterns vary widely. The type of fuel used typically shifts from heavy reliance on firewood to primary reliance on fossil fuels. As petroleum output expanded after mid-century, kerosene began to replace wood as a cooking fuel in Third World cities. It was convenient and, for many urban dwellers, cheaper than firewood. The oil price surge of the seventies reversed this trend, catching many countries unprepared for the dramatic growth in urban firewood demand.

Rising fuel prices and a scarcity of foreign exchange to import oil has forced literally hundreds of Third World cities to turn to the surrounding countryside for cooking fuel. As a result, forests are being devastated in ever-widening circles around cities, particularly in the Indian subcontinent and Africa. No forests remain within 70 kilometers of Niamey, the capital of Niger, or of Ouagadougou, the capital of Burkina Faso.[24]

The country with perhaps the best

Table 3-2. Hong Kong: Energy Use by Source and Sector, 1976

Sector	Liquid Fuel	Electricity[1]	Other	Total	Share of Total
	(terajoules)				(percent)
Domestic	81	43	14	138	18
Commercial	97	64	9	170	22
Industrial	148	73	12	233	31
Transport	216	1	0	217	29
Total	542	181	35	758	100

[1]All electricity was generated from oil at the time of this survey.
SOURCE: Adapted from Kenneth Newcombe, in Ian Douglas, *The Urban Environment* (Baltimore, Md.: Edward Arnold Publishers, 1983).

data on this process is India, where satellite images have been used to monitor deforestation. One study reports that for nine of India's principal cities, the area of closed forest within 100 kilometers fell sharply between the mid-seventies and early eighties. (See Table 3–3.) In well under a decade, the loss of forested area ranged from a comparatively modest 15-percent decline around Coimbatore to a staggering 60-percent decline around Delhi.

Unfortunately for low-income urban dwellers, this return to fuelwood has boosted prices. (See Table 3–4.) Data for 41 Indian cities show a 42-percent rise in fuelwood prices from 1977 to 1984. Even though food prices in India have remained remarkably stable, escalating fuelwood prices means that the cost of cooked food is rising.[25]

As forests recede from Third World cities, the cost of hauling wood rises. Eventually it becomes more profitable to convert the wood into charcoal, a more concentrated form of energy, before transporting it. This conserves transport fuel, but charcoal typically has less than half of the energy contained in the wood

Table 3-3. India: Changes in Closed Forest Cover Around Major Cities, 1972–75 to 1980–82

City	1972–75	1980–82	Change
	(square kilometers)		(percent)
Bangalore	3,853	2,762	−28
Bombay	5,649	3,672	−35
Calcutta	55	41	−25
Coimbatore	5,525	4,700	−15
Delhi	254	101	−60
Hyderabad	40	26	−35
Jaipur	1,534	786	−49
Madras	918	568	−38
Nagpur	3,116	2,051	−34

SOURCE: B. Bowonder et al., *Deforestation and Fuelwood Use in Urban Centres* (Hyderabad, India: Centre for Energy, Environment, and Technology and National Remote Sensing Agency, 1985).

used in its manufacture, providing yet another example of how urbanization boosts energy consumption and accelerates the loss of tree cover.[26]

If firewood harvesting could be evenly distributed throughout a country's forests, this renewable resource could sustain far larger harvests with proper management than is now the case. But

Table 3-4. India: Fuelwood Prices in Leading Cities, 1960–84

City	Fuelwood Price Per Ton			Average Annual Change in Price	
	1960	1977	1984	1960–77	1977–84
	(1960 rupees)			(percent)	
Ahmedabad	90	94	114	0.2	2.8
Bangalore	47	69	94	2.3	4.5
Bombay	84	111	180	1.6	7.2
Calcutta	93	94	140	0.1	5.9
Coimbatore	73	74	103	0.1	4.9
Delhi	100	122	162	1.2	4.1
Hyderabad	66	74	106	0.7	5.3
Jaipur	78	91	113	0.9	3.1
Madras	85	87	117	0.1	4.4
Nagapur	60	48	99	−1.3	10.9

SOURCE: B. Bowonder et al., *Deforestation and Fuelwood Use in Urban Centres* (Hyderabad, India: Centre for Energy, Environment, and Technology and National Remote Sensing Agency, 1985).

because the demand is often heavily concentrated around cities, nearby forests are decimated while more distant ones are left untouched. As people congregate in cities, this inability to manage national forest resources for the maximum sustainable yield could prove to be economically costly and ecologically disastrous over the long term.

As world oil production falls, cities are beginning to turn to renewable sources of energy, including hydroelectricity, waste-fueled electrical generation, solar collectors, and geothermal energy. Some cities are well along in the transition from fossil fuels. A World Bank-supported effort to reduce dependence on imported oil by developing indigenous hydropower resources is steadily boosting the hydroelectricity share of many Third World energy budgets. Hydropower and firewood dominate energy use in scores of Third World economies, but, as noted earlier, a major future role for firewood is contingent on better management of existing forests and a far greater tree planting effort than is now in prospect.[27]

The list of cities relying on renewable energy is as diverse as the sources they are drawing on: Munich derives 12 percent of its electricity from burning refuse. A 55-megawatt power plant near Rotterdam annually converts over 1 million tons of garbage into electricity. In Jerusalem and Tokyo, both located in countries that lead in solar water heater installations, rooftop collectors are commonplace. The transport system in São Paulo relies heavily on alcohol fuels distilled from sugarcane produced on nearby farms. San Francisco is deriving more and more of its electricity from nearby geothermal fields and wind farms. Reykjavik has long used geothermal energy for most of its space heating, while Philippine cities such as Manila are deriving a growing share of electricity

from geothermally powered generating plants.[28]

As oil becomes more costly in the nineties and as the world turns to alternative, more geographically diffuse sources of energy, the economics of energy use will favor cities less than in the past. Just as cities were shaped by the shift from wood to coal and then even more dramatically by the shift from coal to oil, so too will their future be shaped by a necessary shift from fossil fuels to renewable energy. This energy transition, already under way, raises questions about the optimal size of cities and a desirable rural-urban balance.

FEEDING CITIES

When agriculture began, world population probably did not exceed 15 million, no more than live in Greater London or Mexico City today. The first cities were fed with grain surpluses produced in the immediately surrounding countryside, since the lack of efficient transportation prevented long-distance movement of food.

With the Industrial Revolution this changed, as Great Britain began to export industrial products in exchange for food and raw materials. The practice spread, and soon much of Europe followed this trade pattern. On the eve of World War II, Asia, Africa, and Latin America, as well as North America, were all net grain exporters. Rural areas of these regions were producing grain to exchange for the manufactured products of European cities. Cities in the industrial countries were tapping not only the food surplus of their own countryside, but that produced far away as well.

These distant sources of food for cities grew in importance after World War II, as agricultural advances in North America created a huge exportable surplus of grain. Between 1950 and 1980, the continent's grain shipments increased from 23 million to 131 million tons. (See Table 3–5.) Since mid-century, North America's food surplus has underwritten much of the world's urban growth. Close to half of North America's grain exports are consumed in African and Asian cities half a world away.

Recently, Western Europe—for over two centuries the dominant food-importing region—has become a net exporter. This shift is attributable to agricultural support prices well above world market levels, advancing agricultural technology, and near-stationary population sizes. Like cities in North America, those in Western Europe can now be supplied entirely with grain produced in the surrounding countryside. In good crop years, such as 1986, Latin America can also feed people in its cities.

Although Asia is now the leading grain importer, India and China, the two countries that dominate the region, have recently achieved food self-sufficiency and are thus providing food for their own cities. Both could conceivably continue to do so as long as they can afford the energy to keep intensifying their agricultural production.[29]

Thus three major geographic regions —Asia (excluding India and China), Africa, and Eastern Europe and the Soviet Union—still depend on grain from abroad, principally North America. Major cities in these regions, such as Leningrad, Moscow, Cairo, Lagos, Dacca, and Hong Kong, depend heavily on grain produced in North America. And the Soviet Union is Argentina's main export market. In Africa, formerly a grain exporter, some of the world's fastest-growing cities are being fed largely with imported grain.

Occasionally logistics provide a sound reason to import food. It is sometimes easier to supply Third World coastal cities with food from abroad than from the local countryside. China, for instance, imported several million tons of grain annually for many years because it lacked the internal transportation to move grain from its agricultural interior to the major coastal cities.

As China worked toward national self-sufficiency in cereals, some of its major cities were seeking self-sufficiency in the production of perishables, particularly fresh vegetables. To reach this goal, Shanghai, a city of 11 million, extended its boundaries into the surrounding countryside, increasing the city area to some 6,000 square kilometers. This shift of nearby land to city management

Table 3-5. The Changing Pattern of World Grain Trade, 1950–86[1]

Region	1950	1960	1970	1980	1986[2]
	(million metric tons)				
North America	+23	+39	+56	+131	+102
Latin America	+ 1	0	+ 4	− 10	− 4
Western Europe	−22	−25	−30	− 16	+ 14
E. Eur. and Soviet Union	0	0	0	− 46	− 37
Africa	0	− 2	− 5	− 15	− 22
Asia	− 6	−17	−37	− 63	− 73
Australia and New Zeal.	+ 3	+ 6	+12	+ 20	+ 20

[1]Plus sign indicates net exports; minus sign, net imports.   [2]Preliminary.
SOURCES: U.N. Food and Agriculture Organization, *Production Yearbook* (Rome: various years); U.S. Department of Agriculture, *Foreign Agriculture Circulars*, various issues.

greatly facilitated the recycling of nutrients in human wastes. As of 1986, Shanghai was self-sufficient in vegetables and produced most of its grain and a good part of its pork and poultry. Vegetables consumed in Shanghai typically travel less than 10 kilometers from the fields in which they are produced, often reaching the market within hours of being harvested.[30]

India and China have recently achieved food self-sufficiency and are providing food for their own cities.

Hong Kong, a city of 5 million occupying an area of just over 1,000 square kilometers, has a highly sophisticated urban agriculture system, which provides 45 percent of its fresh vegetables. It produces 15 percent of its own pork by feeding the pigs with indigenous food wastes, including some 130,000 tons per year from restaurants and food-processing plants, and with imported feedstuffs. Relying on imported feed, the city also produces 60 percent of its live poultry supply. Some 31 percent of Hong Kong's agricultural land produces vegetables. Fish ponds, occupying 18 percent of the agricultural land, are commonly fertilized with pig and poultry manure and yield 25–74 tons per hectare, depending on the particular species and practice used.[31]

In the industrial West, European cities have traditionally emphasized urban community gardens. After the oil price hikes of the seventies, many American cities also launched urban gardening projects, offering undeveloped land to inner-city residents. State governments, particularly in the Northeast, have organized farmers' markets in cities, producing a direct link between local farmers and consumers. Popular with urban dwellers, they are a valuable adjunct to the more traditional roadside stands in heavily populated areas.[32]

The most effective urban food self-sufficiency efforts are those where city governments orchestrate land use, nutrient recycling, and marketing, as in Shanghai. Increased local production of perishable vegetables facilitates the recycling of nutrients from waste and yields fresh produce at attractive prices. Another bonus is that shorter supply lines reduce dependency on energy-intensive transportation.

NUTRIENT RECYCLING

Each day thousands of tons of basic plant nutrients—nitrogen, phosphorus, and potassium—move from countryside to city in the flow of food that sustains urban populations. In turn, human organic wastes—society's most ubiquitous disposable materials—are created. Worldwide, over two thirds of the nutrients present in human wastes are released to the environment as unreclaimed sewage, often polluting rivers, streams, and lakes. As the energy costs of manufacturing fertilizer rise, the viability of agriculture—and, by extension, cities—may hinge on how successfully urban areas can recycle this immense volume of nutrients. Closing nutrient cycles is thus one of the building blocks of ecologically sustainable cities.[33]

The collection of human wastes (known as night soil) for use as fertilizer is a long-standing tradition in some countries, particularly in Asia. People use door-to-door handcarts to collect night soil in many of the older neighborhoods of Seoul, South Korea, for recycling to the city's green belt. The World Bank estimated as recently as 1981 that

one third of China's fertilizer requirements were provided by night soil.[34]

European cities began fertilizing crops
with human wastes in the late nineteenth
century to minimize water pollution and
to recycle sewage. By 1875, nearly 50
sewage farms existed in Britain, some
serving major cities such as London and
Manchester. These early attempts at nutrient recycling failed for several reasons. The volume of wastes from growing cities soon overwhelmed the capacity
of the sewage farms. As cities grew, sites
to apply the sewage became ever more
distant from the nutrient sources. And
untreated human wastes were recognized as a major source of health problems. Strong taboos developed and the
practice was halted, resulting in an open-
ended nutrient flow.[35]

**Over half the 3.6 million cubic me-
ters of wastewater produced daily
in Indian cities with sewers is being
used to irrigate crops.**

Recently, attitudes toward nutrient
recycling have come full circle. Higher
fertilizer prices, a better understanding of natural resource and ecological
constraints, and improved waste management technologies have renewed interest in nutrient recycling in industrial
and developing countries alike. Such
efforts protect scarce urban resources:
Municipalities that recycle organic
wastes can simultaneously save money,
land, and fresh water for other uses. Recycling treated sewage onto farms surrounding cities also enhances urban self-
sufficiency, as indicated earlier. At least
six Chinese cities produce within their
boundaries more than 85 percent of
their vegetable supplies in part by re-
claiming nutrients from human wastes
and garbage.[36]

Devising a comprehensive recycling
strategy depends on waste composition,
collection, and treatment, and on the
disposable wastes that result. Different
sewage treatment methods yield different end-products, though they all mimic
or enhance natural biological waste degradation. "Wet" or water-borne sewage
systems yield raw or treated solids and
wastewater effluents for recycling. "Dry"
sanitation systems, predominant in developing regions, rely on night soil as
the primary recyclable material.

Two water-borne sewage treatment
methods are now used. In the first, air,
sunlight, and microbial organisms break
down wastes, settle solids, and kill pathogens in a series of wastewater ponds
or lagoons. Because they are inexpensive and land-intensive, lagoons are used
primarily in small urban areas and
throughout developing countries. About
one fourth of the municipalities in the
United States use wastewater lagoons.[37]

The second type of wastewater treatment uses energy and technology to replicate natural processes. Plants receive
large volumes of sewage (domestic
wastes often mixed with industrial
wastes and stormwater), which undergo
a variety of physical, biological, and
chemical cleansing treatments. This
method produces sludge—a substance
of mud-like consistency composed
mainly of biodegradable organic material—and purified wastewater effluent.

Crop irrigation with wastewater
treated in lagoons is practiced worldwide. The effluent is rich in nitrogen,
phosphorus, and other nutrients, and
represents a valuable water resource,
particularly in arid regions. The Kuwaiti
government has turned to nutrient recycling to conserve water and reduce reliance on imported food, and has set goals
of becoming self-sufficient in the production of milk, potatoes, onions, and
garlic. In the Mexican state of Hidalgo,
effluents from Mexico City are recycled

on to 50,000 hectares of cropland in the world's largest wastewater irrigation scheme. Falling water tables and rising energy costs for groundwater pumping are likely to make this practice even more attractive in the future.[38]

Municipal sewage systems currently serve fewer than 4 percent of India's 785 million people. Just over half the 3.6 million cubic meters of wastewater produced daily in Indian cities with sewers is being used to irrigate crops. If all of it were recycled, the World Bank estimates, it would yield 82,000 tons of nitrogen and 24,000 tons of phosphorus annually.[39]

Sewage-fed aquaculture is another way to recycle wastes using wastewater ponds. Here, wastewater purification is complemented by cultivating fish fed on the algae in the lagoons. China, India, Thailand, and Vietnam are leaders in wastewater aquaculture. Fish ponds in Calcutta provide 20 tons of fish per day to city markets.[40]

Sludge is not usually a complete fertilizer substitute because of variations in nutrient content. Nevertheless, it can provide significant quantities of nitro-

gen and phosphorus, while offering other agricultural benefits. Sludge is a soil-builder. It adds organic bulk, improves soil aeration and water retention, combats erosion, and, as a result, boosts crop yields. Added to soil or used as incremental fertilizer, sludge can significantly reduce a farmer's commercial fertilizer bill.

More than 15,000 sewage treatment plants in the United States handled over 26 billion gallons of wastewater daily in 1985, generating 7 million tons of wastewater sludge (dry weight). The U.S. Environmental Protection Agency estimated the nutrient content of this waste, which included 1.4 million tons of nitrogen, at some 10 percent of that supplied to American farmers by chemical fertilizers, worth therefore over $1 billion per year.[41]

Land application of treated sewage sludge has grown markedly over the past two decades. Approximately 42 percent of sludge generated in the United States is applied to land; the rest goes to landfills or incinerators, or is composted. (See Table 3–6.) Western Europe produces over 6.5 million dry

Table 3-6. Sludge Production and Disposal in Selected Industrial Countries, 1983

Country	Annual Sludge Production	Method of Disposal					
		Farm Land	Land-Fill[1]	Inciner-ation	Ocean Dumping	Unspec-ified[2]	Total
	(thousand tons)	(percent)					
United States	6,200	42	15	27	4	12	100
West Germany	2,200	39	49	8	2	2	100
Italy	1,200	20	55	– – 25 – –			0	100
United Kingdom	1,200	41	26	4	29	0	100
France	840	30	50	20	0	0	100
Netherlands	230	60	27	2	11	0	100
Sweden	210	60	– – – – 30 – – – –				10	100

[1]Includes small amounts for land reclamation and forest application.   [2]Mostly sludge retained in lagoons.
SOURCE: A.M. Bruce and R.D. Davis, "Britain Uses Half Its Fertilizer As Sludge," *Biocycle*, March 1984; U.S. data from Robert K. Bastian, U.S. Environmental Protection Agency, Washington, D.C., private communication, September 1986.

tons of sludge each year, a figure that is expected to rise 5 percent annually as more stringent water pollution controls go into effect. Approximately 40 percent of the sludge produced in Western Europe is now used in agriculture.

Composting sludge through biological decomposition is also increasingly popular. Compost is a humus-like substance that is an excellent soil conditioner. Although the nutrient value of composted sludge is reduced due to processing, other benefits, such as the elimination of pathogen populations and reduced water content, make this method of recycling more attractive in some situations. More significantly, compost enhances the ability of crops to draw on both natural and synthetic nutrients. Wheat yields in India increase from 28 to 44 percent with each 5 tons of compost added per hectare.[42]

Appropriate technologies and practices for minimizing sewage-related health risks have been widely adopted in industrial countries, but they have not been fully exploited in developing countries. Installing Western-style sanitation is a luxury few Third World cities can afford. Approximately 40 percent of India's 100 million urban households use dry buckets or latrines from which excreta is collected for disposal; only 20 percent are served by water-borne systems and the rest have virtually no sanitation.[43]

The lack of adequate organic waste collection and treatment in many Third World cities results in serious health and environmental problems. Raw night soil provides a microscopic blueprint of the enteric diseases prevalent in a community. Pathogens present in human wastes include hookworm, tapeworm, and the bacteria that cause typhoid and cholera. Using inadequately treated night soil in agriculture ensures the spread of these pathogens.[44]

U.S. Department of Agriculture scientists have devised a composting method capable of killing virtually all pathogens present in night soil. The technique relies on the same principles as those employed in sludge composting but uses less energy, is labor-intensive, and results in a product with a higher nutrient content. Most important is the extremely low capital cost involved. Adapting such low-technology solutions to night soil management provides an affordable alternative to financially strapped municipalities.[45]

Nutrient recycling is likely to increase in popularity as cities grow and become more concentrated and as waste management strategies improve. Other urban organic disposables—such as household food wastes and the by-products of food processing plants—can add significantly to the share of nutrients recycled from cities handling either wet or dry wastes. Recycling sludge through land application and composting wherever water-borne sanitation exists is cheaper and more environmentally sound than any other disposal option. As part of a broad public health strategy, nutrient recycling can help Third World cities reach simultaneously the goals of better health and sanitation, higher food self-sufficiency, and reduced environmental pollution.

ECOLOGY AND ECONOMICS OF CITY SIZE

Cities require concentrations of food, water, and fuel on a scale not found in nature. Just as nature cannot concentrate the resources needed to support urban life, neither can it disperse the waste produced in cities. The waste output of even a small city quickly overtaxes the absorptive capacity of local terrestrial and aquatic ecosystems. Sustaining urban habitats thus depends on heavy investments in systems to concentrate the essential resources and to treat and disperse the waste products.

Moving large quantities of food, water, and fuel into large cities and moving garbage and sewage out is not only logistically complex, it is energy-intensive. The larger the city, the more complex and costly its support systems become. Nutrient-rich human wastes that are an asset in a rural setting can become an economic liability in an urban environment. Indeed, the collection and treatment of sewage is a leading claim on urban tax revenues, even when it is processed and sold as fertilizer.

As cities grow and their material needs multiply, they eventually exceed the supply capacity of the surrounding countryside. Even water sometimes must be transported over long distances. Early cities were able to satisfy their water needs from local wells, but as urban areas grow their water demands typically outgrow local supplies.

The Greater New York area, for example, which uses 1.9 billion cubic meters of water per year, obtains only 2 percent of it from indigenous underground sources. The remaining 98 percent comes from surface catchments many kilometers from the city proper. Sydney, Australia, a much smaller city that uses only 402 million cubic meters of water per year, obtains only 4 percent of its water from underground sources. (See Table 3–7.)

Hong Kong has a rather different supply pattern. Of the 133 million cubic meters of fresh water used annually, 49 percent comes from underground sources and the rest is from surface catchments, mostly from across the border in China. Thus Hong Kong is one of the few cities that depends heavily on water in another country. Satisfying the water demands of this prosperous commercial city of 6.7 million inhabitants also takes some ingenuity, such as using sea water for industrial processes and to cool electric generating plants.[46]

Many large cities find that they must draw their water from ever more distant sites or deplete the aquifers upon which they sit. Los Angeles, for example, now draws part of its water from northern California, several hundred miles away. The water comes south through the California aqueduct, over the Tehachapi mountains some 2,000 feet above sea level and then into the Los Angeles basin. Some even comes from the Colorado River and is transported a long distance at great cost.[47]

Mexico City faces even greater problems: Its elevated site means it must lift water from progressively lower catchments. In 1982 Mexico City began

Table 3-7. Annual Water Consumption in Three Cities, by Source

City	Underground Water	Surface Catchments	Total	Underground Water Share of Total
	(million cubic meters)			(percent)
New York	48	1,880	1,928	2
Sydney	17	385	402	4
Hong Kong	65	68	133	49

SOURCE: Ian Douglas, *The Urban Environment* (Baltimore, Md.: Edward Arnold Publishers, 1983).

pumping water from Cutzamala, a site
100 kilometers away and 1,000 meters
lower than the city. British geographer
Ian Douglas reports that "augmentation
of the Mexico City supply in the 1990s
will be from Tecolutla, which is some
200 kilometers away and 2,000 meters
lower." Pumping water this far will require some 125 trillion kilojoules of
electrical energy annually, the output of
six 1,000-megawatt power plants. Construction of these plants would cost at
least $6 billion, roughly half the annual
interest payments on Mexico's external
debt. If the costs of expanding Mexico
City's water supply are becoming
prohibitive, as these numbers suggest,
water scarcity may prevent the projected

growth in the city from materializing.
The city is thus faced with three rising
cost curves in water procurement—increasing distance of water transport, increasing height of water lift, and rising
energy costs.[48]

Water scarcity is not the only emerging constraint on urban growth. As
noted earlier, for many Third World cities the rising price of oil, and hence of
kerosene, since 1973 has put pressure
on indigenous fuelwood resources. Research on fuelwood prices in India de-
monstrates a remarkably close relationship between city size and firewood
costs. (See Table 3–8.) In some smaller
cities that are relatively close to forested
areas, such as Darjeeling, fuelwood costs

Table 3-8. India: Fuelwood Prices in Major Cities, by Size, 1984

Rupees per Metric Ton	Population of City		
	Less Than 1 Million	Between 1 Million and 5 Million	More Than 5 Million
Less than 350	Balaghat Darjeeling		
350–400	Srinagar Chikmagalur Asansol		
400–500	Jamshedpur Bhavnagar		
500–700	Bhopal Indore Sambalpur Amritsar Coimbatore Madurai Alleppey	Hyderabad Ahmedabad Bangalore Nagapur Jaipur Madras Kanpur	
Above 700	Gwalior Ajmer Varanasi Howrah		Bombay Calcutta Delhi

SOURCE: B. Bowonder et al., *Deforestation and Fuelwood Use in Urban Centres* (Hyderabad, India: Centre for Energy, Environment, and Technology and National Remote Sensing Agency, 1985).

less than 350 rupees per ton in 1984. As city size increased, so did firewood prices. In the seven cities with populations between 1 million and 5 million, prices ranged from 500 to 700 rupees per ton. For the three cities with more than 5 million residents, fuelwood cost more than 700 rupees per ton, at least twice as much as in smaller cities.

Some small cities also had expensive fuelwood, usually because they were in areas with little remaining forest cover. Thus small cities in India do not necessarily have low fuelwood prices, but all large cities have high prices. Over time this economic differential may begin to affect wage costs, leading industries to move to smaller cities with lower fuelwood prices.

Of all the investments needed to sustain cities, the shortfall is undoubtedly greatest in the treatment and disposal of human and industrial wastes. Reports on the adverse consequences of air pollution in Third World cities, such as Mexico City and Seoul, are legion. An estimated 60 percent of Calcutta's residents are believed to suffer from respiratory diseases related to air pollution. Canadian environmental analyst Vaclav Smil reports that "lung cancer mortality in China is four to seven times higher in cities than in the nation as a whole, and the difference is largely attributable to heavy air pollution."[49]

Water pollution in Third World cities may be even worse than air pollution. Jorge Hardoy and David Satterthwaite of the International Institute for Environment and Development report that only 209 of India's 3,119 towns and cities have even partial sewage systems and treatment facilities. Some 114 towns and cities dump raw sewage into the Ganges, the country's holy river. And in Colombia, 120 kilometers downstream from Bogotá's nearly 5 million residents, the Bogotá River has an average fecal bacteria coliform count of 7.3 million, an

astronomical level compared with the safe drinking water limit of 100 and the safe swimming count of 200. Heavy metal contamination of water supplies is also common around Third World cities. Lake Managua in Nicaragua, for instance, is heavily contaminated with mercury.[50]

Little systematic effort has been made to measure most pollutants in the air and water in Third World cities. Consequently, environmentally induced illnesses are often the first indication of serious pollution. Much of the evidence of deteriorating urban environments is physical and visual. Hardoy and Satterthwaite observe that "when one visits a Third World city, environmental problems, such as smog or smoke irritating the eyes, inadequate provision for garbage collection and disposal, open sewers or no sewers at all, inadequate drainage and noxious and polluted rivers, lakes or seacoasts are usually all too evident."[51]

Whether concentrating the resources needed to sustain a city or dispersing the wastes that threaten to make it uninhabitable, the ecology of cities is a matter of concern. Changes in the ecology of expanding cities are now becoming evident. What is less obvious is that the economics of sustainable cities is also changing, favoring the smaller ones.

SEEKING A RURAL-URBAN BALANCE

The intimate relationship between rural and urban areas stretches far back into history, yet it is a marriage so obvious as to be forgotten by most. Residents of early Greek cities were aware of their dependence on agricultural bounty and sought to limit city size by design. Lewis

Mumford describes the towns of Greece as "both small and relatively self-contained, largely dependent on their local countryside for food and building materials."[52]

A stable and productive farm economy helps ensure long-term food security. At the same time, the improvements in living standards associated with modernization require urbanization as a way to provide basic services and to capitalize on the economies of scale inherent in industrial processes, such as manufacturing. The countries that underwent industrialization and urbanization in the nineteenth century built their cities on successful agrarian foundations.

But the present uncontrolled urban growth in the Third World is the result of failed economic and population policies, driven more by rural poverty than urban prosperity. Economists Michael Todaro and Jerry Stilkind write that "for developing nations, the policy of neglecting agriculture . . . has produced stagnating or inadequate income growth in rural areas, while the policy of importing large-scale, labor-saving technology to achieve instant industrialization has meant that urban job opportunities have not grown as fast as the numbers seeking work." This is nowhere more evident than in Africa, where both per capita agricultural production and urban and rural incomes have fallen back to the levels of the sixties. The challenge now before policymakers is to find a mix of policy approaches that maximizes progress for the entire society.[53]

Third World governments, with only occasional exceptions, have favored cities at the expense of the countryside. Michael Lipton, an analyst of rural-urban relationships in developing countries, graphically describes the conflicts that arise: "The most important class conflict in the poor countries of the world today is not between labor and [those who control] capital, nor is it between foreign and national interests. It is between the rural classes and the urban classes. The rural sector contains most of the poverty and most of the low cost sources of potential advance. But the urban sector contains most of the articulateness and power." As a result, the urban classes "have been able to win most of the rounds of the struggle with the countryside; but in doing so they have made the development process needlessly slow and unfair."[54]

It is not uncommon for developing countries with 70 percent of their populations in rural areas to allocate only 20 percent of their budgets to the rural sector. In such situations, investment per urban dweller can easily be several times that per rural resident. Mexican urban analyst Gustavo Garza notes that between 1970 and 1980, federal spending in Mexico City "far exceeded the worth of the entire existing industrial plant in the city." And Michael Lipton points out that a child from an Indian town or city is 8.5 times more likely than a village child to make it to a university. This strong urban bias in the provision of services, such as education, health, electricity, and water, increases social inequities: It deprives rural individuals of opportunities and societies of sorely needed talent.[55]

Migrants leave rural areas for a complex array of reasons. Landlessness and high rates of rural population growth have foreclosed agrarian futures in every developing region. Some subsistence farmers migrate to cities on a seasonal basis, looking for supplemental employment. But more move permanently in hopes of improving their income propects.

This movement presents several problems. First, the majority of those who migrate, especially in the earliest stages of urbanization, are young men, the primary wage earners in traditional societies. But too few jobs and too many jobseekers lead to 20-percent unemployment rates and 40-percent underemployment in many Third World countries.[56]

Second, due to low domestic agricultural prices and the migration of jobseekers to cities, the food surplus produced in the countryside may dwindle or disappear. Consequently, urban areas become increasingly dependent on imported food. To forestall impending food shortages, governments spend scarce foreign exchange that would be better spent on fertilizer or irrigation pumps; were such investments made, they would expand food output and the national product while creating employment.

Aside from the inherent inequity, the urban bias evident in the economic policies of so many Third World countries wastes both rural human talent and natural resources. Two policies—the official exchange rate that governs the terms of trade between a country and the outside world, and the food price policy that governs rural-urban terms of trade—are the principal means of favoring cities. Official exchange rates are set to make imports cheap, often bringing the price of imported food below that of food produced in the surrounding countryside. The economic stresses being felt in many Third World countries, including potentially unmanageable external debt, are one manifestation of this economic bias.

Food price policies directly affect rural-urban relationships by providing unrealistically cheap food for city dwellers and discouraging private investments in food production and hence rural employment. The resulting distortion in the development process helps explain both the increasing reliance on imported food and the attraction cities hold for the rural unemployed.

Such policies hold down producer prices as well as rural incomes, thereby transferring net income to urban residents. Both Thailand and India have actively restricted foodgrain exports in an effort to dampen domestic urban food prices. In Zambia, consumer maize subsidies are an essential feature of a food policy aimed at encouraging the growth of cities and attracting workers to the mines. Local producers of maize receive well below market rates, encouraging the formation of a pool of labor for mining. At the same time, the low price of food in the cities due to government-subsidized imports helps keep wage costs down.[57]

The World Bank and International Monetary Fund are encouraging heavily indebted governments seeking new loans to abandon the biased policies that have contributed to their dilemmas. Many are being pressed to eliminate the food subsidies that benefit primarily urban dwellers and to adopt agricultural price policies that will stimulate domestic food production and reduce dependence on imported food.

Thailand and India have actively restricted foodgrain exports in an effort to dampen domestic urban food prices.

China offers perhaps the best example of a country that has managed to regulate the growth of cities, by restricting migration and investing heavily in the countryside. The Chinese model will not fit all countries. But the example is particularly instructive in that rural incomes now rival urban ones as a result of widespread agricultural reform. Few Third World governments emphasize agriculture as strongly as the Chinese do, however. What is needed to adequately manage today's cities and to stem the flow of migrants is a set of farsighted national policies that increase national equity. Indeed, the most effective efforts to ameliorate the problems facing cities may well be those to increase investment, and hence employment and productivity, in the countryside.[58]

Third World policymakers face the question of how large cities should be in a world that depends primarily on renewable energy resources. Existing urban projections are keyed to fossil fuels rather than renewable sources, and so may overestimate future urbanization. There is no guarantee that vast cities with tens of millions of people—such as projected for Mexico City or Calcutta, for example—can be sustained or, indeed, should be sustained, if doing so requires heavy subsidies from the countryside. Although the age of renewable energy is only beginning to unfold, both the ecology and the economics of a world economy based largely on these energy sources suggest that the future may favor smaller cities and those who live in rural areas.

4

Reassessing Nuclear Power

Christopher Flavin

At 1:24 a.m. on the 26th of April, 1986, two large explosions destroyed one of four power reactors at Chernobyl in the Soviet Union—a blast heard round the world. Within days, much of Europe was experiencing the highest levels of radioactive fallout ever recorded there; within two weeks, minor radioactivity was detected in Tokyo, Washington, and throughout the northern hemisphere. The Chernobyl accident was by any measure the most serious nuclear accident the world has ever suffered.

The direct costs of the accident are high: 31 deaths as of September 1986; 1,000 immediate injuries; 135,000 people evacuated from their homes in the Ukraine; at least $3 billion of direct financial losses. But the long-term implications are far greater, longer lasting, and less clear. It may not be possible simply to "remove the consequences of

An expanded version of this chapter appeared as Worldwatch Paper 75, *Reassessing Nuclear Power: The Fallout from Chernobyl.*

the accident," as Soviet officials euphemistically put it.[1]

The health of people and of the environment both in the Ukraine and throughout Europe could well be affected for decades. Estimates of future cancer deaths range from a few hundred to more than 100,000. The Chernobyl nuclear cloud showed graphically—and tragically—that we all share the global environment.

The economic and political fallout from Chernobyl may be even more widely felt. Many Europeans have lost faith in government officials whom they believe deliberately understated the health threat from the accident. Public support for nuclear power, already quite slim in most countries, shrank to the lowest levels ever. Several political parties that once strongly favored nuclear power or took a neutral stance have come out strongly against it. In some countries the debate is not over whether to build more reactors but whether to close existing ones. And nuclear power is now a contentious bilateral issue for several neighboring countries with differing nuclear policies.

Most nuclear programs were far from healthy even before Chernobyl. Plant construction worldwide has fallen 45 percent from its peak in 1980, and is likely to be down much further by 1990. Only a handful of countries have steady expansion programs. It now seems almost certain that nuclear power's share of world electricity will be lower in the year 2000 than it is in 1987.[2]

Chernobyl marks a major milestone in the erosion of the world's nuclear programs. The accident has forced a reassessment of nuclear power's role, and a growing portion of the scientific community and the public at large believe that nuclear power as it has so far been developed is unacceptable. Antinuclear advocates are no longer confined to the political fringes: Included now in their ranks are the Prime Minister of Austria, the President of the Philippines, and the leaders of the main opposition parties in Great Britain and West Germany. Prime Minister Ingvar Carlsson of Sweden, once a nuclear power supporter, added up the damage to his country four months after Chernobyl and concluded, "Nuclear power must be got rid of."[3]

As we approach the end of the twentieth century, Albert Einstein's observation that "the unleashed power of the atom has changed everything save our modes of thinking" seems ever more profound.[4] Our technological capacities have produced an energy source whose implications many citizens find profoundly troubling. They argue that nuclear power's long-term costs—in waste disposal, threats of terrorism, and accidents—exceed any conceivable economic benefits. Chernobyl will force the world's governments to consider this possibility far more carefully than they have so far.

CHERNOBYL'S TOLL

From the early accidental discovery of the Chernobyl nuclear cloud in Sweden through weeks of announcements, warnings, misstatements, and corrections, the international community showed it was not even remotely prepared for such an emergency. Yet ever since the first nuclear power plants of the fifties, engineers have recognized the potential for a catastrophic accident that would kill people and contaminate the environment. Elaborate and redundant safety systems are used so that, even in the event of a serious malfunction, these materials will not get into the human food chain or the wider ecosystem. The need to minimize this risk has led to exacting design and construction standards.

At Three Mile Island, where the reactor's core partially melted in 1979 and heavily contaminated the plant, the reactor vessel and containment building kept all but a tiny portion of the dangerous materials from spreading across the Pennsylvania countryside. The Ukrainians were not so fortunate. For the first time ever a large reactor exploded, lifting a 1,000-ton steel cover plate off the reactor and obliterating the containment structure. Much has been made of the fact that Soviet graphite-moderated reactors have relatively weak containments but it is not clear that any containment in use today could have withstood the immense force of the steam explosion caused by the runaway Chernobyl reactor.[5]

Soviet scientists estimate that between 3 and 4 percent of the radioactive materials in the core were released to the environment—about 7,000 kilograms of material containing 50–100 million curies of radioactive isotopes, over 1,000 times the amount released at Three Mile Island.[6]

The immense force of the explosion, combined with a resulting fire in the graphite that surrounded the uranium fuel rods, forced radioactive materials high into the atmosphere. Nearby observers reported a spectacular fireworks display as burning uranium and graphite were hurled into the night sky. Volatile gases, smoke, dust particles, and pieces of the nuclear core itself were found downwind of the plant over the following days, and Soviet scientists found dozens of radioactive isotopes among these materials.[7]

The dispersion of radioactive fallout was left to the winds, as the fire at the damaged reactor raged for 10 days, spewing a radioactive plume into the air. Metropolitan Kiev, home to 2.4 million people, was largely spared due to winds that blew away from the city during the worst period. But several wind shifts brought the nuclear cloud over virtually all of Europe—extending as far north as the Arctic Circle, as far south as Greece, and as far west as the British Isles. Potentially health-threatening levels of radioactive materials were deposited more than 2,000 kilometers from the plant and in at least 20 countries.[8]

The Chernobyl nuclear cloud left an extraordinarily complex pattern of fallout that may never be fully understood. Many parts of Europe directly under the plume received little fallout while others got larger amounts. West German researchers found that over a distance of 100 kilometers, radiation levels varied by a factor of 15. Similarly, levels 100 kilometers northwest of Stockholm reached 10 times those in the capital. Not only was the radioactive cloud composed of many different elements with varying weights and half-lives (the time it takes to decay to half the original concentration), but their deposition was heavily influenced by rainfall. Local topography then caused the radioactive runoff to concentrate along valleys and in reservoirs, forming "hot spots."[9]

A person can be injured by direct exposure to radioactive materials, by inhaling radioactive gases and dust, or by ingesting contaminated food or water. Chernobyl led to all three exposures, but the largest concern outside the immediate vicinity was radiation taken in through the food chain and water supply. Radioactive materials falling onto the soil or grass can be consumed by grazing animals, where the radiation is further concentrated and then enters people by way of meat and dairy products.

Radioactive materials were deposited more than 2,000 kilometers from the plant and in at least 20 countries.

The materials in the nuclear cloud included up to 50 radioactive isotopes with half-lives ranging from two hours to 24,000 years. The two most significant components were iodine 131 and cesium 137, which is particularly hazardous because of its 30-year half-life. Both are chemically reactive elements that are readily absorbed into biological materials, thus contaminating the food chain.[10]

In the first days, iodine 131 was most worrying since it was widely spread and tends to concentrate in the thyroid gland, where it can cause thyroid nodules that can become cancerous. However, iodine 131 has a half-life of 8 days and was largely gone within a few months. This is unfortunately not true for cesium 137, for strontium 90, with a half-life of 27 years, or for plutonium 239, with 24,000 years—all of which were present in the Chernobyl fallout. American scientists estimate that one tenth to one sixth as much cesium 137 was released at Chernobyl as has entered the environment from all above-ground nuclear weapons testing to date.[11]

The health effects of high levels of radiation exposure are well known due to investigations at Hiroshima and Nagasaki as well as from accidents involving workers at nuclear facilities during the past 40 years. Most of the 29 people who died from radiation exposure in the first few months were among the 50 plant workers and firefighters who received direct radiation in excess of 500 rads (units of absorbed radiation).[12]

Doses over 500 rads cause severe damage to the body's tissues, particularly those that grow the fastest. Doctors report that many of the Chernobyl victims died slowly and painfully from radiation burns. The bone marrow that produces the body's red blood cells was also damaged in many patients. Efforts by an international team of doctors to transplant fresh bone marrow or fetal liver cells into about 20 patients were of limited success: Within three months, three quarters of the patients were dead, some killed by infections that overwhelmed their immune systems. Two hundred more people received doses of between 100 rads and 500 rads, and although they are still alive, long-term prospects are not good. They are at increased risk of developing cancer, including leukemia and tumors, for the rest of their lives.[13]

Estimating the health dangers to the wider population is more difficult. It was not until 36 hours after the accident that an armada of 1,100 buses evacuated Pripyat's 49,000 residents and all others within 10 kilometers of the plant. Later, the evacuation zone was widened to 30 kilometers and 94,000 people, and finally to 135,000 people. In Kiev, 80 kilometers south of the plant, all schoolchildren were sent away for an early summer vacation a few weeks after the disaster. The exposures of all these people varied enormously, depending on the path of the plume, how much time they spent outdoors, and what they ate and drank. However, Soviet doctors believe that many of those exposed face serious cancer risks in the years ahead and there is a plan to carefully monitor them for the rest of their lives.[14]

Even low levels of radiation carry some cancer risk, but medical scientists do not know how much. The official Soviet radiation figures indicate that the accident will raise the cancer rate in the European part of the Soviet Union by less than 1 percent according to the consensus of medical scientists. Based on observed fallout patterns, one to three times as many deaths are likely outside the Soviet Union. According to Robert Gale, an American physician who helped treat the victims of Chernobyl, Soviet radiation figures imply that between 5,000 and 50,000 people will die of cancer in the Soviet Union and the rest of Europe.[15]

Frank von Hippel, a physicist at Princeton University's Center for Energy and Environmental Studies, used a computer model to predict between 15,500 and 135,000 extra cancer cases and a maximum of 35,000 extra deaths, mainly as a result of exposure to radioactive cesium. None of the estimates should be considered more than educated guesses. The diverse pathways by which people can receive radiation, the enormous variations in exposure over short distances, and a shortage of local monitoring equipment only compound the uncertainties. And several medical scientists in the United States and Europe believe that Chernobyl's eventual cancer toll will be far higher than the consensus figures indicate.[16]

These figures represent a serious health threat, but one that is exceeded by other risks that societies live with.

Swedish scientists, for example, estimate that people living in heavily contaminated areas are about half as likely to die from cancer caused by Chernobyl as in an automobile accident. And pollution from coal-burning power plants is estimated to kill thousands of people every year who contract heart or respiratory disease or cancer. One thing is certain: Chernobyl has created a huge experiment on the effect of radiation on human health.[17]

In the weeks following the accident, fresh vegetables in many parts of Europe contained levels of radioactivity above limits recommended by health authorities. Cattle grazing on contaminated grass were soon producing milk with significant radioactive materials. This led to both voluntary and mandatory food restrictions throughout Europe. For several months, perhaps 100 million people altered their diets.[18]

In the absence of accepted international standards, national, state, and local governments issued a wide range of regulations and recommendations. In southern Germany, the local government in Konstanz severely restricted milk and vegetable consumption, while the adjacent Swiss canton of Thurgau took almost no precautions. Sweden adopted a comprehensive national program, including extensive monitoring. Eating of spring vegetables, berries, and freshwater fish in some areas was discouraged when they were found to be contaminated with iodine and cesium. Most of Sweden's cattle were restricted to their barns until meadows had been approved for grazing, a process that was not completed until the end of the summer. Although it is hard to quantify, these restrictions probably helped reduce Chernobyl's overall cancer toll in Europe.[19]

Throughout Europe, people were confused and critical of what were perceived as government efforts to placate the public by understating the health dangers. This mixture of paternalism, bureaucratic incompetence, and lack of preparation turned out to be a chaotic brew. In Italy, it was left to local governments and citizens' groups to monitor radiation levels; even four months after the accident, significant amounts of cesium were being discovered in wild mushrooms, veal, rabbit, and mutton. In the United Kingdom, official claims that the country would be spared were followed by a deliberate National Radiological Protection Board effort to downplay the health effects, according to a report in *New Scientist.*[20]

Chernobyl has created a huge experiment on the effect of radiation on human health.

As the Chernobyl cloud passed over eastern France, the government repeatedly stated that the fallout had missed the country and life could continue normally. Weather maps were issued showing sweeping turns in wind currents as they steered around France. But in a few days independent monitors revealed that France had in fact received fallout comparable to that in adjoining nations. The government tried to explain its mishandling of the information by saying that officials were on holiday. Though widely criticized, it still refused to issue significant food restrictions.[21]

International organizations did little either. The International Atomic Energy Agency (IAEA) provided no food or health recommendations. The World Health Organization made no official pronouncement until a week after the accident, and then issued only broad warnings. The European Economic Community (EEC) did adopt interim limits on radiation levels in crops and restrictions on the import of fresh food from Eastern Europe for three weeks. However, the standards were weak and clouded by political compromises. Since the accident, EEC ministers have considered creating a radiological information service and permanent food standards.[22]

Scientists believe that in most areas radiation levels will fall sufficiently to permit resumption of normal life within a year or two—primarily due to the diluting effects of rain, wind, and ploughing. Some problems may persist, however. One example is Switzerland's Lake Lugano, where authorities banned fishing on August 1 when it was discovered that fish had concentrations of cesium up to six times the EEC standard. Radioactive materials may remain in lake sediments and some types of agricultural soils for several years.[23]

In Scandinavia, the Sami people (also known as Lapps) were severely affected. Some 97 percent of the reindeer initially slaughtered in late summer had radioactivity above the level recommended for human consumption, a problem that biologists believe may persist for years. The result is a potential catastrophe for the delicate Lapland ecosystem and for the culturally endangered Sami people who depend on it.[24]

The Soviets have mounted a massive cleanup effort near Chernobyl, bringing in equipment, conscripted workers, and military forces from all parts of the nation. All nearby forests will have to be razed and the topsoil removed and buried. The town of Pripyat may not be habitable, and farmland in the area may have to be abandoned for many decades.[25] In the Soviet Union alone, the direct costs come to $3 billion according to official Soviet estimates and up to $5 billion according to independent economists. (See Table 4–1.) But the eventual costs may be far above even the larger estimates. The cleanup at Three Mile Island, where the reactor

Table 4-1. Soviet Union: Estimated Direct Financial Losses from the Chernobyl Accident, 1986

Loss	Estimated Cost
	(million dollars)
Site cleanup	350–690
Health care for victims	280–560
Relocation of residents	70
Replacement cost of plant	1,040–1,250
Lost agricultural output	1,000–1,900
Lost export earnings	220–660
Total	2,960–5,130

SOURCE: "Economic Consequences of the Accident at Chernobyl Nuclear Power Plant," PlanEcon Reports, Issue 19–20, quoted in "The Cost of Chernobyl," *European Energy Report* (Financial Times Business Information), June 13, 1986.

core remained entirely within the reactor vessel, is still under way seven years later, and cleanup costs will pass $1 billion.[26]

Other countries are also adding up the costs, and some plan to submit their bills to the Soviet Union. In the United Kingdom, sheep farmers have claimed losses of $15 million. In Sweden, total costs are projected at more than $145 million, mainly for radiological monitoring and the compensation of farmers. The West German government reports it will pay farmers at least $240 million for lost sales. Poland estimates that it lost $35-50 million in agricultural sales to Western countries. For East European countries already pressed for hard currency, Chernobyl was a serious blow.[27]

Several Western governments plan to present claims against the Soviet government at the World Court in The Hague, but Soviet authorities say they will not accept the Court's jurisdiction, flatly denying that Western countries have suffered significant damage. Indeed, one top Soviet official has suggested that funds should flow in the opposite direction, to compensate for damage that exaggerated Western press reports did to the Soviet Union. Since no established legal principles underpin most of these claims, experts generally do not expect the World Court to require compensation.[28]

The impact on the Soviet energy economy will be enormous, going far beyond the 2,000 megawatts of power that has been lost indefinitely. Authorities plan significant modifications of all reactors of similar design, though most continued to operate in 1986 after brief shutdowns. By way of comparison, the far less severe Three Mile Island accident resulted in extensive modifications that delayed the completion of dozens of plants and added billions of dollars to their cost. Blackouts have plagued the Ukraine since the accident, and power shortages could persist for years. The country's energy expansion program will inevitably be set back. With one of the world's least energy-efficient economies and with oil revenues sliding, the Soviet Union can ill afford these new blows.[29]

THE POLITICAL FALLOUT

Rarely have so many countries been so affected by a single event. Nuclear power has been politically controversial for more than a decade, and Chernobyl may have decisively tipped the delicate balance of opinion. But the fallout has broader implications, testing the ability of East and West to cooperate in combating a common danger, as well as the public's confidence in government authorities and society's faith in technology.

Despite an avowed new policy of openness, Soviet authorities waited almost three days before announcing the disaster, and that was only in reaction to outcries from Scandinavia. Even then, authorities downplayed the seriousness, refusing to release detailed fallout information and squeezing stories about the accident onto the back pages of *Pravda.* Although the Chernobyl reactor was blown to pieces in the initial seconds of the accident, days later the Soviet Union was assuring the world that the reactor was "under control."[30]

The Soviet silence and deceptions were only slightly more extreme than the behavior of utility officials at Three Mile Island or British officials at the Windscale disaster in 1957. (The first press release issued during the Three Mile Island emergency denied there had been an accident.) Thus, the anti-Soviet reaction was relatively brief in most countries and was soon replaced by more immediate concerns such as whether it was dangerous to go for a walk or drink the water, and whether nearby nuclear facilities were safe.[31]

This focus was a natural outgrowth of public opposition to nuclear power that began to appear in Europe in the mid-seventies. Opposition was generally locally based, stirred up by the presence of nearby nuclear facilities. National opposition was led by citizens' groups concerned with environmental and peace issues. But most major political parties, both left and right, remained committed to nuclear power during this time. By 1986, most of Europe's antinuclear groups had peaked and were in decline.[32]

All of this changed on April 26. (See Table 4–2.) By the summer of 1986, there had been a rebirth of large antinuclear demonstrations throughout Western Europe, including massive rallies in Rome and at several controversial nuclear facilities in West Germany, where hundreds of demonstrators and police were injured. By late August, over 1 million Italians had signed petitions calling for a referendum on the nuclear program. Switzerland too announced its

Table 4-2. Reactions to Chernobyl in Selected European Countries

Country	Citizen Response	Political Response
Austria	Antinuclear movement victorious at home; protests in neighboring countries.	Government decides to dismantle sole plant; develops formal non-nuclear stance.
Finland	Opposition doubles, to 64 percent; 4,000 women go on childbearing strike.	New orders postponed.
France	Public angered by disinformation on fallout but opposition limited.	All major parties remain pro-nuclear; safety study ordered.
Italy	100,000 protest in Rome; 1 million petition for nuclear referendum.	All major parties turn against the nuclear program; conference on nuclear power planned.
Poland	3,000 petition government to halt construction until inspection by IAEA.	Government affirms nuclear plans; safety study ordered, upgrade promised if found necessary.
Sweden	Heavy fallout redoubles non-nuclear consensus; many call for rapid phaseout.	Government establishes commission to consider detailed plans for previously agreed phaseout.
United Kingdom	Opposition to new plants up 18 points, to 83 percent; citizens block waste sites.	Conservative government affirms nuclear course; Labor and Liberal parties call for phaseout.
West Germany	Large demonstrations; Green Party gains in state elections.	Government establishes cabinet-level post for nuclear safety; Social Democrats call for phaseout.
Yugoslavia	Opposition nearly doubles in size; local antinuclear groups are formed.	Planned plants postponed pending safety evaluation.

SOURCES: Various news articles and personal contacts.

third nationwide antinuclear referendum in six years. British public concern has focused on the low-level waste disposal program; hundreds of families blocked village roads in order to stop test drilling.[33]

The opposition cuts across ideological lines. Thousands of Swedish hunters and fishers have taken up the antinuclear cause. Farmers from northern Sweden dumped 10 tons of cesium-laden hay in front of government buildings in Stockholm. In the Netherlands, power company workers voted even before Chernobyl not to work on new nuclear projects. In the United Kingdom, the Labour Party called for a 10-year phaseout of nuclear power in September, despite the opposition of workers employed in the nuclear industry. In Finland, over 4,000 women declared a childbearing strike, pledging not to have children until the government changes its nuclear policy.[34]

Over two thirds of the people in most countries are now against the construction of nuclear plants, a significant increase since before Chernobyl. (See Table 4–3.) About half the people in Europe favor the shutdown of existing facilities. Andrew Holmes of the *Energy Economist* writes, "Nowhere does nuclear power command the enthusiastic assent of a large majority of the population."[35]

Three Mile Island had a similar initial impact, and Americans' faith in nuclear power continued to drift downward in subsequent years. Three Mile Island did not occur in isolation, and the public saw

Table 4-3. Public Opposition in Selected Countries to Building Additional Nuclear Power Plants[1]

Country	Before Chernobyl	After Chernobyl
	(percent)	
United Kingdom	65	83
Italy	—	79
United States	67	78
Yugoslavia	40	74
Canada	60	70
West Germany	46	69
Finland	33	64
France	—	59

[1]All polls asked, essentially, "Are you for or against building additional nuclear power plants?" though wording and polling techniques varied. The data are therefore broadly comparable. Pre-Chernobyl figures are from polls taken between 1982 and 1986.
SOURCE: Worldwatch Institute, based on Gallup and other polls.

it as part of a continuing pattern of technical problems and misinformation. As the most sophisticated and potentially dangerous technology ever harnessed to meet basic needs, nuclear power requires an extraordinary faith by ordinary citizens in their technical elite—a faith that is now badly tattered.[36]

Over two thirds of the people in most European countries are now against the construction of nuclear plants.

In France, Chernobyl's political fallout has been muted. Although the share of the French opposed to further nuclear power development has reached 59 percent, this is the lowest such figure in Europe. French pride in the nuclear program is strongly tied to a desire to be a leading technological power, free of foreign domination. And the French trust their elite. The philosophy, as one top executive puts it, is "it would be totally unhealthy, counterproductive, and damaging for technical issues to be dealt with in public and constantly exposed to criticism and statements by just anyone."[37]

A small crack appeared in this united front two weeks after Chernobyl, when the government admitted it had withheld information on the health threat posed by the nuclear cloud. Soon after, it was revealed that a French plant had suffered a critical malfunction two years earlier but reports of the accident had been quietly entered in official documents and never reached public attention. These revelations resulted in condemnation of what French editorial writers called "nuclear disinformation." However, officials soothed public fears by setting up an interministerial committee to look into the charges, and criticism soon faded.[38]

The Chernobyl accident has also

stirred opposition in Eastern Europe, which has comparatively little nuclear power but some big plans. The radioactive cloud made a deep impression on many East Europeans, in part because the previous lack of a public debate over nuclear issues meant that many had no idea a disaster hundreds of kilometers away could cause such problems. A petition signed by 3,000 Poles and endorsed by the underground Solidarity movement demanded that construction be halted at one plant until it was inspected by the International Atomic Energy Agency.[39]

In Yugoslavia, local opposition groups have sprung up in several republics. In East Germany, citizen activists have petitioned the People's Chamber of Parliament, asking for a national referendum on halting the nuclear program. And in the Soviet Union, the Moscow Trust Group has organized small street demonstrations to protest the government's failure to provide adequate health warnings and to urge that the country's graphite reactors be shut down until they can be operated safely.[40]

Nuclear power has now emerged as an important bilateral issue causing tensions between neighboring countries. Chernobyl demonstrated that the effects of a nuclear accident can cross international borders with impunity, and in Europe, 119 nuclear power plants are located within 100 kilometers (62 miles) of a national frontier. Nuclear plants are often clustered near borders in part because the large rivers that commonly form national boundaries can provide cooling water. Also, it is easier to persuade local communities to accept a nuclear facility if half the affected people live across a frontier and so have no say in the matter.[41]

Denmark, where the parliament voted in 1985 never to develop nuclear power, is close to reactors in East and West Germany as well as across the sound in Swe-

den. Of particular concern is the Swedish plant at Barsebäck, just 30 kilometers across the Øresund Strait and visible on a clear day from Copenhagen. Danish officials fear that the forced evacuation of their capital—whose 1.5 million residents are almost a third of Denmark's population—could cause the virtual collapse of the national economy.[42]

Concern over Barsebäck has risen steadily since the late seventies; after Chernobyl the Danish parliament voted to ask Sweden to close Barsebäck, a request the Swedish government has agreed to consider. In light of a widespread feeling among Swedes that the Danish request is well founded, observers expect a decision to shut the plant down.[43]

Cross-border disputes over nuclear power are not being settled so diplomatically elsewhere. At the French plant at Cattenom, just 10 kilometers from both Luxembourg and West Germany, four 1,300-megawatt reactors (one of the world's largest power complexes) are being built on the Moselle River. Some 334,000 people live within 30 kilometers of the plant and 1.5 million within 50 kilometers.[44]

Public opposition mounted quickly after Chernobyl, and demonstrators from Germany and Luxembourg have crossed the border to protest at Cattenom. Local West German governments have requested that the project be reconsidered. They are opposed to the facility because it is in a heavily populated area, is on swampland that has already caused some buildings to sink, and does not meet German safety standards and so, they say, should not be allowed to jeopardize the health of Germans. French authorities have refused to yield, claiming that the plant is as safe as any. They view the opposition as a manifestation of German "neurotic anxiety" and flatly assert that other countries have no right to question a plant located on

French soil. Cattenom has become a symbolic battle the French are determined to win.[45]

Another battle is brewing over the Wackersdorf nuclear reprocessing plant that West Germany has just started to build in Bavaria near the Austrian border. This facility would eventually handle nuclear spent fuel carried in from German nuclear plants. The reprocessed high-level waste would travel by road or rail over 500 kilometers across one of the most populated areas of Europe for storage in salt caverns in northern West Germany. In protest of these plans, a small chapel has been set up in the woods near the plant; services and demonstrations every Sunday involve thousands of West Germans and Austrians. Authorities have responded by surrounding Wackersdorf with a massive steel fence topped with barbed wire; nearby forests have been razed and the soil churned up to impede demonstrations. Protesters have been met by up to 6,000 riot police, 40 water cannons, 300 vehicles, and numerous helicopters.[46]

Since Chernobyl, concern over Wackersdorf has led to a virtual break in relations between Austria and the German state of Bavaria, including a threat to stop the Austrian Vice-Chancellor from crossing the border to attend a Wackersdorf protest. The Austrian government has formally asked the German government to stop the plant, stating that the facility would pose serious dangers to Austrian citizens. The West German Foreign Minister's reply is that his government is moving forward "without pause for thought."[47]

A border skirmish has also flared up between Ireland and the United Kingdom. Ireland is concerned about several British nuclear facilities that discharge radioactive materials into the Irish Sea, but they are particularly worried about the Sellafield reprocessing plant, which has illegally dumped large amounts of

waste and has a history of mismanagement. A report by the British House of Commons Environment Committee states that the Irish Sea is "the most radioactive sea in the world." Many Irish citizens and politicians have asked that the plant be closed, but British officials refuse to consider it.[48]

Outside of Europe, the most important cross-border dispute is between Hong Kong and China. Hong Kong utilities, the colony's British rulers, and Chinese officials have for years been developing plans to build a two-unit 1,800-megawatt nuclear plant at Daya Bay, just 50 kilometers from Hong Kong. The $3.4-billion plant, the largest joint venture China has ever undertaken, will be financed by Hong Kong banks, and Hong Kong utilities will purchase 70 percent of the power.[49]

Concern over Wackersdorf has led to a virtual break in relations between Austria and Bavaria.

Following Chernobyl, 1 million people—20 percent of the adults in Hong Kong—signed petitions objecting to the Daya Bay plant, mainly due to fears that in an accident the people in Hong Kong would be trapped. China, however, has dismissed the objections and Hong Kong's legislative council has bowed to Chinese pressure and has let the project proceed despite public opposition. It is ironic that in the historic effort to reintegrate Hong Kong with China, scheduled for 1997, a nuclear project conceived by British colonial rulers but now aggressively defended by Beijing has become a major stumbling block.[50]

These disputes highlight a wider point: The question of how nuclear projects are managed and even whether they should be built is fast being recognized as an international issue in which nations have a moral duty to consider the effects on neighboring states. The 1986 IAEA meeting in Vienna resulted in an agreement (supported by the Soviet Union) to provide immediate information in the event of future radioactive leaks that may affect other countries. Similar proposals have been made to the Nuclear Energy Agency, which includes most Western nuclear nations, and to the European Economic Community.[51]

IAEA delegates also agreed on a plan to provide coordinated assistance in the event of future accidents. Some representatives wanted to go further. Hans Blix, the Swedish Secretary-General of the agency, says that there is "growing support" for a study on providing financial compensation in the event of transnational damage caused by future accidents. And the Soviet Union has called for an expert committee to develop international safety standards.[52]

Such proposals are controversial because reactor designs and safety philosophies have always been considered sensitive areas of national sovereignty. Nonetheless, major efforts will undoubtedly be made to implement international standards and controls. It is in many ways shocking that the world has come so far into the nuclear age without such agreements.

REVISING THE NUCLEAR DREAM

The overall scale of the global nuclear enterprise is impressive. As of mid-1986, the world had 366 nuclear power plants in operation, for a generating capacity of 255,670 megawatts. (See Table 4–4.) These facilities generate about 15 per-

cent of the world's electricity, ranging from 65 percent in France to 31 percent in West Germany, 16 percent in the United States, and zero in many nations.[53]

The world's operating reactors represent a cumulative investment of well over $200 billion; an additional $60 billion is spent annually building new plants and operating existing ones. Nuclear development is dominated by the most economically powerful and technologically advanced nations: Five countries have 72 percent of the world's generating capacity. This handful of countries sets the international nuclear pace, an axis of power that revolves mainly around Washington, Paris, Bonn, and Tokyo. Even the Soviet Union has tended to follow the path of the leading capitalist nations.[54]

The experience of most nuclear programs during the past decade can best be summed up in a single phrase: lowered expectations. In the early seventies, when national nuclear programs were being rapidly geared up, planners had lavish ambitions. At one point the IAEA expected 4.45 million megawatts of nuclear power to be in place by the year 2000, with much more to follow. This would require 4,450 1,000-megawatt nuclear plants and is more than double the size of the world's entire electricity system in 1986.[55]

Both national and international projections of nuclear capacity have fallen steadily during the past 15 years. Today, the IAEA projects that the world will have just 372,000 megawatts of nuclear power in 1990 and 505,000 megawatts in the year 2000. (See Table 4–5.) This is almost 90 percent below the agency's 1974 projection, and a 45-percent decline from the 1980 forecast. Yet even the most recent projection is more a hope than a realistic forecast. The current Worldwatch Institute projection is

Table 4-4. Worldwide Nuclear Power Commitment, July 1, 1986

Country	Plants Operating[1]		Plants Under Construction		Total Commitment	
	(number)	(megawatts)	(number)	(megawatts)	(number)	(megawatts)
United States	92	78,618	28	30,849	120	109,467
France	44	38,948	18	22,210	62	61,158
Soviet Union	44	27,338	29	28,950	73	56,288
Japan	33	23,639	11	8,768	44	32,407
West Germany	16	16,114	7	6,877	23	22,991
Canada	17	11,145	5	4,361	22	15,506
United Kingdom	38	11,748	4	2,720	42	14,468
Sweden	12	9,435	—	—	12	9,435
Spain	8	5,682	2	1,979	10	7,661
South Korea	5	3,580	4	3,686	9	7,266
Czechoslovakia	6	2,380	7	3,230	13	5,610
Belgium	7	5,450	—	—	7	5,450
Taiwan	6	4,884	—	—	6	4,884
East Germany	5	1,702	5	2,532	10	4,234
Bulgaria	4	1,760	2	1,906	6	3,666
Italy	3	1,285	3	2,004	6	3,289
Switzerland	5	2,930	—	—	5	2,930
Finland	4	2,310	—	—	4	2,310
South Africa	2	1,840	—	—	2	1,840
India	6	1,244	2	440	8	1,684
Romania	—	—	3	1,680	3	1,680
Hungary	2	820	2	820	4	1,640
Argentina	2	935	1	692	3	1,627
Mexico	—	—	2	1,308	2	1,308
Poland	—	—	2	880	2	880
Cuba	—	—	2	880	2	880
Other Countries	5	1,883	1	300	6	2,183
World Total	366	255,670	140	127,072	506	382,742

[1]Includes several plants in long-term shutdowns that may not be restarted due to safety concerns.
SOURCE: "World List of Nuclear Power Plants," *Nuclear News,* August 1986.

for 325,000 megawatts of nuclear capacity by 1990 and 380,000 megawatts by the end of the century.[56]

The reasons for scaling back nuclear programs are almost as diverse as the countries themselves. (See Table 4–6.) High costs, slowing electricity growth, technical problems, mismanagement,

Table 4-5. Projections of Worldwide Nuclear Power Generating Capacity for 1980, 1990, and 2000

Source and Year of Projection	Projection For		
	1980	1990	2000
	(thousand megawatts)		
International Atomic Energy Agency			
1972	315	1,300	3,500
1974	235	1,600	4,450
1976	225	1,150	2,300
1978	170	585	1,400
1980	137	458	910
1982	—	386	833
1984	—	382	605
1986	—	372	505
Worldwatch			
1986	—	325	380

SOURCES: International Atomic Energy Agency, *Annual Reports* (Vienna: 1972–80); IAEA, "Reference Data Series No. 1," Vienna, September 1982; IAEA, *Nuclear Power: Status and Trends* (Vienna: 1984–86); Worldwatch Institute.

and political opposition have all had an effect. Yet these various problems are closely related. For example, rising costs usually represent some combination of technical problems and mismanagement. Political opposition often arises because of safety concerns or rising costs.

The United States led the world into the nuclear age and appears to be leading it out. The last year a U.S. nuclear plant was ordered that was not subsequently canceled was 1974. Meanwhile, orders for 107 reactors have been withdrawn, representing a capacity comparable to the plants now in operation and under construction. Yet U.S. nuclear capacity continues to rise as projects started in the early seventies are finally completed. In 1986 and 1987, 23 plants are scheduled for completion. But only 4

are scheduled after 1988. Even assuming the usual delays, the U.S. nuclear construction business will have nearly stopped by 1990. U.S. nuclear capacity will likely peak in about 1992 and will then slowly decline as aging plants are decommissioned.[57]

The American nuclear collapse is driven primarily by economic forces. The rate of growth in U.S. electricity consumption has fallen from 7 percent per year in the early seventies to 1.8 percent since 1980. This led to a general scaling back of construction programs that had been designed for an era of rapid growth. Most utility executives cut their nuclear projects first and most heavily, sometimes after spending billions on construction. (Orders and cancellations for coal plants have about balanced since 1980, whereas 54 nuclear projects were canceled and none ordered.)[58]

Nuclear plants in the United States that cost less than $200 per kilowatt in the early seventies carried price tags of $750 per kilowatt in 1980, $1,900 per kilowatt in 1984, and over $3,200 per kilowatt for the 23 reactors scheduled for 1986 and 1987. The industry's own figures indicate that electricity from new plants costs on average at least 12¢ per kilowatt-hour, while new coal plants cost about 6¢ per kilowatt-hour and cogeneration plants cost even less.[59]

The U.S. utility industry, which in the early years was able to sweep these costs under its huge financial rug, has finally been overwhelmed by them. The system is largely made up of private companies that must answer to investors as well as state regulators. For many, the cost overruns have been sufficient to raise prices and damage their financial condition, driving some to the edge of bankruptcy. The U.S. business magazine *Forbes* wrote in 1985 that "the failure of the U.S. nuclear power program ranks as the largest managerial disaster in busi-

Table 4-6. Adjustments to Nuclear Programs Since 1980, Selected Countries

Country	Nature of Shift	Reasons for Shift
Argentina	4 planned plants canceled; one under construction in danger of cancellation.	Financial problems; foreign debt; new civilian government.
Brazil	Government canceled 6 of 8 planned plants in 1986; delayed other 2.	Financial problems; foreign debt; new civilian government.
China	8 of 10 planned plants canceled in 5-year plan of 1986.	Foreign-exchange requirements.
France	Slow down from 6 orders in 1980 to 1 per year; government still plans 90 percent of electricity from nuclear.	Slowdown in electricity demand growth; nuclear overcapacity.
Italy	Planned capacity of 13,500 megawatts in 2000 cut drastically; just one plant nearing completion.	Economics; safety; strong local opposition.
Japan	Capacity goals cut in 1984; construction down to 2 plants per year; government remains committed to program.	Slowing demand growth; technical problems.
Mexico	Plans to build 20 plants scrapped in 1982; third and fourth reactors canceled.	Financial problems; foreign debt.
Spain	5 plants under construction mothballed or canceled, 1984.	Rising costs and technical difficulties; policies of new Socialist government.
Sweden	1980 referendum called for phaseout by 2010; 1986 decisions affirm course.	Safety and waste concerns intensified by Chernobyl.
United States	54 plants canceled, no orders; de facto moratorium by utilities.	Cost overruns; slowing demand growth.
West Germany	No new orders in 10 years; phaseout possible.	Intense political pressure by state governments and opposition political parties; overcapacity.

SOURCES: Diplomatic reports; various news articles.

ness history, a disaster on a monumental scale."[60]

The late eighties will be a strange time for the U.S. nuclear industry. Schedules call for a major increase in nuclear power generation during the next two years, and since these plants are the survivors of an era of massive cancellations, they should be the industry's star performers. Sadly, many are economic disasters that should have been canceled years ago. Safety experts believe that some have serious construction deficiencies as well.[61]

Projected nuclear costs elsewhere range from $2,000 per kilowatt in Canada to less than $1,000 in France, but most are close to $1,500, making nuclear power barely economical in some countries. (See Table 4–7.) Many U.S. nuclear projects have been badly mismanaged,

Table 4-7. Projected Cost of New Nuclear Power Plants in Selected Countries

Country	Cost	Nuclear Share of Electricity, 1985
	(1984 dollars per kilowatt)	(percent)
United States	2,865	16
United Kingdom	2,080	19
Canada	2,019	13
Sweden	1,600	42
West Germany	1,429	31
Japan	1,405	23
France	870	65
Soviet Union	—	10

SOURCES: Nuclear Energy Agency, "Projected Costs of Generating Electricity from Nuclear and Coal-Fired Power Stations for Commissioning in 1995," OECD, Paris, 1986; electricity share from International Atomic Energy Agency, *Nuclear Power: Status and Trends, 1986 Edition* (Vienna: 1986).

and the regulatory process is more chaotic than in most nations. But the main distinguishing characteristic of the American system is its dominance by private utilities. Elsewhere, public authorities are able quietly to pass the financial burden of nuclear power to the public at large.

Nonetheless, most other countries have suffered their own nuclear setbacks. The West German nuclear expansion program has been stalled since the mid-seventies, and the seven plants that remain to be completed include several troubled plants, three of which are in jeopardy of cancellation. Since Chernobyl, a vigorous political debate has begun over when to shut down the country's existing plants. The ruling Christian Democratic Party wishes to wait 30 years, the Social Democratic Party has called for a phaseout in 10 years, and the Green Party wants to finish the job in two. Studies have shown that even a two-year phaseout is feasible, with only minor economic penalties and a slight increase in air pollution.[62]

France's nuclear power program is unique in having largely met its goals of the early seventies. The nation already gets two thirds of its electricity from nuclear power and in 1987 has more nuclear capacity than Sweden, the United Kingdom, and West Germany combined. The French nuclear program is highly centralized and run by state-owned companies. Reactors are built in just six years, and neither local governments nor citizens' groups can impede projects. Socialist President François Mitterand came to power in 1981 promising a reevaluation of the nuclear program, but soon decided to leave it untouched. Since then, the efficacy of the program has been questioned only by those on the fringes of French politics.[63]

Yet despite its achievements, the French nuclear program faces a largely self-inflicted crisis: The overarching commitment to nuclear power has led the state utility, Electricité de France (EDF), to order more plants than the country needs or can afford. EDF now has a debt of $32 billion—exceeding that of most developing countries. The President of EDF admitted in 1986 that the country will have two to four "extra" reactors by 1990, and the French labor union CFDT has estimated overcapacity in 1990 at 19,000 megawatts—the output of 16 nuclear plants, representing all the reactors ordered since 1979.[64]

The Soviet nuclear program is beset by problems that predate Chernobyl.

To justify its massive nuclear investment, EDF has prematurely shut down relatively new oil- and coal-fired power plants, has promoted electricity consumption through a complex pricing system, and is marketing power to neighboring countries. Nonetheless, substantial overcapacity is expected for at least a decade; officials are planning to run most nuclear plants at less than half their rated capacity in the nineties.[65]

A representative for the state-owned nuclear company (Framatome) has said: "One power plant a year is not sufficient to maintain Framatome. We would have to cut employees and close one of our two factories. It would be very difficult to start them up again." Yet one order per year is the best that Framatome can hope for, particularly given the bleak export outlook since Chernobyl. The French nuclear program may turn out to be a costly relative of the Concorde supersonic jet—a technological marvel but a financial albatross.[66]

Japan's nuclear power program has moved forward more slowly but also more steadily than France's. Beyond the

33 plants that now supply 23 percent of the country's electricity, 11 are under construction. Japan has scaled back its initial plans as difficulties developed, but carefully studied and corrected many problems. In 1984, Japan lowered the forecast for its nuclear capacity in the year 2000 by 31 percent. Japanese utilities are now ordering just two reactors per year, a rate more likely to fall than to increase. Public concern over nuclear safety was heightened by Chernobyl, but it has not translated into any effective move to stop nuclear power.[67]

The nuclear program that is hardest to judge is the one most directly affected by the Chernobyl accident. The Soviet Union has followed Western countries into the nuclear age—albeit under a veil of secrecy—and, like France, has concentrated on standardization. Prior to Chernobyl, the Soviet Union and its East European allies had just released their latest nuclear expansion plans, which showed the Soviet Union building two thirds of the nuclear capacity planned worldwide between 1990 and 1995. At the September IAEA meeting, the chief Soviet delegate confirmed these plans.[68]

Despite the confident tone, the Soviet nuclear program is beset by problems that predate Chernobyl. Reports have reached the West of construction mishaps and delays, including problems at the Atommash nuclear manufacturing facility, designed to build equipment for all the Eastern bloc's light-water reactors. The plant required major reconstruction, was completed five years late, and is still not producing at the planned capacity. These and other problems have caused the Soviet Union to miss most of its nuclear targets by margins as wide as any in the West.[69]

Enormous efforts are now being made to fix the graphite-moderated reactors, and by November two of the three surviving units at Chernobyl had been restarted, a remarkable and perhaps risky achievement. (By comparison, it took six years before the reactor adjacent to the damaged unit was restarted at the Three Mile Island plant.)[70]

The restart at Chernobyl and the quick retrofits of similar reactors signal a Soviet commitment to get the nuclear program back on track. It remains to be seen whether this will be accomplished. The public is now concerned about nuclear health and safety issues, but the indirect link between popular opinion and official action makes it difficult to know how the bureaucracy will respond. It also remains to be seen whether the nuclear slowdown in the West will affect the Soviet effort, and it will be several years before the post-Chernobyl trend is apparent in the Soviet Union and Eastern Europe.

Plans for nuclear expansion in the Third World have also been drastically revised. Only a handful of developing countries (mainly South Korea and Taiwan) will have significant amounts of nuclear power in the year 2000. China, once a great hope of nuclear companies looking for export markets, announced in March 1986 that its ambitious plans have been postponed indefinitely.[71]

Latin American programs are in a shambles. Argentina and Brazil are struggling to complete much-delayed and overbudget projects started in the seventies and have put further plans on hold. Brazil's sole operating plant (near Rio de Janiero) was shut down by court order following Chernobyl and work has virtually stopped at the two plants being built. Many development experts now believe that nuclear power has few attractions in the countries most likely to have rapid growth in energy use. (See Chapter 5.) The Third World's precious capital can be used for many more pressing needs.[72]

The world is now in transition from rapid growth of nuclear power in the late seventies and early eighties to very slow growth in the nineties. While 114,400 megawatts of nuclear capacity came on-line between 1981 and 1985, and 123,400 megawatts is scheduled for 1986–90, just 22,900 megawatts is scheduled for 1991–95. (See Table 4–8.)[73]

This represents a 75-percent decline in the nuclear construction industry in just five years. Although these figures do not predict future trends, since more plants can be ordered, they do indicate the general direction in which the world is moving. Indeed, in North America and Western Europe, net additions during the nineties will probably be lower than indicated and could even be negative, particularly since these plans were developed prior to Chernobyl. Official Soviet plans call for 40,000 megawatts of new

Table 4-8. Actual and Planned Worldwide Additions of Nuclear Power Generating Capacity, by Five-Year Intervals, 1971–95[1]

Period	North America	Western Europe	Eastern Europe and Soviet Union	Other	Total Additions
			(thousand megawatts)		
1971–75	32.9	11.0	6.1	5.5	55.5
1976–80	18.2	22.8	8.2	11.2	60.4
1981–85	28.4	49.6	18.5	17.8	114.4
1986–90	35.2	36.2	36.9	15.1	123.4
1991–95	3.0	6.3	4.5	9.1	22.9

[1]Figures based on pre-Chernobyl national plans and utility surveys.
SOURCE: "World List of Nuclear Power Plants," *Nuclear News*, August 1986.

nuclear plants between 1986 and 1990, far more than shown in Table 4-8, but even before Chernobyl it was unlikely that this target would be met. If the Soviet nuclear program instead proceeds at its current pace of 25,000 megawatts each five years, worldwide nuclear power generation could peak before the end of the century.[74]

BEYOND INDECISION

The leaders of many countries rallied behind their nuclear programs soon after the Chernobyl accident. The head of the Soviet delegation to the September IAEA meeting said that "the exploitation of the atom's energy has become a realistic requirement, and is preconditioned by interests of human civilization progress. We shall continue to develop nuclear power in our country in accordance with our plans for the year 2000."[75]

West German Chancellor Helmut Kohl told a national television audience, "Abandoning nuclear power would spell the end of the Federal Republic as an industrialized nation." Energy Secretary Peter Walker of the United Kingdom said, "If we care about the standard of living of generations yet to come, we must meet the challenge of the nuclear age and not retreat into the irresponsible course of leaving our children and grandchildren a world in deep and probably irreversibile decline."[76]

Soon after Chernobyl, Hans Blix, Secretary-General of the IAEA, called nuclear power "a grown up industry, not an infant industry that might be dealt a death-blow by one serious accident." But nuclear power is a sick industry, not a mature one. Moreover, it is propped up by government subsidies and quickly losing the political life-support systems that have kept it going for the past two decades. Indeed, the global nuclear endeavor is like a cancer patient who has also suffered a heart attack—Chernobyl.[77]

Declining faith in nuclear power is reflected by the emergence of non-nuclear energy policies in several countries. This "non-nuclear club" is composed of countries with the capability and the past inclination to rely on nuclear power that have decided to forgo this source of energy. (See Table 4–9.) Several governments decided some time ago not to develop nuclear power, but Chernobyl has swelled the club's ranks.

The accident led Austria's government to confirm a referendum decision first made in 1978, to dismantle the country's only (and never operated) reactor, at Zwentendorf. Similarly, Corazon Aquino, the new Philippines President, announced soon after Chernobyl that the newly completed Bataan nuclear plant would be dismantled. And Greece's Socialist government decided to abandon plans to build the country's first plant.[78]

The global nuclear endeavor is like a cancer patient who has also suffered a heart attack—Chernobyl.

This non-nuclear club may gain some new members in the next few years. In West Germany, although the ruling government is still against the rapid phase-out of nuclear power, the powerful Social Democratic Party is pressing to close down the plants. The future of the nuclear program there will depend on the results of the early 1987 parliamentary elections and related political developments. At a minimum, nuclear power generation will decline slowly during the nineties. But West Germany may have

Table 4-9. The Non-Nuclear Club

Country	Form of Non-Nuclear Policy	When Announced
Australia	Labor government has no-nuclear energy policy.	1983
Austria	Public referendum barred plant from operating.	1978
	Government announced decommissioning.	1986
Denmark	Parliament decision to never build reactors.	1985
Greece	Decision to forgo first nuclear plant.	1986
Ireland	No official policy, but consensus against nuclear power.	late seventies
Luxembourg	De facto moratorium; current government has explicit no-nuclear policy.	early eighties
New Zealand	Labor government policy of Nuclear Free Zone; legislation pending.	1984
Philippines	Government decision to dismantle only nuclear plant.	1986
Sweden	Public referendum to phase out plants by 2010.	1980

SOURCES: Diplomatic reports; various news articles.

largely abandoned nuclear power by the end of the century.[79]

In Italy, all the major parties are against nuclear power, and the country's coalition government may soon develop a plan to shut down the nation's reactors. Switzerland and the United Kingdom are moving slowly in the same direction. Standing strongly against reliance on nuclear power is now not only a respectable political position, it is becoming the official policy of some governments.[80]

Austria's Foreign Minister shocked the international nuclear establishment when as host he addressed the 1986 meeting of the IAEA and explained the government's new stand on nuclear power—a statement considered rude by IAEA standards: "For us the lessons from Chernobyl are clear. The Faustian bargain of nuclear energy has been lost. It is high time to leave the path pursued in the use of nuclear energy in the past, to develop new alternative and clean sources of energy supply and, during the transition period, devote all efforts to ensure maximum safety. This is the price to pay to enable life to continue on this planet."[81]

Opinions on the future of nuclear power are more divided than at any time in the past. No consensus exists among scientists, politicians, or the general public. But despite the diverse opinions, the direction of movement is clear, and it reflects a generational shift. Fewer engineering graduates enter the nuclear industry now, and fewer young politicians advocate its expansion. The world's nuclear programs are now run by older men, many of whom developed enthusiasm for the atom in the forties, when nuclear prospects were bright. Most of their successors have not inherited their optimism.[82]

Getting the nuclear endeavor back on track would require many years of trouble-free plant operation, the speedy resolution of the waste disposal problem, and the elimination of threats of nuclear terrorism. The combination is not likely and may not even be possible. Yet without such developments, a growing number of people are likely to call for an end to nuclear power.[83]

The nuclear industry continues to blame most of its problems on an overly fearful and technologically ignorant public. This argument raises some basic issues about modern societies and the way political institutions deal with complex and potentially dangerous technologies. Although public understanding of nuclear issues is certainly limited and some fears are misplaced, public concerns broadly reflect those of the scientific community.

Local opposition to the disposal of radioactive wastes, for example, may be largely due to the NIMBY ("not in my back yard") syndrome, but it reflects a judgment by many geologists that underground storage of wastes may one day lead to serious public health problems. The fact that the world now has almost 400 nuclear power plants but not a single long-term waste disposal program yet in place must be considered one of the major failings of the nuclear era.[84]

Those who favor nuclear power often say it is held up to unrealistically strict standards. Its environmental and health impacts, they argue, are less than those of coal plants, which are estimated to kill thousands of people each year, mainly through air pollution. Nuclear power, it is said, presents relatively small risks compared with others that modern societies live with. The Bhopal chemical

plant disaster killed more than 2,000 people, for instance, and the Mexico City earthquake killed at least 5,000.[85]

It is true that the direct health impact of nuclear power has been minor so far. But Chernobyl alone may eventually cause tens of thousands of cancer deaths, and this is but the first such accident. It is the long-term and unpredictable consequences of a nuclear accident that people fear the most, and the disturbing truth is that experts do not know how safe nuclear plants are. Moreover, the Chernobyl accident included unexpected phenomena, demonstrating—as Three Mile Island did—that it is impossible to anticipate all problems at nuclear plants.

Although the accident occurred at a plant of uniquely Soviet design, its main cause was the same as at Three Mile Island: operator error. Human beings are by nature capable of making mistakes that cannot be foreseen, and the human element can never be excluded from safety systems. Despite the modifications made after Three Mile Island and the changes the Soviets now plan, reactors remain vulnerable to catastrophic accidents. Safety measures can only reduce their likelihood. It is also disturbing that, in the United States at least, the industry's recent operating record is quite poor. It may be only a matter of time before one of the dozens of serious incidents that occurs each year ends in another disaster.[86]

No one knows how often nuclear disasters will happen. The elaborate probablistic risk assessments conducted in the past decade are now under challenge because they fail to reflect the enormous complexity of nuclear systems and because they have been misused by industry representatives attempting to demonstrate the safety of nuclear power.[87]

Government studies show that core-damaging nuclear accidents should

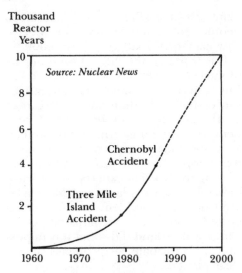

Thousand
Reactor
Years

Source: Nuclear News

Chernobyl
Accident

Three Mile
Island
Accident

Figure 4-1. Cumulative Years of Nuclear Reactor Operation Worldwide, 1960-85, With Projections to 2000

occur only once every 10,000 to 1 million years of reactor operation. (With the number of plants likely to be operating worldwide in the year 2000, this would mean one accident every 20–2,000 years.) However, the Three Mile Island accident occurred after just 1,500 years of reactor operation, and Chernobyl followed after another 1,900 reactor-years. (See Figure 4–1.)[88]

If this accident rate continues, three additional accidents would occur by the year 2000, at which point—with over 500 reactors in operation—core-damaging accidents would happen every four years. Scientists in Sweden and West Germany estimate that there is a 70-percent probability that another such accident will occur in the next 5.4 years.[89]

Not all nuclear accidents are catastrophic. At Three Mile Island, where the reactor vessel was not breached, the damage was confined to the power plant itself, resulting in no immediate deaths and direct economic damages of perhaps $2 billion. But even Chernobyl does not

mark the outer boundary of damage from a nuclear accident. Many plants are closer to large cities than Chernobyl is, and in future accidents the weather conditions may be less favorable.

Moreover, many countries with less regimented societies may have more difficulty dealing with the consequences of a nuclear accident than the Soviet Union did. In the United States, for example, evacuation planning extends only to 16 kilometers, yet the Soviets evacuated everyone within 30 kilometers and all children within 150 kilometers. Worldwide, more than 700 million people live within 160 kilometers (100 miles) of a nuclear plant. (More than 20 million people live that close to the Indian Point nuclear plant in New York State.)[90]

U.S. government studies show that a major accident near a large urban area with unfavorable winds could cause losses as high as $150 billion and result in 140,000 deaths. In Europe, where reactors are generally closer to cities, the figures could be even higher. In some instances an accident might require the permanent evacuation of millions of people and could cause a virtual national collapse.[91]

If this accident rate continues, three additional accidents would occur by the year 2000.

Thus, although the overall risk of a nuclear catastrophe may be small, its potential magnitude could well exceed anything that modern civilization has experienced outside of war. Are people in fact misguided in not wanting to use a technology that poses even a small risk of such a catastrophe?

As a matter of simple practicality, it is

questionable whether countries can or should base their power systems on technologies that much of the public finds objectionable. Although modern societies must deal with many controversial issues, the nuclear endeavor is almost unmatched in the steadily mounting opposition it has faced. Such battles take a toll morally as well as economically. In some countries they have begun to tear at the national political fabric. Does it make sense to pursue nuclear power if to do so leaders will have to struggle continually with those they represent? At what point does the political cost of such campaigns exceed any benefits?

The extent of public opposition to nuclear power also reflects a realization of the ultimate implications of pursuing the nuclear path. By the year 2010 several thousand conventional reactors were to be operating, many of them at the edge of large cities. Hundreds of breeder plants were to be running on plutonium that would ride the world's highways and railroads from the reprocessing plants where it would be refined.

Nuclear waste sites and fuel manufacturing facilities were to be as common in 2010 as steel plants are today. Without a major improvement in industry performance, serious nuclear accidents would have become a regular occurrence in the twenty-first century. Chernobyl gave people a glimpse of the nuclear future, and they did not like what they saw.

The political implications of that future may be just as troubling. Most of the world's nuclear executives point with some envy to the French nuclear program. But that program is made possible by a political system that people in many other nations would find objectionable. Public participation in decision making, for example, is more limited than in most Western nations. Is nuclear power so essential that we should curtail democratic institutions and accept a French-style centrally planned energy system as a fair price to pay?

Reliance on nuclear power for 80–90 percent of electricity (which the French are planning) could also force a government to shut down most of the power system (and economy) in the event of a serious accident. And the threat of terrorism means that nuclear power complexes must be virtual fortresses, with heavily armed security forces and surveillance equipment. Outside the military, modern society has no other facilities that require this scale of protection. A West German government-sponsored study examined the societal implications of a large-scale nuclear power system and found that the security measures needed would make much of West Germany a police state, requiring a curb on states' rights, a suspension of some civil liberties, and perhaps even a change in the constitution.[92]

The world's nuclear leaders have lost their early vision but have not found a new one, leaving many nuclear programs in shambles. Justifying the huge costs of an industry that will supply less than 15 percent of the world's power and 5 percent of its energy in the year 2000 is increasingly difficult. Fast-breeder reactors that just five years ago were assumed to be the successors to conventional plants are in the process of being abandoned as a costly dead end. There is talk of building new, "inherently safe" reactors, but these are at best decades in the future. No one yet knows which designs to pursue or when they might be ready.[93]

One costly side effect of this confusing situation is that efforts to develop non-nuclear technologies and new approaches to energy policy have been paralyzed. Attempts to reduce acid rain are forestalled because energy planners continue to argue that nuclear power is the only real solution. Energy conservation receives short shrift because its success would make it difficult to justify ordering enough nuclear plants to keep the industry profitable. And important reforms of electric utility systems are delayed because the end of utility monopolies could bring the market's verdict down on the remaining nuclear programs.

Nuclear power is advocated and objected to for dozens of reasons, and the rationales on both sides make sense when viewed in isolation. But the ultimate decision should be based on society's wider vision of its future. Cherno-byl's lasting legacy may be that it has helped put such issues squarely on the table.

The conclusion here is that many countries will opt for the deliberate, planned phaseout of nuclear power. Those that do not may believe they are gaining an important technological advantage, but more likely they will be preoccupied with divisive struggles that will weaken them politically as well as economically. In the end, they too will likely move away from nuclear power— a step that is not only an economical option, but the most practical path to follow.

5

Electrifying the Third World

Christopher Flavin

Developing countries have over the past few decades devoted enormous resources to establishing electric power systems, which planners consider essential to the creation of modern societies. The results include many impressive engineering achievements and a rapid growth in the availability of electricity. But they also encompass environmental destruction, the displacement of indigenous peoples, and crippling foreign debt in many nations.

Most Third World electrification programs are currently unsustainable—and so are unlikely to serve broader development goals or help create sustainable societies. Financial difficulties and increasingly frequent blackouts plague many countries. Power systems in some cases are starting to drag developing economies down rather than support them. For the few nations that have attempted

Portions of this chapter appeared in Worldwatch Paper 70, *Electricity For A Developing World: New Directions.*

to follow a nuclear path, the 1986 accident at Chernobyl has forced a reconsideration of those plans. (See Chapter 4.)

Third World electrification efforts are closely modeled on the large utility monopolies and central power plants typical of industrial countries. Western banks lend money for the projects and Western engineers help design them. But conditions in developing countries differ greatly from those in industrial ones. Technical skills are often lacking, management is less rigorous, and populations dispersed in rural areas are harder to reach with electric lines.

Perhaps the most important difference is that for developing countries the bulk of the expansion effort lies ahead. The Third World has just 120 watts of electricity per person, compared with 2,900 watts per person in the United States—a twenty-four-fold difference. Some 1.7 billion people in developing countries, mostly in rural areas, have no electricity at all. Although 80 percent of the people in Costa Rica and 60 percent of those in

China have electricity, fewer than 10 percent in countries such as Bangladesh, Kenya, and Nepal do.[1]

Developing countries need to carve out their own electrification programs based on their needs and resources rather than on Western models. These must be based on a clear vision of the future and a realistic assessment of the financial and physical resources available. Electricity is important to development, but it must be weighed against other needs. In the past, cities and industries have generally been favored over rural villages. In the future, rural energy programs will require more emphasis.

The Third World also cannot afford the inefficient use of electricity that is typical throughout the world today. Programs that improve efficiency can provide developing countries with electricity services at far lower costs than most new power sources being developed. Also, small-scale power plants based on fossil fuels and renewable energy sources often are more suited to Third World power systems than large central plants are. By exploring these options, developing countries can better use electricity to achieve overall development goals.

AN EMERGING POWER CRISIS

Electric utilities are among the stronger institutions in the Third World, thanks both to the magnitude of their financial resources and to their partial autonomy within the political system. Most developing countries are served by large, nationally owned utility systems, many of which were expropriated from foreign-owned private companies in the fifties. Electricity systems dominated by private utilities, as in the United States and Japan, are now rare in the Third World, though a few large nations—Brazil and India, for example—have complex systems mixing both public and private agencies.

Third World nations now use six times as much electric power as they did two decades ago. The rapid development of sizable electric power systems is a major achievement for many developing countries. Compared with industrial countries, however, electricity plays a relatively small role in Third World economies. Wood and crop wastes still provide at least 12 times as much energy as electricity does.

As of 1982, annual per capita electricity use ranged from highs of 1,402 kilowatt-hours in Argentina and 1,192 kilowatt-hours in South Korea to 36 kilowatt-hours in Bangladesh and 23 kilowatt-hours in Nepal, enough to light a 30-watt bulb for a month. (See Table 5–1.) These figures contrast with per capita consumption of 9,600 kilowatt-hours in the United States.[2]

Even in the wealthier developing countries where per capita electricity use is relatively high, a large share of the population may be completely without power. Over half the electricity produced in most developing countries goes to industry, a far larger fraction than in the industrial world. And most of the electricity is used in just a handful of power-intensive industries, often those that produce goods for export. In Mexico, 55 percent of the electricity is used by industry; in South Korea, the figure is 68 percent.[3] Electricity use in the modern office buildings and hotels that dot the skylines of many Third World capitals is also growing rapidly.

Household use of electricity is limited in most developing countries. Many people cannot afford to purchase, let alone operate, appliances that are heavy power

Table 5-1. Per Capita Income and Electricity Use in Selected Developing Countries, 1982

Country	Per Capita Income (dollars)	Electricity Use (million kilowatt-hours)	Per Capita Electricity Use (kilowatt-hours)
Argentina	2,520	39,804	1,402
Brazil	2,240	151,721	1,197
South Korea	1,660	47,197	1,192
Mexico	2,737	80,589	1,103
Costa Rica	1,806	2,500	1,041
Zimbabwe	849	7,614	1,015
Colombia	1,300	22,564	837
Philippines	746	20,560	405
Nicaragua	802	1,153	400
Thailand	764	17,687	365
China	307	327,678	325
Bolivia	932	1,703	290
India	247	138,677	197
Zaire	203	4,392	143
Kenya	420	1,998	110
Senegal	541	633	105
Indonesia	524	12,722	83
Niger	338	350	60
Bangladesh	132	3,305	36
Nepal	136	356	23

SOURCE: World Bank, "1982 Power/Energy Data Sheets for 104 Developing Countries," Washington, D.C., July 1985.

users. Even in cities, only the wealthiest families can pay for refrigerators, electric stoves, air conditioners, and the other appliances that many consumers in the industrial world take for granted. Residents of Manila or São Paulo typically pay as much for electricity as do their counterparts in Washington or Paris, but because their incomes are far smaller, their electric bills consume proportionately more of their incomes.

Projections of growing demand in the Third World led to the first big wave of power plant construction in the sixties. Many oil-fired plants were built because they were relatively inexpensive. Imported oil then cost only $2–3 per barrel. Starting with relatively insignificant power systems, most utility officials estimated a need to expand electricity supplies at over 10 percent annually. This massive construction effort was just gearing up when oil prices soared in the early seventies.

Third World power systems are still heavily dependent on fossil fuels, though hydropower is the predominant and most rapidly growing electricity source in many countries. (See Table 5–2.) In 1980, the most recent year for

Table 5-2. Electricity Generating Capacity in Selected Countries, by Source, 1982

Country	Total Capacity	Share of Capacity Provided by Source			
		Fossil Fuel	Hydro	Geothermal	Nuclear
	(megawatts)	(percent)			
China	72,360	68	32	0	0
Brazil	38,904	15	85	0	0
India	38,808	64	34	0	2
Mexico	21,574	68	31	1	0
Argentina	13,460	48	49	0	3
South Korea	11,597	79	10	0	11
Philippines	5,054	64	25	11	0
Thailand	4,694	71	29	0	0
Colombia	4,660	36	64	0	0
Indonesia	3,513	83	16	1	0
Zaire	1,716	3	97	0	0
Zimbabwe	1,192	41	59	0	0
Bangladesh	990	92	8	0	0
Costa Rica	657	30	70	0	0
Kenya	574	33	62	5	0
Bolivia	508	44	56	0	0
Nicaragua	400	65	26	9	0
Senegal	165	100	0	0	0
Nepal	162	22	78	0	0
Niger	100	100	0	0	0

SOURCE: World Bank, "1982 Power/Energy Data Sheets for 104 Developing Countries," Washington, D.C., July 1985.

which data are available, hydropower supplied 41 percent of Third World electricity, coal supplied 15 percent, and oil, 37 percent. Most of the largest developing countries—with the important exceptions of Brazil and Colombia—obtain at least 60 percent of their power output from fossil fuels and many rely extensively on oil.[4]

Many developing countries have excellent hydropower potential, which is usually associated with mountainous terrain and abundant rain or snow. Managed properly, hydropower is a renewable energy source immune from fuel price increases. Whereas North America and Europe had developed 59 percent and 36 percent of their hydropower potential by 1980, Asia had harnessed just 9 percent, Latin America 8 percent, and Africa 5 percent.[5]

Third World hydropower development involves some of the largest and most expensive civil works projects in history, including the 10,000-megawatt Guri project in Venezuela and the 12,600-megawatt Itaipu plant on the Brazil-Paraguay border, both of which are still under construction. The latter project will produce as much power as 13 nuclear plants. Between 1978 and 1983, Mexico's hydropower capacity rose 43 percent, Brazil's increased 55 percent, and Argentina's, 58 percent.[6]

The World Bank projects that between 1980 and 1990, hydro capacity in the Third World, excluding China, will more than double—rising from 100,000 megawatts to 201,000 megawatts. China has 17,000 megawatts of large hydro projects under construction that will bring the country's total from this source to 41,000 megawatts. The proposed Three Gorges project on the Chang Jiang (Yangtze) River would provide additional capacity of about 13,000 megawatts.[7]

The environmental and human costs of some of these hydropower projects are substantial. Construction of new dams has displaced millions of people, flooded agricultural land, and trapped river silt that once fertilized flood plains. The visions of power planners are now often in direct conflict with the needs of indigenous people.

The Kariba Dam built in Zimbabwe in the sixties uprooted 56,000 people, many of whom never found suitable homes, farmland, or clean drinking water. The Three Gorges project in China would increase the country's power capacity by 15 percent, reduce flooding downstream, and provide additional irrigation for the rich Sichuan Plain. But it would also flood thousands of hectares of rich agricultural land and displace between 300,000 and 1 million people in one of China's most densely populated regions.[8]

Third World governments also wish to increase coal's contribution to electricity generation. The World Bank projects an expansion of coal-fired generating capacity, excluding plants in China, from 35,000 megawatts in 1980 to 92,000 megawatts by the year 2000. Most of this development is concentrated in the few Third World countries with substantial coal reserves, such as India and Colombia. China, which has as much coal in reserves as the Soviet Union and the United States combined,

plans to boost its coal-generating capacity of about 50,000 megawatts to over 140,000 megawatts in the next 13 years. Most of the country's 12,000 megawatts of oil-fired generating capacity has already been converted to coal.[9]

Coal development entails much larger environmental trade-offs than hydropower. Northern Chinese cities are already heavily polluted by coal burning, and evidence of acid rain damage is beginning to appear in some parts of the Third World. The high cost and complexity of pollution control technologies have impeded their widespread use in many developing countries. In addition, coal combustion is a major contributor to atmospheric carbon dioxide levels, which many scientists believe are increasing so rapidly as to severely alter the earth's climate within 30 to 50 years.[10] (See Chapter 9.)

Spending on Third World electrification now approaches $50 billion each year.

Nuclear power, once widely promoted in the Third World, has lost ground in many nations. For developing countries, nuclear power is not only complicated and expensive, it requires more foreign exchange than do most power investments. Major projects in Argentina, Brazil, and the Philippines have run into technical and financial problems; political disputes have drastically slowed programs in Iran, Iraq, and Pakistan. Only in the rapidly industrializing Far East has nuclear power contributed significantly to electricity supplies. In 1986, South Korea had 3,580 megawatts of nuclear capacity (22 percent of its total), and Taiwan had 4,884 megawatts (52 percent of the total). Yet even in these countries there are indications that the accident in Chernobyl may slow plans for additional nuclear plants. (See Chapter 4.)[11]

The cost of building additional generating capacity in the Third World has increased dramatically since the mid-seventies. Not only are hydropower and coal plants inherently more expensive than oil plants, but developers have had to turn to more costly hydro projects since the most attractive sites are already developed. In the sixties, hydro projects costing more than $800 per kilowatt were considered economically questionable, but now many developing countries are building facilities that cost from $2,000 to $3,000 per kilowatt. Construction cost increases have coincided with a period of high interest rates and (until recently) high oil prices.[12]

Spending on Third World electrification now approaches $50 billion each year. Typically, about one third of a power project's cost requires foreign-exchange payments to outside companies, a burden made worse by high interest rates. The World Bank and the regional development banks have devoted about 20 percent of their lending to electricity development and have encouraged commercial banks to invest heavily in Third World power systems. Such projects now account on average for about one quarter of public capital investments in developing countries, or up to 2 percent of gross national product.[13]

Although no precise figures are available, total Third World utility debt can be estimated at over $180 billion, which is one fifth of the Third World's accumulated foreign debt of over $900 billion. National treasuries are in all cases the ultimate guarantors of these debts. A 1985 report to the U.S. Agency for International Development on the situation in Central America concluded that "the region's financial crisis, and its constraints on future development, is significantly the result of huge public power investments in nearly all of the countries." In Costa Rica, 18 percent of the country's foreign debt is attributed to the power sector; in Honduras, the figure is 33 percent.[14]

Electricity consumption in most developing countries is so low and the potential future uses so great that electricity use continues to expand even when the economy does not. The World Bank projects that developing countries will have to invest $60 billion in electric power each year in order to keep up with a demand growth rate of 7 percent.[15] This is more than the Third World receives in development assistance funds annually. These investment goals are for the most part unattainable, and many utilities are not keeping up with demand. The combined pressures of underfinancing and overuse result in inadequate generating capacity and blackouts.

Many Third World utilities are simply no longer credit-worthy.

Financial pressures often cause utilities to cut back on maintenance work, which reduces reliability. In many countries, over 30 percent of the power transmitted is lost because of inadequate maintenance, undersized lines, and illegal tapping of power lines. Pakistan faces some of the worst problems: Losses on the national power system average 38 percent and blackouts occur daily. China's leaders project that the nation's electricity supplies (growing 6 percent annually) will not keep up with needs and so will constrain industrial growth. Already, in Sichuan Province power is cut three days a week to ensure adequate power the other four days.[16]

The financial problems of many electric utilities are getting worse. The

World Bank has projected a $32-billion gap between utility needs and financial capabilities in Latin America and the Caribbean during the next five years. In many cases, the cost of servicing the utility's debt absorbs most of the operating revenues; construction is continually adding to the debt load. Chile is fairly typical, with a planned construction budget of $1.4 billion for 1984–88 and scheduled interest payments of $1 billion, but with projected operating revenues of just $1.1 billion.[17]

Increasingly, government leaders are projecting financial shortfalls and forcing utilities to curtail construction spending. Recent budget negotiations in Brazil and India forced power authorities to halve planned expenditures. A study of Central American utilities concluded that "due to a combination of existing debt obligations and internal organizational problems, the large national utilities could have difficulty financing planned power investments, beginning immediately." Many Third World utilities are simply no longer credit-worthy, and the banks refuse to issue new loans.[18]

The problem is not simply money. Many Third World power systems have also outgrown their own internal management capabilities and are increasingly short of technical expertise. Corruption has become widespread in some countries, as symbolized by the multimillion-dollar payoffs that allegedly passed from the U.S.-based Westinghouse Corporation to the Marcos government in the Philippines in order to secure a contract for the Bataan nuclear plant. In addition, some utilities, having relied for years on expatriate labor and temporary consultants, are now short of people skilled in specialized fields. Many of the best-trained people have left for better-paying jobs in the private sector or overseas.[19]

Selectively trimming construction budgets, strengthening maintenance procedures, raising salaries, and introducing better management techniques are thus essential to any serious program of improvements of Third World power systems. Internal changes and external pressure from lending agencies are moving many utilities in this direction. To meet the ever-growing demand for energy, however, planners need to make even more fundamental changes.

DEVELOPING ELECTRICITY EFFICIENCY

Even analysts who should know better often dismiss the potential to improve energy efficiency in developing countries. Per capita energy use in developing countries is low, they point out—and so rapid growth in energy consumption is assumed to be inevitable. This erroneous assumption threatens to discourage developing countries from investing in one of the essential elements of their energy future.

If energy efficiency is economically attractive when electricity use is relatively stable, it is even more attractive when use is rising rapidly, since it can displace some of the most expensive planned generating capacity. Looked at another way, greater efficiency can increase the productivity of the large number of power plants being built in the Third World.

Research and development have increased the efficiency of many technologies in recent years. In 1985, a U.S. study found that in the past decade the efficiency of new refrigerators increased 52 percent, while that of room air conditioners increased 76 percent. Even greater improvements have occurred in Japan, where companies developed more efficient appliances more rapidly than did their American counterparts.[20]

New Japanese and European fluorescent lights use one fourth as much power as the incandescents now in use. Electric motors, the largest user of electricity in most industries, have been improved. For example, adjustable speed drives can lower the power use of electric motors by 20 to 30 percent. Newly developed aluminum smelters reduce the electricity required in this power-intensive process by 24 percent, and aluminum recycling can lessen power needs by 95 percent.[21]

Several recent studies demonstrate a similar potential to improve electrical efficiency in developing countries where industry, agriculture, and commercial buildings are the main users of electricity. In many cases, they use more electricity than a comparable industrial-country facility does. The equipment used generally was designed years earlier in another country, a clear disadvan-

tage given the improved efficiency of newer appliances.

In some industries, the manufacturing process itself is outmoded and much more energy-intensive than newer processes. In addition, inadequate equipment maintenance can lower efficiency.[22] Using electricity more efficiently would lower production costs and the price of goods, making Third World exports more competitive.

Without such gains, Brazilian planners project that the country's generating capacity will have to grow 150 percent in the next 15 years, at a cost of over $130 billion. Of the 66,000 megawatts of additional power they expect to need, only about 34,000 megawatts is currently planned. A 1986 study concluded that projected electricity consumption just in selected major power uses in Brazil could be cut 30 percent by the year 2000 if a range of cost-effective efficiency measures were adopted. (See Table 5–3.) The $10 billion needed to

Table 5-3. Brazil: Potential Electricity Savings in Selected End-Uses[1] by the Year 2000

Electricity Use	Current Forecast	Savings Potential Amount	Savings Potential Share
	(terawatt-hours)		(percent)
Industrial Motors	177.3	35.5	20
Domestic Refrigerators	28.3	14.8	52
Domestic Lighting	17.7	8.8	50
Commercial Motors	29.7	5.9	20
Commercial Lighting	25.8	15.5	60
Street Lighting	17.9	7.2	40
Total	296.7	87.7	30

[1]These account for about two thirds of total electricity use in Brazil. These projected savings include only efficiency improvements that are economically justifiable based on currently available technologies.
SOURCE: Howard Geller et al., "Electricity Conservation Potential in Brazil," American Council for an Energy-Efficient Economy, Washington, D.C., March 1986.

implement these measures would eliminate the need for 22,000 megawatts of generating capacity that would cost an estimated $44 billion to build.[23]

The cornerstone of a program to improve efficiency is a pricing system that reflects the true cost of providing power. Ideally, this system should charge the consumer just what the utility must pay to deliver additional electricity, providing incentives to use it efficiently. Unfortunately, pricing often becomes a political tool, and prices are kept too low to encourage adequate conservation.

Of course, some subsidizing of electricity prices is inevitable and even beneficial. Few villagers would ever get electricity if in the first few years they were forced to pay what it cost to provide power. The problem occurs when low, subsidized electricity prices continue indefinitely. Recently, many developing countries have bitten the bullet and raised prices to more realistic levels. Some now have "time-of-use" rates for industry to discourage power use during peak demand periods. But politics has slowed the move to price reform and further changes are needed.[24]

Other obstacles block the more efficient use of electricity. In many countries the government guarantees the purchase of manufactured goods at a cost-plus price. Improved efficiency and the resulting cost-saving do not therefore increase a company's profit margin. Even where more efficient technologies are clearly economical based on current electricity prices, consumers often purchase a less efficient appliance. Poor people who have virtually no disposable income cannot afford to buy a slightly more expensive, albeit more efficient, device even if the investment would pay for itself in less than three years.

A broad range of programs can help overcome these barriers. The simplest are educational campaigns to encourage industries and consumers to make in-formed decisions about power usage. Campaigns can promote efficiency labels on appliances, free energy audits for factories or homes, and even simple reminders to turn out lights and maintain appliances. Second, governments can initiate mandatory efficiency standards for appliances, homes, and industrial equipment. Third, governments or utilities can directly assist in the financing of efficiency investments, using either low-interest loans or outright grants. Many countries have tried variations on these approaches, and developing nations no longer need look to the industrial world to find examples of programs that work.

South Korea has one of the highest electricity consumption growth rates in the world and severely limited domestic energy reserves. Not surprisingly, the government has initiated a comprehensive efficiency program, starting with a 1980 "Law Governing Rationalization in the Use of Energy." It regulates energy efficiency of new buildings, requires efficiency labels on new household appliances, and established a national energy conservation center to provide technical support and training. Financial incentives for energy conservation include income tax deductions, reduced tariffs on energy-saving equipment, a one-year depreciation allowance for energy-saving investments, and subsidized loan programs for conservation investments in industrial plants and buildings.[25]

Developing nations no longer need look to the industrial world to find examples of programs that work.

Confronted with the prospect of power shortages, the South Korean government has simply curtailed some power uses. For example, it has banned the use of air conditioners, except for a

40-day period in the summer, and prohibited the use of elevators in the first three floors of buildings. Saving electricity is considered a national priority, because the nation's ambitious economic plans depend on maintaining competitive electricity prices.[26]

Brazil, the Philippines, and Singapore are among the other developing countries that have made energy efficiency a national priority. Among Brazil's programs are an energy labeling program for refrigerators and an electricity price system that penalizes heavy consumers. In the Philippines, the National Bureau of Energy Utilization provides free energy audits to large factories and commercial buildings, and efficiency labels are required on air conditioners. In addition, a U.S.-supported pilot program assists in the financing of energy conservation. Singapore introduced a financial incentives program for energy-efficient buildings in 1979.[27]

One problem many countries face is how to encourage the manufacture of more-efficient equipment. Companies, perceiving that consumers care little about efficiency, neglect potential innovations. In some developing countries, firms manufacture efficient equipment for export while selling less efficient devices domestically. Efficiency standards are probably needed in most countries and can be met by domestic research or by obtaining foreign technologies through manufacturing licenses. Brazil now has a program to support the development of more-efficient refrigerators, lighting systems, heat pumps, and air conditioners.

Internationally certified appliance-testing programs would be a big help. With the international marketing of appliances growing rapidly and several countries already having incompatible standards, future innovations may be hampered without some standardization.

It is too early to assess the impact of energy-efficiency programs aimed at consumers and local industry. Data collection is often inadequate and sorting out the relative importance of different measures is difficult. Nonetheless, many of these programs will undoubtedly yield substantial benefits.

Since efficiency investments can in effect provide additional services in the same way that power plants do, utilities themselves should invest in efficiency whenever it is less expensive than new generating options. Utilities can invest in efficiency improvements in their own generating and distribution systems and in the electricity using technologies owned by industries and consumers.

If efficiency and production programs are kept separate, a utility could be building a power plant that costs $2,000 per kilowatt while the energy ministry is passing up efficiency investments that cost $500 per kilowatt. National utilities have access to relatively low-interest funds; rechanneling 10–15 percent of their construction budgets to efficiency programs could yield enormous returns. Consumers would be better served if electric utilities were gradually converted into energy service companies that would provide efficiency as well as new power supplies—using the same economic criteria.[28]

Only in the industrial world have utilities begun to invest in improved end-use efficiency. The Pacific Gas and Electric Company (PG&E) in northern California, for example, has a peak demand of 13,000 megawatts, more than that of all but five developing nations. PG&E sponsors extensive energy audits, offers zero interest loans for home weatherization, and has rebate incentives for the purchase of energy-saving devices. Company economists calculate that the $80 million spent in 1983 resulted in a savings of 240 megawatts. The savings cost of $350 per kilowatt contrasts sharply with the $2,760 per kilowatt cost of PG&E's only recently completed generating plant—the 2,100-megawatt Diablo Canyon nuclear facility.[29]

In the Third World, the São Paulo utility—Brazil's largest—is one of the few utilities to adopt a modest package of energy-efficiency programs. It is collecting data on the end-uses of electricity and is demonstrating and monitoring the use of energy-efficient electrical equipment. The Public Utilities Board of Singapore provides energy audits for some of its customers. In the Indian state of Karnataka, the state electricity board has set up an "electricity queue" that gives efficient companies priority access to the state's limited power supplies.[30]

ELECTRIFYING RURAL AREAS

Third World electricity programs are largely oriented to providing power for cities and industries. Although two thirds of people in the developing world live in rural areas, political power flows to the cities, and electric power flows with it. Overall, fewer than one third of the people in the rural Third World now have access to electricity. Nonetheless, rural electrification has become integral to the development process and each year millions more people are provided with electricity. Unfortunately, many programs are underfunded, misdirected, or poorly managed. And rural electrification is often promoted as an end in itself, rather than as a means of reaching more basic goals.

In the past two decades, developing countries have given increased priority to rural electrification, which is viewed as a way of unifying countries with different ethnic communities, thereby consolidating political power. Bangladesh's constitution, for instance, includes a guarantee that all villages will eventually get electricity. In most developing countries there is a gap between rhetorical support for rural electrification and the minimal funds devoted to its achievement. Fewer than 10 percent of the Third World's electricity investments go to rural areas, and in many countries that investment is below 5 percent.[31]

The extent of electrification varies widely in different countries. (See Table 5–4.) Overall, just 1 out of 20 rural Africans has power. In Latin America, over one third of those in rural areas lack

Table 5-4. Extent of Electrification in Selected Developing Countries, 1982

Country	Share of Population in Rural Areas	Share of Total Population with Electricity
	(percent)	
Taiwan	29	99
Singapore	0	99
South Korea	43	95
Mexico	30	81
Costa Rica	52	80
China	79	60
Brazil	32	56
Colombia	33	54
Philippines	63	52
Senegal	58	36
Indonesia	78	16
India	77	14
Kenya	84	6
Nepal	94	5
Bangladesh	85	4
Niger	84	3

SOURCES: Population Reference Bureau, *1985 World Population Data Sheet* (Washington, D.C.: 1985); World Bank, "1982 Power/Energy Data Sheets for 104 Developing Countries," Washington, D.C., July 1985.

electricity. Several Asian countries have made great strides in the past 15 years. Virtually all of Taiwan has electricity, and in India 350,000 villages out of more than 600,000 are now connected to an electricity grid. (Even in "electrified" villages, however, often half or more of the houses lack power.)[32]

China has brought power to 500,000 of its 710,000 villages, mostly in the past two decades; the amount of electricity available to rural areas has increased tenfold since 1965. Elsewhere in Asia, progress has been slower. Not even 5 percent of Nepal's rural population has electricity, and in Bangladesh, fewer than 2,000 of 65,000 villages are electrified, notwithstanding the constitutional guarantee.[33]

On the rich agricultural plains of the Far East, rural electrification is easier to justify than in Africa's arid Sahel, where both the population density and income levels are far lower. Isolated mountain communities, such as those in Nepal or Bolivia, are also hard to reach with electricity because population density is low and the terrain makes the installation of power lines difficult. Many developing countries face an almost impossible engineering and financial task in extending power grids into all parts of the nation.

Even at their best, Third World rural electric systems rarely match the reliability taken for granted in industrial countries. People often go for days without power, waiting for a spare transformer to be carried in over rutted roads or for repairs to be made to storm-damaged lines. Nonetheless, electricity can bring sweeping changes to the lives of rural people. Many look back on the arrival of electricity as a turning point in village life. Light bulbs are usually the first purchase, a big improvement over gas or kerosene lamps. Electric irons are also popular, as are radios, televisions, and electric fans; most people, however, do not have appliances such as refrigerators or stoves.[34] (See Table 5–5.)

Table 5-5. Electricity Uses in Homes in Rural Areas of Costa Rica and Colombia That Have Electricity[1]

Appliance	Costa Rica	Colombia
	(percent of homes)	
Lights	100	95
Iron	57	73
Television	54	39
Radio	52	79
Refrigerator	42	19
Blender	39	32
Washing machine	31	—
Electric stove	21	91
Sewing machine	3	26
Fan	—	7

[1]Based on household surveys in the early eighties.

SOURCES: Randy Girer, "Rural Electrification in Costa Rica: Membership Participation and Distribution of Benefits," Masters Thesis, Graduate Program in Energy, Management and Policy, University of Pennsylvania, 1986; Eduardo Velez, "Rural Electrification in Colombia," Resources for the Future, Washington, D.C., March 1983.

Women often benefit more from electricity than men do, since it helps ease household chores, while fans and radios make leisure time more pleasant. Many women report that they have had more free time since electricity became available. Frequently, electric pumps provide a reliable, clean supply of water from a village well for the first time, which makes life easier and improves health.

Several studies have found that electricity promotes literacy by allowing children to study in the evening. In rural India, television-viewing has become widespread, thanks both to electricity and a new satellite that transmits national programming into remote areas. The government broadcasts educational programs, including lessons in preventive health care and new farming techniques.[35]

Like many technologies, rural electrification can perpetuate inequality, particularly in poor villages where only wealthy households can afford power. In the Philippines, for example, newly electrified villages generally have a hookup charge of $30–40, which is beyond the means of many poor families. A survey in India found that it took on average 10 years after initial electrification before poor families could afford to connect to the system. In Costa Rica, although preferential hookup rates and subsidized prices have allowed most homes to obtain power, poor households still use much less electricity than wealthy households do. Special efforts must be made if the benefits of electricity are to be widely shared.[36]

In most villages, even well-designed electrification programs can address only part of the energy problem. The main use of energy in rural areas is for cooking, a task that often is done with wood, crop residues, or dung. These biomass sources provide an estimated 48 percent of all the energy used in the Third World, and in many rural households they supply over 90 percent. Electricity is far too expensive to be used for cooking, even in most cities. (A simple hot plate uses more than 500 watts of power, or 33 times as much as the 15-watt light bulbs that are the main source of light in many village homes.)[37]

Other initiatives must accompany electrification programs in order to address the broad range of rural energy problems. Promising approaches that have been tested successfully in some countries include community tree planting programs, more efficient cookstoves, biogas digesters (to turn biological wastes into flammable methane gas), and solar ovens.

Other important rural energy uses include water pumping, grain grinding, and other mechanical processes. These can be performed with electrically driven motors, but they can also be powered by biomass energy or by human or animal power, particularly if technolo-

gies to improve their effectiveness are developed. However, some applications of electricity have no good substitute. These include high-quality lighting, refrigeration, television, computers, and telecommunications. Comprehensive rural energy planning is needed to introduce a range of appropriate technologies. Although electricity can be beneficial, it should not get exclusive priority.

The real value of electricity is in stimulating economic development. One way this can happen is through the creation of rural industries. So far the record is at best mixed. Where economic expansion has already begun and markets are developing for various products, rural industries have followed electrification. Costa Rica has seen some use of electricity in sawmills, cement factories, and tourist hotels, but electrification has not been a major boost to rural industry. In most countries, development planners find electricity is not enough. Rural industries require a variety of other infrastructure investments in roads, training, and financial credit.[38]

Electricity can also raise agricultural productivity, but so far farm use of power is mainly limited to large plantations owned by the wealthy. Electricity has few affordable uses on most small farms. In Costa Rica, electricity is rarely used in the production of coffee, sugar, or vegetables, but it has helped raise the output of poultry and dairy farms. In Bolivia, planners had hoped that electricity would encourage irrigation, but the harsh climate, salty soils, and lack of financial support cut these plans short. Rural electrification in India and Pakistan is largely directed to developing irrigation in semiarid parts of the country. This has been successful, though it has required heavy subsidies. One study found that Indian farmers were only paying between 7 and 10 percent of the actual cost of providing them with electricity.[39]

Given the many needs of rural people,

investment priorities must be balanced. Electricity can help meet basic needs, but it may not be the fastest or most cost-effective way to do so in sparsely populated areas or regions with mountainous terrain. As a Papua New Guinea Energy White Paper published in 1979 said, "it is clear that investment in electrification is investment foregone in such areas as improved roads, water supply, schooling, and health services."[40]

In the Philippines, rural electric cooperatives have provided power to over 18,000 villages in just 12 years.

Rural electrification is not a magic cure for the ills of village life. Rather, it is one tool that is sometimes appropriate. Since village conditions vary greatly, careful studies should be done before choosing a package of development tools. Health care and simple farming technologies may deserve priority. Electrification should be linked to other energy and development programs, such as the introduction of efficient cookstoves.

One way to make rural electrification part of a comprehensive development program is through the creation of decentralized power agencies. One approach that has proved successful is electric cooperatives—local agencies, owned by the members and managed by local staffs but often supported by a national electrification agency. Most co-ops do not generate their own power but purchase it from the national utility. Electric cooperatives can play a role in encouraging productive uses of electricity by providing low-interest loans and technical extension services for everything from small lumber mills to irrigation systems. And they are more likely than national utilities to support income-generating industries.[41]

Costa Rican cooperatives that were started with U.S. assistance in the sixties provide electricity to about half the families in their areas, and have helped stimulate economic growth. In the Philippines, rural electric cooperatives have provided power to over 18,000 villages in just 12 years. And many of them provide much more than electricity: They have become involved in charcoal production, school lighting, school waterworks, and vegetable gardening. Here, as elsewhere, the effectiveness of electric cooperatives depends on the quality of local leadership and the ability to insulate them from day-to-day political maneuvering. Among the countries now looking seriously at the potential to expand cooperative-based electrification are Bangladesh, India, and Indonesia.[42]

Such approaches can help decentralize the decision-making process and bring local people into energy and development planning. Indeed, rural electrification outside the context of an overall development strategy is bound to fail. Broadly based cooperatives that can also address the cooking fuel issue—the central energy problem in most rural areas—would be even more effective. Co-ops could be used to promote tree planting programs, more efficient cookstoves, and other development efforts.

STRENGTH THROUGH DIVERSITY

Rural electrification to date is concentrated in areas where grid extension is relatively easy and economical—heavily populated agricultural plains and near major urban and industrial centers. Left behind are remote, forested, and mountainous regions where populations are sparse and cash incomes are limited. Examples include much of the Andes region of South America; most of Central America; large sections of India, Indonesia, and Pakistan; and virtually all of Afghanistan, Bhutan, Burma, Laos, and Nepal.

In addition, many island communities will never be reached by grid electricity. The Philippines, for example, consists of over 7,000 islands, and even when the national grid is fully completed, many villages will not be connected. The same is true in Indonesia, large stretches of the South Pacific, and the Caribbean. Full rural electrification, if that is the goal, can never be accomplished by central grids alone.

The next frontier in rural electrification is the use of decentralized technologies that rely on renewable resources. Although these are particularly important in more remote areas, they are also likely to prove useful for small towns, industries, and even the central power grids of developing countries. Most Third World power systems are relatively small and so can more easily accommodate small generators than they can the large coal and nuclear units typical in industrial countries.

Another advantage of small power projects is that they can be built quickly. At a time when future energy trends and economic conditions are uncertain, small projects can be planned to match actual needs rather than tenuous forecasts. Interest costs and foreign-exchange requirements are in turn reduced.

An estimated 580 megawatts of stand-alone diesel systems are now in use in the Third World. Diesel generators of 10 kilowatts or less are used to power individual homes and communications systems, while larger generators of several hundred kilowatts or more can run a whole village. Diesel generators are relatively inexpensive to install but costly to fuel. Total diesel generation costs typically range from 15–50¢ per kilowatt-hour, compared with an average cost of grid electricity in the Third World of about 7¢. Diesel generators need frequent maintenance; neglect commonly leads to breakdowns and time-consuming repairs. Often a damaged generator must be fixed in a distant town, so a village desiring reliable power service has to have a spare ready.[43]

Today, however, a much wider array of small-power options is available, many of them not requiring fossil fuels. Small hydropower is the most mature alternative. Usually classified as less than 15 megawatts in capacity, small hydro's advantage is that the technology is well developed and economical. A study for the U.S. Agency for International Development found that 10,000 megawatts of non-grid-connected small hydro projects had been constructed in the Third World by 1983, and projected that the capacity of stand-alone small hydro systems will reach 29,000 megawatts in 1991. The worldwide potential is probably well over 100,000 megawatts. In many countries the potential exceeds total installed power capacity.[44] (See Table 5–6.)

Since 1980, substantial efforts have been made to develop new approaches to small hydropower development based on local skills and materials. Many micro-hydro projects under 100 kilowatts in capacity are run-of-the-river systems that require less construction and use locally made equipment. As small hydro projects multiply, entrepreneurs in India, Nepal, and Pakistan have started manufacturing pipes, turbines, generators, and load controllers. Similar enterprises have begun to appear in Africa and Latin America. Such innovations have reduced costs from the $3,000–6,000 per kilowatt typical of many heavily engineered systems to $1,000–2,000.[45]

Table 5-6. Decentralized Hydropower Potential in Selected Countries

Country	Small Hydro Potential	1982 Installed Power Capacity[1]	Small Hydro Potential as Share of 1982 Capacity
	(megawatts)		(percent)
Peru	12,000	3,300	364
India	10,000	35,400	28
Philippines	4,000	4,800	83
Costa Rica	2,700	650	415
Thailand	1,100	4,630	24
Indonesia	1,000	5,170	19
Guatemala	1,000	530	189
Nepal	800	138	580
Guinea	560	102	549
Bolivia	500	500	100
Pakistan	300	4,100	7
Madagascar	270	190	142
Sri Lanka	200	500	40
Liberia	150	360	42
Jamaica	100	680	15

[1]Reflects country's total generating capacity, not just small hydropower.
SOURCE: Agency for International Development, *Decentralized Hydropower in AID's Development Assistance Program* (Washington, D.C.: 1986).

The United Mission to Nepal, an indigenous, church-supported organization, has helped establish a private small hydro industry that has installed 65 water-powered mills since the mid-seventies, for grinding grain and sawing logs in areas more than a day's walk from the nearest road. Most of the components are manufactured locally. Although these projects usually involve mechanical mills, many of the lessons can be applied to water-powered electricity generators. Similar efforts have succeeded on a smaller scale in India, Pakistan, Zaire, and elsewhere.[46]

In China, some 76,000 small hydropower plants supply 9,500 megawatts of power, and the country plans to more than double capacity in the next 13 years. These plants are the foundation of what the World Bank terms "the most massive rural electrification effort ever attempted in the developing world." About 40 percent of China's rural townships and one third of its 2,200 counties now get most of their power from small hydro dams.[47]

Although overall plans are developed by China's leadership and some projects get national subsidies, local villages and counties are in charge of much of the planning, execution, and financing of the country's small hydro projects. Many small hydro projects started as autonomous systems, but were later linked together and connected to larger central grids.

Efforts are also under way to develop small-scale power systems using biomass energy sources such as wood and agricultural wastes. The advantage of biomass is that the fuels can be stored for use when needed. Despite the shortage of fuelwood in many regions, some rural areas have ample supplies of biomass, such as rice hulls or coconut shells. In addition, crop or forest plantations can be established to grow biomass specifically for use in power generation.

Among the technologies used, the simplest is direct combustion of biomass, using the heat to run a reciprocating steam engine or a steam turbine, either of which can be connected to a generator. Another approach is to gasify the biomass, using the gas to run a diesel engine or gas turbine. The village of Picon in Indonesia has installed two 40-kilowatt wood gasifiers, for example, using the electricity for pumped irrigation, food processing, and woodworking. Finally, some biomass sources can be converted to liquid fuels such as ethanol or fuel oil. In the Philippines, some small generators are run on coco-diesel, a mixture of coconut oil and diesel fuel.[48]

The Philippines is also the site of the only large-scale effort to supply a central power grid with electricity from wood-fired plants. The National Electrification Administration, with the assistance of foreign lending agencies, started a "dendrothermal" program in the late seventies to help reduce the country's costly dependence on imported oil. Equipment for 17 power plants was imported from the United Kingdom and France, and fast-growing leucaena plantations were started. Like many crash projects, the dendrothermal program ran into trouble. Some plantations were started on poor soil and failed, much of the generating equipment required extensive repairs before it would work properly, and the country's worsening economy forced a cutoff of funds for rehabilitating the program.[49]

Only three dendrothermal plants were working in the Philippines in 1985. This is unfortunate because most of the prob-lems appear to be resolvable, and projections show that the dendrothermal plants can produce power for less than the average cost of electricity in the country. Too often, planners undertake innovative projects like this one but fail to allow for the start-up problems that are inevitable with first-time projects.[50]

Wind power is another source of energy with considerable potential in some developing countries. Used widely by American midwestern farmers in the twenties, before rural electrification, wind generators are proving effective in similar settings in the Third World. The most extensive effort so far is on the remote windswept plains of Inner Mongolia, where nomadic herders use 2,000 small wind turbines for lighting, running televisions, electrifying corral fences, and projecting movies. A portable wind turbine has been designed so that the nomads can carry their power source with them. Three Chinese factories are now producing several thousand wind generators each year for use in Xizang (Tibet), Xinjiang (Sinkiang), and other remote areas.[51]

Grid-connected collections of wind generators known as wind farms show promise as well. Wind farms were first built in California in the early eighties and now supply that state with about 1,100 megawatts of power. Utility-sponsored studies show that the better wind farms can produce power for about 7¢ per kilowatt-hour, which is competitive with conventional power sources.[52]

Several developing countries are now studying the potential of wind farms, and small projects are being tested in China, India, and Pakistan. European and American firms have signed agreements to establish joint manufacturing facilities in these countries. Third World wind-power development is still at an early stage, and detailed wind assessments and feasibility studies are needed. But early evidence indicates that wind power will soon take its place as a decentralized power source that is economical in many areas.[53]

Solar photovoltaic cells are in a sense the ultimate decentralized power source because they rely on sunlight—a more widely available resource than wind, biomass, or falling water. Moreover, solar cells directly produce electricity, requiring no separate generators. If electricity is needed after dark or in cloudy weather, however, storage batteries or a backup generator must be added, which can double the cost. But with or without storage, photovoltaics provide important amenities to villages that cannot afford the alternatives.

It may soon be economical to electrify whole villages using photovoltaics or hybrid photovoltaic-diesel systems.

Since 1980, the use of photovoltaic systems has grown rapidly in the Third World—mainly for communications systems, lighting, and water pumping. Although these systems still cost about $10,000 per kilowatt, for many rural areas that are not connected to a grid, solar cells are already less expensive than the alternatives, including diesel systems.[54]

One of the largest village photovoltaic programs is in French Polynesia, where 2,000 solar electric systems have been installed on 18 islands since 1982. Included in the program are 1,000 homes, 300 freezers, five hospitals, and dozens of radio beacons, street lights, and pumps. The program uses French technology and is partly subsidized by French foreign aid, but less subsidy is needed than for a comparably sized diesel system.[55]

An advantage of photovoltaics is that systems can be installed on a very small scale to provide power for health centers, communications, and education in areas where village-wide electricity will not be affordable for years. It is for these uses that photovoltaics is growing most rapidly. The industry is also beginning to step up marketing and production of solar cells in developing countries. This —together with the fact that the cost of photovoltaics is projected to decline significantly in the next decade—will make solar electricity the power of choice for a growing number of tasks in rural areas. It may soon be economical to electrify whole villages using photovoltaics or hybrid photovoltaic-diesel systems.

The Philippines provides one of the best examples of successful electricity diversification. The country has reduced the oil share of electricity generation from 78 percent in 1978 to 46 percent in 1984 through the development of hydro and geothermal resources. By 1984, the Philippines had 1,654 megawatts of hydropower capacity in place and 894 megawatts of geothermal capacity, out of a total of 5,196 megawatts. An additional 604 megawatts of hydro dams, 110 megawatts of geothermal, and 110 megawatts of coal are being developed. Several small power plants that burn wood and coconut shells are operating or are under construction.[56]

It is notable that throughout the Third World little of the development of the smaller decentralized power systems is the work of national utilities. They are simply not accustomed to executing small projects at the local level. This opens a wider issue: Should the private sector be brought into the power generation business? This concept runs against the grain of power-planning over the past few decades, which has been characterized by public appropriation of private power systems. Nonetheless, it may now make sense to create competitive power systems in which there is some central planning and control, but in which private companies are encouraged to bring innovation and efficiency to the system.

Recent initiatives in opening up the electricity system to competition have occurred where power expansion has run into problems—such as Colombia and Turkey. In Pakistan, the Water and Power Development Authority is already short of capacity by 1,200 megawatts, and forced blackouts are common. Private companies, probably in partnership with foreign corporations, may be offered contracts to build and operate power plants and sell the electricity to the national utility at a fixed price. The foreign partners would help raise the foreign exchange needed and could own equity in the project.[57]

Such efforts are loosely modeled on the Public Utility Regulatory Policies Act passed in the United States in 1978. Under the act, U.S. utilities are required to purchase power from independent producers at the long-run marginal cost of generation. This, together with the availability of tax credits, has resulted in over 30,000 megawatts of proposed small power projects, half of which are fossil-fuel-fired cogeneration (combined production of heat and power) and the rest a diverse mix of wind power, hydropower, wood-fired plants, waste-fired plants, and solar power projects. In California, enough power contracts have been signed to provide more than one third of the state's electricity.[58]

The state of Gujarat may become the California of India. The State Electricity Board offered in 1985 to pay 10¢ per kilowatt-hour for privately generated wind power. It is too early to know the outcome of this offer or whether it will be extended, but Gujarat already has the Third World's first operating wind farm, and the state government has successfully supported the development of other renewable energy sources. In a similar vein, the Chinese government is encouraging local governments and industrial enterprises to pool their resources to build power plants independently from the national Ministry of Water Resources and Electric Power.[59]

Neither a completely government-dominated power system nor an entirely deregulated private approach can capture the ideal mix of economic efficiency and reliable service. However, opening the power system to limited private competition is a way to both bring financial resources to electricity projects and spur the development of innovative technologies. Countries with different political systems and power industries seem to be moving in similar directions, which makes the new developments particularly noteworthy. The end of the era of exclusive government power monopolies will almost certainly open opportunities to improve the reliablity and cost-effectiveness of electricity systems.

No simple prescriptions can be handed out for the Third World's electricity problems. The needs are vast and the available resources small. New initiatives must be carefully designed. Altering the status quo is always difficult, particularly if it involves such a large and politically powerful sector of society. The sheer pace of ongoing construction also undermines attempts to change. But most developing countries simply cannot afford to neglect fundamental problems any longer. For better or worse, electric power is a large and crucial sector of most Third World economies, and if its future growth is misdirected or poorly managed, the development process itself could be jeopardized.

Increased efficiency, more attention to the special energy needs of rural villagers, and the development of decentralized power technologies can together contribute significantly to the viability and effectiveness of Third World power systems. The most fundamental change needed is a philosophical one, however. Electricity is not an end in itself but part of a larger package of initiatives for rural areas. Less effort should be placed on accelerating the pace of power system expansion and more on ensuring that electricity effectively promotes development.

6

Realizing Recycling's Potential

Cynthia Pollock

Residents of New York City collectively discard 24,000 tons of materials each day. The amalgam, considered trash by most of its contributors, contains valuable metals, reusable glass containers, recyclable paper and plastic, and food wastes high in nutrient value. It also contains ever greater amounts of hazardous wastes—mercury from batteries, cadmium from fluorescent lights, and toxic chemicals from cleaning solvents, paints, and wood preservatives.[1]

New Yorkers hold the world record for producing the most garbage per capita, although growing volumes of refuse as well as a scarcity of disposal sites plague cities everywhere. Municipal governments worldwide are struggling to find the best methods for managing their residents' wastes. Particularly in industrial countries, the premium now placed on space and environmental quality is restricting the use of traditional landfills. Increasingly, refuse is either hauled long distances to a sanitary landfill, burned in incinerators designed to recover energy, or separated in order to retrieve valuable materials for recycling.

Most of the products available to consumers are intended for a one-night stand. They are purchased, consumed, and discarded with little regard for their remaining value. The energy, materials, and environmental losses associated with this consumption pattern are staggering. David Morris of the Washington-based Institute for Local Self Reliance puts it well: "A city the size of San Francisco disposes of more aluminum than is produced by a small bauxite mine, more copper than a medium copper mine and more paper than a good sized timber stand. San Francisco is a mine. The question is how to mine it most effectively and how to get the maximum value from the collected materials."[2]

Recycling offers communities everywhere the opportunity to trim their waste disposal needs, and thereby reduce disposal costs, while simultaneously combating global environmental problems. Recycling metals, paper, glass, plastics, and organic wastes would lessen the demand for energy and materials. Producing aluminum from scrap instead of bauxite cuts energy usage and air pollution by 95 percent. Making paper from discards instead of virgin timber not only saves valuable forests, it reduces the energy used per ton by up to three quarters and requires less than half as much water.[3] And since cutting fossil fuel consumption is one of the most effective actions people can take to slow the buildup of carbon dioxide that is warming the earth's atmosphere (see Chapter 9), recycling must be part of the effort to delay climate change.

Managing solid waste is a global problem: Refuse is produced throughout the world. But it is also a local problem in that there is no such thing as a global waste stream. The cumulative waste management decisions made by local and national governments affect global energy balances, the rate at which the atmosphere warms, and the amount of pollution emitted into the environment. They also affect international trade flows and the accumulation of debt. Individuals are not powerless in the face of these problems that sometimes seem too abstract or remote for constructive action. The degree to which people and nations act together to conserve raw materials and energy resources can slow the rate at which the global ecosystem is altered.

Americans spent more for food packaging in 1986 than farmers received in income.

In many areas of the world, recycling has been hampered by a prejudice against used, or postconsumer, materials and the products that incorporate them. Currency is not considered worthless after it has been exchanged, but because refuse collection began as a measure to protect health, many people mistakenly believe that materials that have already been used are dangerous

and dirty. On the contrary, most materials in use today are chosen for their durability. One wearing does not make a rag, nor does one trip through the typewriter or the bottling plant render paper or glass unusable.

An inventory of the world's discards would reveal metal wastes more valuable than the richest ores, paper wastes representing millions of hectares of forests, and plastics wastes incorporating highly refined petrochemicals. That these products rich in raw materials and concentrated energy are frequently considered worthless is indicative of a distorted economic system. We are literally throwing away our future.

THE GARBAGE GLUT

Growing populations, rising incomes, and changing consumption patterns combine to complicate the waste management problem. Total garbage generation expands as a city swells in size, as consumers earning more money increase their consumption of food, beverages, and so-called durable goods, and as strengthening demands for greater convenience encourage the marketing of single-serving and more heavily packaged products. In most areas of the world, the ability to manage waste effectively lags far behind its rate of growth.

Before the days of densely populated urban areas, waste disposal was eased by the absorptive capacity of the surrounding land and water. Farm communities that transferred their food from field to table—bypassing the processor, packager, advertiser, and grocer—created little waste. Vegetable peelings and the like were either fed to the animals or tossed on a compost heap to fertilize the next crop. Moving off the land brings an entirely new consumption pattern.

Homegrown food is traded for products wrapped, sealed, and packaged for convenience.

Industrial societies with smaller farming populations and higher incomes produce considerably more waste per person than developing countries do. New Yorkers, for example, throw out nine times their weight in rubbish each year, while residents of Manila throw away 2.5 times their weight in rubbish. (See Table 6–1.) Part of the reason is that most of the food brought into New York City is shipped hundreds or thousands of kilometers, and the packaging used to keep products fresh and attractive is several times greater than the amounts used at farmers' markets. Nearly $1 out of every $10 spent for food and beverages in the

United States pays for packaging. Preliminary figures released by the U.S. Department of Agriculture indicate that Americans spent more for food packaging in 1986 than farmers received in income. The packaging bill for the year was expected to total $28 billion.[4]

As more women enter the workforce, demand for convenience products continues to grow. Frozen, canned, and vacuum-packed food packages are frequently the eat-at-home substitute for carryout meals. Such prepared dishes do cut down on household organic wastes, but the food trimmings have simply been disposed of elsewhere. In absolute terms, the waste stream is enlarged by the packaging and materials used in the advertising campaign. Transportation to processors and packagers increases the energy intensity of the product. Consumer awareness of the effects of purchasing decisions on waste volumes and disposal needs is only slowly emerging.

In industrial countries, packaging contributes about 30 percent of the weight and 50 percent of the volume of household waste. Food and yard wastes account for most of the remainder. Paper constitutes by far the largest share of packaging, followed by glass, metals, and plastics. Every American discards almost 300 kilograms of packaging each year. The plastics fraction, starting from a negligible base in the sixties, has grown the fastest. Soft drinks, vegetable oils, cleaning products, and toiletries are all available in plastic containers.[5]

In fact, it is becoming almost impossible to buy some of these items in traditional glass containers. Thus, not only is the quantity of packaging increasing, the materials used for packaging are also changing. A growing share of the waste stream is composed of containers that are not easily reusable or recyclable.

The soft drink industry provides a good example of both the changing packaging mix and the way rising afflu-

Table 6-1. Refuse Generation Rates in Selected Cities, Circa 1980

City	Per Capita Waste Generation Rate
	(kilograms per day)
Industrial Cities	
New York, United States	1.80
Singapore	0.87
Hong Kong	0.85
Hamburg, West Germany	0.85
Rome, Italy	0.69
Low-Income Cities	
Lahore, Pakistan	0.60
Tunis, Tunisia	0.56
Bandung, Indonesia	0.55
Medellin, Colombia	0.54
Calcutta, India	0.51
Karachi, Pakistan	0.50
Manila, Philippines	0.50
Kano, Nigeria	0.46

SOURCE: Sandra J. Cointreau, *Environmental Management of Urban Solid Wastes in Developing Countries* (Washington, D.C.: World Bank, 1982).

ence and greater demand for convenience products swell household garbage bins. Until 1975, refillable glass bottles dominated international beverage container markets. Aluminum and steel cans and throwaway bottles accounted for the remainder. By 1981, the ratio in the United States had reversed, and most carbonated beverages were sold in one-way containers.[6]

During the same period, soft drink consumption per capita rose 56 percent. Since then aluminum cans and plastic bottles have overtaken all forms of glass in U.S. markets. By 1985, aluminum cans and plastic bottles achieved a 69-percent market share by volume, while refillable glass retained only a 16-percent share. Carbonated beverage containers frequently account for more than 5 percent of U.S. household wastes.[7]

Aluminum, the most abundant metal on earth, is never found free in nature. Not until the 1820s did Danish and German scientists learn to refine the metal into a valuable product. At $1,200 a kilogram, aluminum was more precious than gold. Since its first use in a toy rattle for Napoleon's son, the use of aluminum has mushroomed. The first 355-milliliter, all-aluminum beverage can appeared on the market in 1963, and such containers are today the largest single use of aluminum, accounting for 22 percent of U.S. shipments. In 1963, 11.5 billion metal beverage cans were used in the United States, of which 11.4 billion were made of steel. By 1985, more than 70 billion beverage cans were used, of which almost 66 billion—94 percent—were made of aluminum.[8]

The advent of low-priced petrochemicals and new technologies ushered in the age of plastics. Two-liter plastic bottles, introduced in 1978, now contain 22 percent of the volume of soft drinks sold in the U.S. market. More plastics are now produced in the United States than aluminum and all other nonferrous metals

combined. Sales have grown at an annual rate of almost 5 percent since 1977. Bottlers of ketchup, canners of soup, and packagers of ice cream are all adopting lightweight, unbreakable, nonbiodegradable plastic containers. In Canada, Japan, and the United Kingdom, beer drinkers may now buy "a six pack in a bottle."[9]

Although the layperson tends to think of plastic as a single material having numerous applications, more than 46 different polymers are actually in common use. A squeezable ketchup bottle, for example, is made of six layers of plastics, each engineered to do a different job, such as to give the bottle shape, strength, flexibility, and impermeability.[10]

Combining plastics with other materials further expands the variety. A brand-name photocopier supplier now offers long lasting "plastic paper" to companies willing to pay 35¢ a sheet. And food packagers are experimenting with composites of aluminum foil and plastic that are less bulky than rigid packages and have a longer shelf life.[11] Unfortunately, as packaging materials increase in complexity, the cost and difficulty of recycling them mounts. And unlike most materials, plastics do not degrade in the presence of sunlight or bacteria.

In a growing number of cities, the volume of discarded materials now surpasses the available managerial and physical capacities to dispose of them. Beijing, Shanghai, Tianjin, and 24 other large Chinese cities are trying to cope with garbage piles that increase by 10 percent each year. Rising living standards in the surrounding countryside have prompted farmers to stop accepting garbage dumping on their fields. Farmers who can afford commercial fertilizers fear that pollution from continued dumping will degrade their land. And in Mexico City, most of the 10,000 tons of trash collected daily was, until recently, thrown into open dumps, where it nourished huge populations of flies and rats that swarmed through poor neighborhoods.[12]

Municipalities in industrial and developing countries alike are watching their garbage piles and problems mount. In some areas the waste management infrastructure has become overloaded; in others, it does not yet exist. Efforts to reduce waste volumes and recover recyclable materials are viable in all regions, however.

Less waste means less demand for expensive garbage-hauling equipment and waste transfer stations, as well as the loss of habitat for disease-spreading insects and rodents. Greater use of recyclable materials cuts the need for imported resources, reduces energy consumption, and curtails water and air pollution. Societies that recycle can more efficiently and less expensively allocate scarce energy and materials among growing populations.

MANAGING SOLID WASTE

Although even the earliest civilizations produced wastes, the refuse problem is basically an urban blight, associated with limited space and dense populations. Where people are scattered sparsely and waste volumes are low, the environment can naturally assimilate discards. But where large numbers of people congregate, unorganized waste disposal becomes an unsightly health hazard.

About 500 B.C., Athens issued the first known edict against throwing garbage into the streets, and organized the first municipal dumps by requiring scavengers to dispose of wastes no less than one mile from the city walls. Like many Greek innovations, the practice of waste removal was lost in medieval Europe.

Parisians continued to toss their trash out the window until the fourteenth century. Several hundred years later, as people thronged to newly industrializing cities to obtain the first factory jobs, the garbage crisis multiplied. City governments ultimately adopted the responsibility for collecting and disposing of refuse.[13]

Once the garbage left the city gate, it was commonly dumped on scattered piles in the surrounding countryside. As cities grew, the available countryside shrank, and the noxious odors and rat infestations caused by the dumps became intolerable. Freestanding piles gave way to pits dug to confine the waste. In densely populated areas of Europe, even this disposal method was soon regarded as requiring too much space and posing an undue threat to groundwater, and a new solution was sought.

The first systematic incineration of municipal refuse was tested in Nottingham, England, in 1874. Burning reduces waste volumes by some 70 to 90 percent, depending on the contents, so waste commissioners on both sides of the Atlantic heralded the development. Densely populated and affluent cities soon built experimental incinerators, but many communities could not justify the expense. Large capital outlays for incinerators only made sense where cheap, unregulated waste burial sites were unavailable. In addition, many cities that did hop on the incineration bandwagon soon jumped off when their air quality deteriorated. Waste burial continued as the most widely practiced disposal method.[14]

Some 90 percent of the refuse in the United States is still buried. But many U.S. landfills are rapidly filling up, and fears of groundwater contamination make landfills unwelcome neighbors. From January 1984 until August 1985, Chicago enforced a moratorium on the development of new landfills until better systems for monitoring and controlling leachate and methane gas migration were devised. According to David Morris and Neil Seldman of the Institute for Local Self Reliance, more than half the cities in the United States will exhaust their current landfills by 1990—just three years from now.[15]

Disposal space is becoming a coveted and more strictly regulated commodity, and prices are beginning to rise accordingly. In Minneapolis, Minnesota, the cost of burying a ton of refuse has risen from $5 to $30, a sixfold increase in as many years. By 1990, cities and towns in California will pay $1 billion annually to get rid of their trash. Philadelphia, a metropolitan area of 6 million people, no longer has access to a local landfill and has sometimes shipped its waste as far away as Ohio and southern Virginia. Since 1980, Philadelphia's disposal costs have risen from $20 to $90 per ton. Even when cities are able to gain access to new, environmentally sound landfills, the sites are usually remote. Disposal costs increase by 50¢ to $1 for every mile each ton of garbage is transported.[16]

Yet, in many areas landfill fees are still artificially low. Until city managers and waste producers are forced to pay the higher costs of diminished capacity and stricter closure requirements, they will not actively pursue other strategies. Maurice Hinchey, chair of New York's legislative commission on solid waste management, believes that "the most critical defect in our present waste economy is the gross under pricing of our disposal capacity. Because landfill charges are set so low, private haulers and municipal waste collection agencies alike have little incentive to sort and salvage recyclable materials from the refuse or to invest in their own materials recovery system." He reasons that since "there is no excess capacity left in the system, the cost of remaining capacity should rise as each new ton of waste is deposited."[17]

Lack of new landfill space coupled with growing waste volumes is prompting a search for new methods of waste management. Support for waste-to-energy plants that burn solid waste to produce either steam or electricity is snowballing. After a number of false starts in the mid-seventies, the technology has been refined, with the help of European experience, and is now being adopted by cities from Alaska to Florida.

A 1986 survey by the U.S. Conference of Mayors found 62 waste-to-energy plants already in operation, 26 under construction, and another 39 in the advanced stages of planning. Some of these plants, known as mass burn, are fired by unsegregated solid waste that is simply shoveled into the furnace. Others, known as refuse-derived fuel plants, remove glass and metals and shred the remaining solid waste to produce either a confettilike or pelletized fuel that can be burned in specially designed boilers or mixed in small proportions with coal.[18]

More than half the cities in the United States will exhaust their current landfills by 1990.

Waste-to-energy plants appeal to city administrators because they require no change in waste collection patterns, their management can be turned over to a private owner if desired, low-cost financing mechanisms are available, and there is a guaranteed market for the energy produced. A 1978 U.S. law requires electric utilities to purchase, at a fair price, electricity offered for sale by private producers. This institutional arrangement is not as readily available to incineration plants elsewhere in the world.[19]

Companies that previously supplied equipment to the now lethargic electric utility industry are actively promoting their newly developed incinerators. The units can be sized to fit a community's needs and range in capacity from less than 100 tons of garbage per day up to 3,000 tons. Both the very small and very large incinerator markets are growing. A dozen plants with capacities of at least 1,500 tons per day are either operating or in the advanced planning stages. As a point of comparison, to burn all of the combustible waste produced in New York City would require 12 incinerators each capable of handling 1,500 tons of waste a day.[20]

Promoters of waste-to-energy plants point to international experience with incinerators as an indicator of their feasibility. Some 350 plants are operating in Brazil, Japan, the Soviet Union, and various nations in Western Europe, which has about half the total. In Denmark, Japan, Sweden, and Switzerland, more than half of household waste is burned (see Table 6–2), but only a portion of these plants produce electricity as a by-product of the combustion. A larger fraction generate steam that is conveyed through ducts to neighboring industries or residential developments. Since 1960, the number of incinerators in Japan has tripled and the overall capacity has swelled 17 times. In the United States, only 3 percent of municipal waste is incinerated. Promoters of the technology predict the figure will reach 40 percent before the turn of the century.[21]

Not everybody is convinced of the merits of waste-to-energy plants. The round of incinerators built throughout the world during the first half of this century have all been retired in large part because they did not meet air quality standards established after their construction. Some analysts are not satisfied that the emissions problems at the newer incinerators have been resolved.

Skeptics point especially to the potential problems of burning materials containing chlorine compounds. (Plastics and bleached paper are the two major sources.) During combustion, these

Table 6-2. Share of Household Waste Sent to Waste-to-Energy Plants in Various Countries, 1985

Country	Amount of Waste Generated Per Year	Amount of Waste Burned Per Year	Share of Wastes Burned	Plants Operating
	(million metric tons)		(percent)	(number)
United States	136.1	4.1	3	58
Japan[1]	71.5	18.7	26	361
West Germany	26.3	9.0	34	46
Sweden	3.5	1.8	51	7
Switzerland	2.5	1.9	75	14

[1]Data for 1983.
SOURCE: Allen Hershkowitz, *Garbage Burning Lessons from Europe: Consensus and Controversy in Four European States* (New York: Inform, 1986); Allen Hershkowitz, *Managing Japan's Waste* (New York: Inform, 1987).

molecules regroup and form members of the chemical families known as dioxins and furans. Some dioxins, such as tetrachlorodibenzo-p-dioxin, are among the most toxic molecules known. They are implicated in weakening the immune system, thereby making the body more susceptible to carcinogens, and they have been shown to affect fetal development and cause chloracne.[22]

From February 1985 until June 1986, Sweden enforced a moratorium on the construction of additional incinerators so that it could investigate the formation, emissions, and health effects of dioxins further. Denmark followed with a moratorium of its own, and concern among West German and American scientists grew. Epidemiological surveys indicated disturbing levels of dioxin in the milk of nursing mothers, and many analysts attribute the prevalence to incinerators.[23]

A growing number of cities around the world are integrating recycling into their waste management plans.

Unanswered questions about the chemistry of the combustion and cooling processes have led to heated arguments by scientists on both sides of the issue.[24] Until the uncertainties surrounding dioxin formation and its health effects are resolved, it would be prudent for cities to proceed slowly and cautiously in their adoption of waste-to-energy plants.

In cities like New York, however, where disposal space is fast running out, waste managers are looking for a quick fix. They want to build five incinerators initially, followed by three more, with a total capacity among the eight incinerators of 17,850 tons of waste per day. The first five plants, with a capacity of 11,200 tons per day, would be constructed simultaneously.[25]

Before any operating experience could be gained at the first plant, the city would issue bonds worth $1.5 billion. This is a risky venture. Investments of this size require careful planning, and the introduction of a relatively new technology should proceed slowly so that the bugs can be ironed out at the first plant before the second is built. Encouraging recycling and developing a new, environmentally sound landfill site, which ultimately will be required anyway for incinerator ash and noncombustibles if not for trash, is likely to be a wiser use of taxpayer funds. Recycling less than 15 percent of New York City's waste would eliminate the need for one incinerator.[26]

No nationwide emissions standards exist for waste-to-energy plants in the United States, nor are there federal guidelines on permissible dioxin levels. Sweden is the only country with specific dioxin regulations. In West Germany, 11 pollutants are regulated and furnaces that violate emissions limits for one hour are required to close. Any plant manager who knowingly violates an environmental standard receives a mandatory two-year jail term.[27]

In addition, all plant workers in West Germany and all plant managers and high-level workers in Switzerland are required to attend two-and-a-half years of practical and theoretical training in resource recovery. Regulators are also concerned about the ash residue from waste-to-energy plants. Because the ash contains heavy metals, Sweden treats it as hazardous waste and California may adopt the same approach.[28]

Waste collection, transportation, and disposal cost cities from $30 to over $100 per ton. Solid waste management is a large and growing share of city budgets. Yet evaluating alternative management practices is frequently left to the system's critics. The purchase-consume-dispose mentality is so well rooted in

Table 6-3. Environmental Benefits Derived from Substituting Secondary Materials for Virgin Resources

Environmental Benefit	Aluminum	Steel	Paper	Glass
		(percent)		
Reduction of Energy Use	90–97	47–74	23–74	4–32
Reduction of Air Pollution	95	85	74	20
Reduction of Water Pollution	97	76	35	—
Reduction of Mining Wastes	—	97	—	80
Reduction of Water Use	—	40	58	50

SOURCE: Robert Cowles Letcher and Mary T. Sheil, "Source Separation and Citizen Recycling," in William D. Robinson, ed., *The Solid Waste Handbook* (New York: John Wiley & Sons, 1986).

public attitudes that even proposals to shift from one disposal site to another—for example, from a landfill to a waste-to-energy plant—are touted as radical.

Recycling programs that require not only a new way of thinking about waste but greater involvement by a host of small, dispersed participants face even greater institutional barriers. Despite these obstacles, a growing number of cities around the world are integrating recycling into their waste management plans. These cities save money by avoiding disposal costs and by selling secondary materials.

RECYCLING TRENDS AND POTENTIAL

Wastes available for recycling theoretically include all consumer discards. In practice, it is necessary to distinguish between quantity and quality. Although some analysts assert that more than half the consumer waste stream can be economically recycled, achieving such high rates requires careful waste handling.

Paper rapidly loses its value when mixed with other refuse, particularly organic food waste. Glass and metals, while less vulnerable to degradation, compete with uncontaminated raw materials in the marketplace. Organic wastes destined for the compost pile are easiest to handle if they are free of inorganics and substances toxic to plants. As a rule, the nearer to the origin of the waste that recovery occurs, the less sorting and processing will be needed before the material can be recycled. The cleanest secondary materials always command the highest prices.

Some consumer wastes, such as refillable glass bottles, only require a thorough washing before reuse. The bottles are about 50 percent heavier than their nonrefillable counterparts and are designed for up to 30 round-trips. Aluminum, nonrefillable glass, and steel require more elaborate processing, but can be recycled almost indefinitely. The energy and materials savings associated with recycling these products are enormous. (See Table 6–3.)

Aluminum is the most energy-intensive commodity in common use, and in some areas of the world, energy is a greater share of the production costs than raw materials. Recycling aluminum requires only 5 percent as much energy as producing it from bauxite and each can recycled saves the energy equivalent of a half can of gasoline. Remelting one ton of aluminum eliminates the need for four tons of bauxite and 700 kilograms of petroleum coke and pitch, while reducing emissions of air-polluting aluminum fluoride by 35 kilograms.[29]

Use of 15–20 percent crushed, post-consumer glass (cullet) was already standard practice in many glass plants prior to the energy price hikes of 1973, but several newer systems, particularly in developing countries, now run furnaces exclusively on cullet. For every ton of crushed glass used in the manufacturing process, some 1.2 tons of raw materials are saved. Every 10 percent of cullet introduced into the furnace results in energy savings of 2–5 percent. The recent adoption of stricter air pollution standards in Japan, Sweden, the United States, and West Germany has led to an increase in the demand for cullet by glass producers because its use reduces emissions.[30]

Recycling is a cost-effective "disposal" option if it requires fewer government subsidies than landfilling or incineration.

Many different grades of paper products are recycled, ranging from the highest quality computer and office paper to corrugated cardboard, newspaper, and mixed miscellaneous sheets. Recycling programs spare millions of hectares of trees, while simultaneously conserving water and energy and reducing the amount of air and water pollution that would otherwise occur. Additional savings are reaped because building a mill designed to use waste paper instead of virgin pulp is 50–80

percent cheaper. In the United States, some 200 mills use only reclaimed paper. Developing countries that rely on waste paper can reserve scarce water for drinking supplies and keep down foreign debts. Simply recovering the print run of a Sunday edition of the *New York Times* would leave 75,000 trees standing.[31]

As literacy rates and paper consumption increase in fiber-poor countries, the expanding domestic industry provides an export market for fiber-rich nations. The largest importers of waste paper are Canada, Italy, Mexico, South Korea, and West Germany. In India, the domestic paper industry was aided until 1985 by stiff duties on wood pulp and paper, but no duty is levied on imported waste paper, which all the mills have the capability of using. Paperboard mills in Finland also import large amounts of used corrugated containers, so municipalities have been given the authority to ban the disposal of corrugated boxes. Waste paper now accounts for one of every four tons of general cargo shipped from the Port of New York.[32]

Materials unsuitable for recycling back into the original product include those composed of many different raw materials and those that are severely degraded. Laminated aluminum, paper, and plastics or simply plastic products made of chemically incompatible resins are generally too expensive to recycle. The costs of separating and processing exceed the value of the resources recovered.

Some degraded materials, however, can be recycled for new uses. Paper, for example, is sold as many different grades depending on its fiber content and brightness. After several rounds through the recycling mill, the fibers become too short for papermaking, but are still valuable as insulation, animal bedding, roofing felt, or fuel. The cleaner the paper is kept at each stage, the more conversions it can undergo.

Recycling rates for such commonly

used materials as aluminum, paper, and glass are on the upswing in many industrial countries. In the past 10 years Austria has tripled and Japan more than doubled its aluminum recycling rate. Glass recycling increased by more than 50 percent from 1981 to 1985 in Austria, the United Kingdom, and West Germany. In Germany the volume of glass collected rose sixfold in the decade through 1984, and in 1985 the country recycled more than 1 million tons. Paper recovery has also increased substantially over the years, but appears to have reached a plateau in many countries. Of the 10 nations listed in Table 6–4, only Austria, Sweden, and Switzerland boosted their paper recovery rates by more than 20 percent during the eighties.[33]

Despite these overall gains, recycling rates could be improved considerably.

Table 6-4. Recovery Rates for Aluminum, Paper, and Glass in Selected Countries, 1985[1]

Country	Aluminum	Paper[2]	Glass
Netherlands	40	46	53
Italy	36	30[3]	25
West Germany	34	40	39
Japan	32	48[3]	—
United States	28	27	10
France	25	34	26
United Kingdom	23	29	12
Austria	22	44	38
Switzerland	21	43	46
Sweden	18	42	—

[1]Includes industrial recycling. [2]Data for 1984. [3]Data for 1983.
SOURCES: Aluminum Association, Inc., *Aluminum Statistical Review for 1985* (Washington, D.C.: 1986); U.N. Food and Agriculture Organization, *Waste Paper Data, 1982–84* (Rome: 1985); *Glass Gazette* (Brussels), October 1986; U.S. glass data from U.S. Department of Commerce, "Current Industrial Reports: Glass Containers," Washington, D.C., May 1986, and Bill Clow, Owens Illinois, private communication, August 28, 1986.

Only a small percentage of these materials are nonrecoverable, such as paper used for cigarettes and books. Yet only the Netherlands collects more than half its aluminum, paper, or glass for recycling. In effect, the country requires no raw materials for making its bottles and jars one year out of two. A minimum 50-percent recovery rate for each of these materials is clearly feasible. In fact, the Organisation for Economic Co-operation and Development estimates that over 90 percent of waste glass could be made available for recovery. Recycling half the paper used in the world today would meet almost 75 percent of new paper demand, and would preserve 8 million hectares of forestland, an area equal to about 6 percent of Europe's forests.[34]

Processes for cleaning plastics are not well developed and the industry is not yet able to turn a used PET (polyethylene terephthalate) soda bottle into a new PET bottle. Containers that are turned in for recycling are sometimes shredded and stuffed into seat cushions or used as insulation in sleeping bags and jackets. Plastic lumber is also an emerging market for applications such as low-maintenance fences and pier supports. Substituting plastic for wood is encouraged in Japan, where plastics consumption has soared in recent years. But in New York State, two thirds of the plastic soft drink containers returned under the deposit system were buried in 1985 because of poor scrap markets.[35]

The economics of recycling depend largely on the alternatives available, the markets for the recovered products, and the costs of operating the recycling program. For years, recycling has been hampered by the belief that it should make money. But recycling is a cost-effective "disposal" option if it requires fewer government subsidies than landfilling or incineration. Lower taxes, energy savings, and a cleaner environment are the real bottom lines. As landfill costs continue to rise because of space constraints and stricter environmental regulations, and as the high capital costs of incinerators and their pollution control technologies sap city budgets, the appeal of recycling will inevitably grow.

In the densely populated northeastern section of the United States, for instance, the average fee for landfill disposal is already more than twice that for any other region. If a system of "shared savings" were implemented, both cities and private recyclers could make money. Taking the extreme example of Philadelphia, a ton of recyclable newsprint sells for $20–25, but costs the city $90 to dispose of. If the city instead paid recyclers half the costs—$45—both sides would come out ahead and the city would save money. Virtually all materials except aluminum are worth more as a cost avoidance mechanism than as raw materials for recycling.[36]

In California, a study conducted by the Waste Management Board found the statewide average cost of collection and disposal of refuse is $60 per ton. According to Board estimates curbside recycling typically costs about $40 per ton, a third less than landfill disposal. The difference in net costs comes from the revenues gained through selling the recyclables rather than paying for their burial.[37]

Prices paid for the materials recovered also factor largely in the economics of recycling. Low and volatile prices are the bane of secondary materials markets. Without a dependable floor price, or ample storage space to maintain price-stabilizing buffer stocks, program planning is impaired. Economically sustainable recycling requires high consumer participation rates, yet households cannot be asked to change their behavior from week to week in order to accommodate market swings.

A curbside newspaper collection service available to 70,000 residences in Montgomery County, Maryland, is guaranteed at least $30 per ton by the mill. In the Netherlands, buffer stocks enable collectors of waste paper to sell to the government-established fund when prices drop below a predetermined level. The stock is sold when prices rise. Such assurances make recycling more appealing to local governments, while providing scrap purchasers with stable supplies of secondary materials.[38]

Unfortunately, opportunities for recycling are sometimes blocked by other community objectives. Flow control ordinances, for example, are designed to ensure that waste-to-energy plants operate at full capacity. Some measures may make it illegal to divert any portion of the waste stream for recycling. But burning is not the most cost-effective or efficient disposal method for many waste products.

Noncombustibles such as metals and glass are valuable when recycled but cause undue wear and tear and take up storage and furnace space at incinerators. Paper and plastics, on the other hand, help generate valuable electricity. Unseparated municipal waste has a heating value of some 8,400 kilojoules per kilogram, approximately half that of coal. The calorific values of paper and plastics are two and four times as high, respectively. Thus the energy recovery potential of the waste diminishes as these materials are culled.[39]

High-grade paper, however, is more valuable as a raw material than as a fuel, and newspaper and corrugated cardboard may be as well. A study done for Garden State Paper Company in New Jersey concluded that if 25–50 percent of newsprint were recycled instead of burned, the energy output of the incinerator would drop by 3.5–7 percent. When the energy required to produce newsprint from virgin fibers was accounted for, the energy savings dramatically offset the incinerator losses. Newspaper recovery rates already exceed 50 percent in a number of cities.[40]

Plastics are a higher value fuel than paper and thus desirable in terms of energy recovery. But according to Dr. Jack Milgrom, a plastics analyst, "Recycling plastics saves twice as much energy as burning them in an incinerator. Producing a fabricated plastic product from scrap instead of virgin resin saves some 85–90 percent of the energy otherwise used, including the energy of the petroleum feedstocks used to manufacture the resin."[41]

In addition, because plastics, especially polyvinyl chloride, contain dioxin precursors, burning them poses environmental risks. In Japan, a 1982 survey by the Ministry of Health and Welfare of 3,255 municipalities revealed that 41 percent collect plastics as part of combustibles and 34 percent designate plastics as one of the incombustibles, or wastes causing difficulties when incinerated. A trial program in Bremen, West Germany, will ask 42,000 households to separate their plastic wastes for a period of six months. The government is hoping that a plastic-free waste stream will reduce the need for additional air pollution control devices at the city's solid waste incinerator.[42]

In deciding how much of a municipality's waste should be incinerated versus recycled, program planners need to include an assessment of the net energy gains possible from each material. Wastes that are more valuable when recycled should be recovered instead of burned. By overbuilding incinerator capacity, cities lose money two ways. The excess capacity represents a capital investment that is not used and the desire (or in some cases contract obligation) to deliver a high volume of wastes to the plant curtails the incentive to reduce and recycle wastes both now and in the future. Only after designing the largest practical recycling program should calculations of incinerator capacity begin. Otherwise, cities commit themselves to producing enough waste to justify their investment.

A growing number of waste management programs are setting explicit goals for the share of wastes that will be recycled or the share that will be diverted from landfills. The Portland, Oregon, metropolitan area, for example, has determined that up to 52 percent of its waste stream is potentially available for reduction, reuse, or recycling and that materials, fuels, or electricity can be recovered from the remainder. Communities within the metropolitan area will be able to devise their own strategies for meeting these targets, but if the goals are not achieved by 1989, waste loads containing a high percentage of recyclable materials will not be accepted at disposal facilities that do not process waste for recovery. The region, home to 1.2 million people, already recycles 22 percent of its waste stream, one of the highest rates in the United States.[43]

SUCCESSFUL RECYCLING PROGRAMS

Getting consumers to participate and establishing markets for recovered materials are the keys to successful recycling programs. Several approaches have effectively increased recovery rates and sales opportunities. Consumers can segregrate their recyclables for pickup, permit others to retrieve the valuable components, or pay for a central processing plant to separate them. They may also return selected items to the place of purchase or take them to a collection or redemption center.

The demand for recovered products can be enhanced by meeting the resource needs of regional industries, exploring new uses for secondary materials, and offering economic incentives to waste processors and companies that use recycled materials as product inputs. Procurement policies that either favor or explicitly do not discriminate against goods made with postconsumer wastes also boost demand. Market stimulation simultaneously requires guaranteed supplies of high-quality secondary materials. Competition from virgin resources and industry standards for the finished product set the operating parameters. If recycled materials are not as reliable, they will not be used.

Programs geared to the recycling of specific products often include a monetary incentive, usually in the form of a deposit. When consumers purchase carbonated beverages or milk jugs, for example, they may be charged separately for the container. If it is returned clean and intact, the consumer receives a refund. Once popular, voluntary deposit programs are now almost extinct and most of today's schemes are spurred by legislation. Nine American states, home to more than 40 million people, require deposits on soft drink and beer containers.[44]

Oregon pioneered the system in 1972, and New York's program, the newest, began in 1983. The 400 million cases of beverage containers sold in New York each year make it a larger market than the other eight states combined. A study conducted by the Beer Wholesalers Association found that within two years of its implementation the New York deposit law had saved $50 million in cleanup expenditures, $19 million on solid waste disposal costs, and $50–100 million on energy, while increasing net employment by at least 3,800 jobs.[45]

Deposits on beverage containers are also used in the Netherlands, Scandinavia, the Soviet Union, and parts of Australia, Canada, and Japan. The West German and Swiss governments are authorized to implement deposits on one-way packages at their discretion. In Ontario, Canada, a soft drink container regulation issued in 1985 ties the use of deposits to the market share of refillable containers and the recycling rate of nonrefillable containers. The policy protects the current 40-percent market share for refillable bottles and requires that all nonrefillable containers achieve a minimum recycling rate of 50 percent within three years of their introduction. Failure of any type of container to achieve the designated 50-percent target will result in a deposit equivalent to that on a comparably sized refillable bottle. A two-liter PET bottle, for example, would carry a deposit of 80¢ Canadian.[46]

The new regulations in Ontario pave the way for introduction of new container materials, but in a manner that ensures they are recycled. Since 1972 refillable bottles and steel cans have been the only legal soft drink containers in the province, with steel cans enjoying a 60-percent share of the market as the only nonrefillable package available. Now, nonrefillable glass and PET bottles will also be allowed, but aluminum cans are not permitted until September 1987.[47]

Some retailers are purchasing reverse vending machines to accept returned containers and disburse deposit refunds. After inserting their containers (as rapidly as one per second), customers are issued either cash or a redeemable voucher, sometimes accompanied by promotional coupons. Most of the machines are designed to accept aluminum, but reverse vending machines that accept glass are already on the market, and at least one company is working to develop a machine for PET bottles.[48]

By the end of 1985, over 12,000 reverse vending machines were in use in 15 countries. Sweden has one third of the total, and another half are found throughout Norway, the United States, and France. Most of the machines can read the universal product code on the container and are equipped with microcomputers programmed to maintain a running inventory of the number, type, and brand of package received. Both indoor and outdoor models are available with a wide range of storage capacity. Beverage distributors like the system because instead of picking up a fraction of each customer's returns, they can pick up all the units in storage and a central accounting system will calculate the credits and debits owed each company.[49]

A few countries have successfully shunned deposit systems in favor of volunteer drop-off programs. In West Germany, for example, 35,000 bottle collection centers are scattered across the country, with some 6,000 igloo-shaped containers in Bavaria alone. Residents of the state of Hesse will soon have access to both a glass and paper receptacle within 500 meters of their homes. In 1985, West German glass container manufacturers bought nearly 1 million tons of domestic scrap, representing about 80 percent of total disposable bottle production, and purchased another 90,000 tons of cullet from importers.[50]

Collection rates are also high in Switzerland, after increasing tenfold in the decade to 1984. On average, 19.7 kilograms of glass per person are recycled, corresponding to about 50 percent of glass consumption. Here, as in West Germany, glass returns are usually separated by color to enhance their value. The demand is greatest for clear and brown cullet, as color-mixed scrap is only usable for making green glass. Long-term contracts for recycled glass have operated at the national level for years in West Germany, Switzerland, and Austria.[51]

In the United States, aluminum can manufacturers promote recycling in all states, not just those with deposit legislation. Since 1981, more than half the 300 billion aluminum cans sold have been returned for recycling. The average can that comes out of a store is remelted and back on supermarket shelves within six weeks. American consumers have received over $1 billion for their efforts. By encouraging recycling and reducing the weight of their cans, the industry used 22 percent less energy to produce a pound of aluminum in 1984 than in 1972.[52]

Long-term contracts for recycled glass have operated for years in West Germany, Switzerland, and Austria.

Official programs for recovering high-value materials are usually lacking in developing countries, but informal, early morning scavenging is often evident in high-income residential neighborhoods. While not encouraged, it is generally tolerated, and frequently well organized. The informal system is commonly based on a network of buyers and their appointed neighborhood agents, typically specialized in only one or just a few categories of materials. Sometimes the rights to scavenge in certain neighborhoods are actually bought and sold.

Scavenging also takes place at stages further along in the waste management system. In Bangkok, Thailand, collection crews spend up to 40 percent of the time while on their service routes recovering and sorting paper, bottles, cans, and plastics. They reportedly earn as much from recycling as they do from their official salary. Collection crews in Manila bring along an extra unpaid member solely for the purpose of sorting.[53]

Recognizing the contributions that this informal sector makes by reducing dependence on foreign imports and lessening the volume of wastes requiring land disposal, the Ministry of Environment in Indonesia is developing strategies aimed at supporting scavenging. In the Philippines, a pilot recycling program in Manila was initiated with the purpose of lessening the stigma attached to house-to-house scavengers. Supported by a widespread public information campaign, workers were trained as ECO-AIDES and provided with clean uniforms emblazoned with the message "pera sa basura," meaning "money from refuse."[54]

Municipal dumps also attract scavengers. In Mexico City, the dump sites are said to support 10,000 people. Waste piles in Cali, Colombia, a much smaller city, supply 400 well-organized workers with salable scrap. Scavengers in Orange County, California, bid each week for the right to salvage from one of the four county landfills. Because of the low living standard and health risks associated with this type of labor, scavenging is not the preferred recovery method. On the other hand, new waste management systems should take into account their displacement of this traditional source of employment and secondary materials.[55]

The fastest growing type of recycling program in industrial countries requires consumers to separate their refuse by material and then place it on the curb for routine collection. In some areas, recyclables and nonrecyclables are collected on the same day in a slightly modified truck. In others, a specially designed, compartmentalized truck with an alternate schedule is used. The materials most often segregated are aluminum, glass, ferrous metals, and newspapers. Some programs also recover corrugated cardboard, used oil, plastics, organic kitchen wastes, and yard and garden debris.

Because the purchase-consume-dispose habit is so well entrenched, especially in industrial countries, promoting a shift to recycling often calls for widespread publicity, incentives, or both.

Colorful, space-saving storage containers appear to elicit greater cooperation, as do reminders from a designated neighborhood leader about the timing of the next pickup and the value of recycling. High levels of participation, essential for a successful program, are also encouraged by offering frequent collections, which mean consumers need to dedicate less household storage space. By lowering the cost of municipal waste disposal, recycling programs also provide tax breaks for local residents.

Source separation programs are in place in many areas of Western Europe and Japan and are increasingly used in the United States. The earliest plans were adopted in small to mid-size cities, some of which now have a decade of experience behind them. Larger cities such as Chicago and New York are engaged in small-scale experimental programs designed to test citywide feasibility. The Office of Recycling in New Jersey recommends that source separation programs be made mandatory for residential and commercial generators. The short-term goal is to reduce the municipal waste requiring disposal by 25 percent.[56]

In the state of Oregon, a Recycling Opportunity Act went into effect on July 1, 1986. Its aim is to make recycling available to all citizens in the state. Residential curbside pickup of recyclables is required at least once per month in cities of 4,000 or more; in smaller communities, recycling depots must be made available at disposal sites. The law explicitly ranks solid waste management options in terms of priority. The most desirable action is to reduce the amount of waste generated, then to reuse the material for the purpose it was originally intended. Next comes recycling of the nonreusable material, followed by energy recovery from "waste that cannot be reused or recycled, so long as the energy recovery facility preserves the quality of air, water and land resources." The last step is to dispose of the remainder by landfilling or other approved method.[57]

Appropriate structuring of waste collection and disposal fees also encourages recycling. Surcharges on landfill costs are one way to discourage dumping. In New Jersey, the 12¢-per-cubic-yard fee, implemented in 1982, is refunded to communities in the form of tonnage grants for materials recycled. The program appears to be working. By 1985, more than half of New Jersey's 567 municipalities offered curbside recycling programs—159 of them mandatory—and collection volumes have increased each year.[58]

The remaining municipalities in New Jersey have at least one recycling depot or a mobile collection vehicle, and more than 80 towns have started composting or mulch programs for yard and garden wastes. A regional 80-ton-per-day recycling facility opened in April 1986 in Camden County will process approximately 60 percent of the recyclable bottles and cans from the county's 37 towns when it is fully operational. Plant managers expect it to be self-supporting within a year.[59]

Recycling programs are most effective when integrated within a city's overall solid waste management plan. If added as an afterthought, and implemented outside of the waste collection system, recycling schemes typically have lower recovery rates. One way to ensure that proposals for materials recovery get a fair hearing is to appoint a full-time recycling coordinator at both the state and municipal level. Cities can also encourage recycling by stipulating that franchises for or contract bids by waste collectors and haulers include a comprehensive curbside recycling program. This approach is working successfully in dozens of cities, but is still a long way from universal adoption. The municipalities that have gone this route usually chose it when they were faced with rapidly rising waste disposal costs or be-

cause environmentally conscious residents demanded it.[60]

The other side of the recycling coin relies on strong and stable markets for secondary materials. Recovery rates are meaningless if there is no demand for the materials collected. On the free market, recyclables compete with virgin resources for industry dollars. As a result, the more consistent the volume collected and the cleaner the wastes, the easier it will be to find a buyer.

To encourage the use of recycled products, governments can require their purchasing agents to buy competitively priced goods that contain a certain percentage of postconsumer stock. Reports, laws, and tax forms printed on recycled paper, government vehicles lubricated with rerefined oil, and public roads paved in part by recovered rubber all represent huge markets.

According to Richard Keller, director of the Maryland paper procurement program, "Use of recycled paper by Federal agencies is important not only because of the volume of Federal purchases (creating a large market demand), but also because Federal procurement arrangements will be used by state, local and private organizations as a model to establish programs of their own to buy recycled paper. Additionally, as the market grows for recycled paper, the unit cost will go down, reducing costs for all organizations."[61]

Surcharges on landfill costs are one way to discourage dumping.

The state of Maryland has had a program to buy recycled paper since 1977. Over 1 million reams of recycled bond and a total of $17 million in recycled paper products have been purchased. The state government is now buying half its bond paper from recycled paper manufacturers and nearly all of its tissue and towel products from reclaimed fiber mills. Enough energy has been saved to heat nearly 9,000 homes for a year.[62]

In Florida, North Carolina, Oregon, and Wisconsin, businesses engaged in recycling pay lower taxes. Two programs are available in Oregon. One administered by the state energy agency granted 27 Oregon firms $13.8 million in tax credits in 1984 for the purchase of recycling equipment. The other is run by the state environmental agency and provides a 50-percent investment tax credit for projects that reduce pollution. In North Carolina, the cost of equipment purchased for recycling may be deducted from income and franchise taxes, and excluded from property taxes. Sales tax exemptions are available to recycling firms in Florida and Wisconsin.[63]

Conducting studies of the inputs used by manufacturers and the degree to which those inputs could be supplied by recycled materials will also stimulate markets. By focusing on regional demand, secondary materials processors can tailor their output. In agricultural areas, for example, they can produce fencing and animal bedding, in coastal regions pier supports and products for export, and in industrial settings pallets, containers, and nonspecialized parts. Plastics recyclers in Rome daily turn old garbage sacks into 350,000 new refuse bags. In East Germany, waste plastic bottles are converted into a polyester backing for carpets and other textiles.[64]

CORNERSTONES OF A RECYCLING SOCIETY

Many of today's tax codes, pricing mechanisms, and marketing practices discriminate against recycling. The obstacles often begin with subsidized raw materials and energy prices and continue through the design stage, where product managers focus on dozens of marketing concerns but are rarely influenced by an item's recycling potential. Throughout the manufacturing, merchandising, and consumption phases, materials selection and purchasing decisions are made without considering a product's afterlife. Characteristics that inhibit reuse, recycling, or disposal are too often either ignored or viewed as somebody else's problem. Removing and overcoming these barriers and establishing markets for secondary materials are essential to making the relationship between producers and consumers a two-way street.

Prices for raw materials, energy, and production inputs rarely reflect their full cost or societal value. Depletion and extraction allowances encourage consumption of virgin resources, while publicly administered mineral and forest leasing programs are chronic money losers. The U.S. Forest Service, manager of 22 percent of the nation's timberlands, lost more than $2 billion on its sales during the last 10 years. Selling timber below cost promotes the depletion of wildlife habitats and continued reliance on virgin materials. The taxpayers charged for these subsidies are effectively paying to shrink the market for their recyclable paper.[65]

Subsidized loans for power plant construction and pollution control equipment compound the problem by masking the true costs of the large amounts of energy used to process materials. Analysts at the Washington-based Center for Renewable Resources estimated that the U.S. government provided $44 billion in subsidies to the energy industry in 1984, a sum equal to one quarter of the federal budget deficit. Other production inputs, such as water, are also sold below cost and at rates considerably less than replacement value, thereby sending erroneous signals to plant managers. The opportunity to trim water usage by three fifths if recycled paper is used instead of pulp will not become cost-effective until water is realistically priced.[66] By underpricing natural resources, governments subsidize the continuation of a throwaway society.

Stricter air and water pollution regulations would also make recycling more appealing. As noted earlier, substituting scrap steel and aluminum for ores cuts smelter emissions by 85 and 95 percent, respectively. Water pollution is scaled back 76 and 97 percent. Already, stricter regulations governing groundwater pollution and methane gas generation at sanitary landfills are starting to tilt the economic scales in recycling's favor.[67]

Superfluous and ill-conceived packaging and advertising further complicate waste management and recycling programs. Products packed in metal, surrounded by plastic, and then placed in paper bags are not uncommon; more elaborate wrappings are also easy to find. And though most wineries and some breweries are still content to use a standard bottle with a unique paper label, many soft drink bottlers and food packagers have adopted the maxim that products have to stand out and be different in order to sell. But the more composites and combinations of materials, and the more designs employed in packaging, the more difficult reuse, recycling, and disposal become. Junk mail, flyers, and coupons are also overused arsenals of the advertising industry.

The key is to design both products and packaging with energy efficiency and waste reduction in mind. Standardized, refillable containers that can be used by multiple producers, such as traditional wine and beer bottles, could be developed for fruit juices, milk, soft drinks, coffee, jams, and so on. In both Denmark and Norway, fewer than 20 different re-

turnable packages for beer and carbonated beverages are permitted on the market. The French government, adopting a different approach, in 1979 directed that beverage containers in household waste be reduced 40 percent and the amount of energy consumed per packaged hectoliter be reduced 12 percent by 1984. The industries affected could develop their own strategies for meeting the target. Unfortunately, lack of diligence resulted in a less than effective program.[68]

Sometimes the materials themselves are the barrier to recycling. The plastics share of U.S. municipal wastes has nearly doubled over the past 10 years, to an estimated 6–8 percent of total volume. According to Mary Sheil, director of New Jersey's Office of Recycling, "These materials have limited recycling markets and often replace recyclable material in product packaging." One of the barriers to further plastics recycling is the inability to distinguish one plastic resin from another. Without separation by type, manufacturers will not even attempt to recycle the scrap. Efforts to develop a plastic identification system for consumers are slowly getting under way.[69]

By focusing on an individual package, the national Coalition for Recyclable Waste, headquartered in Washington, D.C., helped keep the plastic Coca-Cola can off supermarket shelves. In a trial sales campaign in the southeastern United States, experienced recyclers were alarmed by the polyvinyl chloride label, which would contribute to dioxin formation if the can were burned, and by the possible contamination of aluminum recycling programs. If the look-alike plastic cans were added to beverage can collection piles, the sudden flares of heat they release would foul secondary aluminum smelters. Largely because of this public pressure, the can has been sidelined while Coca-Cola works with the recently formed Plastic Recycling Foundation to develop new washing and processing technologies.[70]

In the future, biodegradable plastics may be used for packaging. Scientists working independently at a subsidiary of Imperial Chemical Industries in the United Kingdom and at Belland in Switzerland have come up with a formula for "intelligent plastics" that will degrade either as a result of natural processes or following the application of a reagent. Initial production runs, constrained by high costs and low volumes, limit applications to high-value medical and industrial uses, but both companies project large sales to the consumer products industry within several years. A German subsidiary of Continental Can has already paid to test the technology for making labels on recyclable bottles.[71]

Lawmakers in seven American states and at least as many European capitals have introduced bills to limit or ban some plastics.

Government regulations and fiscal incentives may compel manufacturers to produce recyclable products and packaging. One-way containers, for example, could be taxed to discourage their use, or sales tax exemptions could be implemented for products or packaging composed of at least 50-percent postconsumer waste. Because of the present inability to recycle a large share of waste plastics, lawmakers in seven American states and at least as many European capitals have introduced bills to limit or ban some plastics. Fast-food containers, plastic tampon applicators, and disposable plastic diapers are frequent targets of proposed prohibitions. West Germany has already outlawed PET bottles. And back in 1977, the Danish government, alarmed by the profusion of disposable packaging, banned the sale of almost all one-way soft drink containers, including aluminum cans.[72]

Frustrated by the proliferation of new packages and materials, some public officials are beginning to talk about applying the "cradle-to-grave" management concept from the hazardous waste field to solid waste. Materials production, use, and conversion would be closely monitored so that premature or irresponsible disposal could be avoided or penalized.

Attempts to increase the amount of material available for recycling are on the upswing in many areas. Higher landfill charges, new legislation, and the encouragement of source-separated curbside refuse collection are all increasing the supply of secondary materials. But if governments are going to encourage recycling, they must also take some responsibility for enlarging secondary materials markets.

Simply increasing supply without stimulating demand leads to glutted markets and depressed product prices. The U.S. Resource Conservation and Recovery Act of 1976, along with subsequent amendments, requires all levels of government and government contractors to purchase "items composed of the highest percentage of recovered materials practicable, consistent with maintaining a satisfactory level of competition."[73]

Developing these procurement guidelines for a range of recovered materials is proceeding slowly. Only one final guideline (regarding the use of fly ash in concrete and cement) was issued during the directive's first decade. Thirteen states have tried to take up some of the slack by passing procurement laws of their own. A uniform national standard would, however, have a more far-reaching effect and would free secondary materials processors from trying to comply with different rules in each state.[74]

The potential for increased markets is tremendous. In 1985 federal, state, and local governments employed 16.4 million people and spent an amount equal to 35.4 percent of the gross national product. Stimulating markets for recycled materials could turn household food wastes into soil-enriching compost for public parks and old newspapers into insulation for low-income housing projects. Discarded tires, now fire hazards and breeding grounds for mosquitoes, could help repave and create longer lasting highways.[75]

Governments can also generate markets by encouraging manufacturers to use more discards in their production processes and altering nonessential quality standards. Tax incentives to encourage the purchase of recycling equipment is an approach that appears to be gaining favor. New Jersey is considering a 50-percent tax credit for equipment that makes products containing at least 50-percent recycled materials. Paper brightness and glass clarity standards can also be modified for certain products, thus enlarging the market for recyclables.[76]

The inevitable global transition from dependence on extractive industries to reliance on recycled materials has already begun. Higher energy and materials prices and the development of new technologies are propelling the transformation. The international steel industry is probably the best example of the broad-based shift away from raw materials and toward recycling. By 1983, the industrial market economies produced 30 percent of their raw steel in electric arc furnaces, or minimills, that rely exclusively on scrap for their feedstock. In Argentina, Italy, and Spain, more than half the steel is produced in electric furnaces. Minimills are proliferating while large integrated steel mills that depend on iron ore and energy-intensive production processes are closing their gates or filing for bankruptcy.[77]

As low cost and abundant energy, forest, and mineral resources become a thing of the past, new manufacturing processes and pricing policies are sure to be introduced in other industries. Though the gains made in recovering aluminum, glass, and paper are impressive, tremendous potential remains. Providing a growing world population with wood for housing, paper, and fuel and with metals and glass to build cities, manufacture technical equipment, and package food and medicines will require that resources not be wasted.

Future economic growth depends on the efficient marshaling of energy, raw materials, and scarce financial capital. The countries that make the transition to a recycling society most quickly and smoothly will have the healthiest environments and the strongest economies.

7

Sustaining World Agriculture

Lester R. Brown

World agriculture is in a state of disarray. Per capita food production is rising in some regions, and falling in others. U.S. farmers, the world's most productive, are going bankrupt at a rate not seen since the Great Depression. Western Europe, a grain importer since the Industrial Revolution began, now competes with traditional exporters in world markets.

Over the past decade, the world farm economy has been transformed as the grain shortages of the seventies have become the grain surpluses of the mid-eighties. Unfortunately, this shift has occurred for all the wrong reasons—overplowing, excessive subsidies, and falling food consumption in regions with hungry people.

During this century's third quarter, farmers throughout the world responded to both market demands and subsistence pressures by plowing a record amount of new land. Much of it is highly erodible land that will eventually lose its topsoil and become wasteland unless it is converted to grassland or

woodland first. In addition, agricultural production has been raised to artificially high levels in many industrial countries by government-supported farm prices far above world market levels.

On the demand side, food consumption trends have not followed the script. Improvements in diet that were routinely projected for the Third World have not materialized everywhere. In Africa and Latin America, where malnutrition is common and output should have been rising, per capita food production was actually falling, pulling consumption down with it. Although 1986 was a relatively good crop year for Africa, the amount of grain produced per person was still 14 percent below the postwar peak reached in 1969. And in Latin America it has declined 8 percent from the historical peak in 1981, falling in four of the last five years.[1]

Compilations of world agricultural production data include output produced with agricultural practices that erode soils, lower water tables, or are otherwise unsustainable. A more accurate picture requires an ecological deflator comparable to the deflator economists use to eliminate the effects of price inflation when calculating real economic growth. Such a measure would both help determine "real" production levels in the short run and, by determining which production is ecologically sustainable, facilitate more intelligent planning for long-term food security.

CROPLAND OVEREXPANSION

Between 1950 and 1976, the area planted to cereals, which cover two thirds of the world's cropland, expanded from 590 million to 720 million hectares. Although small compared with growth in world food demand, this 22-percent increase greatly exceeded that for any comparable historical period. Most of this growth came in two surges.[2]

The first surge, in the mid-fifties, was largely a result of Moscow's Virgin Lands project, an undertaking that expanded Soviet cropland by roughly one fifth. The second came during the mid-seventies, when world grain prices doubled following poor 1972 harvests in the Soviet Union and the Indian subcontinent. Several additional poor crop years in the mid-seventies kept prices high and spurred world cropland expansion, principally in the United States and Brazil. Between 1971 and 1975, the U.S. grain area expanded by some 8 million hectares, or roughly one tenth.[3]

Since 1976, the world area in cereals has fluctuated somewhat, but basically changed little. (See Figure 7–1.) The 715 million hectares harvested in 1986 is slightly below the 720 million hectares of 1976. The principal shifts came in 1981, when the United States removed all crop restrictions in a shift to a free-market philosophy, and in 1983, when,

Million
Hectares

Figure 7-1. World Harvested Area of Grain, 1950-86

to correct the imbalance thus created, the U.S. government urged farmers to take a record amount of land out of production.[4]

The experiences of the big three food producers—the Soviet Union, China, and the United States—illustrate well the overplowing that afflicts the world as a whole. For roughly two decades the Soviets sought to maintain the gains from the Virgin Lands expansion, but they finally concluded that much of this land was marginal. As a result, the Soviet grain area has contracted in eight of the last nine years, declining 12 percent overall. To some degree, the shrinkage reflects an increase in fallowed area. But most of it resulted from the abandonment of cropland, and it has coincided with a decline in Soviet grain production of nearly one fifth since the late seventies.[5]

A similar situation existed in China, where the "grow more grain" campaign instituted by Mao Zedong led to an ecologically unsound expansion of cropland. Harvested grain area dropped from 98 million hectares in 1976 to an estimated 88 million hectares in 1986, a decline of one tenth. In China's case, pulling back from marginal land did not lead to production declines as it did in the Soviet Union. The phenomenal surge in production associated with the 1978 shift to a market-oriented farm system completely masked any negative effects on production.[6]

World cropland area may not expand at all during the remainder of this century.

In the United States, with an economic system quite different from either the Soviet Union or China, cropland area expanded markedly in the mid-seventies in response to high grain prices. Farmers reacted to the 1972–74 price increases by plowing grassland in order to plant wheat in the western Great Plains, even though this land is vulnerable to wind erosion. In other regions, farmers drained swampland. World market prices and government policies both fostered a mentality of planting "fencerow to fencerow."

American farmers responded quickly to the growing markets abroad, but often at the expense of their soil. By the late seventies, they were losing nearly as much topsoil as they had during the Dust Bowl years of the thirties. Soil erosion from wind and water exceeded new soil formation on one third of U.S. cropland, much of it in the midwestern agricultural heartland. But the erosion was heavily concentrated on marginal land: Half of the soil loss came from roughly one tenth of the cropland.[7]

Congress responded to these unsustainable practices by incorporating a conservation component in the Food Security Act of 1985, which encouraged farmers to plant their highly erodible cropland to grass or trees under 10-year contracts. The plan provided for the conversion of 45 million acres (1 acre equals 0.4 hectares) to grassland or trees by 1990: 5 million acres in 1986, 10 million acres for each of the following three years, another 5 million acres in 1990, plus 5 million acres to be retired as convenient. Coupled with restrictions on the conversion of grassland to cropland (the "sodbuster" provision) and the draining of wetlands (the "swampbuster" provision), this program is expected to reduce U.S. grain area by roughly one seventh by 1990, on a par with the recent Soviet and Chinese reductions.[8]

Smaller countries with marginal cropland areas are also cultivating less land. In mountainous regions, a combination of small fields and heavily eroded soils is making farming uneconomical. Italy, for example, reduced its grain area from 7 million hectares to less than 5 million between the mid-fifties and the mideighties, a fall of nearly one third. During the same period, Yugoslavia reduced its area in grain by one fourth.[9]

The scheduled shift of 45 million acres of U.S. cropland to grass and trees means the world cropland area may not expand at all during the remainder of this century. If, as projected, another billion people are added to world population over the remaining 13 years of this century, the grain harvested area, which dropped from 0.24 hectares per capita in 1950 to 0.15 hectares in 1986, will shrink to 0.12 hectares per person.[10]

WATER AND FOOD

During the several millennia since irrigation was developed in the Middle East, it has spread gradually throughout the world. By 1900 some 40 million hectares were irrigated; by 1950, the total reached 94 million hectares. Since then, growth has been explosive: The irrigated area nearly tripled between 1950 and 1985, contributing to the record growth of world food production.[11]

The 177 million hectares added to the world's irrigated area during this time entailed heavy use of both surface and underground water resources. Irrigation was a major focus of lending by international development agencies and of investment by those working the land. Farmers drilling wells on their own land with their own capital in the southern U.S. Great Plains and the Gangetic Plain of India achieved impressive gains.[12]

The conditions conducive to irrigation are concentrated in Asia, which has many of the world's great rivers—the Indus, the Ganges, the Brahmaputra, the Chang Jiang (Yangtze), and the Huang

He (Yellow). These rivers originate at high elevations and traverse long distances, providing numerous opportunities for irrigation as they flow seaward. This contrasts sharply with Australia, for example, which has no major rivers and, hence, only 2 percent of its land under irrigation.[13]

One reason that Asia can support half the world's people is that it has two thirds of the world's irrigated area. (See Table 7–1.) North America and Europe (including the European part of the Soviet Union), each with just over one tenth of the world total, account for much of the remainder. Africa and South America are far down the line.

The irrigated area grew most rapidly during the fifties and sixties, when it was expanding at nearly 4 percent annually. During the seventies, however, even though rising food prices stimulated

Table 7-1. Growth in Irrigated Area, by Continent, 1950–85

Region	Total Irrigated Area, 1985	Growth in Irrigated Area			
		1950–60	1960–70	1970–80	1980–85
	(million hectares)	(percent)			
Asia[1]	184	52	32	28	8
North America	34	42	71	14	−11[2]
Europe[3]	29	50	67	33	9
Africa	13	25	80	27	13
South America	9	67	20	28	17
Oceania	2	0	100	0	0
World	271	49	41	26	8

[1]Includes the Asian part of the Soviet Union.   [2]This number, which is for 1980–84 and the United States only, is from U.S. Department of Agriculture, *Farm and Ranch Irrigation Survey-1984*.   [3]Includes the European part of the Soviet Union.
SOURCE: Adapted from W.R. Rangeley, "Irrigation and Drainage in the World," paper presented at the International Conference on Food and Water, Texas A&M University, College Station, May 26–30, 1986; 1980 irrigated acreages prorated from 1970 and 1982 figures as cited in W.R. Rangeley, "Irrigation—Current Trends and A Future Perspective," World Bank Seminar, February 1983.

other agricultural investments, irrigation growth slowed. And the amount of irrigated land has grown on average less than 1 percent per year during the first half of the eighties.

In some countries, such as the United States, the area is actually declining. In 1978, just before the second oil price hike, U.S. irrigated area totaled 20.4 million hectares. By 1934, the last year for which data are available, it had dropped to 18.1 million hectares, a fall of 11 percent. (See Figure 7–2.) Depressed farm prices suggest further declines occurred in 1985 and 1986. California, Colorado, Florida, and Texas—all leaders in irrigation—have registered heavy reductions over the last several years.[14]

Year-to-year changes in world irrigated area reflect the sum of the addition of new capacity and the loss of established capacity due to aquifer depletion, lowered water tables, abandonment of waterlogged and salted land, reservoir silting, and the diversion of irrigation water to nonfarm uses. In Africa, for example, a Club du Sahel review of several Sahelian zone countries where large irrigation projects have been poorly managed concluded that during the last

several years, "the development of new [irrigation] areas has barely surpassed the surface (area) of older ones which had to be abandoned."[15]

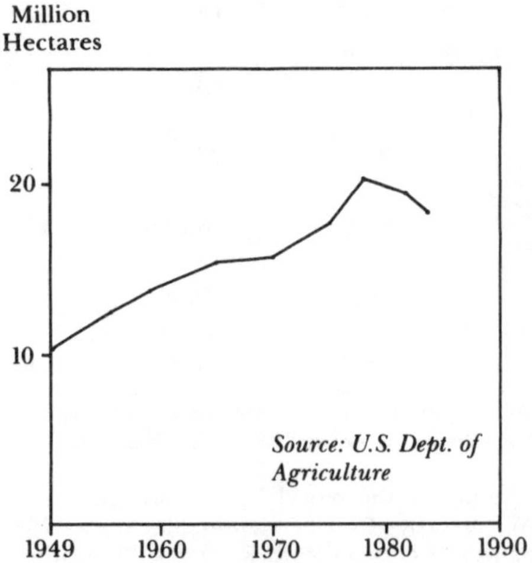

The only large example of fossil aquifer depletion is the Ogallala, which supplies irrigation water in the U.S. Great Plains, from Nebraska to the Texas panhandle. The effect of its falling water level on irrigation has been traumatic: In the six states that rely most heavily on the Ogallala—Colorado, Kansas, Nebraska, New Mexico, Oklahoma, and Texas—irrigated area declined 15 percent between 1978 and 1984.[16]

Although the depletion problem is localized, the overdrafting of rechargeable aquifers can be seen in parts of India, China, and the United States, all leading agricultural countries. In the state of Tamil Nadu on India's southeastern coast, heavy pumping has dropped the water table some 25–30 meters over the past decade. In the Beijing-Tienjin region of northern China and around Phoenix and Tucson in Arizona, the combination of agricultural and urban demands on underground water supplies is lowering water tables several meters per year.[17]

Waterlogging and salting of irrigated fields are forcing some farmers off the land. If underground drainage is not adequate, percolating water gradually accumulates and raises the water table to within several feet of the surface, at which point deep-rooted crops begin suffering. In dry climates the accumulated water begins evaporating through the remaining inches of soil into the atmosphere, leaving salt on the surface and reducing the land's productivity. Glistening white expanses of abandoned cropland that was once highly productive can be seen when flying over Pakistan and the Middle East.

Warren Hall, acting director of the U.S. Department of Interior's Office of Water Resources Research, stated as early as 1973 that "today every arid land

Million
Hectares

Source: U.S. Dept. of
Agriculture

Figure 7-2. Irrigated Land in the United States,
1949-84

region of the world is in some intermediate or final stage of [salinization], and nowhere, it would seem, has there been established a genuine détente with these deceptively simple destroyers of man's vaunted accomplishments." As of the mid-eighties, scientists are making some progress in designing techniques to reclaim land from salt, but on balance salinity is spreading.[18]

In much of the Third World, silting is reducing the storage capacity of surface reservoirs, making it difficult to extend irrigation to new areas. All too often, the engineers who design irrigation systems pay little attention to watershed deforestation. As trees are cut and soil erodes, silt fills reservoirs.

Irrigated agriculture is also threatened by the diversion of water to nonfarm uses, both residential and industrial. This is a problem in several Sun Belt states—Arizona, California, Colorado, Florida, and Texas—where growing populations are bidding water away from farmers. China's northwest and the southwest Soviet Republics are also diverting irrigation water to other uses. Looming water shortages in South Africa may force a reduction of irrigated area there too.[19]

The decision by the Soviet Union to cancel a vast project to divert northbound Siberian rivers southward to the farm belt will markedly lower the expected growth in world irrigation. The two largest, the Ob and the Irtysh, were to expand irrigation massively in central Asia. Even the more modest project to funnel water from northern European rivers to the Caspian Sea basin would cost billions of dollars at a time when capital is scarce. Soviet leaders have simply decided they cannot afford these projects, and are concentrating on raising productivity on the existing cropland and putting their capital into industrial modernization.[20]

As the world demand for electricity increases, governments are being forced to choose whether to use reservoir water to generate electricity or to irrigate farmland. In the Soviet Union, where food is more scarce than energy, the official policy is to maximize irrigated area, even though for some multipurpose projects this has meant reducing electricity generation 30–40 percent.[21]

In the United States, which imports energy and exports food, the decision often goes the other way. A study of potential irrigation expansion in the Pacific Northwest concluded that developing 891,000 hectares would not be economical because, among other things, it would require forgoing electrical generating capacity. The research team concluded that "most irrigation development will be a net loss for the economy, costing more than it returns by at least the power cost and, in some areas, a good deal more."[22]

Depleted aquifers, falling water tables, and growing competition for water from nonfarm sources suggest that only modest increases in irrigation lie ahead. Future output gains from irrigated agriculture will in many regions depend more on gains in water use efficiency than on new supplies—a shift toward efficiency that could parallel the change in oil use that began in 1974.

THE ROLE OF FERTILIZER

The technological foundation for the use of chemical fertilizer to raise land productivity was established in 1847, when Justus von Liebig, a German agricultural chemist, demonstrated that all the nutrients that plants remove from the soil could be added in chemical form. For the next 100 years, however, it was easier for farmers to increase output through organic fertilizers and cropland expansion. It was not until the mid-twentieth century, when the expansion of cropland fell far behind the growth of population, that they began to concentrate their energies on raising land productivity with chemical fertilizers.

World fertilizer use skyrocketed between 1950 and 1986 from 14 million to 131 million tons. (See Table 7–2.) In per capita terms, usage quintupled during this period, from 5 kilograms to 26 kilograms, offsetting a one-third decline in grain area per person. (See Figure 7–3.) This increase was largely responsible for world grain production's climb from 624 million to 1,660 million metric tons.[23]

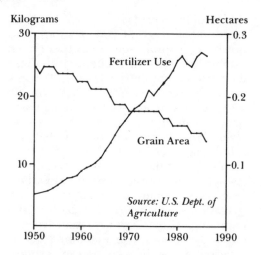

Figure 7-3. World Fertilizer Use and Grain Area Per Capita, 1950-86

Table 7-2. World Fertilizer Use, Total and Per Capita, 1950–86

Year	Total	Per Capita
	(million metric tons)	(kilograms)
1950	14	5
1955	18	7
1960	27	9
1965	40	12
1970	63	17
1975	82	21
1980	112	26
1981	116	26
1982	115	25
1983	115	24
1984	125	26
1985	130	26
1986	131	26

SOURCES: U.N. Food and Agriculture Organization, *Fertilizer Yearbooks* (Rome: various years); Paul Andrilenas, U.S. Department of Agriculture, Washington, D.C., private communication, May 9, 1986; population statistics from United Nations Department of International Economic and Social Affairs; *Statistical Abstract of the U.S.—1986* (Washington, D.C.: U.S. Government Printing Office, 1986).

From mid-century through 1980, growing world fertilizer use was one of the most predictable of global economic trends, moving higher each successive year, with only an occasional interruption. After 1980, however, the pattern became somewhat erratic as the growth in world food demand slowed, as Third World debt soared, as agricultural commodity prices weakened, as diminishing returns on fertilizer use set in, and as many governments reduced fertilizer subsidies. The annual growth in use dropped from 6 percent in the seventies to less than 3 percent in the eighties.[24]

During the fifties and most of the sixties, growth in world fertilizer use was concentrated in the industrial world, but as the adoption of high-yielding, fertilizer-responsive varieties of wheat and rice gained momentum in Asia, so too did fertilizer use. In some agriculturally advanced countries, fertilizer use is now leveling off or declining. In the United States, for example, fertilizer use peaked in 1981, and has fallen since then as farm prices have weakened. (See Figure 7–4.) Given that some 45 million acres of cropland is due to be put into the conservation reserve by 1990, U.S. fertilizer

Million
Tons

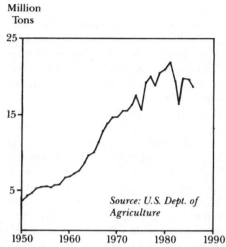

Figure 7-4. Fertilizer Use in the United States,
1950-86

Million
Tons

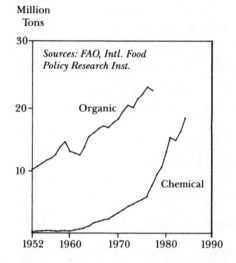

Figure 7-5. Fertilizer Use in China, 1952-84

use may not regain the 1981 level for some years.[25]

In China, now the world's second largest food producer, significant expansion in chemical fertilizer use did not begin until 1960, as planners realized that even the most assiduous use of organic fertilizer could not produce enough food to sustain the country's population. As new fertilizer plants came on-line in the late seventies, usage climbed sharply—more than doubling between 1976 and 1981 in the steepest increase ever in a major food-producing country. (See Figure 7–5.)[26]

Nevertheless, organic fertilizer continues to be a major source of plant nutrients. Over half of China's organic fertilizer comes from livestock manure, principally that of pigs (which Mao referred to as four-footed fertilizer factories) and draft animals. Night soil (human waste), green manure crops, and compost make up most of the remainder.[27]

A crude ratio of world fertilizer use to grain production, ignoring the use of fertilizer on other crops, shows a rather marked shift over the past generation. (See Table 7–3.) In 1950, when nearly

14 million tons of chemical fertilizer were applied, grain production totaled 624 million tons. With fertilizer use expanding far more rapidly than grain production, this ratio gradually declined. Between 1950 and 1980, the ratio of grain production to fertilizer use fell from 46 to 13. During the next six years, the ratio remained remarkably constant, suggesting a reluctance by farmers to push it lower, given current grain/fertilizer price relationships.

Farmers were pushed to use more fertilizers during the seventies not only by the spread of irrigation and high-yielding crop varieties, particularly in India and China, but by extensive fertilizer subsidies in many Third World countries. In the early eighties, these subsidies typically amounted to 50 to 70 percent of fertilizer cost. Urea, for example, was supplied to farmers in Sri Lanka at 56 percent below cost. The Nigerian government went even higher, covering 80 percent or more of costs.[28]

Third World governments subsidize fertilizer use to encourage the adoption of a new technology, to achieve food self-sufficiency, and to stimulate the production of export crops. Although these

Table 7-3. Ratios of World Grain Production to Fertilizer Use, 1950–86

Year	Grain Production	Fertilizer Use	Response Ratio
	(million metric tons)		
1950	624	14	46
1955	790	18	43
1960	812	27	30
1965	1,002	40	25
1970	1,197	63	19
1975	1,354	82	16
1980	1,509	112	13
1981	1,505	116	13
1982	1,551	115	14
1983	1,474	114	13
1984	1,628	125	13
1985	1,674	130	13
1986	1,661	131	13

SOURCES: U.N. Food and Agriculture Organization, *Fertilizer Yearbooks* (Rome: various years); U.S. Department of Agriculture, Economic Research Service, *World Indices of Agricultural and Food Production 1950–85* (unpublished printout) (Washington, D.C.: 1986).

reasons all have merit, chemical fertilizer subsidies do distort resource use in agriculture, and this is now widely recognized. They make agriculture more energy-intensive and less land- and labor-intensive. They also discourage the use of indigenous, organic fertilizers.

In response to budgetary and foreign-exchange imbalances, many governments have reduced fertilizer subsidies during the eighties, and some have eliminated them entirely. Economist Elliot Berg notes that most East Asian countries have abandoned these supports altogether. In addition, he reports that "[subsidies] are declining in Bang-ladesh and Pakistan, and their elimination has been recommended in India. They have been cut back significantly, and are headed for elimination in Senegal, Mali, Niger, Burkina Faso, Benin, and Togo, among other west African countries."[29]

Growth in world fertilizer use is likely to remain slow in the absence of either a substantial improvement in the grain/fertilizer price ratio or technological advances that boost the fertilizer responsiveness of grain. Without these, it will be uneconomical for most farmers, particularly those who already apply large amounts, to use a great deal more fertilizer. A rise in grain prices would stimulate such an increase. But it would also restrict grain consumption among those who are on the lower rungs of the global economic ladder, the very people who most need to increase their consumption of food.

ENERGY TO PRODUCE FOOD

At the turn of the century, farmers relied on livestock to provide both fertilizer and draft power. They were largely self-sufficient in energy, but as the century progressed, the use of fossil fuels began to increase gradually, and then climbed dramatically after mid-century. (See Table 7–4.) Fossil fuels used to operate irrigation pumps and tractors and to manufacture fertilizer account for the lion's share of energy purchased by farmers, and hence have been the key to raising grain yields between 1950 and 1986 from just over 1 ton per hectare to 2.3 tons.[30]

Overall, energy use in agriculture grew at some 7 percent annually during the fifties, then slowed during the sixties and seventies. (See Table 7–5.) During the eighties, growth has fallen to 3.4 per-

Table 7-4. Energy Use in World Agriculture, 1950–85

Year	Tractor Fuel	Irrigation Fuel	Fertilizer Manufacture	Other[1]	Total Energy
	(million barrels of oil equivalent)				
1950	143	17	70	46	276
1960	288	33	133	91	545
1970	429	69	310	162	970
1980	650	139	552	268	1,609
1985	739	201	646	317	1,903

[1]Since no worldwide data are available for other uses of energy such as synthesizing pesticides, manufacturing tractors and other equipment, distributing fertilizer, drying grain, and so on, these were collectively assumed to be 20 percent of the tractor-irrigation-fertilizer total.
SOURCE: Worldwatch Institute estimates based on U.S. Department of Agriculture data; David Pimentel, *Energy Utilization in Agriculture;* Gordon Sloggett, *Energy in U.S. Agriculture;* W.R. Rangeley, "Irrigation and Drainage in the World" and "Irrigation—Current Trends and A Future Perspective."

cent per year, a reflection of markedly slower growth in both the tractor fleet and fertilizer use.

In irrigation, surface diversion systems require heavy energy investments during construction, principally to build the large dams and associated networks of feeder canals. Once constructed, some gravity-fed systems require relatively little energy to operate, although others, such as California's surface water diversion scheme, depend heavily on pumps. By contrast, pump irrigation that draws on underground water maintains a steady claim on energy resources. Since 1970, the amount of energy in this sector has risen rapidly, largely because of the surge in well irrigation in India and China, where millions of pumps have come into use.[31]

The world's tractor fleet has increased from 5.6 million in 1950 to 23 million vehicles today. Although draft animals are still extensively used for tillage in Africa and Asia, as much as two thirds of the world's cropland may now be plowed with tractors. In some major food-producing areas, such as North America, the number of farm tractors has reached an apparent saturation point, with no increase since 1979.[32]

At mid-century, tractors accounted for the lion's share of fossil fuel use in agriculture—a position that has diminished gradually as pump irrigation and fertil-

Table 7-5. Annual Growth in Energy Use in World Agriculture By Decade, 1950–85

Period	Annual Growth
	(percent)
1950–60	7.0
1960–70	6.0
1970–80	5.2
1980–85	3.4

SOURCE: Worldwatch Institute estimates based on U.S. Department of Agriculture data; David Pimentel, *Energy Utilization in Agriculture;* Gordon Sloggett, *Energy in U.S. Agriculture;* W.R. Rangeley, "Irrigation and Drainage in the World" and "Irrigation—Current Trends and A Future Perspective."

izer use have increased. As of 1985, tractors are still the largest user of energy in agriculture, but the lead over fertilizers has narrowed markedly and could disappear well before the end of the century.

In contrast to the other two leading agricultural uses of energy, tractors contribute more to labor productivity than to that of land. In general, farm mechanization has been undertaken primarily to boost labor productivity. Yet some mechanized activities, such as better seedbed preparation and more timely field operations, have helped farmers reap two harvests per year, thus raising land productivity as well. And in much of the world, it is this productivity that is the overriding concern.

The energy intensity of world food output seems certain to increase further.

Perhaps the best measure of agricultural mechanization is growth in the world tractor fleet, although the larger size of tractors today means that the total substantially understates the growth in horsepower used in agriculture. For the United States, a leader in agricultural mechanization, the number of tractors increased from 3.4 million in 1950 to 4.7 million in 1985, while tractor horsepower went from less than 100 million to over 300 million.[33]

The overwhelming trend, therefore, has been for agriculture to become more energy-intensive. The adjustments that lie ahead, as world oil production declines, will challenge the world's agricultural scientists to devise less energy-intensive methods of expanding world food output. (See Chapter 8.) One recent trend, the growth in conservation tillage in the United States, was spurred by the rising fuel costs of the seventies and indicates that the energy intensity of food production can be reduced.

Nevertheless, given the scarcity of good land to plow, the energy intensity of world food output seems certain to increase further. If world food consumption grows 2 percent annually over this century's remaining 13 years—barely enough to maintain current consumption levels—food demand will rise by nearly one third. If it somehow expands at 3 percent per year, as it did from 1950 to 1973—and as it must if malnutrition is to be markedly reduced—then output would have to rise by nearly half. But if cropland area does not expand, as now seems likely, land productivity must rise accordingly.

Using conventional technologies, the world's farmers will have to use far more energy than they now do to boost the average grain yield per hectare from 2.3 tons in 1986 to 3.45 tons in the year 2000. In absolute terms, this would nearly equal the yield gain of 1.3 tons per hectare from 1950 to 1986. Since yields in some countries are already quite high and increasing little, if at all, those in countries where they are still low will have to rise disproportionately if projected needs are to be met.[34]

FOOD SECURITY TRENDS

At the global level, changes in per capita grain production and in grain carry-over stocks (the amount in storage bins when a new harvest begins) provide a broad sense of food security trends. (See Tables 7–6 and 7–7.)

Since grains supply over half of human food energy when consumed directly and a substantial part of the remainder in the form of livestock prod-

Table 7-6. Annual Growth in World Grain Production, Total and Per Capita, 1950–73 and 1973–86

Period	Grain Output	Population	Grain Output Per Capita
		(percent)	
1950–73	3.1	1.9	1.2
1973–86	2.1	1.7	0.4

SOURCES: U.S. Department of Agriculture, Economic Research Service, *World Indices of Agricultural and Food Production 1950-85* (unpublished printout) (Washington, D.C.: 1986); population statistics from United Nations Department of International Economic and Social Affairs.

ucts, per capita production provides some measure of whether the world food situation is improving or deteriorating (although it provides little guidance on individual countries). When falling per capita grain output is not offset by a drawdown in stocks, average consumption also declines.

Grain production per person since 1950 can be divided into two distinct periods. From 1950 through 1973, the year of the first oil price hike, per capita output worldwide climbed some 30 percent. Since then it has increased scarcely 4 percent, with much of this accounted for by spectacular gains in China.[35]

In addition to the global slowdown since 1973, regional production trends have begun to diverge. The production surge in China boosted per capita grain production from scarcely 200 kilograms in 1973 to nearly 300 in 1986, providing a degree of food security unmatched in the country's recent history. With production well above the 180-kilogram subsistence level, not only has China ended its dependence on imports, it also is converting grain into pork, poultry, and eggs to add protein and variety to diets.[36]

At the other extreme, per capita grain production in Africa has fallen by nearly one seventh since 1969, drawing production down close to the survival level for millions of Africans. At these low levels, even a modest weather-induced downturn can become life-threatening, as in 1984 and 1985, when Africans starved to death in record numbers.[37]

With carry-over stocks of grain, the second food security indicator, an increase means that production exceeded consumption during the preceding year. Trends here may be measured in absolute terms or in days of world consumption. Whenever carry-over stocks drop below 50 days of consumption, prices increase dramatically. In 1972, three events coincided to price stocks below this threshold—a U.S. decision to idle a record amount of cropland to boost farm prices and to curry the favor of farmers at election time, the Soviet decision to offset a crop shortfall by imports rather than belt-tightening, and a poor monsoon in the Indian subcontinent.

In response, world grain prices doubled and remained strong through 1975 as poor harvests in major food-producing countries frustrated efforts to rebuild stocks. Despite an all-out production effort during the next few years, it was not until 1976 that carry-over stocks moved above 50 days of consumption and restored some semblance of price stability to the world grain market.[38]

When carry-over stocks range between 55 and 64 days of consumption—as they did from 1976 through 1981—prices are relatively stable, providing a decent return to producers and an assured supply to consumers. But when they exceed 80 days—the situation in 1985 and 1986—world grain prices are severely depressed and government treasuries suffer as they try to support farm prices and maintain farm income. As governments seek to alleviate domes-

Table 7-7. Index of World Food Security, 1960–86

		Reserves		
	World	Grain		Share of
	Carry-over	Equivalent of		Annual World
Year	Stocks	Idled U.S. Cropland	Total	Consumption
		(million metric tons)		(days)
1960	199	36	235	103
1965	142	70	212	81
1970	165	71	236	75
1971	183	46	229	71
1972	143	78	221	67
1973	148	25	173	49
1974	140	4	144	43
1975	148	3	151	44
1976	201	3	204	57
1977	201	1	202	55
1978	231	22	253	64
1979	207	16	223	56
1980	191	0	191	56
1981	227	0	227	57
1982	262	14	276	67
1983	191	97	288	67
1984	240	33	273	62
1985	316	38	354	82
1986	339	51	390	87

SOURCES: Carry-over stocks and world consumption derived from U.S. Department of Agriculture (USDA), *Foreign Agriculture Circular*, FG-5-86, May 1986; idled cropland estimates from Orville Overboe, USDA Agricultural Stabilization and Conservation Service, private communication, June 2, 1986; grain equivalents derived from idled cropland data by assuming a yield of 3.1 metric tons per hectare.

tic surpluses by exporting more grain, competition for markets intensifies and trade wars develop. The cost of carrying unnecessarily large stocks becomes burdensome.

A recent World Bank analysis of Third World nutrition provides some idea of the full picture behind these cold data on food security trends. The study was based on Food and Agriculture Organization/World Health Organization (FAO/WHO) calculations of the amount of food a person needs to function at full capacity in all daily activities. This yardstick was used to establish two reference points for measuring dietary adequacy. The first benchmark was 80 percent of the FAO/WHO standard, a level below which stunted growth and serious health risks are common. The World Bank reported that 340 million people fell short of this consumption level in 1980—half of them in the Indian subcontinent and one fourth in sub-Saharan Africa. Nearly four fifths of this group lived in countries where incomes averaged less than $400 per person annually.[39]

The second benchmark, 90 percent of the FAO/WHO standard, is a level at which growth is not severely stunted but where people do not obtain enough calories to lead a fully productive working life. In 1980, some 730 million people—one third of the developing world outside China—fell short of this standard. Of this total, 470 million lived in the seven countries that make up the Indian subcontinent. Some 150 million were in sub-Sahara Africa, with the remaining 110 million in Latin America, North Africa, and the Middle East.[40]

Between 1970 and 1980 the share of people in the Third World (excluding China) getting less than 90 percent of the FAO/WHO food requirement dropped from 40 to 34 percent. For those who were severely malnourished, the decline was somewhat less. But this good news is tempered by the impact of population growth, which increased the number of malnourished people from some 680 million to 730 million.[41]

No comprehensive surveys comparable to those for 1970 and 1980 have been done since, but per capita grain production trends for Africa and Latin America suggest a deteriorating food situation in both continents since 1980. (See Figure 7–6.) The famine and near-famine conditions in some 22 African countries in 1984 and 1985 attest to this deterioration. Similarly, as Latin American incomes have fallen by nearly one tenth since 1981, the malnourished share of the population has undoubtedly increased as well.[42]

The reduction or elimination of food subsidies in key countries is affecting the nutritional condition of literally hundreds of millions of people in these two

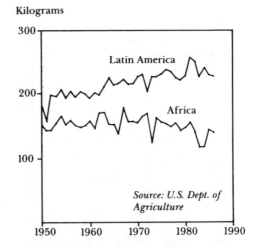

Figure 7-6. Per Capita Grain Production in Africa and Latin America, 1950-86

regions who cannot afford to buy more food. In Egypt, for example, public resistance to a cut in the wheat subsidy led to a less direct reduction—a lowering of the wheat content of a loaf of bread.[43]

Recent developments have brought new sources of food security as well as insecurity. The dramatic growth in irrigation since mid-century has resulted in more reliable harvests. It has also helped diversify agriculture, reducing dependence on a single crop. For example, a quarter-century ago, India depended heavily on a single dietary staple, rice; today it also relies heavily on wheat. (See Figure 7–7.)[44]

Two developments are responsible: the increase in irrigation to make dry season cropping possible and the new earlymaturing wheats and rices. Many Indian farmers can grow a summer rice crop and a winter wheat crop on the same land. Since 1964, wheat production has more than quadrupled, reaching 45 million tons in 1986, compared with a rice harvest of 60 million tons. Wheat may edge out rice as India's lead-

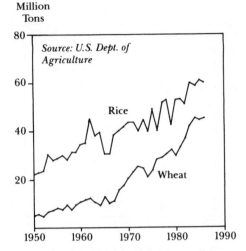

Million
Tons

Source: U.S. Dept. of
Agriculture

Rice

Wheat

**Figure 7-7. Wheat and Rice Production in India,
1950-86**

ing food staple before this century is out.
A similar trend has emerged in China,
although it has not yet progressed as
far.[45]

On other fronts, food security is
deteriorating. Farmers, who have always
faced the uncertainties of weather, now
face the prospect of wrenching climate
change if atmospheric carbon dioxide
continues to rise. The projected rise in
temperatures and shift in rainfall patterns over the next several decades will
dwarf any occurring since agriculture
began. (See Chapter 9.) Heavy capital
outlays in irrigation and drainage will be
required to adjust to the new conditions.
For the first time, many of the world's
farmers will be investing heavily merely
to sustain food output rather than to expand it.

Mounting external debt is a source of
food insecurity in many developing
countries. For those living in the shadow
of debt, the lack of external purchasing
power may have an even greater impact
than reduced individual purchasing
power. Even while food deficits are expanding, some countries are forced by
indebtedness to curb imports.

ESTIMATING SUSTAINABLE
FOOD OUTPUT

As noted earlier, when economists measure economic gains, they distingush between reported and real growth. The
first measures growth in terms of market
value; the second uses a price deflator to
exclude the effects of inflation. To more
accurately measure progress in world
agriculture, and to distinguish sustainable increases in food output from those
that are not, a parallel ecological deflator is needed.

Under the existing economic accounting system, food production can
soar even while the agricultural practices followed are consuming the resource base on which future production
depends. Without an ecological deflator, intelligent long-term planning is
difficult, if not impossible. When
analyzing food production trends, for
example, such a deflator would exclude
food produced on cropland so prone to
erosion that it will not sustain cultivation over the long term. Similarly, it
would not include food produced by
the pumping of irrigation water that exceeds aquifer recharge.

Although production on recently
plowed, highly erodible land cannot be
sustained, it does boost harvests temporarily. As indicated, both the Soviet
Union and the United States have been
guilty of extensive overplowing. In fact,
the 12-percent reduction in Soviet grain
area since 1978 has also lowered economic losses from failed harvests and
preserved the capacity to produce grass
on land that would otherwise have become barren.[46]

In the United States, national soil erosion surveys in 1977 and 1982 showed
large areas of cropland losing topsoil at
a rate that would eventually render it
useless. With the establishment of the
long-term conservation reserve in 1985,

efforts to conserve soil and to manage production were, for the first time, integrated into a single program. The detailed data used by Congress to draft this cropland retirement legislation provide a basis for estimating the unsustainable share of U.S. output due to excessive soil erosion. If 40 million of the 45 million acres to be retired is in grain, and if the grain yield on this rapidly eroding land is two thirds of the national average (1.8 tons per acre), then the unsustainable output amounts to 48 million tons.[47]

In addition to expanding food production by mining the soil, some farmers are also mining underground water supplies, a process that yields dramatic short-run production gains. This depletion can take the form of using water from fossil sources or of withdrawing water in excess of the aquifer recharge. The use of fossil water for irrigation often makes economic sense for individual farmers, though perhaps not for the taxpayers who are paying to idle adjacent rain-fed cropland under farm programs.

Exactly how much food production is based on unsustainable uses of water is not known, but the practice is sufficiently widespread that any global calculation of sustainable output would be misleading if it were not included. In the case of land irrigated from the Ogallala, for example, the unsustainable output is the difference between dryland yields and irrigated yields. For the United States as a whole, roughly a fifth of all groundwater withdrawals are in excess of aquifer recharge and thus cannot be sustained.[48]

Where food output is expanding as a result of the overdrafting of rechargable aquifers, converting to a sustainable basis means reducing output by an amount that will permit the water table to stabilize. A recent study by U.S. Department of Agriculture (USDA) economist Gordon Sloggett reports that the water table is falling by at least six inches, and in some cases up to several feet, per year on over 14 million of the 36 million acres irrigated with groundwater. When this land eventually reverts to dryland farming or rangeland, as outlined in the USDA study, grain production will be reduced by an estimated 9 million tons.[49]

Food production can soar even while the agricultural practices followed are consuming the resource base.

Combining this figure with the grain output on highly erodible land yields a total of 57 million tons of grain output per year—one sixth of recent U.S. grain harvests—as unsustainable over the long term. This provides a way to compare unsustainable U.S. grain output to growth in world grain carry-over stocks. Between 1981, when world stocks totaled 227 million tons (57 days of world consumption) and 1986, when they reached a price-depressing 339 million tons (87 days' worth), carry-over stocks increased by 112 million tons, or 22 million tons per year. This is far less than the unsustainable grain output of 57 million tons produced per year in the United States alone. (See Table 7–8.)

If the 1985 farm bill provisions that restrict the plowing of highly erodible land had been in effect much earlier, the current grain surplus might never have developed. And if in addition water tables were not being drawn down for irrigation, then instead of building up 22 million tons of carry-over stocks each year between 1981 and 1986, the cushion would have been lower. Instead of having 87 days' worth of consumption in storage, reserves would have been closer to the lower end of the historical range.

Table 7-8. Projected Reductions in Annual U.S. Grain Output as Unsustainable Use of Land and Water is Phased Out

Source of Reduction	Reduction
	(million metric tons)
Grain Output on Highly Erodible Land Now Scheduled for Retirement Under Food Security Act of 1985	48
Grain Output Reduction as Irrigation is Discontinued on Land with Falling Water Table	9
Total	57

SOURCES: Worldwatch Institute estimates based on U.S. Department of Agriculture data; Gordon Sloggett and Clifford Dickason, *Ground-Water Mining in the United States;* David Pimentel, *Energy Utilization in Agriculture.*

And the world grain market would be far stronger.

Rapidly eroding land everywhere will eventually be withdrawn from crop production either because national governments follow the United States in diverting it to less eroding uses, such as grazing or firewood production, before it loses all its topsoil, or because it no longer supports agriculture. Recent dramatic examples of cropland abandonment can be seen in Ethiopia, where many of those living in the northern provinces have become ecological refugees, and in Haiti, where topsoil loss has contributed to the halving of per capita food production since 1950.[50]

The use of this ecological deflator allows a comparison of the trends in sustainable food production with projected growth in world food demand. Unfortunately, existing data do not permit a precise worldwide measurement of the share of food output produced by the unsustainable use of soil and water resources. Calculations for other countries comparable to the ones made here for the United States would provide valuable insights into the long-term food prospect.

8

Raising Agricultural Productivity

Edward C. Wolf

After 20 years, the Green Revolution stands as a touchstone in international agricultural development. At a time when famine seemed imminent, new varieties of wheat and rice introduced to Asia and Latin America along with fertilizers, pesticides, and mechanized farm equipment dramatically increased harvests.

This agricultural strategy, which transformed the lives and prospects of hundreds of millions, is considered the most successful achievement in international development since the Marshall Plan and the reconstruction of Europe following World War II. India, whose food prospects formerly seemed bleak, today holds grain reserves that provide insurance against famine. Indonesia, once the world's largest rice importer, is now self-sufficient and exports rice.

But the agricultural progress that made the Green Revolution possible has

An expanded version of this chapter appeared as Worldwatch Paper 73, *Beyond the Green Revolution: New Approaches for Third World Agriculture.*

not been distributed evenly. The aggregate statistics hide a large group who did not benefit from the new technologies: subsistence farmers raising food for their families on marginal, rain-fed land.

High-yielding varieties of wheat and rice have been introduced to less than a third of the 423 million hectares planted to cereal grains in the Third World. The rates of adoption vary widely by region: 36 percent of the grain area in Asia and the Middle East, 22 percent of Latin America's fields, and only 1 percent of those in Africa grow improved varieties of wheat and rice. Other crops—barley, sorghum, potatoes, and especially maize—have also been improved by research and breeding, and new varieties have been distributed to farmers. The local contributions of such advances have been substantial. But none have yet had an effect on total food production, average productivity, and rural incomes as widespread and significant as the Green Revolution wheats and rices.[1]

The case for increasing yields remains as compelling today as it was a generation ago. Nearly 100 million people in Latin America, 280 million in Africa, and over 990 million in Asia raise food under difficult conditions at yields little changed since mid-century. But because grain yields in more agriculturally advanced regions are already near their biological ceilings, this group of nearly 1.4 billion people in the Third World holds the key to future increases in world food production.[2]

There is as yet no research base for achieving high yields in many staple crops.

Over the next 13 years, world population will expand from today's 5 billion to 6.2 billion. Few analysts expect a significant increase in cultivated land by then. Just to maintain current consumption levels will require a 26-percent increase in average grain yields. And by 2020, feeding the projected population of 7.8 billion will require yields 56 percent higher than 1985 levels.[3]

Green Revolution approaches will only be part of the answer for the 230 million families in Africa, Asia, and Latin America whose farming methods are almost identical to those of their ancestors. One reason is energy. Past advances have come from increasing the energy intensity of farming: fuel to run machinery, fossil-fuel-based artificial fertilizers, and diesel fuel or electricity to run irrigation pumps. Few of the rural poor can afford these costly materials and services. Even if they had the income to purchase such inputs, many farmers are not served by roads or markets that could reliably supply them.

In addition, subsistence farmers grow crops that have received comparatively little research attention. There is as yet no research base for achieving high yields in many staple crops. Third World farmers cultivate poor soils under harsh climates that require finely tuned agricultural practices. As rural populations grow, these farmers will need farming improvements that are labor-intensive, rather than capital- and energy-intensive. Such conditions demand research approaches different from those that raised yields in the past.

A new strategy of efficiency and regeneration could help meet the needs of subsistence farmers, and begin to address the environmental and economic problems linked to more intensive cropping practices as well. Such a strategy would stress the efficient use of fertilizers, chemicals, water, and mechanized equipment. Supplementing this, farmers could blend biological technologies and traditional farm practices to increase the contribution that the land's natural fertility makes to food production. The opportunities have never been greater for reaching the quarter of the world's people—and quarter of the world's cropland—left out of the Green Revolution.

PRODUCTIVITY RECONSIDERED

The pursuit of productivity has been central to agriculture since farmers first selected the wild grasses ancestral to today's crops. In recent years, harvests have outpaced population growth, not only because more land has been brought under the plow, but because different plant varieties, more irrigation, newly available fertilizers, and improved tools and equipment have allowed farmers to produce more from each hectare of land and each hour worked. World grain production increased from 624 million metric tons in 1950 to 1,661 million tons in 1986, and the average yield per harvested hectare climbed from 1.1 tons to 2.3 tons. These rapid increases have no precedent.[4]

The postwar increase in yields rested on a simple formula. Researchers and extension agents encouraged farmers to use more fertilizers, pesticides, and irrigation in combination with newly bred crop varieties. According to the conventional approach, substituting these capital- and energy-intensive inputs for the traditional resources of land and labor would allow farmers to expand harvests each year.

Enthusiasm for the conventional productivity formula is understandable. The increase in world food production in the last decade has been associated with a comparable increase in the use of artifi-

cial fertilizers, and the regions that have used the most have reaped the largest benefits. (See Table 8–1.) Asia and North America, source of nearly four fifths of additional world grain production, accounted for 56 percent of the increase in fertilizer use. North America's average harvested area also expanded over this period, but virtually all the growth in Asian harvests came from fertilizer. Yet Eastern Europe and the Soviet Union demonstrate that additional fertilizer does not necessarily mean proportionately larger harvests. Relying on central planning rather than farmers to allocate fertilizer supplies accounted for much of the inefficiency in this region. (See Chapter 10.)

Average grain yields in the world's most populous countries reflect in part

Table 8-1. Increase in Average Grain Production and Fertilizer Use, by Region, Between 1970–74 and 1980–84

Region	Grain Production		Fertilizer Use	
	Total Increase	Share of World Increase	Total Increase	Share of World Increase
	(million metric tons)	(percent)	(million metric tons)	(percent)
Asia	200.3	55	19.2	45
North America	86.0	23	4.6	11
Western Europe	31.3	9	2.8	7
Latin America	23.9	7	3.2	8
E. Eur. and Soviet Union	8.8	2	10.7	25
Oceania	8.4	2	0.6	1
Africa	8.2	2	1.5	3
World	366.9	100	42.6	100

SOURCES: U.S. Department of Agriculture, Economic Research Service, *World Indices of Agricultural and Food Production 1950–85* (unpublished printout) (Washington, D.C.: 1986); U.N. Food and Agriculture Organization, *Fertilizer Yearbooks* (Rome: 1982 and 1984).

variations in rainfall and soil fertility, but they also illustrate the productivity gap that must be closed in the effort to raise the world's average yield above 2.3 tons per hectare. The 11 countries shown in Table 8–2 are home to nearly two thirds of the world's population and represent the entire economic and ecological spectrum. Slightly fewer than a third of the world's people live in four countries where land productivity, measured as tons of grain harvested per hectare of agricultural land, exceeds 3.5 tons, well above the world average. Another third live in the five countries where productivity is less than 2 tons per hectare. Although the highest yields occur in affluent industrial nations, China and Indonesia demonstrate that low income need not be associated with low yields.

Table 8-2. Land Productivity in World's 11 Most Populous Countries, 1985

Country	Average Grain Yield	Population
	(tons per hectare)	(million)
Japan	5.8	122
United States	4.8	241
China	3.9	1,050
Indonesia	3.7	168
Bangladesh	2.2	104
Mexico	2.1	82
Brazil	1.8	143
India	1.6	785
Pakistan	1.6	102
Soviet Union	1.6	280
Nigeria	0.8	105
Total Population		3,182

SOURCES: Population Reference Bureau, *1985 World Population Data Sheet* (Washington, D.C.: 1985); U.S. Department of Agriculture, *World Indices of Agricultural and Food Production 1950–85* (unpublished printout) (Washington, D.C.: 1986).

The first step most countries can take to increase harvests is to correct the inefficient application of chemical fertilizers. Even China's high grain yield conceals a substantial opportunity to expand total harvests by distributing fertilizers more equitably to Chinese farmers. China's remarkable increase in food production from less than 200 million tons in the mid-seventies to over 300 million tons by 1985 was made possible in large part by an equally dramatic increase in fertilizer use.[5]

By 1983, Chinese farmers were applying 115 kilograms of artificial fertilizers per hectare planted, about as much as U.S. farmers. But according to Bruce Stone of the International Food Policy Research Institute, most of this was destined for just a third of Chinese cropland, in the country's most fertile and most market-oriented areas. Adding another sack of fertilizer to these fields now produces much less additional grain than fertilizing neglected areas. Using fertilizer on the other two thirds of Chinese cropland could yield 3 to 15 times more grain per ton of additional fertilizer than the state and market-oriented farms could produce under the existing distribution system.[6]

Another reason for using fertilizer more efficiently is the high environmental costs linked to heavy use. Government subsidies in Europe, Japan, and North America encourage farmers to expand production by applying more fertilizer than either sound agronomic practices or world market conditions warrant. One result is that as much as one fourth of the nitrogen fertilizers used in these regions leaches into groundwater. Increasing concentrations of nitrates in drinking water, which pose a health threat to bottle-fed infants, have been reported in Denmark, France, the Netherlands, the United Kingdom, and West Germany. Ironically, at the levels of fertilizer applied by European farmers, as much as 30 to 45 kilograms of nitrogen may be lost per hectare—more fertilizer than is applied to cropland in many Third World countries.[7]

Farmers in Africa, Latin America, and Oceania have used the least additional fertilizer and contributed least to expanded food supplies. In Latin America, the challenge of managing enormous external debts has forced many countries to curtail imports of fertilizers in an effort to conserve foreign exchange for interest payments. In Africa, few farmers can afford conventional fertilizers, and limited water supplies often make them unprofitable. Yet, African and Latin American farmers need to expand food production, which has fallen behind population growth in both regions. Using additional fertilizer more efficiently would help, but these farmers also need less costly alternatives to the conventional methods of raising productivity.

Correcting inefficiencies in the use of purchased resources is not the only way to raise and sustain agricultural productivity. Farmers have another set of assets that U.S. publisher Robert Rodale has aptly labeled the "internal resources" of agriculture: the inherent fertility of the soil, rainfall and climate patterns, the dynamics of pest populations and their natural enemies—in other words, the natural resource base. The productive potential of these internal resources is sometimes masked or even diminished by heavy use of artificial fertilizers and other farm chemicals.[8]

"The rapid introduction of external inputs into agricultural production over the past century has unnecessarily diminished the strength, vitality, and usefulness of the internal resources of farmers," Rodale argues.[9] Research on nitrogen fixation by legumes shows how this can happen. Microorganisms in the roots of these crops convert nitrogen from the air into a form plants can use;

the excess that remains in the soil can help nourish a subsequent grain crop.

Soil scientist David Bezdicek and his colleagues at Washington State University have found that residual nitrogen from artificial fertilizer can reduce the amount of nitrogen fixed by a legume crop such as chick-peas. A heavy dose of fertilizer applied at the start of the growing season suppresses biological activity, while in some cases a small amount of fertilizer can actually stimulate nitrogen fixation. More nitrogen might be supplied by the correct balance of artificial fertilizer and biological nitrogen fixation than by using artificial fertilizers alone.[10]

Biological approaches can help poor farmers better cope with the risks imposed by erratic rainfall and less fertile soils.

The regenerative approach seeks to maximize such biological contributions to agricultural productivity. It makes the most of natural sources of nitrogen, phosphorus, and potash, as well as the way these nutrients are cycled and conserved in natural ecosystems. Regenerative farming practices include sowing different crops together to use fully the soil's fertility, rotating food grains with nitrogen-fixing legumes, and planting trees and shrubs whose roots draw nutrients from deep soil layers to the surface. Purchased fertilizers and pesticides are used sparingly in these practices. Although regenerative methods require more careful farm management, they are less costly than conventional approaches.[11]

Agricultural research that emphasizes biological approaches to raising productivity can help poor farmers better cope with the risks imposed by erratic rainfall and less fertile soils. Conventional agricultural modernization, based on fossil fuels, will remain beyond the means of many Third World farmers. Offered better methods for managing the internal resources of agriculture, these farmers can reduce their vulnerability to crop failure and famine.

BEYOND THE GREEN REVOLUTION

Two decades have passed since new, high-yielding varieties of wheat and rice were introduced to farmers in Mexico, the Middle East, and South Asia. The new types, more responsive to artificial fertilizers and irrigation than traditional ones, "spread more widely, more quickly, than any other technological innovation in the history of agriculture in the developing countries," according to Dana Dalrymple of the U.S. Agency for International Development.[12]

Modern varieties of wheat were quickly taken up by farmers in Bangladesh, India, and Pakistan. (See Figure 8–1.) New rice seeds spread just as rapidly throughout Southeast Asia. In Latin America, the area planted to new wheat and rice varieties increased from 270,000 hectares in 1970 to 9.6 million hectares by 1983. By the mid-eighties, roughly half the wheat area and nearly 58 percent of the rice area of all developing countries had been sown to high-yielding varieties. In major wheat- and rice-growing regions, the percentages are far higher: Eighty-two percent of Latin America's wheat area and 95 percent of China's rice area were planted to these Green Revolution products in 1983.[13]

The amount of rice and wheat grown in developing countries increased 75 percent between 1965 and 1980, while

Million Hectares

Source: U.S. Agency for Intl. Devel.

Figure 8-1. Area Planted to High-Yielding Varieties of Wheat in South Asia, 1965-82

the area planted to those crops expanded by only 20 percent. The ability to harvest two crops a year with the new seeds contributed to these increases. In 1980, the additional wheat and rice produced by Green Revolution technologies was worth an estimated $56 billion, of which $10 billion was due to the improved genetic potential of the new varieties. This expansion of the food supply has been crucial to many countries with rapidly growing populations.[14]

Africa has benefited least from the Green Revolution. Few of Africa's 50 million rural families grow wheat or rice, and only in the last decade have researchers turned their attention to millet, sorghum, cassava, yams, and cowpeas—the subsistence staples of most rural Africans. Only 6 percent of sub-Saharan Africa's wheat and rice area is planted to modern varieties. Improved maize varieties and hybrids have boosted harvests in such countries as Kenya, South Africa, and Zimbabwe, but on the whole scientific plant breeding has not decisively changed the continent's food prospects.[15]

High-yielding varieties of wheat and

rice are still spreading, however. Though the early Green Revolution seeds were planted almost exclusively by farmers with well-irrigated land who could afford to purchase the necessary supplements of fertilizers and pesticides, modern varieties are now grown by farmers under less-favored circumstances. More than half the high-yielding wheat in Bangladesh is watered only by rain, as is about 85 percent of the high-yielding rice in the Philippines. Varieties bred and released today perform better than traditional varieties even without costly inputs.[16]

The scientists who developed the new varieties of wheat and rice never expected their work to provide an open-ended solution to the world's food problems. Many believed that the new technologies offered a means to buy time until population growth rates could be slowed. Harvests could not increase indefinitely; birth rates would have to fall. Twenty years later, countries like China that both promoted new seeds *and* instituted economic reforms and national family planning programs to lower birth rates have done the most to improve the welfare of their people.

A unique research network launched in Mexico by the Rockefeller Foundation in 1943 may be a more significant contribution of the Green Revolution than the expanded harvests achieved so far. Supported by the Rockefeller and Ford Foundations, plant breeders developed new varieties appropriate for conditions in India, Mexico, Pakistan, and Turkey. Success in these countries led to the creation of the Philippines-based International Rice Research Institute (IRRI) in 1962, the International Center for the Improvement of Maize and Wheat near Mexico City in 1965, and ultimately a system of 13 international agricultural research centers funded through the Washington-based Consultative Group on International Agricultural Research

(CGIAR). The centers' agenda today covers 21 food crops, conservation of the genetic resources used for plant breeding, animal husbandry and livestock diseases, and policy issues related to agricultural research.[17]

A high priority of the CGIAR centers is defending the gains already achieved. Farmers who currently plant high-yielding varieties of wheat and rice need the results of continuous research to sustain their yields. This "maintenance research" emphasizes breeding new varieties to increase crops' natural ability to resist pests and disease. Maintaining stable yields at high levels can be a more complex task than raising yields in the first place. Having varieties on hand to replace old ones that succumb to pests and disease requires a vast breeding program and extensive system of gene banks.[18]

National and international research programs are also turning to a new challenge—developing crops and technologies for farmers who do not irrigate their fields and who lack the income to purchase fertilizers and pesticides. The rice-breeding agenda at IRRI illustrates the shift in research priorities that will help this group. In the sixties, the effort to raise yields of irrigated rice led to IR-8, IRRI's first widely planted high-yielding variety. When IR-8 began to experience serious pest infestation, breeders sought a wider variety of agronomic traits. IR-36 combined high yield with broad genetic resistance to pests, and it matured even more quickly than earlier varieties, permitting two crops to be harvested each year.[19]

IRRI's next successful rice strain, IR-64, was selected both for its resistance to pests and disease and for its more flavorful grain. In the eighties, breeders have further expanded their goals, developing rice varieties suited to adverse growing conditions—varieties that will be profitable for marginal and disadvantaged farmers. IRRI's breeding goals have evolved from a nearly exclusive emphasis on achieving peak yields with inputs of water and fertilizer to dependable production under a range of farming conditions.

Systematic work on cassava and cowpeas in West Africa or potatoes in the Andes is little more than a decade old.

In addition to appropriate crop varieties, poor farmers need alternative sources of plant nutrients. IRRI has begun to investigate opportunities to substitute farm-grown nutrient sources for purchased artificial fertilizers. Promising approaches for Asian farmers include the nitrogen-fixing blue-green algae associated with a fern called *Azolla microphylla* that thrives in flooded rice paddies, and types of bacteria that could enhance soil fertility. Chinese farmers already use some of these methods quite successfully, and researchers in the Philippines have found that farmers who grew *A. microphylla* in their paddies were able to halve their use of purchased fertilizers without lowering yields.[20]

Such innovations are not restricted to Asia. Scientists at the International Institute of Tropical Agriculture in Nigeria have identified a leguminous African shrub called *Sesbania rostrata* that may prove to be a low-cost nitrogen source for African rice farmers. Research in Colombia indicates that farmers can cut their needs for phosphate fertilizers in half by using certain fungi that help plant roots absorb phosphorus. IRRI recently created the International Biofertilizer Germplasm Conservation Center at its Philippines headquarters, where promising microbial sources of plant nutrients can be evaluated, stored, and distributed to researchers all over the world for testing.[21]

A range of other food crops is beginning to receive deserved research attention. Wheat and rice tend to be grown under relatively homogeneous conditions. Breeders of these crops drew on an enormous backlog of improved wheats and rices already available in Japan and North America, varieties whose pedigrees predated World War II. By contrast, improving the staple crops widely grown in Africa, and the potatoes, yams, and legumes grown throughout the Third World, is a much more challenging task. Such crops grow under widely divergent conditions, and have no comparable history of improvement. Systematic work on cassava and cowpeas in West Africa or potatoes in the Andes is little more than a decade old.

Efforts to raise the productivity of all staple crops depend on gathering a wide range of traditional varieties, crop relatives, and wild plants for breeding. Breeders need this genetic sampling to select the traits that strengthen resistance to pests and disease, and to tailor crops to grow under varied ecological conditions. Collecting and storing crop germplasm, coordinated by the International Board for Plant Genetic Resources (IBPGR), is now a major responsibility of all the international centers. IBPGR has initiated genetic resources programs in 50 countries, and national committees concerned with conservation of germplasm have been set up in over two dozen others.[22]

For most major food crops, germplasm collections of modern and traditional crop varieties are impressively broad. (See Table 8–3.) Except for wheat, however, scientists have not thoroughly investigated or collected the wild relatives of these crops. The unique genetic combinations of wild crop relatives are often lost as modern varieties

Table 8-3. Estimated Germplasm Samples Collected for Major Food Crops and Coverage of Traditional Varieties and Wild Species

Crop	Distinct Accessions in Major Genebanks	Share of Diversity Collected	
		Traditional Varieties	Wild Species
	(thousands)	(percent)	
Wheat	125	95	60
Rice	70	70	10
Maize	60	90	n.a.
Barley	50	40	10
Sorghum	20	80	10
Potato	30	95	n.a.
Cowpea	12	75	1

SOURCE: Adapted from Consultative Group on International Agricultural Research, "International Agricultural Research Centers: Achievements and Potential" (unpublished draft), Washington, D.C., August 1985.

and monocultures replace traditional farming methods. Wild species may hold keys to improvements in the productivity of crops such as sorghum and cowpeas that are especially crucial to Africa's food prospects.

Most of the world's food is supplied by a handful of crops that our neolithic ancestors selected millennia ago. While farming technologies have advanced steadily, there have been few significant botanical innovations since the origins of agriculture. Most international research deals with just 16 widely grown crops, although at least 3,000 plants have been used for food at one time or another in history. Crops like teff, a hardy grass grown as a staple grain in Ethiopia, or amaranth, a grain and vegetable crop native to the Americas that is both nutritious and drought-tolerant, may prove better-suited than conventional crops to the environmental and economic conditions facing many Third World farmers.[23]

The network of international research centers will not be the wellspring of work on promising but unproven crops. By their charters, the centers are instructed to work on the most widely grown food crops. Research efforts focus on those with proven potential and regions where the return to research investment is likely to be high. But restricting research to familiar crops may foreclose some important agricultural opportunities.

Naturalist Gary Paul Nabhan, who has studied traditional food and medicinal plants native to the Sonoran desert in the southwestern United States, believes that research on unconventional crops may be as valuable for insights on how to manage familiar crops as for novel agronomic possibilities. He writes, "By evaluating native desert plants as potential economic resources, and comparing them with conventional crops, we stand to learn something about the tradeoffs between short-term productivity and long-term persistence in unpredictable environments."[24]

Independent research centers have an important role to play in pursuing the agricultural opportunities that fall outside the mainstream of international research. The privately funded Rodale Research Center in Pennsylvania coordinates worldwide research on amaranth and maintains a germplasm collection of 1,300 samples from Asia and Latin America. Scientists at Rodale and at the Land Institute in Kansas are investigating perennial grain polycultures as possible alternatives to today's annual corn and wheat monocultures, particularly for marginal lands. Agriculture based on perennials, though probably decades away, would offer several advantages over current practices, including reduced soil erosion, simplified weed control, improved water management, and enhanced soil fertility. Understanding perennial-based cropping practices could shed new light on how to reduce the environmental impact of more conventional farming practices.[25]

New crop varieties and technologies for farmers in developing countries will be essential in the years ahead. Biotechnologies may provide the next generation of seeds to farmers left out of the Green Revolution. But to avoid the environmental and social costs associated with the last generation of agricultural technologies, tomorrow's innovations will have to be more consistent with regional agricultural traditions and better matched to the ecological context into which they are introduced.

REDISCOVERING TRADITIONAL AGRICULTURE

Agricultural research has been needlessly hindered for two decades by pejorative attitudes toward traditional farming. Some scientists assumed that because peasant farmers produced low grain yields, their practices had little relevance to twentieth-century agriculture. Until recently, few researchers recognized the ecological and agronomic strengths of traditional practices that had allowed farmers over the centuries to maintain the land's fertility. In pursuit of higher productivity, many agricultural scientists overlooked the need for long-term sustainability.

The food crisis in India and throughout Asia in the late sixties lent a sense of urgency to efforts to promote the Green Revolution. The strengths of traditional practices and the reasons for their persistence were swept aside. A report by U.S. President Lyndon Johnson's Science Advisory Committee warned in 1966 that "the very fabric of traditional societies must be rewoven if the situation is to change permanently."[26]

Agricultural scientists have recently begun to recognize that many farming systems that have persisted for millennia exemplify careful management of soil, water, and nutrients, precisely the methods required to make high-input farming practices sustainable. This overdue reappraisal stems in part from the need to use inputs more efficiently, and in part from the growing interest in biological technologies. The complex challenge of Africa's food crisis in the early eighties forced scientists to look more closely at the methods used by peasant farmers. Many researchers today seek to "improve existing farming systems rather than attempting to transform them in a major way," according to William Liebhardt, Director of Research at the Rodale Research Center.[27]

Traditional farming systems face real agronomic limits, and can rarely compete ton for harvested ton with high-input modern methods. It is important to recognize these limitations, for they determine both how traditional practices can be modified and what such practices can contribute to the effort to raise agricultural productivity.

First, most traditional crop varieties have limited genetic potential for high grain yields. They are often large-leaved and tall, for example. These traits help farmers meet nonfood needs, supplying thatch, fuel, and fodder as well as food to farm households. Traditional varieties respond poorly to the two elements of agronomic management that make high grain yields possible: dense planting and artificial fertilizer.[28]

Second, peasant farmers often have to plant in soils with serious nutrient deficiencies, where crop combinations and rotations are needed to help offset the limitations. Many tropical soils, for instance, lack sufficient nitrogen to sustain a robust crop. Soils in vast areas of semiarid Africa are deficient in phosphorus. High-yielding varieties, more efficient in converting available nutrients into edible grain, can rapidly deplete soil nutrients if they are planted in monocultures by peasant farmers who cannot purchase supplemental fertilizers.[29]

Traditional agriculture, practiced under biological and physical limitations, often breaks down under growing population pressure. As rural populations grow, farmers try to squeeze more production from existing fields, often accelerating the loss of fertility. Or they may cultivate new, marginal, or sloping land that is vulnerable to soil erosion and unsuited to farming.

Nonetheless, traditional methods can make an important contribution to efforts to raise agricultural productivity. They offer what Gerald Marten of the East-West Center in Hawaii calls "principles of permanence." They use few external inputs, accumulate and cycle natural nutrients effectively, protect soils, and rely on genetic diversity. "Neither modern Western agriculture nor indigenous traditional agriculture, in their present forms, are exactly what will be needed by most small-scale farmers," notes Marten. "The challenge for agricultural research is to improve agriculture in ways that retain the strengths of traditional agriculture while meeting the needs of changing times."[30]

Farming methods like the traditional agroforestry systems of West Africa's Sahel region offer improvements in water-use efficiency and soil fertility that subsistence farmers can afford. Sahelian farmers traditionally planted their sorghum and millet crops in fields interspersed with a permanent intercrop of *Acacia albida* trees. Acacia trees fix nitrogen and improve the soil. In the Sahel, grain yields are often highest under an acacia's crown.[31]

Fields that include acacia trees produce more grain, support more livestock, and require shorter fallow periods between crops than fields sown to grain only. Acacia naturally enhances productivity by returning organic matter to the topsoil, drawing nutrients from deep soil layers to the surface, and changing soil texture so that rainwater infiltrates the topsoil more readily. All of these benefits make farming on marginal lands more productive and profitable without requiring the farmer to purchase fertilizers year after year.[32]

Equally important, such improvements in soil structure, organic matter content, water-holding capacity, and biological nitrogen fixation allow the most productive application of conventional fertilizers. Programs promoting acacia-based agroforestry could complement fertilizer extension in semiarid countries with agroforestry playing a role analogous to irrigation. Governments with modest fertilizer-promotion programs may find that they can maximize the benefits of fertilizers by promoting agroforestry as well.[33]

In the Sahel, grain yields are often highest under an acacia's crown.

Legume-based crop rotations and traditional intercropping systems husband organic material and nutrients much more carefully than do modern monoculture practices. While organic manures and composts contribute significant amounts of nutrients in their own right, they can, like agroforestry, also magnify the contribution of small amounts of artificial fertilizers.

Research in Burkina Faso illustrates the complementary effect. (See Table

8–4.) This study looked at the contributions of straw, manure, and compost to sorghum yields with and without the addition of small amounts of artificial nitrogen. The results showed that the most productive organic method, applying compost, increased sorghum yields from 1.8 tons per hectare to 2.5 tons. Artificial fertilizer alone produced grain yields slightly higher than any of the organic practices. But the best result was achieved by combining compost with artificial fertilizer; this raised sorghum yields to 3.7 tons per hectare. The three organic practices increased the efficiency of nitrogen application by 20 to 30 percent. Given responsive crop varieties and small amounts of artificial fertilizer, traditional practices that cycle organic materials effectively would raise yields in the same manner.[34]

Intercropping, agroforestry, shifting cultivation, and other traditional farming methods mimic natural ecological processes, and the sustainability of many traditional practices lies in the ecological models they follow. This use of natural analogies suggests principles for the design of agricultural systems to make the most of sunlight, soil nutrients, and rainfall.

Shifting cultivation practices, such as bush-fallow methods in Africa, demonstrate how farmers can harness the land's natural regeneration. Farmers using bush-fallow systems clear fields by burning off the shrubs and trees. Ashes fertilize the first crop. After a couple of seasons, as nutrients are depleted, harvests begin to decline, so farmers abandon the field and move on to clear new land. Natural regeneration takes over; shrubs and trees gradually reseed the field, returning nutrients to the topsoil and restoring the land's inherent fertility. After 15–20 years, the land can be burned and cultivated again.[35]

The bush-fallow system has obvious limitations. It requires enormous amounts of land, and when population growth pushes farmers to return too quickly to abandoned fields, serious environmental deterioration can result. Declining land productivity in crowded countries like Rwanda is testimony to this danger. But even disintegrating sys-

Table 8-4. Burkina Faso: Complementary Effect of Artificial and Organic Fertilizers on Sorghum Yields, 1981

	Sorghum Yield	
Treatment	Without Artificial Fertilizer	With Artificial Fertilizer[1]
	(metric tons per hectare)	
No Organic Treatment	1.8	2.8
Sorghum Straw[2]	1.6	3.4
Manure[2]	2.4	3.6
Compost[2]	2.5	3.7

[1]At 60 kilograms of nitrogen per hectare.   [2]All organic materials applied at a rate of 10 tons per hectare.
SOURCE: M. Sedogo, "Contribution à la Valorisation des Résidus Culturaux en Sol Ferrugineux et Sous Climat Semi-aride" (doctoral thesis), Nancy, France, ENSAIA, 1981, quoted in Herbert W. Ohm and Joseph G. Nagy, eds., *Appropriate Technologies for Farmers in Semi-Arid West Africa* (West Lafayette, Ind.: Purdue University International Programs in Agriculture, 1985).

tems offer a basis for designing productive and sustainable farming practices.

Researchers at the Nigeria-based International Institute of Tropical Agriculture, for instance, have adapted the principles of natural regeneration in bush-fallow systems to a continuous-cultivation agroforestry system called alley cropping. Field crops are grown between rows of nitrogen-fixing trees; foliage from the trees enhances the soil organic matter, while nitrogen fixed in root nodules increases soil fertility. A high level of crop production is possible without a fallow interval. Traditional shifting cultivation provided the model for this system.[36]

Biotechnologies may offer cheaper and quicker ways to improve Third World staples.

Traditional practices exemplify efficiency and the regenerative approach to agricultural development. Yet until recently, a kind of myopia has kept the research community from recognizing the opportunities for agricultural innovations that lie in traditional practices. In West Africa, for example, 70–80 percent of the cultivated area is sown to combinations of crops in traditional intercropping systems. Cowpeas, one of Africa's most widely grown food staples, are always planted as an intercrop. But only about 20 percent of the research effort in sub-Saharan Africa focuses on intercropping.[37]

As these African examples show, researchers can use traditional principles to develop new techniques that preserve the land's stability and productivity even as populations increase. Though traditional methods have limitations, they are not archaic practices to be swept aside. Traditional farming

constitutes a foundation upon which science can build.

Toward Appropriate Biotechnology

Most agricultural innovations of the past have been based on gradual refinements of technologies known at least since the Industrial Revolution and in some cases since the dawn of farming. But the 1953 discovery of the structure of DNA and the 1973 development of recombinant DNA (gene-splicing) techniques promise to change irretrievably the familiar landscape of agricultural development. Biotechnologies based on these insights allow scientists to identify the genes that control certain physical traits and to combine the genes of distantly related or unrelated plants and animals—two barriers that conventional plant breeders could never overcome. Many analysts believe that agricultural applications of biotechnology will mark a watershed in the effort to raise productivity.

From 1920 to 1950, agriculture in industrial countries was dominated by mechanical technologies that dramatically increased the amount of food produced per worker and per hour. Shortly after World War II, the mechanical age gave way to the chemical age as farmers worldwide began to adopt artificial fertilizers and synthetic chemical pesticides. Biotechnologies shift the focus of research toward crop plants themselves. They have inaugurated a new era of agriculture likely to reshape research, development assistance, and farmers' choices. Biotechnologies may offer cheaper and quicker ways to improve Third World staples—including millet, cassava, and yams—than the costly innovations of the mechanical and chemical eras.[38]

The new technology encompasses an array of tools and applications that allow researchers to manipulate the genetic material of plants, microbes, and animals. These methods provide ways to modify the characteristics that are passed from one generation to the next. The vaccines, antibiotics, and reproductive technologies created through biotechnology and genetic engineering are already revolutionizing animal husbandry. Biotechnologies are not yet as widely applied to cultivated crops, in part because scientists understand less about plant genetics and physiology than about domestic animals.

Technical hurdles are not the only constraints on agricultural applications of biotechnology. So far, advances have been made in industrial countries, where public scrutiny is intense. The environmental risks posed by releasing gene-spliced microbes or plants into the environment remain poorly understood. The development of regulations and guidelines for the newly emerging technologies has led to a contentious public debate about genetic engineering.

Biotechnologies that affect agriculture in the years ahead will have a decidedly private-sector cast.

In the United States, concerns have centered on proposals to release bacteria modified to retard the formation of frost on strawberry and potato plants. Because the bacteria could reproduce in the natural environment and thus spread beyond the fields where they were released, predicting environmental impacts is both more crucial and more complex a task than with many other technologies. Developing the predictive ecology that critics say is necessary for thorough environmental review and enacting regulations that guard against the uncertainties will slow the marketing of commercial biotechnology products to industrial-country farmers.[39]

The genetic engineering of plants is far harder than modifying microbes, but it is also less controversial on environmental grounds. Crops with modified traits are under a farmer's direct control, and their reproduction and spread in the environment are both slower and more predictable. Crop characteristics like drought-tolerance, ability to withstand salty water, and pest resistance—the traits that have always concerned breeders—are a likely focus of the new technologies.

Thus, the major applications of biotechnologies to Third World crops will complement rather than replace conventional plant breeding. Developing new crop varieties can be an extraordinarily laborious and intricate process. Identifying desirable characteristics, crossing parents, planting and growing the first generation of the cross, selecting the progeny that have the right mix of desired traits, and refining those characteristics through further breeding and screening can easily take a decade or longer. Conventional breeding of a new variety of wheat may involve thousands of carefully selected crosses.

By contrast, tissue culture, gene transfer, and other genetic techniques allow much of this work to be done in the laboratory, because researchers can manipulate single cells rather than entire plants. This saves space and time. Gene-splicing techniques permit researchers to transfer only specific traits into a crop. Such precision can help reduce the need to identify and eliminate full-grown plants carrying undesired genetic baggage—a problem when distantly related species or varieties are crossed.

Given the ability to modify virtually any plant characteristic and to tailor plants in precisely defined ways, biotechnology would seem to offer tools well-suited to agricultural development strategies that emphasize resource efficiency and farming's internal resources. According to the U.S. Office of Technology Assessment, "Most emerging technologies are expected to reduce substantially the land and water requirements for meeting future agricultural needs."[40] For example, it should eventually be possible to modify a plant's physiology to improve its efficiency in photosynthesis, enabling grains to produce more carbohydrates, and thus higher yields. The adaptations that allow some plants to lose very little water through their leaves in transpiration, transferred to more widely grown crops, could reduce irrigation needs.

Nothing in the nature of biotechnologies renders them inherently appropriate to a strategy of efficiency and regeneration, however. Many biotechnology innovations pose trade-offs rather than clear-cut benefits. One such trade-off centers around herbicide resistance, a relatively uncomplicated genetic trait that is therefore an attractive research target. Researchers have already put considerable effort into developing crop plants that resist herbicides, allowing farmers to apply more of these chemicals. Much of this work is supported by the chemical companies that market herbicides.[41]

Herbicides now play a major role in industrial-country farming. High fuel costs and the need to conserve soil have prompted U.S. farmers to adopt reduced-tillage practices on 42 million hectares. These methods, which involve less plowing and leave topsoil covered with crop residues, rely on herbicides rather than cultivation to control weeds. Conservation tillage is also being advocated for the Third World; scientists at the International Institute for Tropical Agriculture are investigating more labor-intensive forms of these practices

for small farmers to protect fragile tropical soils. Yet in both industrial and developing countries, the soil and energy-saving benefits of conservation tillage could be offset by the hazards of increased reliance on chemical herbicides if herbicide-resistant seeds are widely planted.[42]

The most significant influence on the direction of agricultural biotechnology is the rapid shift of research from the public to the private sector. This is especially evident in the United States. For nearly a century, public agricultural experiment stations and land grant universities sponsored by the U.S. Department of Agriculture (USDA) performed most agricultural research. Private seed companies often used the plant varieties developed by government-supported breeders. Over the last three decades, however, the private sector has assumed control of research efforts. Private companies now perform two thirds of U.S. agricultural research.[43]

In biotechnology, the deck is stacked even more in favor of the private sector. USDA's Agricultural Research Service and Cooperative State Research Service support most public work in agricultural biotechnology, and these two federal programs spent less than $90 million on biotechnology research in 1984–85. Monsanto, which has the largest but by no means the only plant biotechnology research program among private U.S. corporations, has already invested $100 million in agricultural biotechnology development. Biotechnologies that affect agriculture in the years ahead will have a decidedly private-sector cast. With the exceptions of mechanization and the development of hybrid corn, that has not generally been true of important innovations in agriculture.[44]

Leaving research priorities to the marketplace may eclipse promising opportunities. Research efforts on crops will be proportional to the value of the crop and the size of the market. Because improving crops for small farmers in developing countries means producing low-cost agronomic innovations, many of which must be site-specific and thus not suitable for mass-marketing, crop improvement for the vast majority of the world's farmers offers little profit. Few private companies are likely to enter such an unpromising market. Consequently, investigations of minor crops like sorghum and millet, grown primarily by Third World subsistence farmers, will be neglected.

The private-sector domination of biotechnology raises questions about the role new technologies will play in international research programs. Private companies may become competitors with the CGIAR-sponsored centers, particularly when it comes to improvements in major, widely traded crops such as wheat and rice. The full exchange of scientific information that is essential to the international centers may be curtailed if it appears to compromise proprietary corporate research. Moreover, international centers may increasingly have to purchase or license new technologies that were formerly freely available through public channels. Finally, private firms will compete with the centers for scientific talent, and the centers may be unable to match the salaries, facilities, and security that corporate laboratories offer.[45]

Uncertainties cloud the prospects for national biotechnology programs as well. A few developing countries, notably Indonesia, the Philippines, and Thailand, have established national programs in agricultural biotechnology. The Philippines views its program as the first step toward an industrialization strategy based on biological materials that can help free the country from dependence on imported oil. Philippine scientists hope to use crop residues and by-products as raw materials to produce liquid fuels and industrial chemicals, and to develop food-processing industries with biotechnology methods. According to W.G. Padolina, of the National Institute of Biotechnology and Applied Microbiology at the University of the Philippines, "The national strategy is to transform biomass biologically into food, fuel, fertilizers, and chemicals."[46]

Achieving these goals is certain to be costly. Few countries can afford the investment in equipment that major biotechnology programs entail, and some lack sufficient numbers of trained scientists to staff such programs. Agricultural biotechnology contrasts sharply in this regard with conventional plant breeding programs, which require relatively modest capital investments.

Biotechnologies offer promising tools for more resource-efficient and sustainable agriculture. Technical hurdles must be overcome and environmental risks evaluated before that potential can be realized. But more troublesome from the standpoint of Third World agriculture is the degree to which the private sector will dominate agricultural biotechnologies. An expanded commitment to public research, at both the national and international levels, is needed to correct distortions of the research agenda and ensure that Third World priorities command attention.

TWO-WAY TECHNOLOGY TRANSFER

The sense of urgency with which the Green Revolution was launched has largely disappeared from international agricultural development efforts. That several developing countries, formerly food importers, now have achieved food self-sufficiency has led some policymakers to question the value of assisting poor countries to raise production further.

But for Third World farmers who never shared in the agricultural advances of the Green Revolution, the issue is economic survival. Only by husbanding their scarce resources, regenerating their land, and raising their yields can these farmers improve their economic prospects. The reorientation of agricultural research and development assistance needed to meet their needs has begun, but it deserves more attention and support.

One bellwether of trends in international agricultural research is the funding of the 13 CGIAR-sponsored research centers. The budget grew from $21 million in 1972, when the system included just four centers, to over $100 million by 1980. This growth expanded the research mission to new crops and ecological zones. Spending increased more slowly to a level of about $170 million by the mid-eighties. Although support for the centers remains strong, sufficient financial resources in the years ahead to underwrite more complex research tasks and changing technologies are by no means assured.[47]

CGIAR centers have established an important foundation of basic knowledge about staple food crops in the last 15 years. Opportunities to apply that knowledge could slip away if funding support stagnates. A large measure of responsibility for adapting crop research to local conditions rests with national research programs. Scientists at CGIAR hope that such programs will assume most of the responsibility for crop breeding in the years ahead. This would allow the international centers to focus on more strategic issues, including coordinating the conservation of crop genetic resources and applying biotechnology to staple crops.[48]

Private foundations, which funded much of the work that led to the Green Revolution, can help kindle interest in new research priorities. In 1983, the Rockefeller Foundation redirected its program in agricultural sciences to emphasize biotechnology research on rice, the grain of least interest to private firms in industrial countries. And in 1986, the foundation outlined a new agenda that included plans to extend biotechnology research to the improvement of sorghum, millet, and other neglected staple food crops—partly to counterbalance the private-sector emphasis on more widely grown commercial crops.[49]

The public research agenda can complement and compensate for the interests of the private sector in other ways as well. One way is to focus some portion of agricultural research on ecology. Robert Barker of Cornell University argues that public institutions like the U.S. land grant universities should shift their attention to the "development of the ecosystem sciences."[50] Designing agricultural technologies and practices that emphasize efficient use of resources and regenerative approaches is more likely to draw on the insights of ecology and evolutionary biology than on biochemistry.

At the international level, CGIAR centers have begun to acknowledge the importance of agricultural sustainability. The directors of the centers agreed in May 1986 to devote more research to raising crop productivity in ways that avoid environmental deterioration. The new emphasis on resource management goes beyond crop yield to encompass soil conservation, water management, and ways to help farmers reduce their reliance on purchased chemicals and fertilizers. In addition, the centers will work to develop technologies that can restore degraded croplands.[51]

Several international research centers have adopted a new approach to better understand the constraints faced by farmers on marginal lands. "Farming systems research" involves farmers and rural households directly in the research process. But how can a handful of scientists in national and international research begin to reach a quarter of a billion households and refine technologies to match their individual circumstances? The answer must be a far more decentralized research effort that builds on farmer-scientist collaboration and equips farmers to produce innovations for themselves.[52]

The reappraisal of traditional practices is a step toward this collaboration. According to Paul Richards of University College in London, who has worked with Nigerian farmers, indigenous agricultural knowledge is "the single largest knowledge resource not yet mobilized in the development enterprise." In his book *Indigenous Agricultural Revolution,* Richards documents how traditional farmers in West Africa have modified farming practices on the basis of carefully controlled experiments, ranging from selection of rice varieties to the control of grasshoppers. He suggests that mainstream researchers have as much to learn from the partnership with small farmers as vice versa.[53]

The challenge for agricultural research at all levels is no longer a problem of one-way technology transfer, as so many people perceived the Green Revolution. Innovations and insights that help raise agricultural productivity will flow in both directions—between researchers and farmers, between developing and industrial countries. Success in the low-productivity fields of the Third World can suggest new ways of managing agricultural resources that farmers in Iowa or France could use as well.

The world is far from having solved the problems of agricultural productivity. The conventional approach to raising productivity—combining new crop varieties with fertilizers, pesticides, and heavy use of energy—succeeded dramatically in increasing food production in industrial countries and in parts of the Third World. But new approaches are needed to reach farmers who could not afford to follow this path, as well as to correct inequities in the distribution of resources and to confront widespread environmental problems. Complementing the use of conventional resources with innovative biological technologies that maximize agriculture's internal resources can begin to achieve affordable and sustainable gains in agricultural productivity.

9

Stabilizing Chemical Cycles

Sandra Postel

Over the last two centuries—a mere instant of geologic time—industrial societies have altered the earth's chemistry in ways that may have staggering ecological and economic consequences within our lifetimes or those of our children. Three stand out as particularly threatening and costly to society: diminished food security from a changing climate, the demise of forests from air pollution and acid rain, and risks to human health from exposure to chemical pollutants in the environment. These consequences arise from everyday activities that collectively have reached a scale and pace sufficient to disrupt natural systems that evolved over millions of years.

Much scientific uncertainty surrounds each of these threats, and more research is urgently needed. Yet waiting for a

An expanded version of this chapter appeared as Worldwatch Paper 71, *Altering the Earth's Chemistry: Assessing the Risks.*

definitive picture of how each threat will unfold invites costly and potentially disastrous effects. By the time researchers document a marked change in climate, for example, it will be irrevocable, and the consequences unavoidable. Such irreversibility requires citizens and political leaders to act before the consequences of chemical pollution fully emerge.

An unsettling element of surprise also pervades environmental threats. Natural systems—including climate, forests, and the human body—may absorb stresses for long stretches of time without much outward sign of damage. A point is reached, however, when suddenly conditions worsen rapidly. Scientists may anticipate such sudden changes—variously called jump events, thresholds, or inflection points—but rarely can they pinpoint when they will occur. As the scale and pace of human activities intensify, the risk of overstepping such thresholds increases.

DISRUPTION OF CHEMICAL CYCLES

Just six elements—carbon, oxygen, nitrogen, hydrogen, phosphorus, and sulfur—constitute 95 percent of the mass of all living matter on earth. Since the supply of these elements is fixed, life depends on their efficient cycling through the atmosphere and the rocks, soils, waters, and organisms of the biosphere, a process called biogeochemical cycling. In recent years, researchers have learned that human activities have significantly disrupted these cycles, notably those of carbon, nitrogen, and sulfur.[1]

Since 1860, the combustion of fossil fuels has released some 185 billion tons of carbon to the atmosphere. Annual emissions rose from an estimated 93 million tons in 1860 to about 5 billion tons at present, a fifty-three-fold increase. The bulk of these emissions occurred since 1950 as the rapid rise in oil use added substantially to carbon releases from coal.[2] (See Figure 9–1.)

Earlier in this century, the clearing and burning of forests to make way for cropland and pasture contributed even more carbon to the air each year than fossil fuels did. Scientists estimate that between 1860 and 1980 forest clearing released to the atmosphere more than 100 billion tons of carbon. Today, land conversion—principally deforestation in the tropics—is estimated to cause a net release of between 0.6 billion and 2.6 billion tons of carbon annually, or between 12 and 50 percent of that released each year by fossil fuel combustion.[3]

Scientists voiced concern about this addition of carbon to the atmosphere as long as a century ago. Until fairly recently, many assumed that the oceans—the biggest reservoir in the carbon cycle—would remove this element added by human activities. Then in the late fifties, researchers atop Hawaii's Mauna Loa began to measure the concentration of atmospheric carbon dioxide (CO_2), and found that it was rising. Between 1959 and 1985, the annual average CO_2 concentration increased from 316 parts per million (ppm) to about 346 ppm, or 9 percent. With CO_2 levels prior to 1860 estimated at 260–270 ppm, human activity had increased the atmospheric concentration of carbon dioxide by about 30 percent in just 125 years.[4]

The central role of carbon dioxide in regulating the earth's temperature has long been suspected. Like a one-way filter, CO_2 lets energy from the sun pass through but it absorbs the longer wavelength radiation emitted from the earth's surface. Researchers have mathematically modeled this phenomenon, dubbed "the greenhouse effect," to predict how the earth's climate would respond to higher concentrations of CO_2. From the models' results, a consensus has emerged that should the concentration of atmospheric CO_2 reach double preindustrial levels (which under existing trends will occur around the middle of the next century), the earth's average

Billion Tons

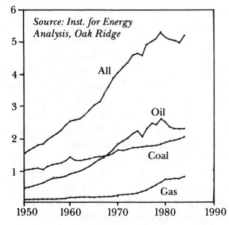

Figure 9-1. Carbon Emissions from Fossil Fuel Combustion Worldwide, 1950-84

temperature will rise between 1.5 and 4.5 degrees Celsius.[5]

Such a change, while seemingly small, would have profound effects on the world's climate. During the last Ice Age, when vast sheets of ice covered much of Europe and North America, the earth's average temperature was only about 5 degrees colder than it is today. The predicted change from a doubling of CO_2 would make the earth warmer than at any time in human history.[6]

Recently scientists have begun to raise concerns about another carbon compound: methane. Studies of ancient air trapped in polar ice show that the atmospheric concentration of methane remained constant for many thousands of years, but then began rising around the year 1600. It has since more than doubled, and is now increasing 1–2 percent per year. The exact cause of this increase remains uncertain.[7]

Most gaseous methane is produced by bacteria that decompose organic matter in oxygen-deficient environments. Bacteria in the digestive tracts of cows and the soils of rice paddies worldwide produce on the order of 140 million tons of methane annually, perhaps double the amount released from natural swamps and wetlands. Like carbon dioxide, methane acts as a greenhouse gas, trapping heat from the earth. Researchers estimate that methane's buildup in the atmosphere by the year 2030 could add to the global warming expected then from carbon dioxide by between 20 and 40 percent.[8]

Only a partial picture exists of the global nitrogen budget, but human activities clearly have altered the cycling of this key element as well. The combustion of fossil fuels releases oxides of nitrogen (NO_x) to the atmosphere. Power plants, automobiles, and industries are large emitters of these compounds. In the United States, NO_x emissions rose from 9.3 million tons in 1950 to 20.2 million tons in 1973, and have since remained at roughly this high level. Current estimates peg worldwide NO_x emissions from human activities as equal to those from lightning, soils, and other natural sources combined.[9]

Parts of the nitrogen cycle have also been accelerated by the increasing intensity of crop and livestock production. To meet growing world food demands, farmers have applied large amounts of nitrogen-based fertilizers to the land and have stepped up meat production by raising cattle in feedlots. Scientists believe that the fertilization of soils, the concentration of animal wastes, and, to a lesser degree, fossil fuel combustion release substantial quantities of nitrous oxide, known to many people as laughing gas. Unlike the NO_x compounds, which settle or rain out after a relatively short life in the atmosphere, nitrous oxide may remain for a century or more. Concern about this compound has intensified with the discovery that it, too, is a greenhouse gas. The projected concentration of nitrous oxide in the year 2030 is expected to increase the global warming by between 10 and 20 percent over the level expected by then from carbon dioxide.[10]

Unlike nitrogen and carbon, sulfur maintains no major reservoir in the atmosphere, yet a portion of it cycles through the air as it moves between the land and sea. Each year volcanoes, sea spray, wetlands, and tidal flats release some 90 million to 125 million tons of sulfur to the atmosphere. The greatest human influence on the cycle comes from industrial activity—mainly the combustion of coal and oil and the smelting of sulfur-bearing metallic ores. These sources emit the compound sulfur dioxide (SO_2). (Every two tons of sulfur dioxide emitted adds one ton of sulfur to the air.) Worldwide, humanity's annual contribution of sulfur to the atmosphere now roughly equals that of all natural sources combined—about 100 million tons, essentially doubling the annual cycling of sulfur through the biosphere.[11]

Once aloft, NO_X and SO_2 react with other chemicals in the lower atmosphere. NO_X and hydrocarbons, for example, are both emitted by the combustion of oil in automobiles. Under intense sunshine, they help form ozone, a principal ingredient in the "photochemical smog" that blankets many urban areas. These pollutants can migrate from the cities to the countryside, sometimes carried great distances by prevailing winds. In many rural areas of Europe and North America, summer ozone concentrations now measure two to three times higher than natural background levels.[12]

Similarly, acid deposition stems from a complex set of reactions involving sulfur and nitrogen compounds. In the mid-nineteenth century, English chemist Robert Angus Smith studied the precipitation falling around Manchester, England, and found higher sulfuric acid levels in town than in the surrounding countryside. Over the last several decades, however, acid rain has spread widely throughout rural areas in industrial countries. The increase in emissions of acid-forming pollutants, along with tall smokestacks designed to disperse them away from cities, converted acid rain from a localized urban problem to one regional and continental in scale.[13]

Industrial activities have also turned metals into troublesome pollutants. Metals occur naturally in soils and rock; in the forms and concentrations found in nature, they pose little hazard. But with the growth of fossil fuel combustion, smelting, incineration, and other high-temperature processes, metal concentrations in the environment have increased markedly. For nearly a dozen metals, releases to the atmosphere from human activities now greatly exceed those from soils, volcanoes, and other natural sources. (See Table 9–1.) Emissions of cadmium have been increased twentyfold, and of zinc twenty-three-fold. The use of lead in gasoline, which began in the twenties, has boosted lead emissions worldwide to 2 million tons annually—333 times greater than estimated releases from natural sources.

Like emissions of acid-forming pollutants, metals return to earth and are deposited in soils, streams, and lakes. Scientists do not know the regional or global extent of metal deposition, since it has not been monitored extensively. Yet a team of North American researchers found from a literature survey covering nearly 300 sites worldwide that metal deposition rates in rural areas were between 10 and 100 times greater than in the remote North Atlantic. In urban

Table 9-1. Estimated Annual Global Emissions of Selected Metals to the Atmosphere from Human Activity and Natural Sources, Circa 1980

Metal	Human Activity	Natural Sources	Ratio of Human to Natural Contribution
	(thousand tons)		
Lead	2,000	6	333
Antimony	38	1	38
Zinc	840	36	23
Cadmium	6	0.3	20
Copper	260	19	14
Selenium	14	3	5
Arsenic	78	21	4
Nickel	98	28	4
Vanadium	210	65	3
Chromium	94	58	2

SOURCE: James N. Galloway et al., "Trace Metals in Atmospheric Deposition: A Review and Assessment," *Atmospheric Environment*, Vol. 16, No. 7, 1982.

areas, the rates were between 100 and 10,000 times greater. They concluded that mercury and lead "are now being deposited in some areas at levels toxic to humans" and cadmium, copper, mercury, lead, and zinc "at levels toxic to other organisms."[14]

Besides altering the cycling of natural elements such as carbon, nitrogen, sulfur, and metals, society has introduced to the environment over the last half-century thousands of substances that have no natural counterparts. Their early creators probably never imagined that these chemicals might severely damage natural systems. Yet in the early seventies, scientists warned that one family of synthetic compounds—the chlorofluorocarbons (CFCs)—could destroy the life-protecting layer of ozone in the upper atmosphere.

Ironically, ozone—the chemical that in the lower atmosphere forms irritating urban smog—in the upper atmosphere performs a vital function. It absorbs ultraviolet radiation from the sun that, if it reached the earth, would cause skin cancers, damage crops, and have other harmful effects. Once aloft, chlorofluorocarbons migrate to the upper atmosphere, where the sun's intense rays break them down, releasing atoms of chlorine. This chlorine in turn drives a series of reactions that destroy ozone. Largely as a result of worldwide CFC emissions, stratospheric concentrations of chlorine are now more than twice natural levels.[15]

Production of CFC-11 and CFC-12, the most worrisome members of the CFC family, rose steadily from the early thirties to the early seventies as demand grew to use them as propellants in aerosol cans, as foam-blowing agents, and as coolants for refrigerators. Production declined from the mid-seventies through 1982 after a number of industrial nations responded to scientists' warnings by banning or restricting aerosol uses of CFCs. Yet because of increasing demands for CFC products in Third World countries and for unrestricted CFC uses in industrial nations, this downward trend appears to have reversed. Estimated production (excluding the Soviet Union, Eastern Europe, and China) rose 16 percent between 1982 and 1984.[16]

Humanity's annual contribution of sulfur to the atmosphere now roughly equals that of all natural sources combined.

Assuming modest emissions growth rates for related atmospheric gases and a 3-percent annual increase in CFC emissions, the U.S. National Aeronautics and Space Administration has projected a 10-percent depletion of the ozone layer by the middle of the next century. According to a study by the U.S. Environmental Protection Agency, such a depletion could result in nearly 2 million additional skin cancer cases each year, damage to materials such as plastics and paints worth as much as $2 billion annually, and incalculable damage to crops and aquatic life.[17]

Concern about the pace and predictability of ozone depletion was heightened recently with findings of roughly a 40-percent decrease in the ozone layer above Antarctica each October, shortly after sunlight reappears following the continent's dark winter. Scientists had not anticipated such a loss, and whether it portends a more-rapid-than-expected depletion of the ozone layer globally remains unknown.[18]

Chlorofluorocarbons also add to the threat of climate change, both indirectly by their attack on the ozone layer and directly by acting as greenhouse gases. The expected ozone depletion will alter the energy budgets of the upper and lower atmospheres, tending to warm the earth. Since CFCs themselves effectively trap heat radiated from the earth, their buildup in the atmosphere will add substantially to the greenhouse warming. In October 1985, scientists from 29 nations meeting in Villach, Austria, concluded that the climate-altering potential of greenhouse gases other than CO_2—such as methane, nitrous oxide, and the CFCs—"is already about as important as that of CO_2." Taken together, the rising concentrations of carbon dioxide and all other greenhouse gases could lead to the equivalent of a doubling of CO_2 over preindustrial levels by "as early as the 2030s."[19]

The long-term effects of the thousands of other synthetic chemicals applied to croplands, emitted from factories, and deposited as waste onto the land are largely unknown. As with many industrial products, the benefits of using chemicals are easier to quantify than the costs. Pesticides, for example, have helped control such dreaded diseases as malaria, bubonic plague, typhus, and sleeping sickness, saving many millions of lives. They kill insects that can devastate crops, and thus have arguably helped reduce hunger and avert famine. Yet research has revealed that pesticides and other chemicals pose serious and often insidious long-term risks.[20]

Few people could have known when the pesticide DDT came into widespread use in the early forties that it would interfere with the formation of normal eggshells in peregrine falcons, bald eagles, and other predatory birds, thus nudging these species toward rarity and extinction. Still fewer would have guessed that DDT would find its way to penguins in the Antarctic; that within three generations, most Americans would have measurable quantities of DDT in their blood and fat; or that more than a decade after being banned from use in the United States, DDT would still be found in carrots and spinach sold in San Francisco supermarkets.[21]

How extensively alterations in the earth's chemistry will affect people and natural systems remains unknown. With built-in mechanisms of checks and balances, the biosphere tends toward a steady state, much as the human body maintains a constant internal temperature regardless of the temperature outdoors. Yet any self-regulating system can be so perturbed by external stresses that it destabilizes and loses its ability to function.

RISKS TO FOOD SECURITY

Over the centuries, farmers have geared their cropping systems to nature's normal offering of rain and warmth. Departures from these seasonal conditions can severely undermine crop production, farmers' livelihoods, and, ultimately, food security. Because of the rising concentrations of carbon dioxide, chlorofluorocarbons, and other greenhouse gases in the atmosphere, a marked change in the earth's climate may occur over the next 50 years. Existing models cannot capture all the complexities of the world's climate, nor can they predict precisely the changes in temperature and rainfall that will occur in specific regions. Yet they clearly indicate the need for some major and costly adjustments to maintain global food security.[22]

Although the climate will change gradually as the concentrations of greenhouse gases increase, most modelers focus their predictions on what will occur from the equivalent of a doubling of carbon dioxide over preindustrial levels. They generally agree that temperatures will rise everywhere, though by greater amounts in the temperate and polar regions than in the tropics. Since a warmer atmosphere can hold more moisture, average precipitation worldwide is expected to increase by 7–11 percent. In many regions, however, this additional rainfall would be offset by higher rates of evaporation, causing soil moisture—the natural water supply for crops—to decrease.[23]

Recent model results indicate a substantial summertime drying out of the mid-continent, mid-latitude regions of the northern hemisphere.[24] Soil moisture for summer crop production would diminish in large grain-producing areas of North America and the Soviet Union. Together, Canada and the United States account for more than half of the world's cereal exports, and the United States alone accounts for 72 percent of the world's total exports of corn. (See Table 9–2.)

In large portions of these areas, lack of water already limits crop production. A drier average growing season, along with more frequent and severe heat waves and droughts, could lead to costly

Table 9-2. Share of World Cereal Exports in 1984 from Major Countries Where Summer Moisture is Expected to Decrease

Country	Corn	Rice	Wheat	All Cereals
	(percent)			
Canada	1	0	19	11
Soviet Union	0	0	2	1
United States	72	17	37	44
Total	73	17	58	56

SOURCE: U.N. Food and Agriculture Organization, *1984 FAO Trade Yearbook* (Rome: 1985).

crop losses in these major breadbaskets. As a rule of thumb, for example, corn yields in the United States drop 10 percent for each day the crop is under severe stress during its silking and tasseling stage. Thus, five days of temperature or moisture stress during this critical period, which would likely occur more frequently in much of the U.S. Cornbelt with the anticipated climate change, would cut yields in half.[25]

Temperatures will rise everywhere, though by greater amounts in the temperate and polar regions than in the tropics.

Although some key food-producing regions may dry out, prospects for expanding production in other areas could improve. Warmer and wetter conditions in India and much of Southeast Asia might increase rice production in these areas. The picture remains unclear for Africa. But reconstructions of the so-called Altithermal period some 4,500 to 8,000 years ago, when summertime temperatures were higher than at present, suggest that northern and eastern Africa could get substantially more rainfall. If so, average flows of the Niger, Senegal, Volta, and Blue Nile rivers would increase, possibly aiding the expansion of irrigation. In northern latitudes, higher temperatures and milder winters might open vast tracts of land to cultivation. Agricultural production in Canada, northern Europe, and the Soviet Union might expand northward.[26]

Unfortunately, shifting crop production to areas benefiting from climate change would not only be costly, it would have to overcome some serious constraints. Thin, nutrient-poor soils cover much of northern Minnesota, Wisconsin, and Michigan, so a northward shift of the U.S. Cornbelt in response to higher temperatures would result in a substantial drop in yield. Poor soils will also inhibit successful northward agricultural migrations in Scandinavia and Canada. It would take centuries for more productive soils to form. Though during the Altithermal period the present desert regions of North Africa were savannas suited for grazing, these lands also would require a long time to regain their former fertility.[27]

Climate change could carry a global price tag of $200 billion for irrigation adjustments alone.

Low-lying agricultural areas face the threat of a substantial rise in sea level from the altered climate. Since water expands when heated, oceans will rise with the increase in global temperature. Warmer temperatures will also melt mountain glaciers and parts of polar ice sheets, transferring water from the land to the sea. From the global warming expected by the middle of next century, sea levels could increase as much as one meter, threatening large tracts of agricultural lowlands—where much of the world's rice is grown—with inundation. Of particular concern are the heavily populated, fertile delta regions of the Ganges River in Bangladesh, the Indus in Pakistan, and the Chang Jiang (Yangtze) in China.[28]

The productivity of major food crops will respond not only to changes in climate, but directly to the higher concentration of CO_2 in the atmosphere. Carbon dioxide is a basic ingredient for photosynthesis, the process by which green plants transform solar energy into the chemical energy of carbohydrates. Experiments suggest that as long as

water, nutrients, and other factors are not limited, every 1 percent rise in the CO_2 concentration may increase photosynthesis by 0.5 percent.[29]

Yet, other factors could offset potential gains in yield. Crops might need more nitrogen and other nutrients to achieve the greater productivity made possible by higher CO_2 levels. Damage from insect pests could increase, since the warmer climate would likely enhance insect breeding. Yields of some crops—notably corn—could also suffer from greater competition from weeds.[30]

Whatever the outcome for individual regions, adapting to climate change will exact heavy costs from governments and farmers. The expensive irrigation systems supplying water to the 270 million hectares of irrigated cropland worldwide were built with present climatic regimes in mind. These irrigated lands account for only 18 percent of total cropland, yet they yield a third of the global harvest. Irrigated agriculture thus plays a disproportionately large role in meeting the world's food needs. Shifts in rainfall patterns could make existing irrigation systems—including reservoirs, canals, pumps, and wells—unnecessary in some regions, insufficient in others. Moreover, seasonal reductions in water supplies because of climate change could seriously constrain irrigated agriculture, especially where competition for scarce water is already increasing.[31]

A look at one key food-producing region—the western United States—highlights how costly climate change could be. Though by no means conclusive, climate models suggest that much of this area could experience a reduction in rainfall along with the rise in temperature. Since rates of precipitation and evaporation largely determine any region's renewable water supply, supplies in the West would diminish. Assuming a 2-degree Celsius increase in temperature and a 10-percent decrease in pre-

Table 9-3. Water Supplies Under Present and Postulated Climate, Western United States

Water Resources Region	Average Annual Supply		Change	Ratio of Demand in Year 2000 to Altered Supply
	Present Climate	Altered Climate[1]		
	(billion cubic meters)		(percent)	
Missouri	85.0	30.7	−64	1.2
Arkansas-White-Red	93.5	43.2	−54	0.4
Texas Gulf	49.2	24.7	−50	0.7
Rio Grande	7.4	1.8	−76	3.7
Upper Colorado	16.4	9.9	−40	1.7
Lower Colorado	11.5	5.0	−57	2.7
California	101.8	57.1	−44	0.7
All Regions	350.9[2]	165.3[2]	−53	0.9

[1]Assumes a 2-degree Celsius temperature increase and a 10-percent reduction in precipitation. [2]Does not equal sum of column because a portion of Lower Colorado flow is derived from Upper Colorado. SOURCE: Roger R. Revelle and Paul E. Waggoner, "Effects of a Carbon Dioxide-Induced Climatic Change on Water Supplies in the Western United States," in National Research Council, *Changing Climate* (Washington, D.C.: National Academy Press, 1983).

cipitation, supplies in each of seven western river basins would be reduced some 40 to 76 percent. (See Table 9–3.)

Such reductions would create severe imbalances in regional water budgets. Projected water consumption 13 years from now would exceed supplies available under the current climate only in the Lower Colorado region. With the assumed climate change, however, consumption in the year 2000 would exceed the renewable supply in four regions, with local shortages probably occurring in the other three.[32]

Since agriculture is by far the biggest consumer of water, balancing regional water budgets would likely require that irrigation cease on a substantial share of cropland. This is happening now in portions of the Lower Colorado, where consumption already exceeds the renewable supply. Correcting the large imbalances resulting from such an altered climate could require that as many as 4.6 million hectares be taken out of irrigation in

these seven western U.S. regions— roughly 35 percent of the area currently irrigated.[33]

A reduction of that magnitude would have high costs, measured either by the capital investments in dams, canals, and irrigation systems rendered obsolete or by the replacement value of that irrigation infrastructure. Investment needs for expanding irrigation vary widely, but assuming expenses of $1,500 to $5,000 per hectare, replacement costs could range from $7 billion to $23 billion in the United States alone. Worldwide, maintaining food security under the altered climate could require new irrigation systems beyond those that would be added anyway as world food needs increased. If such additional systems were needed for the equivalent of 15 percent of existing irrigated area, climate change could carry a global price tag of $200 billion for irrigation adjustments alone.[34]

The need for new drainage systems,

flood control structures, cropping patterns, and crop varieties would greatly magnify the costs of adapting to a changed climate. According to some ballpark estimates, the annual cost of a greenhouse gas-induced warming of 2.5 degrees Celsius could amount to 3 percent of the world's gross economic output. Much of this expense would result from the loss of capital assets in agriculture. Poorer countries would have the most difficulty adapting, and as food production typically generates a relatively large share of their incomes, their people would suffer disproportionately.[35]

Moreover, as climate expert William W. Kellogg points out, the need to adapt to climate change will arise "against a backdrop of increased world population, increased demands for energy, and depletion in many places of soil, forests, and other natural resources." The disruptions wrought by a changing climate may thus bring new pockets of famine, losses of income, and the need for huge capital investments that many countries will find difficult to afford.[36]

CHEMICAL STRESSES ON FORESTS

Growing threats to forests from changes in the chemistry of the atmosphere constitute another set of potentially costly consequences during the coming decades. In the autumn of 1983, the West German Ministry of Food, Agriculture, and Forestry galvanized both scientists and the citizenry with an unsettling finding: 34 percent of the nation's trees were yellowing, losing needles or leaves, or showing other signs of damage. Preliminary evidence pointed to air pollution and acid rain as contributing, if not

the leading causes. A more thorough survey in 1984 confirmed that the unusual tree disease was spreading. Foresters found that trees covering half of the nation's 7.37 million hectares of forests were damaged, including two thirds of those in the southwestern state of Baden Württemberg, home of the fabled Black Forest.[37]

Spurred by West Germany's alarming discovery, other European nations took action to assess the health of their own forests. Different methods of surveying and estimating damage were used in various countries, so the results are not strictly comparable. Nonetheless, the assessments collectively suggest that 14 percent of Europe's forests, or 19.3 million hectares—an area the size of Austria and East Germany combined—exhibit signs of injury. (See Table 9–4.) The key symptoms for the conifer species, the hardest hit, parallel those found in West Germany: yellowing of needles, casting off of older needles, and damage to the fine roots through which trees take up nutrients. In eight countries—Austria, Czechoslovakia, Finland, Luxembourg, the Netherlands, Poland, Switzerland, and West Germany—a quarter to half the forested area is damaged.[38]

National estimates in some cases belie the extent of damage in specific regions. Total damage in Sweden is placed at about 4 percent, but an estimated 20 percent of the forested area in the south is affected. In Yugoslavia, 1 out of 10 trees is damaged nationwide, but 1 out of 3 exhibits injury in Slovenia. In 1984, foresters in France surveyed portions of the French Jura and Alsace-Lorraine, adjacent to West Germany's Black Forest, and found that more than a third of the trees were injured, at least 10 percent of them severely.[39]

Indeed, the alpine region spanning portions of Austria, France, Italy, Switzerland, and West Germany exhibits the worst damage. Swiss officials have

Table 9-4. Estimated Forest Damage in Europe, August 1986

Country	Total Forest Area	Estimated Area Damaged[1]	Portion of Total Area Damaged
	(thousands of hectares)		(percent)
Austria	3,754	960	26
Belgium	616	111	18
Czechoslovakia	4,600	1,200	26
East Germany	2,900	350	12
Finland	19,400	6,790	35
France	15,075	280	—[2]
Hungary	1,670	184	11
Italy	6,363	318	5
Luxembourg	82	42	51
Netherlands	309	155	50
Norway	8,330	400	5
Poland	8,677	2,273	26
Sweden	26,500	1,000	4
Switzerland	1,200	432	36
West Germany	7,371	3,824	52
Yugoslavia	9,500	1,000	10
Other	19,687	—	—
Total	136,034	19,319	14

[1]Estimates were made in 1984, 1985, or 1986, and are generally the most recent available.   [2]24 percent of the 1.16 million hectares surveyed exhibit damage.
SOURCES: *Allgemeine Forst Zeitschrift*, Munich, West Germany, No. 46, 1985 and No. 41, 1986.

warned that avalanches and landslides resulting from the loss of tree cover will damage houses and farms, and may force people to evacuate some areas. Estimates for some East European countries include a large share of severely damaged trees. In Poland, for example, dead and dying trees cover 450,000 hectares, 20 percent of the total area damaged. No data are available for Greece, Ireland, or Portugal, and Spanish officials report no significant damage.[40]

Unusual tree injury in North America is largely confined to high-elevation forests of the eastern mountain ranges. There, red spruce trees are undergoing a serious dieback, a progressive thinning from the outer tree crown inward. More subtle signs of ill health come from the discovery that pine trees in a broad region of the U.S. Southeast grew 20–30 percent less between 1972 and 1982 than they did between 1961 and 1972. In a November 1985 report, U.S. Forest Service analysts stated that the net annual growth of softwood timber in the Southeast "has peaked and turned downward after a long upward trend."[41]

Though less well documented, unexpected growth declines appear to have occurred throughout the Appalachians, extending north into New England. In written testimony presented to the U.S. Senate in February 1984, soil scientist Arthur H. Johnson drew an unsettling parallel by noting that similar growth reductions preceded the "alarming incidences" of forest damage in Europe.[42]

Hundreds of scientists in the affected countries continue to search for the cause of this unprecedented forest decline. Collectively they offer a bewildering array of hypotheses, attesting to the difficulty of unraveling a mystery within a complex natural system. Most agree, however, that air pollutants—probably combined with natural factors, such as insects, cold, or drought—are a principal cause. Explanations focus on acid rain, gaseous sulfur dioxide, nitrogen compounds, heavy metals, and ozone, which singly or in combination cause damage variously through the foliage, forest soils, or both.[43]

Changes in soils present the most troubling prospects as they may be irreversible for the near future. A severely damaged forest in Eastern Europe offers evidence that alterations in the soil are indeed taking place. Large portions of the Erzgebirge mountains northwest of Prague, Czechoslovakia, now resemble a wasteland. Near the industrial city of Most, where power plants burn high-sulfur coal, SO_2 concentrations average 112 micrograms per cubic meter, much higher than in other industrial areas, and 13 times higher than in a seemingly undamaged rural forest about 160 kilometers to the southeast. Peak concentra-

tions register several times higher than the average. The numerous dead and dying trees in this industrial region may thus be succumbing to the "classic smoke injury" known to occur near large sources of uncontrolled pollution.[44]

Detailed measurements of the chemistry of runoff from the Erzgebirge mountain watershed also suggest, however, that acidification has profoundly altered the soil's ability to support a forest. Czech geochemist Tomas Paces found that losses of the nutrients magnesium and calcium from the damaged forest were on average, respectively, 6.8 and 7.5 times greater than from the undamaged rural forest. (See Table 9–5.) Less than half of these increased nutrient losses can be explained by the higher rates of precipitation and thus of atmospheric chemical inputs in the damaged forest.[45]

Runoff of aluminum, which normally remains bound up in soil minerals, was 32 times greater from the damaged forest than from the undamaged one. With the loss of calcium and other elements that can buffer incoming acidity, aluminum mobilizes to serve as the buffering agent. In soluble forms, this metal can be toxic to trees. Finally, outputs of nitrate exceeded those from the undamaged forest by a factor of 20. Paces believes this reflects the damaged forest's

Table 9-5. Chemicals in Runoff from Forested Watersheds, Czechoslovakia, 1976–82

Chemical	Undamaged Rural Forest[1]	Damaged Forest[2]	Ratio of Damaged to Undamaged
	(kilograms per hectare per year)		
Potassium	1.9	6.8	3.6
Magnesium	3.8	26.0	6.8
Calcium	9.9	74.0	7.5
Sulfate	9.0	96.0	10.7
Nitrate	0.6	12.0	20.0
Aluminum	0.1	3.2	32.0

[1]Average for 7 years, 1976–82.　[2]Average for 5 years, 1978–82.
SOURCE: Tomas Paces, "Sources of Acidification in Central Europe Estimated from Elemental Budgets in Small Basins," *Nature*, May 2, 1985.

inability to properly recycle nitrogen—a loss of basic ecosystem function.

Forests in the industrial regions of Eastern Europe have borne inordinately heavy pollutant loads over the last few decades. Few forests outside these regions have so drastically collapsed. Yet ecological theory firmly supports the possibility of more widespread destruction as chemical stress accumulates over time. According to C.S. Holling of the University of British Columbia, natural systems may so successfully absorb stress that for long periods change occurs very slowly. Eventually, however, systems may reach a stress point, and "a jump event becomes increasingly likely and ultimately inevitable."[46]

Substantial economic losses already are occurring from the existing level of pollution stress on forests, and they will magnify greatly if the prospects of large-scale forest decline become reality. The Czechoslovakian Academy of Sciences estimates the cost of acid pollution at $1.5 billion annually, with forest damage accounting for much of the total. In West Germany, researchers at the Technical University of Berlin project from current trends that German forest industries will suffer direct losses averaging $1 billion annually through the year 2060. Yet besides supplying timber, healthy forests help protect the quality of streams and groundwater supplies, control the erosion of soils, and provide recreational enjoyment for residents as well as tourists. Adding in projected losses of these functions, the Berlin researchers estimate that the total cost of forest damage in West Germany over the next several decades will average $2.4 billion per year.[47]

In the United States, field and laboratory experiments, combined with the findings of greatly reduced tree growth, strongly suggest that ozone—already known to be diminishing crop yields—is reducing the productivity of some commercial forest species. Researchers at

Cornell University subjected four species—white pine, hybrid poplar, sugar maple, and red oak—to a range of ozone concentrations spanning those typically found in the United States. In all four species, net photosynthesis, which is a measure of a tree's growth, decreased linearly with increasing ozone concentrations. Thus, even with no outward sign of injury, trees covering large regions are very likely losing vigor and growing slower. Growth reductions of just 1–2 percent per year amount to a substantial loss of timber over a tree's lifetime.[48]

Chronic pollution stress now places a substantial share of the industrial world's forests at risk. In just one year, forest damage in West Germany jumped from 34 percent to 50 percent. The 1985 damage survey showed just a slight increase, to 52 percent, perhaps because of weather conditions favorable for the forests.[49] No one knows how much the forest damage in all of Europe—now estimated as 14 percent—will increase. Nor does anyone know how many of the injured trees will eventually die, or when thresholds may be reached beyond which forest damage rapidly worsens. Whether the unexplained growth reductions in eastern U.S. forests portend a similar decline there also remains unknown. Meanwhile, with each passing year of continued pollution stress, the costs of lost forest productivity mount, as do the risks of more extreme forest decline and death.

THREATS TO HUMAN HEALTH

In 1775, during England's industrial revolution, epidemiologist Percival Pott identified the first environmental carcinogen. He found surprisingly high rates of scrotal cancer among British chimney sweeps, and uncovered the cause to be their unusually high exposure to soot, a by-product of combustion.[50]

Since then, the health hazards of environmental pollutants have spread widely to the general population. The same fossil fuel pollutants damaging forests and crops also harm people. Metals released into the environment have become a growing cause for concern. Most recently, the proliferation of synthetic chemicals applied to crops, dispersed into the air, and disposed of on land has added new dimensions to environmental health risks.

Just as scientists cannot unequivocally prove that air pollutants cause forest damage, health researchers rarely can prove that pollution causes specific cases of human illness and death. Yet as an added stress on the human body, air pollutants reduce the productivity and life spans of susceptible people, just as they do with trees. The U.S. Office of Technology Assessment estimates that the current mix of sulfates and particulates in ambient air may cause 50,000 premature deaths in the United States each year—about 2 percent of annual mortality. As many as 4 out of every 10 Americans are exposed to high ozone concentrations during the spring and summer, when weather conditions favor ozone's formation. Especially vulnerable are the more than 16 million people already suffering from emphysema, asthma, and other chronic respiratory disorders.[51]

In growing Third World cities, uncontrolled emissions from power plants, factories, and automobiles have added substantially to those from the burning of firewood and coal in homes. Between 1976 and 1980, annual sulfur dioxide concentrations in São Paulo, Brazil, averaged 25 percent higher than the U.S. standard set to protect human health. Similarly, in Beijing, China, sulfur dioxide concentrations for 1982 averaged

eight times higher than the nation's primary standard; average levels in the southwest city of Chongqing registered 21 times higher. Health officials in Shanghai reportedly hold air pollution primarily responsible for a higher rate of lung cancer deaths there than elsewhere in the country.[52]

Heavy metals released to the environment during combustion, smelting, incineration, and other industrial processes are of growing concern. Some metals—including copper, iron, and zinc—are essential nutrients needed by the body in small amounts. Others, such as lead, cadmium, and mercury, serve no nutritional function. If introduced to the body in large enough amounts, either type can cause varying toxic effects, including cancer, and can damage the liver, kidneys, and central nervous system.[53]

The same fossil fuel pollutants damaging forests and crops also harm people.

Scientists have long known that high levels of lead in a person's blood can cause serious health damage. Since the twenties, when petroleum refiners began adding lead to gasoline, people's exposure to this heavy metal has increased greatly. An estimated 675,000 young children in the United States have high concentrations of lead in their blood. The effects vary with the quantities present, but include damage to the kidney, liver, nervous system, and reproductive system; impaired growth; and interference with blood synthesis. With the burgeoning use of automobiles over the last few decades, millions of children worldwide have become exposed to potentially toxic amounts of lead.[54]

Risks from some metals—for example,

cadmium, lead, and mercury—amplify with their ability to increase in concentration as they move up the food chain. In the United States, dangerous levels of mercury led the Wisconsin Department of Natural Resources to issue a warning in April 1985 against eating certain species of fish from 15 lakes in that state. Similarly, in Poland's Gdansk Bay, quantities of mercury found in herring, cod, and flatfish have exceeded permissible levels considerably.[55]

In recent years, scientists have found that acid rain may magnify health risks from metals. Surveys of regions receiving acid precipitation, along with experiments in which lakes are purposely acidified, show that aluminum, cadmium, mercury, and lead become more soluble as acidification progresses. Acidic water can thus leach metals from soils and lake sediments into underground aquifers, streams, and reservoirs, potentially contaminating edible fish and water supplies. It can also dissolve toxic metals from the pipes and conduits of municipal or home water systems, contaminating drinking water. In New York's Adirondack Mountains—a region receiving high rates of acid precipitation—drinking water samples have had lead concentrations up to 100 times higher than standards set to protect human health.[56]

Acid rain's ability to mobilize aluminum, the most abundant metallic element in the earth's crust, appears particularly disturbing. Aluminum normally remains bound up in soil minerals and is thus harmless to living organisms. Rendered soluble by increasing acidification, however, its concentration in lakes and streams has risen to levels harmful to aquatic life, and in some soils may be damaging to trees.[57]

Recently, some researchers have suggested a possible link between aluminum and Alzheimer disease, a pervasive, degenerative form of dementia commonly associated with severe loss of memory and cognitive function. The association came to light from studies of the abnormal clumps of nerve-cell fibers —called neurofibrillary tangles—found at autopsy in the brains of Alzheimer victims. Using sensitive X-ray techniques, Dr. Daniel Perl, a neuropathologist at the University of Vermont, found significant accumulations of aluminum in the tangles, which were absent from normal control samples. Corroborating evidence comes from Perl's studies of native populations in Guam and two other locales of the western Pacific. All three populations have exhibited unusually high incidences of neurodegenerative disorders; all three regions have soils rich in bauxite, an ore of aluminum.[58]

Just how aluminum gets into the damaged nerve cells of Alzheimer victims— and whether its presence is a cause or an effect—remains unknown. The destructive effects of aluminum on fish and trees suggest that these organisms have not adapted successfully to the altered chemistry of their environs. According to Perl, we can only speculate at this point as to whether humans will find themselves "in a similar vulnerable state."[59]

A third set of health hazards, along with fossil fuel pollutants and metals, stem from the introduction of synthetic chemicals to the environment. Some 70,000 chemicals presently are in everyday use, with between 500 and 1,000 new ones added to the list each year. Estimates of the share of cancer deaths caused by these substances vary, but the most widely accepted range from 1 percent to 10 percent.[60]

Compared with tobacco—which in the United States causes an estimated 30 percent of cancer deaths and nearly one fifth of all deaths—known risks from synthetic chemicals pale in importance. Nonetheless, some investigators believe these compounds account for tens of thousands of deaths each year in the

United States alone. Because of the long lag time—often 20–40 years—between exposure to a cancer-causing chemical and the appearance of disease, the number of cancers induced by synthetic substances may increase markedly over the coming decades.[61]

No information on toxic effects is available for an estimated 79 percent of the chemicals in commerce.

Moreover, perhaps the greatest risks posed by manufactured chemicals derive not from what *is* known about their health effects, but rather from what is *not* known. So few data exist on the toxicity of chemicals now in use and on the extent of human exposure to them that estimates of the total health risk they collectively present can only be educated guesses at best.

The U.S. National Research Council (NRC) estimates that about 53,500 chemicals are used commercially in the United States. From available listings, these chemicals fall into five categories: pesticides and pesticide ingredients, cosmetics, drugs, food additives, and a broad category of "chemicals in commerce" consisting of compounds listed in the inventory of toxic substances prepared by the Environmental Protection Agency (EPA). This latter category includes most industrial chemicals. They and the pesticides present the greatest threats to the general population through inadvertent exposure. Pesticides may leave residues in food, leach to underground water supplies, or spread through the air. Similarly, industrial chemicals may be released to the air or, when stored or disposed of on land, may seep into drinking water.[62]

Despite the potential for widespread human exposure, most synthetic chemicals have received little or no testing for toxicity. No information on toxic effects is available for an estimated 79 percent of the chemicals in commerce. Fewer than a fifth have been tested for acute effects, and fewer than a tenth for chronic (e.g., cancer-causing), reproductive, or mutagenic effects. Moreover, the NRC found that chemicals produced in large volumes were tested no more frequently or thoroughly than those produced in smaller volumes.[63] Given how little is known about the extent of people's exposure to these substances, their introduction to the environment is akin to playing Russian roulette with human health.

Pesticides have generally received more extensive testing, but serious gaps remain. Charles Benbrook, executive director of the Board on Agriculture of the National Academy of Sciences, estimates that between 60 and 75 percent of the pesticides used on food and put on the market within the last decade have met EPA's current standards for toxicity testing. Bills that moved through Congress in the fall of 1986 (but that did not pass) called for speeding up the retesting of older compounds, hundreds of which were marketed before the full health dangers of pesticides were understood. Since these older pesticides typically cost less than the newer ones, they are still especially widely used by farmers in the Third World.[64]

In the absence of adequate testing, knowledge of adverse chemical exposure may come only after serious health consequences arise. A classic example involved diethylstilbestrol, which caused vaginal cancer in daughters of women given this compound during a critical period of their pregnancy. Men reportedly have suffered reproductive effects from occupational exposure to a variety of chemicals, including vinyl chloride, kepone, lead, and some common pesticides. Indeed, at least 20 chemicals have been associated with adverse reproductive effects in men or women, typically through exposure in the workplace. Harm to the general population is much more difficult to detect and prove.[65]

Recent findings of widespread human contamination, however, raise concerns that pervasive hazards may exist. Some investigators now believe, for example, that dioxins—among the most toxic chemicals known—are present in virtually everyone living in industrial countries. The levels detected in the general population are far below that known to cause acute toxic effects in humans, but the long-term effects of low-level contamination remain unclear.[66]

Dioxins have produced tumors in animals and have been linked with certain rare cancers in people. Recent evidence also suggests that they may damage the immune system, which would weaken people's ability to fight disease. Breastfeeding babies appear especially at risk from any toxic effects. Researchers have calculated that through the dioxin-contaminated fat in breast milk, an infant nursed for one year could acquire 18 times the "allowable" lifetime exposure set by the U.S. Centers for Disease Control.[67]

Additional evidence of widespread chemical hazards comes from research at Florida State University that points to environmental chemicals as contributing to a decline in male fertility. In American men, sperm density—a measure of fertility—has apparently diminished significantly since mid-century. A 1979 study of 132 university students showed that nearly one out of four men had sperm densities low enough to reduce their reproductive success. Each sample of seminal fluid contained synthetic chemicals, including pentachlorophenol (a widely used pesticide and wood preservative), polychlorobiphenyls, and metabolites of DDT. According to the researchers, toxic substances accounted for more than a quarter of the variation in sperm density found among the students.[68]

Arthur J. Vander, a professor of physiology at the University of Michigan, points out that when considering how the body metabolizes environmental chemicals, "we must never assume that children are simply little adults." Defensive enzyme systems are not fully mature in newborn babies or in very young infants. Babies may have limited access to the environment, but they are exposed to environmental chemicals through their mothers. Virtually all chemicals present in a mother's blood will get into her milk, which an infant may then ingest. Also, since the placenta is designed for diffusion, chemicals in a pregnant woman's bloodstream may pass, in varying amounts, into the developing fetus. The concentration of DDT in fetal blood, for example, is typically almost half that in maternal blood.[69]

With advances in medical technologies and more sophisticated epidemiological studies, evidence linking chemicals to adverse health effects seems likely to grow. Researchers are now investigating the possibility, for example, that Parkinson's disease is associated with exposure to environmental chemicals.[70] More research is needed to unravel the complex and sometimes subtle ways in which chemicals affect the human body. Since many toxic effects appear several decades after exposure to the offending chemical, the full implications of the chemical age will take time to realize.

MINIMIZING RISKS

Industrial societies have spawned multiple and rapidly increasing changes in the earth's chemistry. The resulting threats to food security, forests, and human health pose substantial risks over the years ahead. A strategy of minimizing human-induced chemical change—where possible, through measures that remedy several problems simultaneously—deserves immediate support.

Because of society's past and present dependence on fossil fuels, a change in the world's climate is already inevitable. Yet since carbon dioxide is the key variable in the climate equation, the magnitude of climatic change and the pace at which it unfolds will depend greatly on the future use of coal, oil, and natural gas. If worldwide carbon emissions from fossil fuels return to their pre-1973 rate of growth—more than 4 percent per year—the atmospheric concentration of CO_2 will reach double preindustrial levels in about 40 years. (See Table 9–6.) On the other hand, holding that growth to 1 percent per year would delay a CO_2 doubling for more than a century.

The goal of limiting the annual growth of carbon emissions to 1 percent may have seemed utterly unrealistic 10 years ago. Now, however, it appears entirely feasible. For the decade following 1973, worldwide carbon emissions grew at an encouragingly low average rate of 1.1

Table 9-6. Projected Dates for a Doubling of CO_2 Over Preindustrial Levels Given Different Rates of Growth in Fossil Fuel Emissions

Annual Worldwide Growth in Fossil Fuel Emissions	Year CO_2 Concentration Will Have Doubled
(percent)	
4	2026
3	2036
2	2054
1	2100

SOURCE: Adapted from William W. Kellogg and Robert Schware, *Climate Change and Society* (Boulder, Colo.: Westview Press, 1981).

percent per year, just one quarter the pre-1973 rate. Carbon emissions actually fell for four consecutive years, 1980 through 1983. But with the recent drop in oil prices and strong economic growth in many countries, maintaining this low rate will require substantial investments in energy efficiency and alternative energy sources beyond what the market alone would induce. Moreover, maintaining a 1-percent worldwide rate of growth will mean putting a virtual cap on carbon emissions from industrial countries to allow for needed growth in energy use in the Third World.[71]

No nation has yet taken steps explicitly geared toward limiting carbon emissions. Such limits also would curb other fossil fuel pollutants, reducing acid rain and air pollution and thereby relieving threats to forests and to human health. Indeed, without West Germany's 8-percent decline in total energy consumption between 1979 and 1984, air pollution damage to the nation's forests might have progressed even further than it has.[72] By focusing only on pollution control technologies—such as scrubbers for power plants and catalytic converters for automobiles—virtually all nations are neglecting opportunities to limit acid-forming pollutants and CO_2 buildup simultaneously.

As indicated earlier, synthetic chlorofluorocarbons damage the earth's protective layer of ozone and also contribute substantially to climatic change. Lessening these threats requires reductions in CFC emissions, and a worldwide ban on nonessential aerosol uses of CFCs would be a cost-effective first step. A few nations have already restricted or banned such uses. This action actually proved beneficial to the U.S. economy, with readily available substitutes saving consumers an estimated $165 million in 1983 alone. In September 1986, a trade group representing U.S. manufacturers and users of CFCs announced that it would support international limits on CFC production, a significant policy shift. International negotiations regarding CFCs are in progress under the auspices of the United Nations Environment Programme, but as of November 1986 had resulted only in a framework for adopting control measures if they are deemed necessary.[73]

Preserving forests and planting trees can do much to minimize the threat of climate change. The clearing and burning of tropical forests adds perhaps 20 percent to the amount of carbon released to the atmosphere each year through fossil fuel combustion. Trees also remove carbon dioxide from the air during photosynthesis, so increasing global forest cover would help stabilize atmospheric CO_2 levels. In mid-1985, a promising development emerged with the unveiling of an ambitious tropical forest protection plan. Designed by an international task force coordinated by the World Resources Institute of Washington, D.C., and supported by leading aid agencies, it calls for investments totaling $8 billion over five years in tree planting projects and efforts to arrest deforestation.[74]

Threats to health from increased exposure to lead could be reduced cost-effectively by phasing out the use of lead in gasoline. In 1973, the United States initiated regulations controlling lead in fuel, which have substantially reduced the amount of lead in the environment. EPA determined in 1985 that a further reduction in the allowable lead content of gasoline from 1.1 grams per gallon to 0.1 would yield health benefits far exceeding the added costs petroleum refiners would incur. The agency estimated net benefits of at least $1.3 billion (1983 dollars) for 1986 alone. That new lower limit is now in effect. Many European nations are just introducing unleaded fuel, and standards are minimal or nonexistent in most Third World countries. Besides reducing health risks, use of unleaded fuel is essential for catalytic converters, the state-of-the-art technology for controlling the carbon and nitrogen compounds emitted by automobiles.[75]

More extensive toxicity testing of synthetic chemicals is urgently needed. Thorough testing of a chemical, using mice or rats, can take as long as five years and cost up to $500,000. Short-term tests costing only a few hundred dollars offer a useful screening mechanism for setting priorities for additional testing. Adequately protecting the public, however, will require that industries profiting from the sale of chemicals take more responsibility for ensuring chemical safety.[76]

Under the amended U.S. law regulating pesticides, manufacturers must show that new products do not pose unacceptable health risks. Laws on other categories of chemicals, however, require government regulators to demonstrate that a chemical poses an unacceptable risk before taking action to restrict or ban it. Besides creating backlogs and requiring large expenditures of tax dollars, such a policy can allow harmful chemicals to remain in use for many years. J. Clarence Davies of the Conservation Foundation points out that additional toxicity testing, though expensive, in most cases amounts to a small share of the total cost of producing a chemical.[77]

Reduced reliance on potentially harmful chemicals could also help minimize health risks. Over the last two decades, for example, agricultural researchers have developed techniques collectively known as integrated pest management (IPM), which seeks to limit pest damage while minimizing pesticide use. It may include, for example, introducing natural predators to prey on pests, monitoring pest population levels and applying chemicals only when necessary, or applying pesticides at the most vulnerable point of a pest's life cycle. By reducing chemical costs, IPM usually benefits farmers economically. In the Texas High Plains, IPM programs to control the cotton boll weevil increased farmers' annual net profits by $27 million.[78]

No nation acting alone can avert the costly consequences of altering the earth's chemistry. Air pollutants and acid rain waft easily across political boundaries. Carbon dioxide emissions anywhere contribute to climate change everywhere. Pesticides produced in one country may freely be traded for use in others. Yet translating shared risks into cooperation aimed at minimizing them is no easy task. A decision to place a hefty tax on fossil fuel combustion, for example, would have serious political and economic repercussions. Few nations would view it as in their interest to adopt such a preventive measure without guarantees that others will do likewise.

Many different institutions can help build the cooperation needed among governments. The United Nations Environment Programme, the U.N. Economic Commission for Europe, the European Economic Community, the World Meteorological Organization, and others have in various ways been instrumental in achieving progress toward global environmental management. But only with leadership from individual nations will concrete measures result. Swe-

den's efforts to make acid rain a top priority on the international environmental agenda, West Germany's call for stricter pollution controls on European power plants, and the recent enactment by Austria, Sweden, and Switzerland of automobile pollution control standards roughly equivalent to those in the United States are examples of the kind of leadership needed.

Action by just a few countries can lead to action by many. (See Chapter 11.) Ten nations initially made the commitment in March 1984 to reduce their sulfur dioxide emissions by 30 percent within a decade; at present, 21 nations have joined in this pledge. Meaningful reductions in worldwide carbon emissions could begin with concerted measures by just three nations—China, the Soviet Union, and the United States, the world's largest users of coal.

Fossil fuels and chemicals have figured prominently in society's pursuit for economic growth and higher standards of living. Yet changes in the earth's chemistry wrought by their use threaten the integrity of natural systems upon which future growth and human well-being depend. Alternatives to the present course exist. By failing to act, we thrust upon ourselves and the next generation potential crises we have the capacity to avert.

10

Designing Sustainable Economies

William U. Chandler

The choice of who allocates resources is crucial. In *The Wealth of Nations,* Adam Smith compiled spectacular examples of government mismanagement and argued that the market should be left free to allocate resources. Markets alone, he reasoned, could assemble and convey essential information about scarcity and value. Prices and profits would work to maximize production and minimize resource use.[1]

Though overcutting of forests had already become an issue in England by 1776, when Smith published his classic book, he argued that market mechanisms were sufficient to protect forests. Growing scarcity would drive up the price of wood, reduce consumption, as well as prompt landowners to plant more trees in anticipation of higher prices.

He could not have predicted that acid rain would kill forests in Western

Europe, or that the subsequent oversupply on the timber market would hold down prices. On the other hand, he might have felt vindicated by the price-induced energy conservation response in the West since 1973, arguably the most significant conservation achievement of our time.

Traditional economics asks how to produce what for whom. Sustainable economics examines these same questions, but includes future generations in the "for whom." It asks how irreplaceable resources—water, air, soil, and fish and wildlife—can be adequately conserved. It also recognizes that economic mechanisms that do not efficiently and equitably satisfy human needs are not likely to be sustainable.[2]

Sustainable economics analyzes issues complicated by politics, ideology, and nationalism. It tries to ascertain what works to make resource use more efficient. How do people behave in relation to their natural resources? How does a country's economic system alter its prospects for survival? The beginnings of an

An expanded version of this chapter appeared as Worldwatch Paper 72, *The Changing Role of the Market in National Economies.*

answer can be formed by measuring national performance in food security, energy efficiency, environmental pollution, and equity.

The issue is not socialism versus capitalism; it is the efficacy with which economic systems achieve their intended ends. Ideally, nations could be graded for degree of market orientation and assessed for changes in resource use. But no one has yet invented a grading system for economic philosophy or environmental sustainability. It is instructive, nonetheless, to categorize nations as centrally planned or not and to assess their resource-use efficiency. A centrally planned economy is one that through price controls, state ownership, or allocation of capital effectively manages more than half of a nation's industrial and agricultural production.

From the end of World War II until recently, centralized state planning has served as a model for almost half the world. Newly independent Third World countries faced with the choice between centralized control and market orientation usually chose the former. That their foreign rulers had been capitalists turned them against market systems, while the tradition of colonialism eased the transition to tight central control. In the postwar era, many military states and even most market-oriented nations also expanded the role of government in the day-to-day management of their economies.

The world today is at a turning point in economic management. The abrupt Chinese shift to market mechanisms is the most dramatic example, not only because of the vast number of people affected, but because of the reform's spectacular early successes. Many African nations, plagued with agricultural decline, have begun to extend market incentives for agriculture. Latin Americans, burdened with debt, have moved to sell off state-owned companies. Meanwhile the Soviet Union, its confidence in

uninterrupted growth shaken, is debating the need for economic reform. Ironically, although Western governments have also begun to sell off state-owned concerns, they increasingly subsidize private agriculture, restrict trade, and permit concentration of economic power in industrial conglomerates.

The efficiency with which nations produce food and consume energy provides a useful indicator of their progress toward sustainability. Countries of all political stripes seek to avoid excessive dependence on food imports. Air and water pollution and land degradation are closely associated with agricultural production and energy-use efficiency. Thus, if market pricing and competition provide greater efficiency, both economists and environmentalists have a stake in the changing role of the market in the world's economies.

EFFICIENCY IN AGRICULTURE

Some environmentalists reject both markets and bureaucratic planning as incapable of dealing with the crisis of sustainability.[3] Putting a sober twist on an old joke, "In capitalism, man exploits man; in socialism, it's the other way around," they say both exploit nature. But important differences exist between systems, as shown by comparing their efficiency in agricultural production.

Agricultural production can critically affect the consumption and disruption of resources—water, wood, and air. Soil erosion and deforestation can result from low agricultural productivity if new, marginal lands are pressed into production to make up for lost potential. Overuse of chemicals can cause water pollution. Efficiency is consequently an essential ingredient of agricultural sustainability.

Economists define efficiency, roughly,

as maximizing output while minimizing input. When farmers produce a given value of grain with a least-cost combination of land, labor, fertilizer, and machinery, production is efficient. When grain production increases faster than consumption of the inputs, productivity and the outlook for sustained production improve. When productivity declines, a society is headed for trouble. Inflation, the need for costly imports, even famine can result.

Land and labor productivity, two partial but important measures of performance, reveal several advantages of market orientation. Crop production per hectare is generally higher in market-oriented countries. Of course, factors other than the economic system affect these ratings, such as rainfall levels, inherent soil fertility, and farm price policies that may either encourage or discourage farm efficiency. Japan's population pressure, for example, has pushed it to increase land productivity, but this explains only about a third of the more efficient record it has than the Soviet Union. The remainder is attributable to policies that, among other things, keep prices high, encourage larger numbers of people to farm, and keep farm size low. Similar policies have placed market-oriented Hungary even higher in land productivity.[4]

Ranking nations by agricultural labor productivity shows a dramatic advantage for market economies. West European countries enjoy labor productivity rates often double those of Eastern Europe, while the United States outperforms the Soviet Union by a factor of almost 20. Only one third of the difference between the United States and the Soviet Union is due to the greater resource endowment of the former; the rest is due to policy. Labor productivity naturally tends to be higher when farmers earn high incomes, which in turn indicates higher levels of development, a central goal of economic policy. Again, Hungary ranks among the highest in Eastern Europe.[5]

The Hungarian model holds important lessons for the rest of the world, for it shows that market economics can work even in the absence of private landownership, as long as the producers effectively control their work. It was the Hungarian experiment, moreover, that paved the way for the Chinese reforms. Though inefficiency and shortages are often associated with collective agriculture, three fourths of Hungarian agricultural land is state- or cooperative-owned. Ironically, three fourths of Poland's agricultural land, with a much lower productivity, is in private hands.[6]

Crop production per hectare is generally higher in market-oriented countries.

István Láng, Secretary General of the Hungarian Academy of Sciences, explains the Hungarian-Polish paradox in terms of incentives. Hungary produces two thirds more grain per hectare than Poland. Láng maintains that only 30 percent of this difference can be explained by the fertility of Hungarian soil, that is, by the resource endowment. The rest is attributable to policy measures—incentives for production, and the technological improvements these measures bring. Noting that Hungarian farms are run mainly by cooperatives, he says that the cooperatives "are real cooperatives," meaning that they are self-managing. The cooperatives, not the central state apparatus, decide what they will grow and how they will grow it. If they choose to raise potatoes when meat is in demand, then they lose money. But if they respond to the market and use their food production resources efficiently, they profit. They have an incentive to work hard and efficiently to produce what is needed.[7]

Hungarian state farms, though having a relatively small share of total output, manage grain production on contract. Growing specific products at set prices, the managers can earn additional income from more efficient production. The nation distributes these products without the excessive losses in storage and transportation common elsewhere in Eastern Europe. The overall result is an exportable food surplus and land productivity that compares favorably with the West. Hungary is the answer to critics who say that the Chinese agricultural experiment is succeeding only because "China is China." The lines to buy food so common in the centrally planned economies do not exist in Hungary.

The low Polish agricultural land productivity cannot be attributed to private ownership per se, but rather to the impasse resulting from the central control imposed on Poland's farmers. Strictly regulated prices reduce profitability for farmers, and deprive them of capital to invest in machinery and fertilizers to raise productivity. Following World War II, Polish farmers were reluctant to make such investments for fear that their holdings would be nationalized, and the state was unwilling to invest in private land. As a result, Poland still has 1.6 million horses doing the work of tractors and trucks. It is not uncommon to see farmers harvesting wheat or hay by hand, using only scythes. Poland, once the breadbasket of Europe, now has to import food from the West.[8]

Land productivity says little about the "total factor" productivity of an agricultural system, which also takes into account inputs of labor, fertilizer, and machinery or animals. Efficiency can be distorted and productivity diminished by poorly crafted policies. For example, high price subsidies and protective trade barriers account for part of the relatively high land productivity in Japan. Consumers bear the cost of these distortions, paying almost three times the import price for rice and other commodities.[9]

Total factor productivity is relatively easy to determine in a perfectly competitive economy. Ideally, price signals instruct farmers on how much to spend on production, and they maximize their earnings by choosing the least-cost combination of labor, land, machinery, and fertilizer. According to microeconomic theory, they produce at the level at which the cost of their last, or marginal, unit of production—their most expensive ton of grain—just equals the price they receive. They maximize profits in this case, making efficiency and productivity almost synonymous. In nonmarket economies, on the other hand, prices of resources usually do not reflect their scarcity, and so resources must be allocated by plan, a fact that directly affects productivity.

Lung-Fai Wong, a U.S. economist, has extensively analyzed productivity trends in centralized agricultural economies. Between 1960 and 1980, total agricultural productivity declined in the Soviet Union, China, and all Eastern European countries. The Soviets, Romanians, and Poles experienced declines of more than one third. By contrast, the United States and Japan over this period increased total productivity—and from far higher levels. (See Figure 10–1.) If the long-term decline of total productivity in Soviet agriculture continues, it will become more difficult to sustain the country economically.[10]

Wong notes that while total productivity declined in centrally planned nations' farm sectors, land and labor productivity increased. He attributes this apparent inconsistency to inefficient allocation of fertilizer and machinery. Bonuses paid to Soviet state farms to meet quotas push them to use excessive amounts of fertilizer. Their incentive is not to maximize yields while cutting costs, but to meet quotas. Soviet cooperatives have

Index

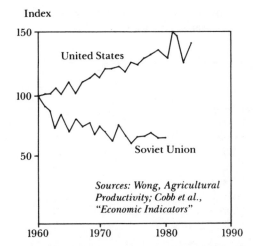

Sources: Wong, Agricultural
Productivity; Cobb et al.,
"Economic Indicators"

**Figure 10-1. Total Agricultural Productivity for
the United States and the Soviet Union, 1960-84**

more incentive to cut costs, but resources are allocated by central government planners rather than at the farm
level. Overall, improvements in yields
per hectare and per worker have been
won at the expense of inefficient use of
fertilizer and tractors.[11]

Post-Mao China provides a rare and
vast laboratory for testing the effect of
greater reliance on market mechanisms
in agriculture. Farming in China until
1978 was modeled on the Soviet system.
But in December of that year the Chinese decided to switch to market-oriented agriculture. The shift boosted
grain output by a third between 1978
and 1986, and yielded improvements in
per capita consumption that stand in
marked contrast to Soviet trends. The
change also doubled oilseed production
and raised that of meat 80 percent. Significantly, this growth was achieved
along with a 4-percent reduction in cultivated area, as highly erodible land was
idled, and a decline in water and pesticide use. Shifting to the market spurred
a dramatic increase in fertilizer use, a
near doubling within eight years. The
increases in output and efficiency translated into higher rural incomes, which

have grown as much since 1978 as during the preceding 30 years.[12]

In the West, resource efficiency in the
agricultural sector is frequently undermined by heavy farm production subsidies, both with trade barriers and direct
budgetary expenditures. In 1980, these
policies cost the United States the equivalent of 18 percent of the value of U.S.
agricultural output. But by 1983, they
cost almost half the total value. Tax-
payer subsidies alone were projected to
exceed $30 billion in 1986.[13]

The United States is by no means
unique among market-oriented countries in failing to adjust agricultural policies properly. Japanese farm price policies cost that nation's consumers and
taxpayers 62 percent of the value of
Japan's agricultural output in 1980,
though this was reduced to 51 percent
by 1983. Common Market countries' agricultural policies drive prices one fourth
above world market levels on most products. Such subsidies hurt not only domestic consumers, but also Third World
exporters who could produce more efficiently and sell cheaper. The policies
have the aim of preserving and sustaining the farm sector and its way of life.
But the goal could be equally well served
without the damage caused by price distortions if governments substituted direct income transfers for agricultural
price supports.[14]

Western nations, nonetheless, have
long satisfied basic food and fiber needs,
and government policies have played a
major role in this success. When policies
such as minimum price supports are introduced in order to ensure food security and stabilize markets—that is, when
supports are set below international
market levels—they can be useful. When
supports exceed world market levels,
however, they interfere with trade, stimulate environmentally disruptive over-
production, and waste taxpayers' and
consumers' money. These distortions,

like their more pervasive counterparts in planned economies, have political motivations that may well be worthy. But their impact on environmental and economic sustainability cannot be ignored. Ultimately they become counterproductive.

ENERGY EFFICIENCIES

Energy sustains modern societies. It not only reduces drudgery and makes inhospitable climates habitable, it substitutes for scarce resources. Energy permits us to replace copper with aluminum, wood with iron, time with speed. It has been sanctified by economists with a place in their production functions—equations that incorporate labor, capital, and other factors into least-cost combinations. Energy inefficiency can undermine a society's sustainability. In the worst case, pollution resulting from inefficient use may make entire regions uninhabitable.

Romania and Hungary each use twice as much energy per unit of gross national product as the United States, and five times as much as France or Sweden. (See Table 10–1.) Stated otherwise, if Eastern Europe and the Soviet Union were to increase their incomes to Western levels, they would need twice as much energy per capita as Western nations. Their poor ranking is related in part to their stage of development—they have poorly developed service sectors. But their industries are highly energy-inefficient in both the economic and the physical sense. And sustained development, of any type, is unlikely without energy efficiency as fossil fuel supplies dwindle and the environmental impacts of fuel use worsen.[15]

No national economy is more energy-inefficient than Hungary's. José Bognár, who helped develop that country's New

Table 10-1. Efficiency of Energy Use, Selected Countries, 1983

Country	Energy Use
	(megajoules per dollar of GNP)
Market-Oriented	
France	8.6
Sweden	8.6
Japan	9.7
Spain	11.8
West Germany	11.8
Italy	12.9
United Kingdom	17.2
United States	19.3
Centrally Planned	
Yugoslavia	21.5
Poland	26.9
East Germany	29.0
Czechoslovakia	30.1
Soviet Union	32.3
Romania	37.6
China[1]	40.9
Hungary[1]	49.5

[1]Though the agricultural sectors of these economies are now market-oriented, their industrial sectors are centrally controlled.

SOURCE: Worldwatch Institute, based on energy consumption data and dollar GNPs in World Resources Institute/International Institute for Environment and Development, *World Resources 1986* (New York: Basic Books, 1986); dollar GNPs for the Soviet Union and Eastern Europe are adjusted 1980 levels estimated in Paul Marer, *Dollar GNPs of the USSR and Eastern Europe* (Baltimore, Md.: The Johns Hopkins University Press, 1985).

Economic Mechanism, attributes this fact to markup pricing. Industry determines prices for its finished products on a cost-plus basis; the higher the input costs, the larger its net share of revenues. Because the net "profits" are distributed as bonuses, managers and workers actually have an incentive to consume energy.[16]

Hungarian economist János Kornai describes this phenomenon in terms of "soft and hard budget constraints." A budget constraint is soft if cost increases can be passed on, or if government will bail out an industry rather than lose the firm's production or create unemployment. In such a case, little discipline or incentive exists to bring about energy efficiency improvements. International trade, to some extent, does provide an impetus to cut costs in order to compete with more efficient producers. Heavy dependence on trade is an important reason why resource-poor Japan is so efficient. Hungary also depends heavily on exports, which the government often subsidizes to earn foreign exchange. The soft budget constraint reflects policies governing all of Eastern Europe, the Soviet Union, much of the Third World, and an increasing share of the Western economies.[17]

Sustained development is unlikely without energy efficiency as fossil fuel supplies dwindle and the environmental impacts of fuel use worsen.

Gábor Hoványi, a Hungarian industrial economist, argues that in addition to markup pricing and soft budgets, energy efficiency is affected by policies that reduce trade, limit foreign exchange, distort wages, and reduce investment. These factors critically affect innovation, which is essential if growth is to continue without exhausting resources. Innovations for energy efficiency in steelmaking offer a basis for comparing performance in market-based and centrally planned economies because steel has long been an essential component of industrialization. It is also the world's foremost energy-consuming industrial activity.[18]

Though the Soviet Union now leads the world in total tons of steel produced, it is close to last in energy efficiency, using 31 gigajoules of energy per ton compared with the Japanese standard of 19 gigajoules. An important reason for this is a lag in innovation of new technology. The Soviet Union, like all of Eastern Europe, trails far behind the West in the use of the more efficient basic oxygen furnace. In Japan, this furnace has, along with the electric-arc one, completely replaced the obsolete open-hearth furnace. The Soviets, however, still use the open hearth to produce over half their steel.[19]

Other centrally planned economies also rely heavily on this outmoded, inefficient technology. Even East Germany, with its reputation for technical prowess, uses the open-hearth furnace for 45 percent of its steel production. Moreover, the Soviets recycle very little steel. They have lagged far behind the West in the adoption of the electric-arc furnace, which is usually fed almost exclusively with recycled scrap instead of virgin iron ore.[20]

A clear demarcation thus exists between market-oriented and centrally planned economies in energy as well as agriculture. Where governments directly control industrial production, energy efficiency is low. Centrally planned economies would probably create more goods and services with a given level of resources if they relied more on markets. But that does not mean that markets alone can keep nations within the bounds of sustainable development. Even less does it mean that the market alone will solve problems of inequity and human need.

EQUITY QUESTIONS

Any change in economic policy will touch the most basic human concerns. At stake are this generation's ability to buy food, shelter, and fuel, and future generations' prospects to produce these necessities from the resources they will inherit. Those prospects depend on the resource husbandry of the present generation, for depletion of soils, forests, fisheries, and energy sources can be catastrophic. The consequences of neglect can be seen in the famine and relocation of people in northern Ethiopia, where soils will no longer support agriculture and forests have disappeared. For this reason, the fairness with which centrally planned and market-oriented systems distribute resources among people and between generations is vital.

Equity means different things to different people. Definitions range from equal incomes to equal opportunities. Equity can be gauged with such measures as income distribution, longevity, and infant mortality. Calculation of the equity ratio permits easy comparison of how income is distributed between the rich and the poor within a nation. The equity ratio is the income share of the richest 20 percent of a population divided by that of the poorest 20 percent. Here, income share includes nonmonetary benefits such as special shopping privileges, housing allowances, and recreational facilities provided for an elite in some countries.

Ranking nations by equity ratio shows no clear advantage for either centrally planned or market economies. (See Table 10–2.) East Germany and Romania are slightly more egalitarian than most, but many Western nations—much richer ones—have similar distribution levels. The equity ratios of Japan and West Germany are only slightly worse than that of East Germany. A poor West German would on average be much richer in absolute terms—by over $900 per year—than a poor East German. A poor East German, on the other hand, would on average be more than $100 per year richer than a poor American,

Table 10-2. Income in 1983 and Income Distribution, Circa 1980, for Selected Countries

Country	Economy Type[1]	Equity Ratio[2]	Average Income of Poorest Fifth of Population
			(1983 dollars)
Romania	C	3	1,690
East Germany	C	3	3,660
Japan	M	4	4,545
Soviet Union	C	4	2,345
West Germany	M	5	4,570
Poland	C	5	1,630
Spain	M	6	1,680
United Kingdom	M	6	3,170
Hungary[3]	C	6	1,650
Sweden	M	6	4,340
India	M	7	90
Yugoslavia	C	7	970
Italy	M	7	1,905
South Korea	M	8	600
United States	M	8	3,522
China[4]	C	8	n.a.
Thailand	M	8	240
France	M	9	2,600
Philippines	M	10	190
Brazil	M	13	470

[1]Centrally planned (C) or market-oriented (M). [2]Ratio of income received by richest and poorest fifths of the population, rounded to the nearest whole number. [3]Refers to total economy; the market-oriented agricultural sector represents only one fifth of the economy. [4]Distribution figures used here predate the December 1978 economic reforms.
SOURCES: World Bank, *World Development Report 1986* (New York: Oxford University Press, 1986); Christian Morrisson, "Income Distribution in East European and Western Countries," *Journal of Comparative Economics*, June 1984.

though a poor American would be nearly $1,200 per year richer than a poor Soviet. Countries that have justified central control for equity purposes have little advantage in equity and compare poorly in absolute income.[21]

Income statistics reveal only one aspect of equity. Ready access to health care, for example, is another important factor in the equation. Longevity and infant mortality rates reveal much about the quality of life and human services in a country. A ranking based on average life spans shows market-oriented countries at the top, although both market and nonmarket countries (China, Egypt, the Philippines, and South Korea, for example) are found in the lower ranks. Market-oriented countries also have the lowest rates of infant mortality. Their relative advantage probably lies in higher-quality health care made possible with higher incomes. Smoking and drinking tend to be less prevalent in the West, which means reduced disease.[22]

Leaders who would make their economies more market-oriented may also pause to consider the problem of unemployment. Chronic unemployment and the spawning of a permanent underclass rank among the West's most serious problems. The Soviet Union's accomplishment of zero unemployment, though it has been achieved at the cost of great labor inefficiency, may nevertheless be seen as an important attainment, particularly when compared with 7 percent unemployment in the United States and 10 percent average unemployment in Western Europe.[23]

At the same time, reformers in Eastern Europe understand that the only short-term alternative to inefficiency and stagnation may be to "shed labor." The pain of this step can be eased by providing a social safety net of unemployment benefits or "make-work," but these require the political skill to effect an income transfer from the employed. There may

be a direct conflict between efficiency of resource use and unemployment, which may be seen as a conflict between generations, for inefficiency in resource use reduces future prospects.

Future generations, if they could participate in the matter, might well ask how market-oriented and centrally planned economies are husbanding the resources on which their well-being will depend. Although the environmental problems of the West are well known, information from centrally controlled economies is sketchy. But evidence is mounting that environmental disruption in these nations is severe. When Marshall Goldman wrote *The Spoils of Progress,* in 1972, he showed that environmental pollution problems are as familiar to socialism as to capitalism. Today, however, the efficiency improvements made by Western market-oriented nations, combined with regulatory policies to correct market failures, have begun to ameliorate pollution problems while those in centrally planned economies worsen.[24]

Even in the early seventies it was becoming difficult to find an unpolluted river in the Soviet Union. Goldman reported that fish kills had occurred all over the country, especially in the Volga, Ural, and Dnepr rivers. He found water use in steel mills to be 40 to 150 percent higher than in the United States, and similar water-use inefficiency in refineries and agriculture. Sulfur dioxide and nitrogen oxide emissions approached lethal levels in some areas, not unlike the deadly smogs of Donora, Pennsylvania, and London, England, of many years ago. Toxic emissions of lead and fluoride were permitted in large quantities. Lead concentrations in one city in eastern Kazakhstan reached 14 times the maximum permissible level.[25]

Timber in the Ukraine had nearly disappeared, Goldman reported, and coal surface-mining, with its profoundly disruptive effects, had proliferated. Natural areas, including spectacular Lake Baikal, the world's largest and oldest freshwater lake, have been exploited and seriously disrupted. Some 50 factories were built during the sixties along Lake Baikal's shores and four fifths of them discharged their raw wastes into the water. Goldman concluded, "Unfortunately the rape of Lake Baikal shows that public greed and lust can be as destructive as private greed and lust."[26]

Forests around Katowice show clear effects of sulfur dioxide, ozone, and hydrocarbon emissions.

More recently, Goldman noted that the Soviet Union has made some progress in environmental protection. Fish have returned to the Moscow River, and air and water pollution have been reduced. The Soviets may also be relying more heavily on natural gas to reduce environmental burdens. But the scant literature available in the West on Soviet pollution suggests that the problems remain serious and uncorrected. The recent disaster at the Chernobyl nuclear power plant reinforces the impression that Soviet safeguards against environmental disruption are weak.[27]

Poland is another example of the failure of central planning to control pollution. American analyst Stanley J. Kabala recently noted that a by-product of that country's Stalinist economy is "hundreds of miles of rivers unfit for *any* use and air pollution in nearly every major city 50 times worse than permissible limits" (emphasis in original). An analysis of Poland's environment prepared by planner Andrzej Kassenberg confirms this observation. Kassenberg has mapped extensive areas of environmental disruption due to toxic pollution, acid rain, and oxygen depletion in rivers. A visit to Upper Silesia reveals uncontrolled sul-

fur dioxide and particulate emissions that pour over populations living in industrial squalor. Ancient buildings and a wealth of history and culture in Kraków are being damaged by the pollution. Forests around Katowice show clear effects of sulfur dioxide, ozone, and hydrocarbon emissions. One third of the forest area in southwestern Poland has been affected; many young trees are already dead or dying.[28]

China also exemplifies the fact that central planning does not internalize environmental pollution costs but leaves them for future generations to bear. Environmental destruction existed in China before the communist military victory in 1949, but it has intensified since. Deforestation is China's biggest environmental problem: Large areas of trees were cut down to provide charcoal for backyard steel furnaces during Mao's Great Leap Forward. Planned tree-cutting in Sichuan Province during the sixties exceeded sustainable yields by 160 percent. Overall, forest area between 1949 and 1980 declined by a quarter. One reform recently undertaken to reverse this is to give incentives to peasants to plant and nurture trees: "Whoever afforests the land owns the trees." The goal is to extend forest cover to 20 percent of land area by the year 2000.[29]

The environmental failures of centrally planned nations thus rank alongside those of market-oriented economies. The former failed to internalize environmental costs because incentives were provided to managers to boost production. Moreover, the resources allocated to the managers reflected no scarcity value, no opportunity cost, no real price—the cost of using the resource was essentially irrelevant. The absence of prices and competition led to inefficiency as well as widespread environmental abuse.

Energy productivity trends show a marked divergence between some centrally planned and most market-oriented economic systems. Energy use per unit of output from 1970 to 1983 increased in Bulgaria, Romania, the Soviet Union, and Yugoslavia. West European countries meanwhile reduced consumption per unit of output by an average of 14 percent over that 13-year period. Since 1970, the United States dramatically reduced energy consumption per unit of output—by 30 percent. The Soviet Union, however, still requires an additional 1.2 percent of energy for each 1 percent of economic growth.[30] (See Figure 10–2.)

Increasing energy use bodes ill for future generations not only because fuels could be exhausted. Energy use is directly related to air, water, and land degradation, as extensive damage in Europe related to acid rain makes clear. Comparing nations' performances in controlling sulfur emissions provides a more direct measure of how economic systems affect future generations by diminishing the resource base.

Ranking nations by sulfur dioxide emissions per dollar of GNP shows a sharp demarcation between East and West. (See Table 10–3.) Czechoslovakia's rate is eight times that of West Ger-

Table 10-3. Sulfur Dioxide Emissions, Selected Countries, 1982

Country	Emissions
	(kilograms per $1,000 GNP)
Market-Oriented	
Japan[1]	1
Sweden	4
France	5
West Germany	5
United States	7
United Kingdom	8
Canada[1]	18
Centrally Planned	
Soviet Union	19
Romania	28
Hungary	31
East Germany	35
Czechoslovakia	40

[1]Data for 1980.
SOURCE: Worldwatch Institute, based on data in OECD, *OECD Environmental Data, Compendium 1985* (Paris: 1985); N. H. Highton and M. J. Chadwick, "The Effects of Changing Patterns of Energy Use on Sulfur Emissions and Depositions in Europe," *Ambio*, Vol. 11, No. 6, 1982; World Bank, *World Development Report 1984* (New York: Oxford University Press, 1984); and Paul Marer, *Dollar GNPs of the USSR and Eastern Europe* (Baltimore, Md.: The Johns Hopkins University Press, 1985).

many. The Soviet rate is almost triple that of the United States. Though the United States emits a quarter of sulfur dioxide gas worldwide, since the early seventies it has cut per capita sulfur dioxide emissions by a third while the Soviet Union has increased emissions by a similar proportion.

East European and Soviet rates of sulfur emissions are high as a result of their economic strategy, as well as the dependence on coal in Eastern Europe and an almost complete lack of emissions control there and in the Soviet Union. This is paralleled in the West by West Germany's absence of auto emissions controls and by the failure of the United States and the United Kingdom to join

Megajoules

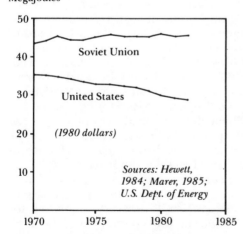

Figure 10-2. Energy Consumption Per Dollar of GNP for the United States and the Soviet Union, 1970-82

nations agreeing to reduce sulfur dioxide emissions by 30 percent. But in damage per unit of output, Western nations do far better than centrally planned ones.

Sustainable economics, in summary, puts forward two criteria for choice of investment or consumption as being particularly valuable: the net present-value criterion and the conservation criterion. The former represents efficiency and merely says that the investment has to be a good one, one that maximizes output while minimizing the cost of inputs. Under the theory of sustainability, it is a condition that can be met, however, only as long as the conservation criterion is met. That is, the use of agricultural land can be maximized as long as the productivity of the resource can be maintained.

Only if the conservation criterion is met first and the present-value criterion fulfilled second can both inter- and intragenerational equity be achieved. Markets alone cannot accomplish this, but to a large degree they offer a self-administering check on resource waste: The resource user pays for inefficiency. Nonmarket systems lack this internal correction. Theoretically, centrally planned economies could make resource conservation a high priority. But the evidence to date shows that they have not. And economic as well as psychological theories suggest that without meaningful price signals as a prompt, they are not likely to do so effectively.

CHANGING RELIANCE ON MARKETS

If the nineteenth century was the age of the free market, the twentieth is the age of the state. Current trends, however, could well make the next century better balanced between the two. A shift back toward markets has been prompted by five recent developments: Mao's death and his legacy of underdevelopment in China, the debt crisis in Latin America, the crisis of famine and underdevelopment in Africa, chronic underdevelopment in South Asia, and burgeoning deficits in the West. These economic dilemmas have their roots in resource use, and policy responses to them concern environmentalists as well as economists.

Worldwide, government enterprises produce about one third of the world's industrial output. Dependence on state firms ranges from being almost exclusive in the Soviet Union to being minimal in the United States. (See Table 10–4.) Western nations generally own or control less than 10 percent of their national output, with the important exceptions of the United Kingdom, Italy, and France. Even in Hungary, the most market-oriented East European nation, two thirds of nonagricultural output is produced by state enterprises. Third World countries fall between the East and West on the spectrum of state ownership.

The Chinese reforms announced in December 1978 represented a major turning point in world economic management. Mao's Great Leap Forward of the late fifties had caused enormous losses of production, even famine. That policy was followed by retrenchment, then by the violent Cultural Revolution from 1966 to 1976. During this period China decentralized economic control, but put decision-making authority in the hands of local and provincial bureaucrats rather than the marketplace.

Economic stagnation followed Mao's campaign to make China's regions self-sufficient, and pressure mounted for change. In the countryside, where 80 percent of the Chinese live, incomes in the two decades before the death of Mao

Table 10-4. Estimated Role of State-Owned Enterprises in Selected Economies, Circa 1980

Country	Share of Steel Industry	Share of Coal Industry	State Share of Total Capital Investment
	(approximate fraction)		(percent)
Romania	all	all	95
Soviet Union	all	all	95
Hungary	all	all	66
China	all	all	66
Poland	all	all	66
Egypt	n.a.	—	48
Pakistan	—	all	47
India	¾	all	34
Mexico	¾	all	33
South Korea	¾	¼	33
Brazil	¾	all	23
United Kingdom	¾	all	17
Italy	¾	—	15
Spain	½	½	15
Thailand	—	—	13
France	¾	all	12
Japan	0	0	11
West Germany	0	½	11
Australia	0	0	10
United States	0	0	4

SOURCES: "Privatization: Everybody's Doing It, Differently," *The Economist,* December 21, 1985; Mary M. Shirley, *Managing State-Owned Enterprises,* World Bank Staff Working Paper No. 577 (Washington, D.C.: World Bank, 1983).

grew by less than 10 percent. Rationing was common, and a third of the grain consumed in cities had to be imported. Over a third of the state-owned enterprises lost money in 1976.[31]

The 1979 reforms have within only a few years increased China's agricultural output by more than half, rural incomes by two thirds, and industrial production by two thirds. By 1986, private retailers supplied Beijing with a third of its vegetables, eggs, and beef, and Hebei Province with two thirds or more of its vegetables and eggs.[32]

New pricing policies gave farmers incentives to increase output. At first, they were obligated to deliver a minimum quota to the government at a fixed price. A higher price for deliveries over quota was then applicable, a premium that reached 50 percent for grain. Because retail prices were still set artificially low, budget subsidies for agriculture reached approximately $23 billion in 1983, some 42 percent of budget revenues. The state's contract procurement system did not match the demand of consumers with new yuan to spend, and the government accumulated expensive Western-style surpluses. Producer prices and quotas were consequently reduced for many items in 1985, and retail prices were increased.[33]

Other developing countries have been pushed by fiscal difficulties and mounting external debt to sell state-owned companies. (See Table 10–5.) Brazil owns almost 500 companies, five times as many as in 1960. It intends to sell the smaller of these, and to sell shares of energy-related concerns that dominate the state-company budget of Brazil. Shares of Petrobras, the national oil company, were already up for sale in 1985, though the main motivation may have been to avert the need to raise $400 million in taxes to pay for Petrobras' losses. Brazil is not likely to relinquish control of the larger state-owned enterprises.[34]

Brazil's new civilian government finds itself confronted not just with a foreign debt of $100 billion—and with a debt service that costs 5 percent of gross domestic product (GDP)—but with an entrenched economic bureacracy. The World Bank estimates that the government itself allocates resources to or controls enterprises producing 40–46 percent of GDP. This fact, according to one Bank study, suggests "that governmental decisions have, to a considerable extent, replaced the price mechanism in determining the composition of investment and, hence, the emerging structure of productive capacity."[35]

Mexico outranks even Brazil in number of state-owned enterprises. The government reserves to itself production of oil, steel, chemicals, shipbuilding, and railroads. State ownership has concentrated debt and thus contributed to Mexico's crisis. The government announced that it will sell 200 of its enterprises, partly to shed debt, and in 1985 it sold some hotels and small industries.[36]

African nations, many of which imi-

Table 10-5. Movements Toward Market Orientation of Industry in the Eighties, Selected Countries

Country	National-ization[1]	Reforms Announced[2]
Argentina	1946	Sell SOEs, 1986
Bangladesh	1971	Sell SOEs, 1982
Brazil	1940s	Sell SOEs, 1983
China	1953	Permit POEs, 1983
France	1981	Sell SOEs, 1986
Hungary	1949	Pricing, 1980s
India	1956	Deregulation, 1982, 1986
Indonesia	1957	Promote POEs
Italy	—	Sell SOEs, 1983
Japan	—	Sell SOEs, 1985
Mexico	1950s	Sell SOEs, 1985
Nigeria	1960s	Sell SOEs, 1986
Pakistan	1972	Deregulation, 1979
Philippines	—	Sell SOEs, 1986
South Korea	—	Deregulation, 1986
Spain	1939	Sell SOEs, 1980s
Thailand	—	Sell SOEs, 1980s
Turkey	—	Sell SOEs, 1985
United Kingdom	1960s	Sell SOEs, 1979
United States	—	Deregulation, 1979
West Germany	—	Sell SOE shares, 1984

[1]Includes both partial and total nationalizations of the industrial sector. [2]SOEs=state-owned enterprises; POEs=privately owned enterprises. SOURCE: Worldwatch Institute.

tated Maoist and Stalinist economic policies, have been slow to adopt reforms despite the pressure of near collapse. Tanzania under President Julius Nyerere copied the Maoist model. Nyerere has retired, but Tanzania remains exceedingly poor and underdeveloped, yet wedded to a Chinese model that no longer exists.

Nyerere's friend in revolution, President Robert Mugabe of Zimbabwe, has been determined not to repeat Tanzania's mistakes. Mugabe has retained market mechanisms while implementing specific measures to reduce inequity and underdevelopment. Most notably, he has provided incentives for farmers on tribal lands while permitting larger commercial farms to continue to operate. Programs to reduce infant mortality and to provide birth control measures have received high priority. Zimbabwe under Mugabe's rule is one of the few success stories on a troubled continent.[37]

Egypt, with a population approaching 50 million and an economy riddled with subsidies and inefficiencies, must import massive amounts of almost everything. Twenty-five percent of the country's national budget goes to pay for food and energy price subsidies. State-owned enterprises have dominated the industrial sector of the Egyptian economy since 1961, when the means of production were nationalized. Almost 20 percent of GDP is used for public investment. Public enterprises are expected to serve social goals in the process of producing goods, particularly to absorb labor. The enterprises are virtually powerless to fire unproductive workers.[38]

Throughout Africa, agriculture remains underdeveloped and low in productivity, a situation for which some governments bear direct responsibility. The Organization of African Unity heads of state met in 1985 and adopted a measure recommending allocation of at least 20 percent of total investment to agriculture. Their Priority Programme also calls on nations to provide necessary incentives for farmers, including price incentives.[39]

Manufacturing accounts for only 11 percent of African economic output, and progress remains slow. The African Development Bank associates industrial lethargy with nonmarket control. But it notes that markets are becoming more important in Africa's economies. A recent report concluded that "it would seem that the overall direction of change is towards more market freedom, more emphasis on producer incentives, increased resource allocation to agriculture, and the reform of the public sector to ensure greater profitability."[40]

The African Development Bank cites Ghana, Mali, Zaire, and Zambia as examples of nations that have begun the difficult reforms. Ghana has devalued its currency, freed up prices, and removed subsidies, especially for petroleum products. Mali has privatized many of its state-owned enterprises. Zambia has devalued its currency by 60 percent.[41]

Markets are becoming more important in Africa's economies.

South Asia suffers from neither Latin America's debt nor Africa's famine, but is experimenting with economic change because its economies also remain seriously underdeveloped. India has led the way in reform, although Pakistan and Bangladesh have also made changes. India had in 1956 formally restricted to state enterprises the rail, air, communications, power, insurance, heavy extractive, and defense industries. These sectors were given additional flexibility in 1982 when a dual-price policy—one for delivery of government quotas, one for the open market—was implemented. Described as a radical change, it was designed to help overcome the shortages that have stymied the economy since the sixties.[42]

The cement industry in India has shown the first positive results. In the early eighties, for the first time, it more than met its production goals. The increase in cement production from 1980 to 1985, in fact, equalled that of the preceding 25 years. Indian agriculture has also been liberalized, with the government mainly providing price guarantees that have generally been unnecessary, as they have been set below acceptable market prices.[43]

Western nations, meanwhile, are also becoming more market-oriented in industrial policy. Japan, France, and West Germany have all begun to sell state-owned enterprises and their shares in companies. Western Europe in particular has been forced by large budgetary deficits to denationalize industry.

The United States, at least in terms of ownership of the means of production, remains the most market-oriented major economic power in the world. With only a small percentage of GNP generated by state companies and some private defense contractors that are virtually government appendages, the country has moved even further to reduce government's role in the economy. It recently closed down the mammoth Synthetic Fuels Corporation, for example, which the Carter administration created to subsidize oil substitutes. The most important market reorientation, however, came when President Carter deregulated petroleum prices. He also set in motion other important efforts at deregulation, particularly in trucking and air transportation.[44]

Yet governments worldwide have resisted market reforms for agriculture. Western nations continue to subsidize farm production, and distortion of agricultural prices everywhere in the West has become extreme. Rice is heavily protected and subsidized in Japan. Western Europe and the United States also maintain policies that create large distortions. (See Table 10–6.) As indicated earlier, these programs cost the U.S. government at least $30 billion in 1986.[45]

Table 10-6. Wheat and Rice Producer Prices in Selected Countries, Compared with World Market Price, Circa 1982

Country or Group	Wheat	Rice
	(percent of world price)	
Japan	380	330
South Korea	220	210
Turkey	120	190
Kenya	165	145
European Common Market	125	140
United States	115	130
Bangladesh	75	85
India	100	80
Philippines	n.a.	80
Pakistan	85	75
Thailand	n.a.	75
Brazil	n.a.	65
Tanzania	n.a.	50
Egypt	95	45
Yugoslavia	55	n.a.

SOURCES: World Bank, *World Development Report 1986* (New York: Oxford University Press, 1986); Hans Binswanger and P.L. Scandizzo, "Patterns of Agricultural Protection," World Bank, Washington, D.C., November 15, 1983; World Bank, *Commodity Trade and Price Trends* (Baltimore, Md.: The Johns Hopkins University Press, 1985).

Elsewhere, governments hobble agriculture with underpayment rather than overpayment. The Soviet Union, which under Stalin paid farmers only about one eighth of the value of their products, continues to underpay them. The global imbalance in agricultural policy reached a new height in 1986 when the United States agreed to export part of a wheat surplus—created by subsidies—to fill a Soviet wheat deficit created by central planning.[46]

Worldwide, market reorientation through the mid-eighties has left the environmentally important natural resource industries almost untouched. Though private companies still control oil production in Australia, Canada, the

United Kingdom, the United States, and West Germany, governments control oil supplies in Brazil, Mexico, Nigeria, Saudi Arabia, the Soviet Union, and Venezuela.[47]

Over half of all coal, perhaps the most noxious fuel, is produced or consumed by government plan. The largest state producers are China and the Soviet Union, which together produce and use over one third of the world's coal. Many major market-oriented nations own their coal-producing enterprises, including 100 percent of the coal industry in France, India, and the United Kingdom and half of it in West Germany.[48]

The century-long trend toward greater government control has ended.

At least half of all steel, and the attendant environmental burden, is produced by governments. The Soviet Union and Eastern Europe produce almost one third of all steel. The governments of Brazil, France, India, Italy, Mexico, South Korea, and the United Kingdom own at least three quarters of their nations' steel-producing capacity, and those of Belgium and Spain own half of theirs. Of the major steel-producing countries, only in Australia, Canada, Japan, the United States, and West Germany are the companies almost completely privately owned.[49]

Government control of the production and prices of oil, coal, and steel has led to excessive consumption of these resources. Some governments, however, have usefully intervened to conserve these resources. By adding taxes to the price of fuels, for example, to account for the environmental, security, and intergenerational costs of energy consumption, they have reduced excessive use. Many nations now apply taxes to oil

products that drive their prices to twice the U.S. retail price, which is largely unaffected by controls or taxes.

In sum, a dramatic shift has occurred in the structure of national economies: The century-long trend toward greater government control has ended. This shift has not involved the essential macroeconomic measures that balance and stabilize economic systems, but rather the details of production and allocation of resources. Government intervention for enhancing the environmental sustainability of nations is increasing, though possibly not quickly enough. But many nations, having drawn the boundaries of sustainability, are increasingly leaving the internal workings of economies to market mechanisms. Those that have shifted—notably China, Hungary, and Zimbabwe—are reaping the rewards. Those that have not—Brazil, Mexico, and Egypt—are headed for trouble. Nations falling between these extremes—India and Pakistan—are making slow progress toward greater economic and environmental efficiency.

TOWARD A BALANCE

The world of the late eighties faces a growing rift in incomes and resource-use efficiency. Agricultural productivity has fallen in virtually every centrally planned nation over the last 20 years, while it continues to increase in market-oriented nations. Energy consumption per unit of output is highest in centrally planned economies. Fuel consumption per unit of output continues to rise in the Soviet Union while it is decreasing in Western Europe, Japan, and the United States. Emissions that cause acid rain are being reduced in market economies, but continue to grow in centrally planned ones.

Greater productive efficiency in market nations has reduced environmental pressures, while inefficiency in centrally planned countries has increased them. Income distribution is comparable in both types of economies, but market ones enjoy higher life expectancy and lower infant mortality, indicators that suggest greater overall well-being. Absolute income levels are much higher in market-oriented economies.

A given level of industrial production —a given level of wealth—is thus being created more efficiently under market conditions than elsewhere. This fact derives from at least two advantages that markets have over central planning. The first is that they are largely self-administering. The price mechanism brings demand more or less automatically into equilibrium with supply.

The second advantage is that the prices are meaningful. That is, under competition they reflect real scarcity values—values based both on the difficulty of winning new resources from the earth and on the relative priorities that consumers place on them. Higher prices alert resource consumers to the cost of overconsumption; they transmit critical information between the environment and the economy.

Central planners, if they did their jobs well, would replicate these functions of the market. But the difficulty of assembling the mountain of information required, coupled with the problem of competing priorities of resource conservation and political stability, hinders their ability to set meaningful prices and to allocate resources efficiently.

Beyond a point, the creation of wealth by market economies brings new problems, characterized by the prodigious consumption of gasoline in the West. This contradiction between efficiency and high per-capita consumption highlights the role of sustainable economic policy. A boundary—a limit on consumption of some resources—can avert

threats to sustainable development. Limitations on fishing can ensure that the supply of fish is not depleted faster than it can be replenished, for instance. Similar measures can be implemented to protect other resources.

When constraints are needed, they work best when applied on the macroeconomic level. Gasoline, for example, would not be rationed on an individual basis, but would be taxed to limit total consumption. Price mechanisms would then allocate the fuel to its most productive uses. Equity problems may follow, but nations can manage these through income policies, without resort to rationing or planned allocation of resources.

Recent history suggests that economies worldwide might benefit from finding some common new path. This new model would veer away from central planning toward market reliance for microeconomic decisions. It would not, however, deny the necessity of government intervention at the macroeconomic level to keep economies in balance and to control external costs. It would not deny the necessity for societies to act as a whole through their political processes to improve their lot beyond the capabilities of market economics.

In the mid-eighties, many countries have begun to reorient their economies. Eighteen of the world's 20 most populous nations are initiating measures to sell state-owned industry, relax price controls, or increase competition. This reorientation affects two thirds of the world's people.

Hungarian economist János Kornai cautions against overoptimism in economic affairs. He directed this advice particularly to American readers: "There are unsolvable dilemmas, because each of us has conflicting goals and adheres to conflicting ethical postulates." He is aware that "hard budgets" are more efficient, but efficiency means unemployment, and nations like Hungary may not have the resources to redistribute income quickly enough to reduce the human suffering that comes with economic readjustment.[50]

At the same time, Hungary and other socialist countries do not have the resources to continue the enormous inefficiency of central planning and soft budgets. Western countries have used market economics to create wealth efficiently. Yet to the extent that they fail to address the problems of underemployment, unemployment, and hunger amidst plenty, they undermine the credibility of market solutions.

11

Charting a Sustainable Course

Lester R. Brown and Edward C. Wolf

Until recently, responsibility for charting the course of development was left to economists. Appropriate economic policies, ones that ensured high rates of savings and investment, were expected to drive the engine of economic growth. But as populations expanded and pressures on natural support systems intensified, national development policies based on economic considerations alone often failed to guarantee improvements in living standards. A rekindling of progress now depends on a careful integration of economic, population, and environmental policies.

Deforestation, soil erosion, acidification, and desertification are undermining economic progress in scores of countries. Efforts to devise sustainable development policies will be further complicated by the global warming induced by greenhouse gases, the depletion of the ozone layer, and the wholesale loss of biological diversity associated with tropical deforestation. These new threats to progress confront industrial and developing countries alike. Future improvements in living standards rest more heavily than ever on international cooperation. And time has suddenly become one of the scarcest of all resources.

"Overall, we are locked in a race," observed biologist E.O. Wilson of Harvard University at the 1986 National Forum on Biodiversity in Washington, D.C. The race, as he sees it, pits humanity's ability to gather information about the earth's rich evolutionary inheritance of plant and animal life against the uncontrolled degradation of tropical environments, which threatens an episode of extinction as large as any in the planet's history.[1]

Michael McElroy, Director of Harvard's Center for Earth and Planetary Physics, is one of the creators of a new branch of atmospheric science that investigates the global atmosphere as a single system. McElroy and his colleagues hope that this research will yield insights that allow humanity to manage, rather than submit to, a changing climate. "There is no longer any doubt that we are in a high-stakes race with the pace of atmospheric change," wrote Jonathan Leonard, profiling McElroy's work. The steps required to adjust to such change may be drastic; unfortunately, the enormous gaps in our understanding of atmospheric processes make it difficult to know exactly what to do. This counterpoint of urgency and uncertainty will dominate human affairs as the twentieth century draws to a close.[2]

The environmental and economic problems we face and the course corrections they will require are complex. Simply determining how basic human activities, such as producing food and burning fossil fuels, are altering the biosphere and atmosphere poses unprecedented scientific problems. These are not questions that can be answered within a year or two with a crash research program. Rather, they require a sustained research commitment on a scale that is massive by any previous yardstick.

The more serious challenge faces political institutions that must respond to the emerging scientific consensus on global problems. Changes in the atmosphere, on land, and in the earth's biological endowment will require cooperative global responses. National leaders who fail to comprehend the fundamental alteration in the relationship between the 5 billion of us who now inhabit the earth and the natural systems and resources on which we depend will find themselves plagued by intractable problems and locked into economic decline.

THE SCIENTIFIC CHALLENGE

Few human activities have grown as rapidly in this century as the worldwide scientific effort. The number of scientists and engineers has expanded three times faster than world population and twice as fast as the global economy; the inten-

sity of scientific inquiry has increased accordingly. Despite this dramatic expansion, unanticipated and unwelcome discoveries in recent years have raised questions about the adequacy of current research efforts.[3]

The existing scientific effort falls short of what is needed to assess the impacts of human activity on the global environment.

The spread of forest damage in central Europe is one phenomenon that caught scientists by surprise. Despite intensive research on air pollution, acid rain, and the ecological dynamics of forests, scientists have not yet put the pieces of the puzzle together in a model that can fully account for the unfolding pattern of forest decline. More recently, the discovery of a "hole" in the layer of stratospheric ozone over Antarctica each September and October has confounded atmospheric scientists. None of the widely accepted models of the ozone layer predicted it.

These and other after-the-fact discoveries suggest that the existing scientific effort falls short of what is needed to assess the impacts of human activity on the global environment. Current research suffers from disciplinary specialization, geographic fragmentation, and a lack of long-term commitment.

Recognizing these limitations, the international scientific community has proposed a new initiative—called the International Geosphere-Biosphere Program, or simply the Global Change program—that is interdisciplinary and global, and that involves a time commitment measured in decades rather than years. The proposed inquiry is by far the most comprehensive, cooperative effort in the history of international scientific collaboration. First outlined in Ottawa, Canada, at a 1984 meeting of the International Council of Scientific Unions (ICSU), the Global Change program received a ringing endorsement in Bern, Switzerland, in September 1986 from the 71 national scientific academies and 23 professional societies that constitute ICSU.[4]

The Global Change program will focus on the interactions between the geosphere (the earth's physical systems and resources) and the biosphere. In essence, the focal point will be the physical, chemical, and biological processes that support life on earth. In the words of atmospheric scientist Thomas Malone, an organizer of the 1984 meeting, its central thrust will be "to describe and understand quantitatively the interactive physical, chemical, and biological processes that regulate the total earth system, the unique environment it provides for life, the changes that are occurring in that system and the manner in which they are influenced by human actions."[5]

Strong support for the new initiative has come from the U.S. National Aeronautics and Space Administration (NASA), which in 1982 had proposed its own international Global Habitability research program. NASA officials were undoubtedly impressed by some of the resource degradation they could see from space—deforestation, desertification, soil erosion, and other environmental disruptions brought about by human activities. For example, NASA satellites photographed the progress of giant dust plumes from the Sahara across the North Atlantic, and monitored the formation of a new island in the Bay of Bengal as silt was carried to the ocean from the Himalayas and the Gangetic Plain in India. NASA's Earth Systems Science Committee will join the National Science Foundation and the National Academy of Sciences in sponsoring the Global Change study.[6]

Among the issues where incomplete understanding is deterring action are the atmospheric buildup of carbon dioxide (CO_2) and trace gases, and the dynamics of the ozone layer. The amount of CO_2 produced by fossil fuel combustion can be readily estimated, but the amounts released by deforestation and land degradation are poorly known. Estimates vary by a factor of two. Coupled with this range of uncertainty is inadequate knowledge of the rates at which the oceans absorb atmospheric carbon dioxide.[7]

Renewed attention to the ozone layer has also yielded more surprises than satisfactory explanations. Alarmed by the unexpected decline in ozone over Antarctica, the U.S. National Science Foundation organized a research expedition to the continent in August 1986 to chart changes in atmospheric chemistry as the Antarctic spring progressed. Three general hypotheses had been proposed to account for the seasonal decline in ozone concentrations. Measurements of ozone and other chemicals in the Antarctic atmosphere proved inconsistent with two of them. Team leader Susan Solomon concluded, "We believe that a chemical mechanism is fundamentally responsible for the hole." Scientists will attempt to untangle the chemistry involved—including the extent to which chlorofluorocarbons (CFCs) play a role.[8]

In October 1986, a NASA investigator reported a smaller "hole" in the ozone over the Arctic that seemed analogous to the puzzling Antarctic phenomenon. This hole, like the one observed in the southern hemisphere, appears to be linked to very cold atmospheric temperatures. Whether the two seasonally transient "holes" are related to a global depletion of the ozone layer—and whether similar processes generate them at the two poles—are scientific questions whose answers could literally alter the course of life on earth.[9]

Both soil chemistry and soil fertility, seemingly more mundane concerns, contain equally large uncertainties. The link between changes in soil chemistry and the forest die-off in Europe has generated a wide-ranging, so far unresolved debate in the scientific community. And while monitoring soil erosion on agricultural land would seem to be an obvious and urgent priority, only the United States has undertaken a comprehensive national soil erosion survey.[10]

The largest international scientific collaboration in the world today is not the Global Change study but the U.S. Strategic Defense Initiative.

Land use patterns have changed dramatically over the last generation, but little effort has been made to determine how these alterations have affected the hydrological cycle. It has been demonstrated experimentally, and indeed it is obvious even to untrained observers, that removing vegetation from the land increases rainfall runoff. This in turn reduces the percolation that recharges aquifers and the evaporation that contributes moisture to the air and may promote cloud formation. Yet there is little documentation of how vegetation losses have affected water supplies and rainfall patterns. As a result, scientists cannot predict the full consequences of deforestation and land degradation.

The uncertainties surrounding physical resources and processes are matched by uncertainties about the distribution and abundance of living organisms. Estimates of the total number of plant and animal species range from 5 million to 30 million, but only about 1.6 million organisms have been described. A full

taxonomic accounting has never been done; E.O. Wilson laments "we do not know the true number of species on Earth even to the nearest order of magnitude." As a result, estimates of the rate and implications of species extinctions are rough extrapolations based on ecological theory and limited field studies—hardly a basis for the redesign of development policies that may be needed to conserve biological diversity.[11]

Dispelling this ignorance of planetary processes will be time-consuming and intellectually demanding but not prohibitively costly. The Global Change program is expected to cost about $1 billion over a decade. Compiling a thorough inventory of living species—which though not part of the Global Change agenda is equally critical to a sound understanding of human impacts on the biosphere—might require 25,000 professional lifetimes devoted to collecting, analyzing, and describing unique plants and animals. At current levels of funding and scientific effort, fewer than 1 percent of the world's species are being investigated. Scientific enthusiasm for both these initiatives is building. New technologies including satellites, powerful computers, and analytic techniques that monitor chemicals at concentrations of parts per trillion put such ambitious research objectives within grasp.[12]

New constraints on funding for scientific research could do more than technological limitations to compromise progress on the Global Change program. The largest international scientific collaboration in the world today is not the Global Change study, from which all nations could benefit, but the U.S. Strategic Defense Initiative, or Star Wars program. Since it was begun in 1983, $9 billion has been committed to this research. Reagan administration plans call for spending $33 billion on Star Wars between 1986 and 1991. Israel, Japan, the United Kingdom, and West Germany have signed agreements to participate in the research, and France and Italy are expected to conclude formal agreements that will guarantee them a share of Pentagon contracts for exotic defense technologies.[13]

Although the Star Wars program will not necessarily rule out research on the global environment, the enormous distortion of U.S. federal research funding will certainly make it more difficult to carry out components of the Global Change program or to fund neglected disciplines like biology. According to Gerard Piel, past President of the American Association for the Advancement of Science, "if the [Star Wars] program goes forward there will be enough funds to hire half of all the country's physicists." Star Wars is gathering momentum despite a broad consensus among U.S. scientists that its aims are not feasible.[14]

A turning point could be reached when institutions more concerned with worldwide economic advance than with narrow definitions of national security recognize the contribution that the Global Change study could make to their work. The World Bank, for example, plans to use satellite remote sensing to create a global data base on environmental trends in the Third World. The pace at which climate change unfolds as a result of greenhouse gas warming has obvious implications for Bank-financed investments in drinking water supply, irrigation, and rural development. The modest cost of a Global Change program could be considered a down payment toward more sustainable development in the twenty-first century.[15]

The International Geophysical Year of 1957–58 and the International Biological Program, both sponsored by ICSU, offer precedents for the worldwide collaborative effort needed if the Global Change study is to succeed. Without this new "mission to Planet Earth," we may lack the information needed to arrest the deterioration of the earth's habitability.[16]

Yet action to avert the consequences of global change need not await the outcome of long-term scientific research. Ample reason already exists to move ahead on at least three broad fronts. An international commitment to complete the demographic transition, restrain carbon emissions, and launch a second energy revolution could provide a yardstick by which worldwide progress toward sustainability might be measured.

COMPLETING THE DEMOGRAPHIC TRANSITION

In the late eighties, the straightforward economic division of the world into the North and the South is yielding to a more significant demographic division based on differential population growth rates. As noted in Chapter 2, in one set of countries, which contain nearly half the world's people, populations are growing slowly or not at all and incomes are rising. In the second group, populations are growing rapidly and incomes are falling, or risk doing so if rapid population growth continues.

Dozens of countries in the latter group, all in the Third World, have crossed key environmental thresholds and are now experiencing income declines. They need to slow population growth quickly lest they fall into the demographic trap. This will be particularly difficult because the economic and social improvements that normally help reduce family size are no longer operating. The urgent need to slow population growth under such trying circumstances presents a situation for which the experiences of other countries offer little guidance.

China narrowly avoided this demographic trap. Government projections in the late seventies showed that even if Chinese families averaged just two children, the country's population would still grow by several hundred million and would overwhelm support systems and resources, undermining the economy and reducing living standards. China's leaders saw the decline coming and took preemptive action to head it off. They adopted the only alternative—an unprecedented program to encourage one-child families.[17]

The key to the Chinese success was a national effort to foster public understanding of the consequences of the demographic path China was on. Using the long-term projections, they calculated future per capita supplies of cropland, water, energy, and jobs. These numbers formed the basis of a broad public education effort on population policy.

One consequence of this effort was a shift in the focus of childbearing decisions. Couples whose concerns would traditionally have centered on how many children they would need to support them in their old age began to consider how the size of their family would affect the world in which their children would live. This subtle shift from narrow self-interest to a concern for the well-being of future generations may hold the key to completing the demographic transition.

Attempting to slow population growth quickly when living standards are deteriorating is one of the most difficult, politically complex undertakings any government can face. Many nations face a demographic emergency. Failure to check population growth will lead to continued environmental deterioration, economic decline, and, eventually, social disintegration.

In this new situation, some policymakers are beginning to consider new approaches to lowering birth rates. Nigerian economist Adebayo Adedeji, Executive Secretary of the U.N. Economic Commission for Africa, urges research on "the use of the tax system as a means for controlling population growth and discouraging rural/urban migration." Such a recommendation, suggesting an unprecedented approach to Africa's population problems, indicates the urgency that some African decision makers are at last beginning to attach to escaping the demographic trap.[18]

Many nations face a demographic emergency.

In Africa, the Indian subcontinent, Latin America, the Middle East, and Southeast Asia, progress toward the final stage of the demographic transition is uneven. Stopping population growth in these five high growth regions does not depend on new technologies. Existing contraceptives and family planning services have already sharply reduced fertility in almost half the world. The missing ingredient is leadership.

A dozen countries—10 in Western Europe and 2 in Eastern Europe—have completed the demographic transition. (See Table 11–1.) These nations contain some 247 million people, or 5 percent of world population. A second group, 8 countries with an annual growth of 0.5 percent per year or less, has nearly reestablished equilibrium between births and deaths. Unless fertility levels change, they too should reach stability within a matter of years. Eight percent of world population will soon live in countries with stationary populations.

Not too far behind are several coun-

Table 11-1. Countries That Have Completed the Demographic Transition, 1986

Country	Crude Birth Rate	Crude Death Rate	Annual Rate of Increase or Decrease[1]	Population
	(per 1,000 population)		(percent)	(million)
Austria	11	12	−0.1	7.6
Belgium	12	11	+0.1	9.9
Denmark	11	11	0.0	5.1
East Germany	14	14	0.0	16.7
Greece	12	10	+0.2	10.0
Hungary	12	13	−0.1	10.6
Italy	10	10	0.0	57.2
Luxembourg	11	11	0.0	0.4
Norway	13	11	+0.2	4.2
Sweden	12	11	+0.1	8.4
United Kingdom	13	13	0.0	56.6
West Germany	10	11	−0.1	60.7
Total				247.4

[1]Excludes immigration.

SOURCE: Worldwatch Institute estimates based on data in the United Nations, *Monthly Bulletin of Statistics*, New York, monthly.

tries whose populations are expanding between 0.5 and 1 percent per year. This group includes some of the world's most populous nations, such as China, Japan, the Soviet Union, and the United States. Japan, growing at 0.6 percent per year, and the United States, at 0.7 percent, are now well below replacement-level fertility, indicating that reaching zero population growth is only a matter of time.[19]

Of the five geographic regions where population growth is between 2 and 3 percent per year, Southeast Asia may have the best chance of lowering its fertility and moving into the final stage of the demographic transition. Within the region, wide variations in population growth rates exist. Indonesia and Thailand have been rather successful in going from a high to a moderate rate. Other societies, however, like Burma,

Malaysia, the Philippines, and Vietnam, have made little progress to date.[20]

More worrisome are the billion people in the Indian subcontinent, three fourths of them in India. Although it was the first country to enact an official family planning program, India's commitment has wavered. An overzealous effort to slow population growth in the mid-seventies led to reports of coercive sterilizations. The public resistance that followed dealt a severe setback to the overall family planning program.

India is beginning to reinvigorate its family planning program. The Seventh Five-Year Plan endorses a two-child family norm and aims to achieve replacement-level fertility by the year 2000. Specific goals of the plan include 31 million sterilizations, 21 million insertions of intrauterine devices, and 62 million conventional contraceptive users by 1990. Recollections of the political and social costs of coercion should prevent the excesses of a decade ago as policies to accomplish these goals are enacted.[21]

Whether India can slow its population growth before deforestation, soil erosion, and desertification undermine its economy remains to be seen. Severe regional shortages of water and food are likely in the not-too-distant future if population growth is not arrested. If India's annual population growth persists at 2.3 percent, meager gains in per capita food production could turn into a decline in food availability, as it has in Africa.

With the most rapid population growth of any continent in history, Africa's economic and nutritional difficulties remain acute. Only 3–4 percent of the couples in most African countries use contraception. This figure will have to rise severalfold in order to reduce birth rates substantially. The World Bank, reviewing the constraints on Africa's prospects in late 1986, announced that lending for population control had become "its highest priority in Africa." The Bank plans to double its spending on African family planning programs by 1990.[22]

Despite African political leaders' new awareness of population problems, family planning success stories in Africa are few. The most progress has been achieved in Zimbabwe, where one third of the women now use contraception. Strong support from Prime Minister Robert Mugabe and a well-organized program headed by Dr. Esther Boohene have been the keys to success. Zimbabwe has chosen to keep the family planning program largely separate from the Ministry of Health so it can be carefully managed and monitored. Dr. Boohene credits this decision with part of the success achieved in some 300 family plan-

ning clinics dispersed throughout the country.[23]

Some Latin American countries are trying innovative approaches to boost family planning practices in their societies. Brazil, the most populous country in Latin America, is launching a program to give all women information on birth control methods and a free supply of pills. Spending will total $254 million per year, or roughly 10 percent of the social security ministry's budget. Mexico launched an unusual media campaign using soap operas, athletes, and popular music to publicize the importance of family planning.[24]

In just over half the world, time is running out in the effort to slow population growth by reducing birth rates. Unfortunately, not all national leaders recognize the basic relationship between population growth, ecological support systems, and economic trends. Even those who understand the links do not consistently support effective family planning programs. Perhaps the most tragic failure in this area is the United States. Traditionally a leader in the international family planning movement, the U.S. government announced in August 1986 that it was withdrawing all financial support from the U.N. Fund for Population Activities (UNFPA), the U.N. agency responsible for coordinating family planning programs in 134 countries.[25]

The ostensible reason for the Reagan administration's decision was reports of forced abortions in China, a recipient of UNFPA support. China denied the allegations, but the United States disputed that denial. The more salient issue, one ignored by U.S. policymakers, was whether other countries in need of family planning assistance should be penalized because of the Chinese program. Playing politics with family planning assistance counters progress toward completing the demographic transition. For some countries, it increases the likelihood that population growth will slow because of rising death rates rather than falling birth rates.[26]

BALANCING THE CARBON EQUATION

Carbon dioxide constitutes just 0.03 percent of the earth's atmosphere by volume, ranking fourth, behind nitrogen (78.1 percent), oxygen (21.0 percent), and the inert gas argon (0.9 percent). Yet in this relative scarcity lies carbon dioxide's special importance to living things, its vulnerability to human activity, and the possibility that the human impacts on CO_2 levels can be managed. Restoring equilibrium to the global carbon cycle is both imperative and achievable.[27]

Industrial and developing countries alike share responsibility for human-induced disturbance of the carbon cycle. The burning of fossil fuels, mainly by industrial countries, releases about 5 billion tons of carbon to the atmosphere each year. The clearing and burning of forests, principally in tropical developing countries, contributes between 0.6 billion and 2.6 billion more tons of carbon to the air. As a result, the total amount of carbon stored in the atmosphere, about 700 billion tons, is slowly increasing.[28] (See Chapter 9.)

Although the carbon cycle is a vigorous one, with billions of tons of carbon fixed annually by plants through photosynthesis and released by respiration and the decay of plants and animals, levels of carbon dioxide have been relatively stable through most of human history. Regular measurements of atmospheric carbon dioxide levels did not begin until 1958. Public concern about the effects of rising CO_2 on climate and the economy is even more recent.

An enormous effort is required to reduce CO_2 emissions, but it can be done, and it is likely to be far cheaper than adjusting to CO_2-induced climate change. Energy price increases have already arrested the growth in one component of the CO_2 buildup. Between 1950 and 1979, total carbon emissions from fossil fuel combustion more than tripled, from 1.6 billion to 5.1 billion tons. (See Table 11–2.) Since 1979, however, these emissions have remained fairly stable, with a total in 1986 less than 2 percent above the 1979 level. This will continue to boost atmospheric carbon dioxide levels, but not nearly as fast as if the 1950–79 trend had continued.

Fossil fuel consumption has temporarily leveled off at a time when enormous potential remains for increasing energy efficiency in the world economy. No country has yet come close to realizing the full gains in this sector that modern technology makes possible, and only a handful of countries have extensively substituted renewable energy sources for fossil fuels.

Reversing the net contribution of CO_2 from deforestation is the other crucial component of efforts to restore balance to the carbon cycle. Progress may be made indirectly as policymakers recognize that continued deforestation will confront tropical countries with unacceptable economic costs. Once forest cover is removed, many tropical soils deteriorate rapidly. Productive agriculture cannot be sustained on such land.

The World Bank, which has financed colonization of Brazil's western Amazon, temporarily withdrew support for part of the Polonoroeste Project in Rondonia State in 1985 because of environmental and social problems. A phase of the project that originally envisioned resettling 15,000 families was scaled back to 5,000 families due to low soil fertility.[29] An al-

Table 11-2. Carbon-Emissions Intensity of World Economic Output, 1950–86

Year	Total Carbon Emissions From Fossil Fuels	Gross World Product[1]	Carbon Per $1,000 of GNP
	(million metric tons)	(trillion dollars)	(kilograms)
1950	1,583	2.94	538
1955	1,975	3.78	522
1960	2,495	4.68	533
1965	3,037	5.99	507
1970	3,934	7.67	513
1975	4,453	9.42	473
1980	5,058	11.27	449
1981	4,931	11.43	431
1982	4,875	11.59	421
1983	5,013	11.80	425
1984	5,105	12.33	414
1985	5,180	12.68	408
1986[2]	5,225	13.10	399

[1] 1980 dollars.   [2] Preliminary figures.
SOURCES: Worldwatch Institute estimates based on data from United Nations, U.S. Department of Energy, U.S. Department of State, and British Petroleum of North America.

ternative to settlement of rain forest areas is to enact real land reform that will distribute existing farmland more equitably, and to organize family planning programs to slow population growth.

Planting trees also restrains pressures on the tropical forests that remain, and helps slow the CO_2 buildup by incorporating more carbon into growing trees. South Korea, beginning in the early seventies, launched a reforestation effort to replant barren hillsides that could supply the wood needed in rural villages. In less than a decade, Korean villagers planted an area in fast-growing pines that approximates two thirds of the area in rice, the national food staple.[30]

A similar situation is unfolding in China, though on a much larger scale. The share of the country's territory covered by trees has increased from just 8 percent in 1960 to 12.7 percent today. The goal is to have 20 percent of the country forested again by the end of the century, assuring wood supplies and restoring stability to degraded lands. Reaching this target will store millions of tons of carbon in trees. Unfortunately, Chinese energy plans also call for a heavy increase in coal burning during this same period.[31]

Reforestation in industrial countries can also contribute needed carbon storage. Tree planting in England and Scotland is restoring cover to land that has been bare of forests for centuries. Italy encourages reforestation on abandoned hillside farmland.[32]

In the United States, Congress in effect endorsed a major carbon storage program with passage of the Food Security Act of 1985. The aim is to plant grass and trees on 45 million acres (18 million hectares) of highly erodible cropland, designated as a conservation reserve. Farmers are paid to enroll erosion-prone land in the reserve. Although unusually high crop subsidies in 1986 slowed the sign-up, more normal market conditions will make the reserve an attractive economic option. Most of the land is likely to be seeded to grass, but an estimated 5 million acres will be planted to trees. Both grass and trees will store more carbon than cropland that is plowed each year.[33]

Balancing the carbon equation is not the only step needed to slow global warming. Methane, nitrous oxide, synthetic chlorofluorocarbons, and other trace gases—some of which are increasing in concentration more rapidly than carbon dioxide—collectively may contribute as much to the greenhouse warming as CO_2 does. But because virtually every country either burns fossil fuels or is losing forests, a commitment to restore equilibrium to the carbon cycle is one all countries could embrace.[34]

A SECOND ENERGY REVOLUTION

Over the 14 years since the Organization of Petroleum Exporting Countries (OPEC) first engineered an oil price increase, world energy demand has increased only modestly. Efforts to ameliorate the effects of higher prices through energy conservation led to innovative technologies and policies that helped nations use energy more efficiently than ever before. The energy used per unit of world economic output has declined by over 12 percent since 1973. And this fall appears likely to continue for the foreseeable future, though it may slow temporarily due to the weakening of oil prices.[35]

Though the first post-OPEC energy revolution is far from having run its course, a second revolution is now needed—one that responds to longer-term environmental and economic concerns. Designing an energy strategy that will maintain the earth's habitability will be far more demanding than allowing price signals alone to set the course. The challenge facing policymakers and energy planners is to reduce emissions of CO_2, sulfur dioxide, and nitrogen oxides by further increasing energy efficiency and accelerating the shift to renewable sources of energy.

The first energy revolution succeeded in stabilizing CO_2 emissions from fossil fuels. The aim of the second revolution is to reduce emissions of carbon dioxide to slow the warming trend now under way. Enormous opportunities exist to boost the energy efficiency of the world economy, ranging from increasing the fuel efficiency of automobiles to designing and distributing more-efficient wood cookstoves in Third World cities.

The existing world automobile fleet travels an average of 18 miles per gallon of fuel, a poor reflection of the technical possibilities. (See Table 11–3.) The most efficient cars today include the gasoline-powered Honda Civic, which gets 47 miles to the gallon, and the Volkswagen diesel, which travels 45 miles per gallon. Test vehicles under study in the United States and Europe go far beyond this, achieving 60–100 miles per gallon. When vehicles like these become commercially available, doubling the fuel efficiency of the world fleet will simply be a matter of time. With an average fuel

Table 11-3. Fuel Efficiency of Selected Four-Passenger Automobiles

Car	Status	Fuel Economy (miles/gallon)	Curb Weight (kilogram)
1981 VW Rabbit (gasoline)	commercial	30	945
1981 VW Rabbit (diesel)	commercial	45	945
Honda City Car (gasoline)	commercial	47	655
VW Experimental Car 2000	prototype	62	786
Volvo LCP 2000	prototype	65	707
Cummins/NASA Lewis Car	design	79	1,360
Volvo LCP (potential)	design	85	—
Pertran Car (diesel version)	design	100–105	545

SOURCE: Robert H. Williams, "Potential Roles for Bioenergy in an Energy-Efficient World," *Ambio*, Vol. 14, No. 4–5, 1985.

efficiency of 36 miles per gallon, a world fleet 50 percent larger than today's could run on 25 percent less fuel.

Appropriate policies can yield efficiency gains of this magnitude in relatively short order. In the United States, standards adopted for automobiles in 1976 nearly doubled the fuel efficiency of new cars in little more than a decade, from 14 miles per gallon in 1974 to 26 in 1986. A government decision to double efficiency again by the turn of the century could slow the increase in CO_2 emissions and acid rain in the late twentieth and early twenty-first centuries. Unfortunately, two of the major U.S. automobile manufacturers, General Motors and Ford, convinced the government to reduce the fuel efficiency standard from 27.5 to 26 miles per gallon for cars sold after 1985.[36]

By contrast, significant progress toward increasing the energy efficiency of electrical household appliances has been achieved, driven largely by market forces. Added impetus came in August 1986, when environmentalists and U.S. appliance manufacturers agreed in principle on standards for all refrigerators, freezers, water heaters, air conditioners, dishwashers, furnaces, and kitchen ranges marketed in the United States. Congress passed the National Appliance Energy Conservation Act in October 1986, which requires major appliances to be 15–25 percent more energy-efficient by 1990 than they were in 1985.[37]

Unfortunately, President Reagan "pocket vetoed" this bill while Congress was out of session in early November, so the measure will have to be reintroduced in 1987. This legislation could reduce consumer energy bills by an estimated $28 billion by the end of the century. The need to build 22,000 megawatts of new electrical generating capacity would be avoided, restraining CO_2 emissions commensurately.[38]

Patterns of energy use are dramatically different in the Third World, but the same principles of policy and technology can be applied to increase energy efficiency. In West Africa, Burkina Faso has launched a nationwide effort to encourage more efficient cookstoves in both rural and urban areas. The U.N. Sudano-Sahelian Office and the Swedish government have cooperated to develop four types of improved stoves that use 40–60 percent less fuelwood than traditional three-stone hearths. The new stoves, which cost between $2 and $4 apiece, also take advantage of standardization—they are designed to accommodate Burkina Faso's four standard cooking pots, saving on materials and making mass production cheaper.[39]

Renewable energy sources are destined to play a much larger role during the second energy revolution. Hydropower is the source that can most quickly make a large contribution to energy supplies. Canada, with 100,000 megawatts of undeveloped hydropower potential, is looking south, toward the U.S. market. Increased U.S. reliance on Canadian hydropower could help some regions shift from dependence on oil- and coal-fired power, which produces CO_2 and the acid precipitation that has recently soured U.S.-Canadian relations. Canadian utilities already market electricity in New England, New York State, the upper Midwest, and the West Coast.[40]

China expects to develop 13,000 megawatts of generating capacity at the Three Gorges site on the Chang Jiang (Yangtze) River, in the world's largest hydropower project. At least 300,000 Chinese would be resettled from the reservoir site and 13,000 hectares of cropland would be inundated. Chinese planners are weighing the costs of these environmental and social disruptions against those of generating 13,000 megawatts with coal, the country's principal alternative. China's stakes in averting a global warming are high, because the country's most densely settled provinces are coastal and thus at risk from a rise in sea level.[41]

The large-scale development of any energy source has always involved such environmental trade-offs. The need to balance local environmental costs against transboundary and global consequences has become especially acute. The British are considering constructing a barrage across the Severn Estuary that would capture the energy in estuarine tidal flows, producing some 7,200 megawatts of power at a price competitive with coal-fired or nuclear electricity.[42]

Other European countries, which bear the brunt of England's sulfur dioxide emissions, would undoubtedly welcome the Severn project. But the biological effects of the possible disruption of estuarine processes are poorly understood. Because tidal flows would be restrained, pollutants from adjacent communities might accumulate more rapidly in the estuary. A consortium of private power companies, the Central Electricity Generating Board, and the British government is now doing feasibility studies of this project.[43]

As discussed in Chapter 9, several European countries have begun to map out energy strategies that reflect a decided step away from fossil fuels. Before Chernobyl, West Germany's planned shift to non-fossil-fuel generating capacity included a significantly expanded reliance on nuclear power—although support for this approach diminished following the accident. Sweden is embarking on a more ambitious and progressive path that includes a planned phaseout of nuclear power as well as a reduction in oil use. Energy savings in new buildings and homes will help cut total energy demand, and wind, water, and cogeneration will provide incremental energy supplies.[44]

The benefits of the second energy revolution are impossible to measure precisely. Progress must be evaluated not only in strict economic terms, but in averted climate change, reduced acidification, and the avoided damages and costs of adjusting to these changes. One such estimate has been made by H.C. Cheng and his colleagues at Brookhaven National Laboratory, who analyzed how adoption of energy-efficient technologies could affect global CO_2 emissions by the year 2050. They assumed roughly the same reliance on fossil fuels as at present, and found that an aggressive commitment to energy efficiency could hold power plant emissions of CO_2 to 7 billion tons worldwide. By contrast, if efficiency remained at levels reached in the mid-seventies, annual CO_2 emissions would rise to 17 billion tons.[45]

CENTERS OF DECISION

As with the new science research agenda, policies to complete the demographic transition, balance the carbon cycle, and launch the second energy revolution will have to be global, cooperative, and interdisciplinary. The consequences of domestic policies no longer stop at national borders. Irresponsible energy policies in one country can lead to undesired acidification of the environment in dozens of others. Failed population policies contribute to uncontrolled migration of people in search of jobs. Slow progress on energy efficiency can force countries to invest in generating capacity that will accelerate global climate change.

The question facing the world's leaders is how responsibility for the new global problems will be shared in the international community. Continued population growth, the accumulation of greenhouse gases, and the clearing of tropical forests are a class of problems whose consequences are cumulative, whose causes are interactive, and whose effects transcend national boundaries. The world has few effective models for managing such complex problems. The

U.S. National Research Council has pointed out "the frequently large mismatch between the scales or jurisdictional boundaries of management authority and the scales of ecological phenomena involved."[46]

For some of the major adjustments facing humanity, a relatively small number of countries hold the key to success.

The issues are global, but in the absence of global authorities only national governments can implement policies. For example, goals for restraining CO_2 emissions can be set at the international level, but programs to reach those goals will be carried out by national authorities. For some of the major adjustments facing humanity, a relatively small number of countries hold the key to success. Identifying those centers of decision and building momentum in key countries can help the world avoid the potentially disastrous global changes now in prospect.

The first imperative, and one toward which the world is making hesitant progress, is the balancing of birth rates and death rates needed to complete the demographic transition. Responsibility for stopping population growth lies both in the remaining high-growth regions that have the highest stake in averting the consequences of continued rapid population growth, and in the low-growth regions that can provide the financial and technical assistance for successful family planning programs.

World population increased by 83 million in 1986. Two countries, India and China, adding 18 and 11 million, respectively, accounted for 35 percent of this increment. If world population is to be slowed, each of these population giants will have to play a major role. China is already doing so. With its one-child program, it has reduced its annual addition from a peak of 22 million in 1971. If China stays on course, its population will stop growing by the end of the century or shortly thereafter.[47]

Overall food production gains in India since the Green Revolution began two decades ago have eliminated imports, but they have raised per capita food consumption only marginally. In addition, these national trends mask vast regional disparities that embrace what Indian economist Ashok Rudra has called "islands of modern agriculture" in a sea of traditional technology. These regional imbalances, and the political stresses they generate, could undermine India's future.[48]

The United States and the Soviet Union generate 23 and 18 percent of global CO$_2$ emissions, respectively.

India cannot remain in the middle stage of the demographic transition much longer. It needs to project the interplay of the country's demographic, environmental, and economic trends to the year 2010. The Indian National Trust for Art and Cultural Heritage, a nongovernmental organization chaired by Prime Minister Rajiv Gandhi, has already published some insightful reports on India's environment and natural resources and might provide a forum for thoughtful analysis of the country's future by many Indian institutions. Such an exercise could establish the analytical underpinning needed for new policy initiatives and the information needed to raise public awareness of the threat posed by continuing population growth and related problems.[49]

Certain countries play a disproportionate role in shaping regional prospects as well. In Africa, Nigeria and

Egypt account for one quarter of the continent's 26 million annual births. And in Latin America, Brazil and Mexico are responsible for more than half the births. If the regions of the Third World with rapid population growth are to escape the demographic trap, rapid fertility declines in these key countries are essential.[50]

Developing countries that have successfully initiated fertility declines—such as China, Thailand, and Zimbabwe—can assist other Third World countries to develop family planning programs. Such South-South cooperation, though it holds great promise, has not yet been exploited. And the industrial countries that are approaching zero population growth can play an instrumental role in helping the world complete the demographic transition. These nations carry most of the burden for research and development of new contraceptives, and provide much of the financial assistance that supports Third World family planning programs.

Family planning needs are quite different in high-growth/low-income societies than in those that have achieved population stability. Long-acting, inexpensive contraceptives are needed by Third World women whose contact with clinics and physicians is sporadic at best. Some promising methods on the horizon include a birth control vaccine, now being tested in Australia, that prevents pregnancy for up to two years, and a pill that can be used to induce menstruation after intercourse. Methods like these could help prevent pregnancy and space births better than existing contraceptives, improving the health of mothers and children.[51]

But several forces in industrial countries make progress toward these and other effective contraceptives slower than it need be. Private companies have little incentive to develop such long-acting, low-cost contraceptives. The skyrocketing cost of liability insurance in the United States is forcing some pharmaceutical companies to abandon their efforts to develop new birth control methods altogether. And public ambivalence toward contraception and abortion in the United States is eroding support for the government-sponsored research that could counterbalance private-sector biases. Worldwide, research spending on reproductive health, new contraceptives, and birth control safety declined by over one third in real terms between the early seventies and the early eighties.[52]

Coupled with the uncertainty surrounding U.S. official family planning assistance, this decline in contraceptive research and development is cause for concern. Family planning choices are still largely limited to methods that have been available for at least 25 years—while the world population continues to grow and the share of the population entering its childbearing years reaches unprecedented size. Governments that could be doing the most to produce safer and more effective contraceptives matched to the needs of high-growth regions have been slow to accept responsibility for helping to complete the demographic transition.

The centers of decision for balancing the global carbon cycle are fewer. Although all countries contribute some CO_2 emissions by burning fossil fuels, a few countries account for the lion's share. (See Table 11–4.) The United States and the Soviet Union generate 23 and 18 percent of global CO_2 emissions, respectively. With the addition of China, three countries account for nearly half of the global total. Although an effective response by these three giants would not ensure sufficient control over the CO_2 buildup, it could enhance greatly the global chance of success. And other countries would likely follow their lead.

The role of the United States, the Soviet Union, and China is even greater than their current share of carbon emis-

Table 11-4. Carbon Emissions from Fossil Fuel Burning, 1983

Country	Emissions	Share
	(million metric tons)	(percent)
United States	1,138	23
Soviet Union	911	18
China	440	9
Japan	224	4
West Germany	179	4
United Kingdom	141	3
Poland	113	2
France	103	2
Italy	91	2
East Germany	82	2
All Other	1,591	32
World	5,013	100[1]

[1]Does not add to 100 due to rounding.
SOURCES: Worldwatch Institute estimates based on data from United Nations and from World Resources Institute/International Institute for Environment and Development, *World Resources 1986* (New York: Basic Books, 1986).

sions indicates because they also possess nearly two thirds of the world's remaining coal—by far the most abundant fossil fuel. Their decisions about exploiting these coal resources will bear heavily on future world climate.[53]

To halt tropical deforestation, which contributes carbon to the atmosphere and also diminishes biological diversity, dozens of tropical countries have a role to play. But within this group, forest management in three key countries could play a disproportionate role in carbon storage. Brazil, Indonesia, and Zaire encompass 577 million hectares of remaining rain forests—48 percent of the closed forests in the tropics in 1980. Unfortunately, Brazil and Indonesia are both pursuing national resettlement programs that will reduce the remaining rain forest area, and Zaire has shown little leadership in the management of the largest expanse of tropical forest on the African continent.[54]

The problems of acidification and CFC emissions relate to processes that are currently concentrated in industrial countries. But efforts to reduce acidification need to be focused on all countries heavily dependent on grades of coal with high sulfur content and in those with large automobile fleets. For the most part, controlling acidification lies in the hands of the northern tier of industrial countries. China and India, however, are now burning enough coal to create serious acidification problems.

The number of industrial countries manufacturing chlorofluorocarbons is also relatively small. As the consensus on depletion of the ozone layer takes shape, curbing the production of these industrial gases should not be unmanageable. A promising step was taken in September 1986 by a consortium of U.S. firms. An industry group called the Alliance for Responsible CFC Policy announced that its 500 members were prepared to support international limits on CFC production.[55]

Although the announcement endorsed limits on only the rate of growth in production, rather than setting an absolute ceiling, it marked a departure for a trade group that in the past opposed global controls and disputed the scientific evidence suggesting danger to the ozone layer. The announcement offers a promising precedent for the balancing of public and private interests on which sucessful efforts to restrain global changes will rest.

If the second energy revolution succeeds, it will be because research and development efforts emphasize energy technologies suited to the needs of Third World countries that face rapid growth in the demand for energy. Industrial countries have traditionally been the developers of innovative technologies; unfortunately, industrial-country interests have tended to promote Third World adoption of technologies that have failed economic and environmental tests in their own societies. Aggressive promotion of nuclear power, the clearest and most costly example, has slowed in the aftermath of the Chernobyl accident.

No widely shared vision exists of the need for worldwide progress to stabilize population, control carbon emissions, and revolutionize energy-using technologies. No agenda or five-point plan has been drafted that confronts or even acknowledges the most serious challenges facing the world in the decades ahead. It is characteristic of what historian Barbara Tuchman has called the "Age of Disruption" that leaders find their time and imagination eroded by immediate crises; few devote their talents to the statecraft and "planetcraft" that global problems demand.[56]

Responsible decision making in an age of global effects requires more information on the consequences of our actions than ever. The international scientific community has taken the lead by proposing the Global Change study. But simply studying global dynamics and global disruptions is not enough. Social, economic, and political initiatives commensurate with global changes are needed. The values that guide the management of technology in modern societies have not been clearly articulated, and the need for cooperation is not yet widely recognized in a world where diplomacy remains tied to anachronistic definitions of national sovereignty.

Technological and demographic changes are leading us into the twenty-first century with political institutions inherited from the nineteenth. The need to comprehend our responsibility in time to exercise it successfully presses upon us. That we know so little about the consequences of our activities is humbling. That we have brought so much responsibility upon ourselves is sobering.

The threats that emerge as we cross

natural thresholds are no longer hypothetical. Already environmental deterioration and mounting external debt are combining to reduce living standards in scores of Third World countries. Incomes in Africa have fallen by nearly one fifth since 1970, and in Latin America by several percent since 1981. Reversing these trends will not be easy.

A sustainable future calls upon us simultaneously to arrest the carbon dioxide buildup, protect the ozone layer, restore forests and soils, stop population growth, boost energy efficiency, and develop renewable energy sources. No generation has ever faced such a complex set of issues requiring immediate attention. Preceding generations have always been concerned about the future, but we are the first to be faced with decisions that will determine whether the earth our children inherit will be habitable.

The course corrections needed to restore a worldwide improvement in the human condition have no precedent. And they may not be possible if the militarization that is hampering international cooperation and preempting leadership time, fiscal resources, and scientific personnel continues. Anyone contemplating the scale of the needed adjustments is drawn inescapably to one principal conclusion: The time has come to make peace with each other so that we can make peace with the earth.

Notes

Chapter 1. Thresholds of Change

1. National Science Foundation, "National Ozone Expedition Statement," press release, Washington, D.C., October 20, 1986; National Aeronautics and Space Administration (NASA), "Present State of Knowledge of the Upper Atmosphere" (draft), Washington, D.C., January 1986; United States Environmental Protection Agency (EPA), "Analysis of Strategies for Protecting the Ozone Layer," prepared for the Working Group Meeting, Geneva, Switzerland, January 1985; National Research Council, *Causes and Effects of Changes in Stratospheric Ozone: Update 1983* (Washington, D.C.: National Academy Press, 1984).

2. P.D. Jones et al., "Global Temperature Variations Between 1861 and 1984," *Nature*, July 31, 1986; "Warming of Alaskan Tundra Linked to Use of Fossil Fuels," *New York Times*, November 1, 1986.

3. "World's Population to Reach Milestone of 5 Billion Today," *Washington Post*, July 7, 1986; figures on the number of young people entering reproductive years over the next generation derived by Worldwatch from Population Reference Bureau, *1986 World Population Data Sheet* (Washington, D.C.: 1986).

4. Philip Shabecoff, "Action is Urged To Save Species," *New York Times*, September 28, 1986; Roger Lewin, "A Mass Extinction Without Asteroids," *Science*, October 3, 1986; Boyce Rensberger, "Scientists See Mass Extinction As Rainforests Are Cleared," *Washington Post*, September 29, 1986.

5. "Ukrainian Nuclear Fire Spreads Wide Tragedy With Radiation Cloud," *Wall Street Journal*, April 30, 1986; "Soviet Union Hit By Nuclear Disaster," *Christian Science Monitor*, April 30, 1986.

6. For more information on the Food Security Act of 1985, see R. Neil Sampson, "A Landmark for Soil Conservation," *American Land Forum Magazine*, Spring 1986; Tim T. Phipps, "The Farm Bill, Resources and Environmental Quality," *Resources*, Winter 1986.

7. Herman E. Daly, "Toward a New Economic Model," *Bulletin of the Atomic Scientists*, April 1986.

8. See G.H.M. Krause et al., "Forest Decline in Europe: Possible Causes and Etiology," paper presented at the International Symposium on Acid Precipitation, Ontario, Canada, September 1985; see also Susan Tifft, "Requiem for the Forest," *Time* (international edition), September 16, 1985.

9. Cropland area from United States Department of Agriculture (USDA), Economic Research Service (ERS), *World Indices of Agricultural and Food Production 1950–85* (unpublished printout) (Washington, D.C.: 1986).

10. Der Bundesminister Für Ernährung, Landwirtschaft, und Forsten, "Neuartige Waldschäden in der Bundesrepublik Deutschland," Bonn, West Germany, October 1983; Federal Ministry of Food, Agriculture, and Forestry, "1984 Forest Damage

Survey," Bonn, West Germany, October 1984.

11. See Sandra Postel, "Protecting Forests from Air Pollution and Acid Rain," in Lester R. Brown et al., *State of the World-1985* (New York: W.W. Norton & Co., 1985).

12. D.W. Schindler et al., "Long-Term Ecosystem Stress: The Effect of Years of Experimental Acidification on a Small Lake," *Science*, June 21, 1985.

13. Byron W. Bache, "The Acidification of Soils," and B. Ulrich, "Production and Consumption of Hydrogen Ions in the Ecosphere," in T.C. Hutchinson and M. Havas, eds., *Effects of Acid Precipitation on Terrestrial Ecosystems* (New York: Plenum Press, 1980); Tomas Paces, "Sources of Acidification in Central Europe Estimated from Elemental Budgets in Small Basins," *Nature*, May 2, 1985; Jan Nilsson, "Soil is Vulnerable Too," *Acid* (Sweden), August 1986.

14. J.P. Malingreau et al., "Remote Sensing of Forest Fires: Kalimantan and North Borneo 1982–83," *Ambio*, Vol. 14, No. 6, 1985.

15. Ibid.

16. World Bank, "The 1983–84 Drought in Sub-Saharan Africa—Short Term Impact —Desertification and Other Long-Term Issues" (draft), Washington, D.C., May 1984.

17. Lester R. Brown, "Conserving Soils," in Lester R. Brown et al., *State of the World-1984* (New York: W.W. Norton & Co., 1984).

18. Preindustrial concentration of CO_2 from Eric W. Wolff and David A. Peel, "The Record of Global Pollution in Polar Snow and Ice," *Nature*, February 14, 1985; atmospheric levels of CO_2 at Mauna Loa from Charles D. Keeling, Scripps Institution of Oceanography, private communication, June 26, 1986, updating C.D. Keeling et al., "Measurements of the Concentration of Carbon Dioxide at Mauna Loa Observatory, Hawaii," in William C. Clark, ed., *Carbon Dioxide*

Review (Cambridge: Oxford University Press, 1982).

19. Robert E. Dickinson and Ralph J. Cicerone, "Future Global Warming From Atmospheric Trace Gases," *Nature*, January 9, 1986.

20. B.B. Vohra, *The Greening of India* (New Delhi: The Indian National Trust for Art and Cultural Heritage (INTACH), 1985); B.B. Vohra, *Land and Water: Towards a Policy for Life Support Systems* (New Delhi: INTACH, 1985); Janaki Nair, "Many Faces Of Drought," *Economic and Political Weekly*, May 3, 1986.

21. Peter M. Vitousek et al., "Human Appropriation of the Products of Photosynthesis," *BioScience*, June 1986.

22. Ratios of tree cutting to tree planting from United Nations Food and Agriculture Organization (FAO), Forest Resources Division, *Tropical Forest Resources*, Forestry Paper 30 (Rome: 1982); Eneas Salati and Peter B. Vose, "Amazon Basin: A System in Equilibrium," *Science*, July 13, 1984.

23. The amount of energy (oil equivalent) used in agriculture is a Worldwatch Institute figure based on the amount of oil embodied in the manufacture and maintenance of farm machinery and inputs such as fertilizers and pesticides, and the amount of energy needed to run tractors and irrigation pumps. No aggregate data exist for global pesticide use, so this was assumed to be 20 percent of the total energy for all other categories. Energy used in the manufacture of fertilizer and fabrication of farm machinery based on David Pimentel, *Handbook of Energy Utilization in Agriculture* (Boca Raton, Fla.: CRC Press, 1980); energy consumed by tractors based on USDA, *Agricultural Statistics* (Washington, D.C.: U.S. Government Printing Office, various years); energy for irrigation pumping based on Gordon Sloggett, *Energy and U.S. Agriculture: Irrigation Pumping, 1974–83* (Washington, D.C.: U.S. Government Printing Office, 1985); total fertilizer

consumption from FAO, *Fertilizer Yearbooks* (Rome: various years); world irrigated area from W.R. Rangeley, "Irrigation and Drainage in the World," paper presented at the International Conference on Food and Water, Texas A&M University, College Station, May 26–30, 1985, and from W.R. Rangeley, "Irrigation—Current Trends and a Future Perspective," World Bank Seminar, February 1983.

24. World oil production data from American Petroleum Institute (API), *Basic Petroleum Data Book* (Washington, D.C.: 1986); growth in world grain production from USDA, ERS, *World Indices.*

25. Oil production 1973–85 and world oil production in 1985 from API, *Basic Petroleum Data Book;* grain production from USDA, ERS, *World Indices.*

26. U.S. oil imports from British Petroleum Company, *BP Statistical Review of World Energy* (London: 1986).

27. Indian flooding due to deforestation in the Himalayan watershed from John Spears, "Preserving Watershed Environments," *Unasylva,* No. 137, 1982; siltation in the hydroelectric facilities of Central America from Catherine Caufield, *Tropical Moist Forests: The Resource, the People, the Threat* (Washington, D.C.: Earthscan/International Institute for Environment and Development, 1982).

28. Amount of carbon released into the atmosphere, total and per person, from Gregg Marland and Ralph M. Rotty, *Carbon Dioxide Emissions from Fossil Fuels: A Procedure For Estimation and Results For 1950–81* (Washington, D.C.: U.S. Department of Energy, 1983).

29. Information on the West German wood market from Von H. Steinlin, "Waldsterben und Raumordung" (draft), Albert-Ludwigs University, Freiburg, West Germany, 1986; H.J. Ewers et al., "Zur Monetarisierung der Waldschäden in der Bundesrepublik Deutschland," paper presented at Symposium on Costs of Environmental Pollution, Bonn, West Germany, September 12–13, 1985.

30. Debora MacKenzie, "Acid Rain May Trigger Alpine Avalanches," *New Scientist,* January 2, 1986.

31. Ann Henderson-Sellers and Kendall McGuffie, "The Threat From Melting Icecaps," *New Scientist,* June 12, 1986.

32. Ibid.

33. Joseph Lelyveld, "Dutch Inaugurate Dike, a $2.4 Billion Marvel," *New York Times,* October 5, 1986.

34. Thorkild Jacobsen and Robert M. Adams, "Salt and Silt in Ancient Mesopotamian Agriculture," *Science,* November 21, 1958; Diane E. Gelburd, "Managing Salinity: Lessons from the Past," *Journal of Soil and Water Conservation,* July/August 1985.

35. Jacobsen and Adams, "Ancient Mesopotamian Agriculture"; Gelburd, "Managing Salinity."

36. Jacobsen and Adams, "Ancient Mesopotamian Agriculture."

37. Norman Hammond, "The Emergence of Mayan Civilization," *Scientific American,* August 1986; Robert J. Sharer, "Mathematics and the Maya Collapse" (a review of *The Dynamics of Apocalypse*), *The Sciences,* May/June 1986.

38. Sharer, "Mathematics and the Maya Collapse."

39. John W.G. Lowe, *The Dynamics of Apocalypse* (Albuquerque, N.M.: University of New Mexico Press, 1985).

40. Per capita grain production in Africa and Latin America from USDA, ERS, *World Indices.*

41. For a discussion of food-related riots, see Lester R. Brown and Edward C. Wolf,

"Assessing Ecological Decline," in Lester R. Brown et al., *State of the World-1986* (New York: W.W. Norton & Co., 1986).

42. Earth System Sciences Committee, *Earth System Science Overview: A Program for Global Change* (Washington, D.C.: National Aeronautics and Space Administration, 1986).

43. Additions to world population from Population Reference Bureau, *1986 World Population Data Sheet.*

44. W.H. Lindner, World Commission on Environment and Development, Geneva, Switzerland, private communication, November 5, 1986.

Chapter 2. Analyzing the Demographic Trap

1. The demographic transition theory is a term first used by Frank W. Notestein in 1945 in reference to the experience of Western Europe; it was later applied to the Third World. See Regina McNamara, "Demographic Transition Theory," *International Encyclopedia of Population,* Vol. 1 (New York: MacMillan Publishing Co., 1982).

2. Frank W. Notestein, Dudley Kirk, and Sheldon Segal, "The Problem of Population Control," in Philip M. Hauser, ed., *The Population Dilemma* (Englewood Cliffs, N.J.: Prentice Hall, Inc., 1963).

3. Population figures throughout this chapter, unless indicated otherwise, from Population Reference Bureau, *1986 World Population Data Sheet* (Washington, D.C.: 1986).

4. United Nations Food and Agriculture Organization (FAO) and United Nations Fund for Population Activities (UNFPA), *Expert Consultation Report on Land Resources for Populations of the Future* (Rome: 1982).

5. Ibid.

6. Ibid.

7. World Bank, *Desertification in the Sahelian and Sudanian Zones of West Africa* (Washington, D.C.: 1985).

8. Ibid.

9. James Nations and H. Jeffrey Leonard, "Grounds of Conflict in Central America," in Andrew Maguire and Janet Welsh Brown, *Bordering on Trouble: Resources and Politics in Latin America* (Bethesda, Md.: Adler & Adler, 1986).

10. Three stages in the population/natural support system relationship are discussed in Kenneth Newcombe, *An Economic Justification for Rural Afforestation: The Case of Ethiopia,* Energy Department Paper No. 16 (Washington, D.C.: World Bank, 1984).

11. Herbert R. Block, *The Planetary Product in 1980: A Creative Pause?* (Washington, D.C.: U.S. Department of State, 1981).

12. Ibid.; International Monetary Fund, *World Economic Outlook* (Washington, D.C.: May 1986).

13. Grain production data derived from U.S. Department of Agriculture (USDA), Economic Research Service (ERS), *World Indices of Agricultural and Food Production 1950–85* (unpublished printout) (Washington, D.C.: 1986).

14. For a discussion of Mexico's debt problems, see John C. Pool and Stephen C. Stamos Jr., "Devising a Bankruptcy Plan for Mexico," *New York Times,* June 8, 1986, and Robert Pear, "Hard Times in Mexico Cause Concern in U.S.," *New York Times,* October 19, 1986; Brazil's foreign debt discussed in Alan Riding, "Brazil Gets Back on the Fast Track," *New York Times,* October 12, 1986; U.S. federal debt reported in U.S. Census Bureau, *Statistical Abstract of the United States 1986* (Washington, D.C.: U.S. Government Printing Office, 1986).

15. USDA, ERS, *World Indices.*

16. Ibid.

17. Changes in per capita income 1979–84 from B. Blazic-Metzner, Economic Analysis and Projections Department, World Bank, Washington, D.C., private communication, July 25, 1986; per capita income data for 1985 from David Cieslikowski, Economic Analysis and Projections Department, World Bank, Washington, D.C., private communication, October 22, 1986; data for 1986 from USDA, ERS, *World Situation and Outlook Report* (Washington, D.C.: June 1986).

18. Radha Singha, *Landlessness: A Growing Problem* (Rome: FAO, 1984).

19. Ibid.

20. Inderjit Singh, *Small Farmers and the Landless in South Asia* (draft) (Washington, D.C.: World Bank, July 1981).

21. For information on Brazil's resettlement programs, see Philip M. Fearnside, "Spatial Concentration of Deforestation in the Brazilian Amazon," *Ambio*, Vol. 15, No. 2, 1986, and Mac Margolis, "Land Disputes Trigger Wave of Violence in Brazil," *Washington Post*, August 29, 1985; Indonesia's resettlement program is described in Nicholas Guppy, "Tropical Deforestation: A Global View," *Foreign Affairs*, Spring 1984.

22. Singha, *Landlessness: A Growing Problem.*

23. Nazli Choucri, *Population and Conflict* (New York: UNFPA, 1983); Howard Wiarda and Iêda Siquiera Wiarda, *Population, Internal Unrest, and U.S. Security in Latin America* (Amherst, Mass.: International Area Studies Programs, 1985).

24. Sergio Diaz-Briquets, *Conflict in Central America: The Demographic Dimension*, Population Trends and Public Policy No. 10 (Washington, D.C.: Population Reference Bureau, 1986).

25. Georgie Anne Geyer, "Our Disintegrating World: The Menace of Global Anarchy," in Encyclopedia Britannica, Inc., *1985 Britannica Book of the Year* (Chicago: 1985).

26. "Africa Struggles for Food Security," *Journal of Commerce*, May 22, 1986.

27. Wiarda and Siquiera Wiarda, *Population, Internal Unrest, and U.S. Security.*

28. Jorge Castaneda, "Mexico's Coming Challenges," *Foreign Policy*, Fall 1986.

29. Ibid.

30. Ibid.

31. Ibid.

32. Grain production data in Egypt from USDA, ERS, *World Indices.*

33. Paul Jabber, "Egypt's Crisis, America's Dilemma," *Foreign Affairs*, Summer 1986.

34. John Kifner, "Egypt's Army Praised in Quelling Riots, But For Mubarak, Crisis Is Not Over," *New York Times*, March 9, 1986; Hirsh Goodman, "The Terrible Tide," *New Republic*, March 24, 1986. See also John Kifner, "The Egyptian Economy Has No Place To Turn," *New York Times*, July 6, 1986.

35. Per capita income distribution in Central America from Diaz-Briquets, *Conflict in Central America.*

36. Data on income distribution from World Bank, *World Development Report 1986* (New York: Oxford University Press, 1986).

37. USDA, ERS, *World Indices.*

38. John C. Pool and Stephen C. Stamos Jr., "Devising a Bankruptcy Plan for Mexico," *New York Times*, June 8, 1986.

39. Robert J. Sharer, "Mathematics and the Maya Collapse" (a review of *The Dynamics of Apocalypse*), *The Sciences*, May/June 1986.

Chapter 3. Assessing the Future of Urbanization

1. Number of people living in cities in 1950 from Bertrand Renaud, *National Urbanization Policies in Developing Countries*, Staff

Working Paper No. 347 (Washington, D.C.: World Bank, 1981); number in 1986 from Population Reference Bureau, *1986 World Population Data Sheet* (Washington, D.C.: 1986).

2. For a discussion of the historical evolution of cities throughout the world, see Lewis Mumford, *The City in History* (Orlando, Fla.: Harcourt, Brace, Jovanovich, 1961).

3. Renaud, *Urbanization in Developing Countries.*

4. Mumford, *The City in History.*

5. Percentage of British living in cities in 1800 from Andrew Lees, *Cities Perceived: Urban Society in European and American Thought, 1820–1940* (New York: Columbia University Press, 1985).

6. Population Reference Bureau, *1986 World Population Data Sheet.* The definition of an urban area differs from country to country and by region. What is considered a city in relatively unurbanized Africa may not be considered a city in Asia; minimum city size for the purposes of definition may vary from 10,000 to over 20,000 people. Global and regional percentages used throughout this chapter are United Nations averages based on individual country censuses.

7. Rafael M. Salas, *The State of World Population 1986* (New York: United Nations Fund for Population Activities (UNFPA), 1986).

8. Ricardo Jordan, "Population and the Planning of Large Cities in Latin America," paper presented at the International Conference on Population and the Urban Future sponsored by UNFPA, Barcelona, Spain, May 19–22, 1986.

9. Aderanti Adepoju, "Population and the Planning of Large Cities in Africa," paper presented at UNFPA Conference.

10. Aprodicio A. Laquian, "Population and the Planning of Large Cities in Asia," paper presented at UNFPA Conference.

11. Ibid.

12. Salas, *The State of World Population 1986.*

13. Lees, *Cities Perceived.*

14. Jeffrey Bartholet, "Mediterranean's 'Pearl' Now Awash in Raw Sewage," *Washington Post,* August 21, 1986.

15. Survey on African households from Adepoju, "Large Cities in Africa."

16. Weltstädte defined in Lees, *Cities Perceived;* Salas, *The State of World Population 1986.*

17. Jonathan Kandell, "Nation in Jeopardy: Mexico City's Growth Once Fostered, Turns Into Economic Burden," *Wall Street Journal,* October 4, 1985.

18. For urban economic concentration in Mexico, the Philippines, and others, see Jorge E. Hardoy and David Satterthwaite, "Third World Cities and the Environment of Poverty," *Geoforum,* Vol. 15, No. 3, 1984.

19. Andrew Hamer, *Brazilian Industrialization and Economic Concentration in Sao Paulo: A Survey* (Washington, D.C.: World Bank, Water Supply and Urban Development Department, 1982).

20. United Nations Department of International Economic and Social Affairs (DIESA), *Population Growth and Policies in Mega-Cities: Metro Manila,* Population Policy Paper No. 5 (New York: 1986).

21. Food prices rise in the 1972–76 period from International Monetary Fund, *International Financial Statistics Yearbooks* (Washington, D.C.: various years).

22. For information on Egypt's subsidies and the economic burden they impose, see Christopher S. Wren, "Cairo Seems to Lose a Chance to Prosper in a Time of Peace," *New York Times,* August 23, 1986, and John Kifner, "The Egyptian Economy Has No Place To Turn," *New York Times,* July 6, 1986. A detailed discussion of different kinds of subsidies and their various ramifications can be found in Grant Scobie, "Food Consumption

Policies" (background paper prepared for World Bank, *World Development Report 1986*), Ruakura Agricultural Research Center, Hamilton, New Zealand, August 1985.

23. Total energy used in the United States food system from David Pimentel, *Handbook of Energy Utilization in Agriculture* (Boca Raton, Fla.: CRC Press, 1980).

24. Sandra Postel, "Protecting Forests," in Lester R. Brown et al., *State of the World-1984* (New York: W.W. Norton & Co., 1984).

25. B. Bowonder et al., *Deforestation and Fuelwood Use in Urban Centres* (Hyderabad, India: Centre for Energy, Environment, and Technology and National Remote Sensing Agency, 1985).

26. The energy efficiency of charcoal making is roughly twice the yield by weight from the wood burned. Energy efficiency ranges from 20 percent to 50 percent, depending on the type of charcoal production method used, whether with earthen mounds or steel kilns. A more detailed discussion of this topic can be found in Gerald Foley, *Charcoal Making in Developing Countries* (Washington, D.C.: Earthscan/International Institute for Environment and Development, 1986).

27. For a discussion of World Bank efforts to boost hydroelectric capacity in the Third World, see Christopher Flavin, *Electricity For a Developing World: New Directions*, Worldwatch Paper 70 (Washington, D.C.: Worldwatch Institute, June 1986).

28. Walter Sullivan, "Parley is Told of European Gains from Burning Waste and Garbage," *New York Times*, May 11, 1978; Christopher Flavin and Cynthia Pollock, "Harnessing Renewable Energy," in Lester R. Brown et al., *State of the World-1985* (New York: W.W. Norton & Co., 1985).

29. Food self-sufficiency in India and China derived by Worldwatch from United States Department of Agriculture (USDA), Foreign Agricultural Service (FAS), *Foreign Agriculture Circular—Grain Reference Tables For Individual Countries* (Washington, D.C.: various years); USDA, FAS, *Foreign Agriculture Circular—Rice Reference Tables For Individual Countries* (Washington, D.C.: various years).

30. Yue-Man Yeung, "Urban Agriculture in Asia," The Food Energy Nexus Programme of the United Nations University, Tokyo, September 1985.

31. Ibid.

32. John Spitler, "Many Hard-Pressed U.S. Farmers Sell Produce Directly to Public," *Christian Science Monitor*, November 12, 1986.

33. Nutrients present in human wastes that are lost through disposal is a Worldwatch Institute estimate based on figures from A.M. Bruce and R.D. Davis, "Britain Uses Half Its Fertilizer As Sludge," *Biocycle*, March 1984; Robert K. Bastian and Jay Benforado, "Waste Treatment: Doing What Comes Naturally," *Technology Review*, February/March 1983; Hillel I. Shuval et al., *Wastewater Irrigation in Developing Countries: Health Effects and Technical Solutions* (Washington, D.C.: United Nations Development Program and World Bank, 1986); United States Environmental Protection Agency (EPA), *Environmental Regulations and Technology: Use and Disposal of Municipal Wastewater Sludge* (Washington, D.C.: 1984).

34. Seoul's night soil collection system described in United Nations, DIESA, *Population Growth and Policies in Mega-Cities: Seoul* (New York: 1986); China's use of night soil in Hillel I. Shuval et al., *Appropriate Technology for Water Supply and Sanitation: Night-soil Composting* (Washington, D.C.: World Bank, 1981).

35. The First Royal Commission in England set a precedent with guidelines and suggestions for the land application of sewage wastes in 1865. A detailed discussion of the history of nutrient recycling in European cities can be found in Shuval et al., *Wastewater Irrigation in Developing Countries*.

36. Yeung, "Urban Agriculture in Asia."

37. EPA, *Primer for Wastewater Treatment* (Washington, D.C.: 1984).

38. Kuwait's wastewater recycling plans from "From Effluents to Affluence?" *Technical Review: Middle East,* May/June 1986; information on Hidalgo from Shuval et al. *Wastewater Irrigation in Developing Countries.*

39. Shuval et al., *Wastewater Irrigation in Developing Countries.*

40. An excellent discussion of wastewater aquaculture in practice in a number of countries can be found in Peter Edwards, *Aquaculture: A Component of Low Cost Sanitation Technology* (Washington, D.C.: United Nations Development Program and World Bank, 1985).

41. Robert K. Bastian, EPA, Washington, D.C., private communication, September 1986, updating Bastian and Benforado, "Waste Treatment: Doing What Comes Naturally."

42. S.C. Talashilkar and O.P. Vimal, "From Nutrient-Poor Compost to High Grade Fertilizer," *Biocycle,* March 1984.

43. Martin Strauss, "About Wastewater and Excreta Use in India" (draft), World Health Organization International Reference Centre for Wastes Disposal, Duebendorf, Switzerland, June 1986.

44. Detailed discussions of the pathogens found in human wastes and the treatments and management strategies necessary to safely recycle wastes for agricultural purposes can be found in Richard G. Feacham et al., *Health Aspects of Excreta and Sullage Management—A State of the Art Review* (Washington, D.C.: World Bank, 1980), in Shuval et al., *Wastewater Irrigation in Developing Countries,* in Shuval et al., *Night-soil Composting,* and in World Health Organization, *The Risk to Health of Microbes in Sewage Sludge Applied to Land* (Copenhagen: 1981).

45. Beltsville Aerated Rapid Composting System, designed by USDA scientists, discussed in Shuval et al., *Night-soil Composting.*

46. Hong Kong's water supply is discussed in Ian Douglas, *The Urban Environment* (Baltimore, Md.: Edward Arnold Publishers, 1983).

47. Catherine Caufield, "The California Approach to Plumbing," *New Scientist,* February 21, 1985.

48. Douglas, *The Urban Environment.*

49. Quoted in Hardoy and Satterthwaite, "Third World Cities and the Environment of Poverty."

50. Ibid.

51. Ibid.

52. Mumford, *The City in History.*

53. Michael P. Todaro and Jerry Stilkind, *City Bias and Rural Neglect: The Dilemma of Urban Development* (New York: Population Council, 1981).

54. Michael Lipton, "Urban Bias and Food Policy in Poor Countries," *Food Policy,* November 1975.

55. Garza quoted in Kandell, "Nation in Jeopardy"; Lipton, "Urban Bias and Food Policy in Poor Countries."

56. Todaro and Stilkind, *City Bias and Rural Neglect.*

57. Scobie, "Food Consumption Policies."

58. Ye Shunzan, "Current Policies and Tendency of China's Urbanization," prepared for Conference on Population Growth, Urbanization, and Urban Policies in the Asia-Pacific Region, East-West Center, Honolulu, Hawaii, April 8–12, 1985; Martin King Whyte and William L. Parish, *Urban Life in Contempory China* (Chicago: University of Chicago Press, 1984).

Chapter 4. Reassessing Nuclear Power

1. USSR State Committee on the Utilization of Atomic Energy, "The Accident at the Chernobyl Nuclear Power Plant and its

Consequences," draft, Information Compiled for the International Atomic Energy Agency (IAEA) Experts' Meeting, Vienna, August 25–29, 1986; direct financial losses from "The Cost of Chernobyl," *European Energy Report* (Financial Times Business Information), June 13, 1986.

2. Worldwatch Institute projections, based on trends discussed in detail later in this chapter.

3. "Swedish Chief Assails Nuclear Power," *New York Times*, August 18, 1986.

4. Quoted in Ralph E. Lapp, "The Einstein Letter That Started It All," *New York Times Magazine*, August 2, 1964.

5. Gordon Thompson, "What Happened at Reactor Four," *Bulletin of the Atomic Scientists*, August/September 1986.

6. USSR State Committee, "Accident at Chernobyl."

7. Ibid.

8. C. Hohenemser et al., "Chernobyl: An Early Report," *Environment*, June 1986; Bureau Européen des Unions De Consommateurs, *Chernobyl: The Aftermath* (Brussels: 1986).

9. Hohenemser et al., "An Early Report"; Torkel Bennerstedt et al., *Chernobyl: Fallout Measurements and Consequences* (Stockholm: The Swedish Institute of Radiation Protection, 1986).

10. USSR State Committee, "Accident at Chernobyl."

11. Bureau Européen des Unions De Consommateurs, *Chernobyl: The Aftermath*; Stuart Diamond, "Long-Term Chernobyl Fallout: Comparison to Bombs Altered," *New York Times*, November 4, 1986.

12. Michael McCally, "Hospital Number Six: A First-Hand Report," *Bulletin of the Atomic Scientists*, August/September 1986; Herbert L. Abrams, "How Radiation Victims Suffer," *Bulletin of the Atomic Scientists*, August/September 1986.

13. Dr. Robert Gale, University of California at Los Angeles, presentation at "Symposium on Chernobyl: How the Soviet System Responded," Russian Research Center, Harvard University, October 6, 1986; McCally, "Hospital Number Six."

14. USSR State Committee, "Accident at Chernobyl."

15. Stuart Diamond, "2 Experts Foresee Deaths of 24,000 Tied to Chernobyl," *New York Times*, August 27, 1986; Gale, at "Symposium on Chernobyl."

16. Frank von Hippel and Thomas B. Cochran, "Chernobyl: Estimating Long-Term Health Effects," *Bulletin of the Atomic Scientists*, August/September 1986.

17. "Sweden: Health Consequences of Chernobyl Assessed," *Nuclear News*, July 1986.

18. Bureau Européen des Unions De Consommateurs, *Chernobyl: The Aftermath*.

19. Hohenemser et al., "An Early Report"; Bennerstedt et al., *Chernobyl: Fallout Measurements and Consequences*.

20. "Italy Three Months After Chernobyl," *WISE News Communique* (Amsterdam), September 5, 1986; David Webster, "How Ministers Misled Britain About Chernobyl," *New Scientist*, October 9, 1986.

21. Judith Miller, "Trying to Quell a Furor, France Forms a Panel on Chernobyl," *New York Times*, May 14, 1986; "Le Gouvernement Tente D'apaiser la Polémique sur les Effets de L'accident de Tchernobyl," *Le Monde*, May 13, 1986.

22. World Health Organization, "Chernobyl Reactor Accident: Report of a Consultation," Copenhagen, May 6, 1986; "EEC Proposes Nuclear Safeguards," *European Energy Report* (Financial Times Business Information), August 8, 1986.

23. "Swiss Plan Nuclear Meeting," *European Energy Report* (Financial Times Business Information), September 19, 1986.

24. Francis X. Clines, "Chernobyl Shakes Reindeer Culture of Lapps," *New York Times*, September 14, 1986.

25. "Cost of Chernobyl," *European Energy Report;* "Chernobyl Costs Put at $3 Billion," *Journal of Commerce,* September 22, 1986.

26. USSR State Committee, "Accident at Chernobyl"; L.M. Toth et al., *The Three Mile Island Accident: Diagnosis and Prognosis* (Washington, D.C.: American Chemical Society, 1986); "Costs at $3 Billion," *Journal of Commerce.*

27. Susan Tirbutt, "Farmers Claim £10 Million Chernobyl Damages," *The Guardian* (Manchester), August 27, 1986; David Winder, "Swedes Come Unglued Over Atomic Energy," *Christian Science Monitor,* September 9, 1986; "West German Farmers to be Compensated for Chernobyl-Related Losses," *World Environment Report,* August 12, 1986; Jackson Diehl, "Poland, Facing Hardships, May Try Liberalizing," *Washington Post,* August 29, 1986.

28. Walter Pincus, "Chernobyl Is Focus of IAEA Session," *Washington Post,* September 30, 1986; Stephen Wermiel, "Chernobyl Raises Questions on Liability of Soviets for Damage in Other Countries," *Wall Street Journal,* May 12, 1986.

29. Gary Lee, "Soviets Begin Recovery from Disaster's Damage," *Washington Post,* October 27, 1986; Three Mile Island figure is author's estimate; problems of Soviet energy economy from Theodore Shabad, Soviet energy expert, presentation at "Symposium on Chernobyl."

30. Alexander Amerisov, "A Chronology of Soviet Media Coverage," *Bulletin of the Atomic Scientists,* August/September 1986.

31. John Kemeny et al., *The Need for Change: The Legacy of TMI* (Washington, D.C.: U.S. Government Printing Office, 1979); Walter C. Patterson, "Chernobyl: Worst But Not First," *Bulletin of the Atomic Scientists,* August/September 1986; Barton J. Bernstein, "Nuclear Deception: the U.S. Record," *Bulletin of the Atomic Scientists,* August/September 1986.

32. Author's observations based on discussions with antinuclear activists in five European countries in August and September 1986.

33. "Chernobyl: Western Europe's Reaction," *European Energy Report* (Financial Times Business Information), May 16, 1986; "Massive Response to Chernobyl in FRG," *WISE News Communique* (Amsterdam), June 13, 1986; Italian figure from Laura Radiconcini, Amici della Terra, Rome, personal communication, July 31, 1986; Michael Parkin and Edward Vulliamy, "Villagers Foil Nuclear Dump Tests," *The Guardian* (Manchester), August 19, 1986, and "Villagers Win Round Two," *The Guardian* (Manchester), August 20, 1986.

34. "Sweden After Chernobyl," *WISE News Communique* (Amsterdam), September 5, 1986; Netherlands vote from Asa Moberg, "Nuclear Power in Crisis: A Country by Country Report," Lima, Sweden, unpublished, June 1986; "End of the Line for Italian Nuclear?" *European Energy Report* (Financial Times Business Information), September 19, 1986; "A Fight to the Finnish," *Sierra,* October 1986.

35. Andrew Holmes, "The Ratchet Turns Again on Safety and Economics," *Energy Economist* (Financial Times Business Information), June 1986; poll information in Table 4-3 from "Gallup Poll: Alarm Over Atomic Power," *Sunday Telegraph* (London), March 16, 1986, and from Andrew Holmes, Financial Times Business Information, private communication, September 25, 1986; "A Referendum to Halt All Nuclear Activities in Italy," *Nucleonics Week,* May 15, 1986; Washington Post-ABC News Poll, "78% of Americans Balk at New Nuclear Reactors," *Washington Post,* May 24, 1986; Hubert Poznaril, Eco-Institute, Ljubljana, Yugoslavia, private communication, September 25, 1986; Gallup of Canada, pri-

vate communication, September 24, 1986; Gallup Institute of Finland Poll, "Nuclear Opposition Doubles in Finland," *Journal of Commerce*, May 9, 1986.

36. "78% of Americans Balk at New Nuclear Reactors," *Washington Post*; "More Than Just a Soviet Problem," *U.S. News and World Report*, May 19, 1986.

37. David Dickson, "France Weighs Benefits, Risks of Nuclear Gamble," *Science*, August 27, 1986.

38. "Le Gouvernement Tente D'apaiser," *Le Monde;* Miller, "France Forms a Panel"; "France Discovers the Nuclear Scare," *New Scientist*, May 29, 1986.

39. Jackson Diehl, "Chernobyl's Other Losers," *Washington Post*, June 8, 1986; Michael T. Kaufman, "Three Weeks Later, 'The Cloud' Still Bothers the Poles," *New York Times*, May 20, 1986; "Poles Protest Construction of Nuclear Plant," *Washington Post*, May 17, 1986.

40. "Confusion Reigned in Yugoslavia," *Nucleonics Week*, May 15, 1986; "International Briefs: A Call for a Referendum in East Germany," *Nuclear News*, August 1986; M. Medvedkov, former member, Moscow Trust Group, Vienna, personal communication, September 26, 1986.

41. Worldwatch Institute calculations based on map included in "Von der Atomruine zum Atomruin," Aktion Mühleberg Stillegen, Bern, Switzerland, 1986.

42. Author's assessments based on meetings with government officials and nongovernmental observers and activists in Stockholm, August 11–12, 1986, and in Copenhagen, August 13–14, 1986.

43. "Sweden Agrees to Study Early Barsebäck Phase-Out," *Nuclear News*, July 1986.

44. Erich Wiedemann, "Cattenom: Storfall fur die gute Nachbarschaft," *Der Spiegel*, September 1, 1986; Michael Dobbs, "Fission Splits France, W. Germany," *Washington Post*, August 4, 1986.

45. Wiedemann, "Cattenom"; Dobbs, "Fission Splits France."

46. "Police Break Up Protest at West German A-Plant," *New York Times*, April 1, 1986; author's observations in travel to Wackersdorf, August 31, 1986.

47. "Nuclear Protests Cross Borders," *European Energy Report* (Financial Times Business Information), July 11, 1986; Robert McDonald, "German-Austrian Tensions Mount Over Planned Wackersdorf Reprocessing Plant," *Nuclear Waste News*, Sample Issue, 1986; James A. Markham, "Spreading the Anti-Nuclear Gospel in Europe," *New York Times*, August 3, 1986.

48. Karen DeYoung, "Massive Nuclear Site Disturbs Britons," *Washington Post*, May 19, 1986; "Ireland vs. Sellafield," *WISE News Communique* (Amsterdam), April 4, 1986.

49. Lee Yee, "China's Plan for Nuclear Plant Illuminates Hong Kong Politics," *Wall Street Journal*, September 29, 1986; "Showdown Over Daya Bay," *Asiaweek*, September 14, 1986.

50. Yee, "Hong Kong Politics"; "Showdown Over Daya Bay," *Asiaweek*.

51. Paul Lewis, "94 Nations Urge Reactor Safeguards," *New York Times*, September 27, 1986; "Making Safety International," *European Energy Report* (Financial Times Business Information), June 6, 1986.

52. Pincus, "Chernobyl is Focus."

53. Electricity shares from IAEA, *Nuclear Power: Status and Trends, 1986 Edition* (Vienna: 1986).

54. Worldwatch Insitute estimates based on numbers of plants and current average construction costs worldwide of about $1,500 per kilowatt.

55. IAEA, *1974 Annual Report* (Vienna: 1974).

56. Worldwatch Institute projection based on assumed completion of 70,000 megawatts by 1990 and 55,000 additional megawatts in

the nineties, mainly in the Soviet Union and Eastern Europe. The year 2000 estimates are highly speculative but are more likely to be overestimates than underestimates.

57. Atomic Industrial Forum (AIF), "Historical Profile of U.S. Nuclear Power Development," Bethesda, Md., January 1, 1986; U.S. Department of Energy (DOE), Energy Information Agency (EIA), *Nuclear Power Plant Construction Activity 1985* (Washington, D.C.: U.S. Government Printing Office, 1986).

58. DOE, EIA, *Monthly Energy Review,* June 1986; AIF, "Historical Profile"; coal data from DOE and Kidder, Peabody, and Co., New York, private communications.

59. DOE, EIA, *Nuclear Power Plant Construction Activity 1985;* coal and nuclear costs per kilowatt-hour based on ibid. and AIF, "Economic Survey," Bethesda, Md., September 25, 1986.

60. James Cook, "Nuclear Follies," *Forbes,* February 11, 1985.

61. Union of Concerned Scientists, *Safety Second: A Critical Evaluation of NRC's First Decade* (Washington, D.C.: 1985).

62. Ulrich Steger, State of Hesse Minister of Economics and Technology, "The Nuclear Power Debate in West Germany after Chernobyl," presented at International Energy Seminar, The Johns Hopkins University School of Advanced International Studies, September 18, 1986; Mark Hibbs, "Study of Costs of Closing German Nuclear Plants Fuels Debate," *Nucleonics Week,* September 18, 1986.

63. Dickson, "France Weighs Benefits, Risks."

64. "EDF Under Fire Over Tariffs," *European Energy Report* (Financial Times Business Information), October 17, 1986; "Power Too Cheap to Meter but Only on the Night Shift," *Energy Economist* (Financial Times Business Information), September 1985; "CFDT: Supercapacité Nucléaire: Mettre sa

Voiture a la Casse et Achèter une Diesel . . . Pour Rouler 10,000 km par An," *WISE Bulletin International* (Paris), June 15–30, 1986.

65. "Power Too Cheap to Meter," *Energy Economist.*

66. Jacques Neher, "France: N-Power Expertise Aimed Overseas," *Boston Globe,* March 9, 1986.

67. "World List of Nuclear Power Plants," *Nuclear News,* August 1986; "Japan Lowers Nuclear Capacity Forecast, Citing Conservation, Political Opposition," *Electric Utility Weekly,* January 16, 1984; Sub-Committee on Nuclear Energy of Advisory Committee for Energy, Japanese Ministry of International Trade and Industry, "Nuclear Energy Vision: Perspectives of Nuclear Energy for the 21st Century," Tokyo, September 1986.

68. Theodore Shabad, "News Notes," *Soviet Geography,* April 1986; "Statement by the Head of the USSR Delegation to the Special Session of the IAEA General Conference," Vienna, September 24, 1986.

69. George Stein, "Soviet Nuclear Industry Riddled with Problems," *Los Angeles Times,* May 16, 1986; Dusko Doder, "Problems Reportedly Plague Soviet Nuclear Reactor Plant," *Washington Post,* November 29, 1983; "USSR: Best Year Yet, But Improvements Still Needed," *Nuclear News,* February 1986.

70. Lee, "Soviets Begin Recovery from Disaster's Damage."

71. Jasper Becker, "China Abandons Nuclear Plans," *Journal of Commerce,* March 11, 1986.

72. John J. Fialka and Roger Cohen, "Nuclear-Plant Projects in Nations Like Brazil Falter After Accident," *Wall Street Journal,* June 5, 1986; James Bruce, "Brazil Changes Nuclear Course," *Journal of Commerce,* August 11, 1986; Gregory Kats, "Importing Insolvency; Nuclear Energy: The Investment That

Doesn't Work," *Multinational Monitor,* May 1986.

73. Estimates based on Worldwatch analysis of "World List," *Nuclear News,* adjusted and updated with press reports, private communications, and comparisons with AIF, "International Survey," Bethesda, Md., January 1986; IAEA, *Status and Trends, 1986;* Andrew Holmes, "World Status: Nuclear Power," *Energy Economist* (Financial Times Business Information), January 1986; and Shabad, "News Notes."

74. The figures in Table 4-8 are for firmly scheduled plants listed in "World List," *Nuclear News.* They include almost all the Western and Third World plants planned by 1995, and probably are overestimates for some countries. However, Soviet and East European planners plan far more plants in 1991-95 than are included in the table.

75. "Statement by Head of USSR Delegation to Special Session of IAEA."

76. "Nuclear Power Controversy Balloons in West Germany," *Journal of Commmerce,* September 22, 1986; David Fairhall, "No Retreat from Nuclear Age, says Walker," *The Guardian* (Manchester), June 27, 1986.

77. Blix quoted in Bill Rankin, "Hashing Over the Political Fallout from Chernobyl," *Energy Daily,* October 9, 1986.

78. David Fishlock, "Chernobyl's First Victim is Zwentendorf," *Energy Daily,* June 12, 1986; William Branigin, "Chernobyl Prompts Philippines to Reassess Reactor," *Washington Post,* May 16, 1986; Costis Stambolis, "Greek Utility Announces Major Wind Energy Program," *Solar Energy Intelligence Report,* September 16, 1986.

79. Tony Catterall, "No Nukes, Says Bonn Party," *Energy Daily,* August 18, 1986; "Kohl Fails to Calm Reaction to Chernobyl," *Nuclear News,* July 1986.

80. "End for Italian Nuclear?" *European Energy Report;* "Swiss Launch Anti-Nuclear Initiative," *European Energy Report* (Financial Times Business Information), September 5, 1986; "Labour Halt on Nuclear Power," *The Guardian* (Manchester), September 4, 1986.

81. Peter Jankowitsch, Federal Minister for Foreign Affairs of Austria, "Statement at the First Special Session of the General Conference of the IAEA," Vienna, September 24, 1986.

82. "Making Safety International," *European Energy Report;* Moberg, "Country by Country Report."

83. Nuclear Control Institute, "Report of the International Task Force on Prevention of Nuclear Terrorism," Washington, D.C., 1986.

84. U.S. Congress, Office of Technology Assessment, *Managing the Nation's Commercial High-Level Radioactive Waste* (Washington, D.C.: U.S. Government Printing Office, 1985).

85. Bernard L. Cohen, "Exaggerating the Risks," in Michio Kaku and Jennifer Trainer, eds., *Nuclear Power: Both Sides* (New York: W.W. Norton & Co., 1982); Centre for Science and Environment, *The State of India's Environment 1984–1985* (New Delhi: 1985); Jonathan Kandell, "Mexico City's Growth, Once Fostered, Turns into Economic Burden," *Wall Street Journal,* October 4, 1985.

86. See, for example, Joshua Gordon, "1984–1985 Nuclear Power Safety Report," Critical Mass Energy Project, Washington, D.C., 1986; U.S. Nuclear Regulatory Commission, "List of Significant Operational Events and Regulatory Problems," report to Representative Edward J. Markey, Chairman, U.S. House of Representatives, Committee on Energy and Commerce, Sub-Committee on Energy Conservation and Power, Washington, D.C., May 4, 1986.

87. See, for instance, William Cannell, "Chernobyl, Challenger and the Numbers Game," *Energy Economist* (Financial Times Business Information), September 1986;

Charles Perow, *Normal Accidents: Living with High-Risk Technology* (New York: Basic Books, 1984); Jim MacKenzie, "Finessing the Risks of Nuclear Power," *Technology Review*, February/March 1984.

88. U.S. Nuclear Regulatory Commission, "Reactor Safety Study: An Assessment of Accident Risks in U.S. Commercial Nuclear Power Plants," WASH-1400 (Washington, D.C.: U.S. Government Printing Office, 1975).

89. S. Islam and K. Lindgren, "How Many Reactor Accidents Will There Be?" *Nature*, August 21, 1986.

90. "Soviet Union Showed the World How to Evacuate," *New Scientist*, September 4, 1986; Stuart Diamond, "Chernobyl Causing Big Revisions in Global Nuclear Power Policies," *New York Times*, September 27, 1986.

91. Sandia National Laboratory, "Estimates of the Financial Consequences of Nuclear Power Reactor Accidents," prepared for the Nuclear Regulatory Commission, Washington, D.C., 1982.

92. Klaus Michael Meyer-Abich and Bertram Schefold, *Die Grenzen der Atomwirtschaft* (Munich, West Germany: Verlag C.H. Beck, 1986).

93. Ronald Klueh, "Future Nuclear Reactors—Safety First?" *New Scientist*, April 3, 1986; Richard K. Lester, "Rethinking Nuclear Power," *Scientific American*, March 1986.

Chapter 5. Electrifying the Third World

1. Per capita estimates based on figures in World Bank, "1982 Power/Energy Data Sheets for 104 Developing Countries," Washington, D.C., July 1985, and in World Bank, *China: The Energy Sector* (Washington, D.C.: 1985); 1.7 billion figure is Worldwatch Institute estimate based on figures in several regional and country studies. In China, half the rural households, representing 400 million people, do not have electricity. In other developing countries an average of 75 percent of the 1.7 billion rural people do not have power. Even in "electrified" villages, many homes lack power.

2. World Bank, "1982 Power/Energy Data Sheets"; Edison Electric Institute, "Electric Output," Washington, D.C., April 30, 1986.

3. World Bank, "1982 Power/Energy Data Sheets."

4. World Bank, *The Energy Transition in Developing Countries* (Washington, D.C.: 1983).

5. World Energy Conference, *Survey of Energy Resources, 1980* (Munich: 1980).

6. Figures compiled by Worldwatch Institute from various sources; Christopher Flavin and Cynthia Pollock, "Harnessing Renewable Energy," in Lester R. Brown et al., *State of the World-1985* (New York: W.W. Norton & Co., 1985).

7. World Bank, *China: The Energy Sector.*

8. Patricia Adams and Lawrence Solomon, *In the Name of Progress: The Underside of Foreign Aid* (Toronto: Energy Probe Research Foundation, 1985); Ken Lieberthal, "Energy Decision-Making in China," lecture at The Johns Hopkins School of Advanced International Studies, Washington, D.C., February 5, 1986.

9. World Bank, *Energy Transition in Developing Countries;* World Bank, *China: The Energy Sector.*

10. World Bank, *China: The Energy Sector;* Massachusetts Division of Air Quality Control, "Acid Rain and Related Air Pollution Damage: A National and International Call for Action," unpublished, Boston, Mass., August 1984.

11. "World List of Nuclear Power Plants," *Nuclear News*, August 1986.

12. Hugh Collier, *Developing Electric Power: Thirty Years of World Bank Experience* (Baltimore, Md.: The Johns Hopkins University Press, 1984).

13. A. Heron, "Financing Electric Power in Developing Countries," *IAEA Bulletin,* Winter 1985; Edward S. Cassedy and Peter M. Meier, "Planning for Electric Power in Developing Countries in the Face of Change" (draft), in *Planning For Changing Energy Conditions* (New Brunswick, N.J.: Transaction Inc., forthcoming).

14. Worldwatch Institute estimates, based on figures available for selected countries; National Rural Electric Cooperative Association (NRECA), "Central America Rural Electrification Study," report to U.S. Agency for International Development (AID), unpublished, Washington, D.C., 1985.

15. Heron, "Financing Electric Power"; World Bank, *Energy Transition in Developing Countries.*

16. Robert Ichord, AID, presentation at meeting of Society for International Development, Washington, D.C., September 12, 1985; "Power Shortage a Priority," *China Daily,* April 29, 1986.

17. World Bank, "Latin America and Caribbean Region Power Sector Finances," unpublished, Washington, D.C., April 22, 1985.

18. Mohan Munasinghe, World Bank, private communication, May 19, 1986; NRECA, "Central America Rural Electrification Study."

19. Robert J. Saunders and Karl Jechoutek, "The Electric Power Sector in Developing Countries," *Energy Policy,* August 1986; Fox Butterfield, "Filipinos Say Marcos Was Given Millions for '76 Nuclear Contract," *New York Times,* March 7, 1986.

20. Howard S. Geller, "Progress in the Energy Efficiency of Residential Appliances and Space Conditioning Equipment," in *Energy Sources: Conservation and Renewables* (New York: American Institute of Physics, 1985).

21. Ibid.; Amory Lovins, "Saving Gigabucks with Negawatts," *Public Utilities Fortnightly,* March 21, 1985.

22. Howard S. Geller, "End-Use Electricity Conservation: Options for Developing Countries," American Council for an Energy-Efficient Economy, Washington, D.C., March 1986.

23. Howard S. Geller et al., "Electricity Conservation Potential in Brazil," American Council for an Energy-Efficient Economy, Washington, D.C., March 1986. Additional electricity supplies in developing countries cost on average about $2,000 per kilowatt, including about $500 per kilowatt for transmission and distribution; see Heron, "Financing Electric Power."

24. Mohan Munasinghe and Jeremy J. Warford, *Electricity Pricing: Theory and Case Studies* (Baltimore, Md.: The Johns Hopkins University Press, 1982).

25. Geller, "End-Use Electricity Conservation."

26. Ibid.

27. Ibid.

28. The 10–15 percent figure is based on data from Brazil, developed by Howard S. Geller, American Council for an Energy-Efficient Economy, Washington, D.C., private communication, May 2, 1986.

29. Pacific Gas and Electric Company, *1985 Energy Management and Conservation Activities* (San Francisco: 1984).

30. Geller, private communication.

31. Douglas V. Smith et al., "Report of the Regional Rural Electrification Survey to the Asian Development Bank" (draft), Manila, Philippines, October 1983.

32. World Bank, "1982 Power/Energy Data Sheets"; Randy Girer, "Rural Electrification in Costa Rica: Membership Participation and Distribution of Benefits," Masters Thesis, Graduate Program in Energy, Management and Policy, University of Pennsylvania, 1986; World Bank, "Electricity Use in India: Third World Rural Electrification

Project," Staff Appraisal Report, Washington, D.C., May 7, 1986.

33. World Bank, *China: The Energy Sector;* Smith et al., "Report to the Asian Development Bank."

34. AID, *Rural Electrification: Linkages and Justifications* (Washington, D.C.: 1979).

35. Douglas F. Barnes, "Electricity's Effect on Rural Life in Developing Nations," paper prepared for the United Nations University and the International Development Research Center, Ottawa, September 1984.

36. Douglas F. Barnes, *Electric Power for Rural Growth: How Electricity Affects Rural Life in Developing Countries* (Boulder, Colo.: Westview Press, 1986); Girer, "Rural Electrification in Costa Rica."

37. Barnes, "Electricity's Effect on Rural Life."

38. Barnes, *Electric Power for Rural Growth.*

39. Girer, "Rural Electrification in Costa Rica"; AID, *Bolivia: Rural Electrification* (Washington, D.C.: 1980); Barnes, *Electric Power for Rural Growth.*

40. Cited in Smith et al., "Report to the Asian Development Bank."

41. AID, *The Product is Progress: Rural Electrification in Costa Rica* (Washington, D.C.: 1981).

42. Author's observations based on travel in northern Luzon Province, Philippines, with the National Electrification Administration, November 1985; Samuel Bunker, NRECA, Washington, D.C., private communication, January 24, 1986.

43. "Remote Power Market is Predicted to Swell," *Renewable Energy News,* July 1985; Smith et al., "Report to the Asian Development Bank."

44. AID, *Decentralized Hydropower in AID's Development Assistance Program* (Washington, D.C.: 1986).

45. Allen R. Inversin, "Pakistan: Villager-Implemented Micro-Hydropower Schemes," NRECA, Washington, D.C., 1983; Smith et al., "Report to the Asian Development Bank"; AID, *Decentralized Hydropower.*

46. NRECA, "Nepal: Private-Sector Approach to Implementing Micro-Hydropower Schemes: A Case Study," Washington, D.C., 1982.

47. "Small Power Units Rise," *China Daily,* April 2, 1986; World Bank, *China: The Energy Sector;* Robert P. Taylor, *Decentralized Renewable Energy Development in China* (Washington, D.C.: World Bank, 1982); Eugene Chang, "Little Plants Give Lots of Power," *China Daily,* December 14, 1985; He Quan, "Nation Tags 100 Counties for Mini-Hydro Experiment," *China Daily,* April 16, 1986.

48. Alan S. Miller et al., *Growing Power: Bioenergy for Development and Industry* (Washington, D.C.: World Resources Institute, 1986); Abubakar Lubis et al., "Solar Villages in Indonesia," *SunWorld,* Vol. 9, No. 2, 1985; Philippines Ministry of Energy, *1984 Annual Report* (Manila: 1984).

49. Frank H. Denton, *Wood for Energy and Rural Development: The Philippines Experience* (Manila: Frank H. Denton, 1983).

50. Recent appraisals based on author's discussion with Filipino and AID officials in Manila, November 1985.

51. Xu Yuanchao, "Remote Areas Switch on to Windmills," *China Daily,* February 27, 1986.

52. Robert Lynette, "Wind Turbine Performance: An Industry Overview," *Alternative Sources of Energy,* September/October 1985.

53. Donald Marier, "Developments in Wind Projects Overseas," *Alternative Sources of Energy,* November/December 1985.

54. Christopher Flavin, *Electricity from Sunlight: The Emergence of Photovoltaics* (Golden, Colo.: Solar Energy Research Institute, 1985).

55. P. Jourde, "Solar Electrification of the French Polynesian Islands," G.I.E. Soler, unpublished, 1985.

56. Philippines Ministry of Energy, *1984 Annual Report.*

57. Ichord, at Society for International Development.

58. Christopher Flavin, "Reforming the Electric Power Industry," in Lester R. Brown et al., *State of the World-1986* (New York: W.W. Norton & Co., 1986).

59. Michael Farmer, GALT Asiatic Corporation, New York, private communication, January 9, 1986; "China Power Sector Decentralized," *China Daily,* June 6, 1985.

Chapter 6. Realizing Recycling's Potential

1. Environmental Defense Fund (EDF), *To Burn or Not to Burn: The Economic Advantages of Recycling Over Garbage Incineration in New York City* (New York: 1985).

2. David Morris, "A National Resource Recovery Policy Emerging," *Building Economic Alternatives* (Co-op America, Washington, D.C.), Spring 1985.

3. Robert Cowles Letcher and Mary T. Sheil, "Source Separation and Citizen Recycling," in William D. Robinson, ed., *The Solid Waste Handbook* (New York: John Wiley & Sons, 1986).

4. "Waste Reduction," *RE:SOURCES* (Environmental Task Force, Washington, D.C.), Summer 1986; "Cost of Packaging Food Could Exceed Farm Net," *Journal of Commerce,* August 12, 1986.

5. Evelin Hajek, "The Importance of Packaging in Household Waste," in A. Bridgewater and K. Lidgren, eds., *Household Waste Management in Europe: Economics and Techniques* (New York: Van Nostrand Reinhold Co., 1981); L.L. Gaines and A.M. Wolsky, "Resource Conservation Through Beverage Container Recycling," *Conservation & Recycling,* Vol. 6, No. 1/2, 1983.

6. National Soft Drink Association (NSDA), "The Soft Drink Industry of the United States: Statistical Profile 1982," Washington, D.C., 1983.

7. Ibid.; Stephen Christophe, financial analyst, NSDA, private communication, September 1986.

8. Reynolds Metals Company, "Aluminum's Centennial: Reynolds Role," 1985 Annual Report, Richmond, Va., February 1986; Aluminum Association, Inc., *Aluminum Statistical Review for 1985* (Washington, D.C.: 1986).

9. Christophe, private communication; "Current Business Statistics," *Survey of Current Business,* August 1986; Jonathan Puth, "Take Back That Trash," *Environmental Action,* July/August 1985.

10. Community Environmental Council, *Solid Waste Managment Plan City of Berkeley* (Santa Barbara, Calif.: 1986); Kenneth R. Sheets, "The New High-Tech World of Plastics," *U.S. News & World Report,* February 24, 1986.

11. "Market Update," *Resource Recycling,* July/August 1985.

12. "Mounting Garbage Threatens Cities," *Beijing Review,* February 18, 1985; Richard J. Meislen, "Mexico City Gets Too Big a Million Times a Year," *New York Times,* September 8, 1985.

13. Martin V. Melosi, *Garbage in the Cities: Refuse, Reform, and the Environment, 1880–1980* (College Station: Texas A & M University Press, 1981).

14. Ibid.

15. "City Expands Landfill Moratorium; Sets New Task Force," *The Neighborhood Works* (Chicago), March 1985; David Morris and Neil Seldman, "New Ways to Keep a Lid on

America's Garbage Problem," *Wall Street Journal,* April 15, 1986.

16. Morris and Seldman, "New Ways"; Neal Peirce, "Garbage-to-Energy Plants a Golden Opportunity," *Journal of Commerce,* February 6, 1985; William K. Stevens, "Philadelphia Trash: Too Much and Nowhere to Go," *New York Times,* March 9, 1986; costs of shipping from David Morris, "The Cost of Burning Garbage," *Alternative Sources of Energy,* April 1986.

17. Maurice D. Hinchey, "Elements of a Materials Policy for New York State," presented to the Conference on Materials Recycling and Composting, Albany, N.Y., October 9, 1985.

18. United States Conference of Mayors, "Resource Recovery Activities," *City Currents* (Washington, D.C.), April 1986.

19. For a discussion of the Public Utility Regulatory Policies Act, see Christopher Flavin, "Reforming the Electric Power Industry," in Lester R. Brown et al., *State of the World-1986* (New York: W.W. Norton & Co., 1986).

20. John Reilly, "Garbage Has Promise as a Power Source," *USA Today,* May 22, 1984; Donald Marier, "Waste-To-Energy Project Updates," *Alternative Sources of Energy,* April 1986; EDF, *To Burn or Not to Burn.*

21. Colin Leinster, "The Sweet Smell of Profits from Trash," *Fortune,* April 1, 1985; Allen Hershkowitz, *Garbage Burning Lessons from Europe: Consensus and Controversy in Four European States* (New York: Inform, 1986); Plastic Waste Management Institute (PWMI), *Plastic Waste: Resource Recovery and Recycling in Japan* (Tokyo: 1985); Matthew L. Wald, "Converting Waste to Energy," *New York Times,* April 18, 1985.

22. Christoffer Rappe et al., eds., *Chlorinated Dioxins and Dibenzofurans in Perspective* (Chelsea, Mich.: Lewis Publishers, Inc., 1986); Susan Okie, "Dioxin May Weaken Ability to Fight Disease," *Washington Post,*

April 18, 1986; Richard E. Hoffman et al., "Health Effects of Long-Term Exposure to 2,3,7,8-Tetrachlorodibenzo-p-Dioxin," *Journal of the American Medical Association,* April 18, 1986; proposed U.S. Environmental Protection Agency rule, *Federal Register,* December 19, 1985.

23. Maurice D. Hinchey, "Resource Recovery and Solid Waste Management in Norway, Sweden, Denmark and Germany: Lessons for New York," New York State Legislative Commission on Solid Waste Management, Albany, N.Y., December 1985; Hershkowitz, *Garbage Burning Lessons.*

24. Walter Liong-Ting Hang and Steven A. Romalewski, *The Burning Question: Garbage Incineration Versus Total Recycling in New York City* (New York: New York Public Interest Research Center, 1986); J.E. Helt and K.M. Myles, *Energy from Municipal Waste—Assessment of Control Technologies for Stack Gas Emissions* (Argonne, Ill.: Argonne National Laboratory, 1983).

25. EDF, *To Burn or Not to Burn.*

26. Ibid.; Hang and Romalewski, *The Burning Question.*

27. Morris, "Cost of Burning Garbage"; Asalie Larrson, Office of Science and Technology, Swedish Embassy, private communication, July 29, 1986; Hershkowitz, *Garbage Burning Lessons.*

28. Hershkowitz, *Garbage Burning Lessons;* Hinchey, "Lessons for New York"; Martha Gildart, California Waste Management Board, private communication, November 6, 1986.

29. James S. Kennedy, "Energy and the Primary Aluminum Industry," International Trade Administration, U.S. Department of Commerce, Washington, D.C., January 1985; William U. Chandler, *Materials Recycling: The Virtue of Necessity,* Worldwatch Paper 56 (Washington, D.C.: Worldwatch Institute, October 1983); Letcher and Sheil, "Source Separation and Citizen Recycling."

30. Organisation for Economic Co-operation and Development (OECD), *Household Waste: Separate Collection and Recycling* (Paris: 1983).

31. Mill costs from Shigeo Egusa, "A Second Life for Wastepaper," *Journal of Japanese Trade & Industry*, No. 6, 1985; reclaimed mills from Richard Hertzberg, "Searching for Common Ground: The Third National Recycling Congress," *Resource Recycling*, November/December 1984; "National Science Test II," *NOVA* Series, WGBH-Boston, broadcast on May 6, 1986.

32. "Waste Paper Recovery," *Resource Recycling*, May/June 1985; Mal Tariff, "India Paper and Paperboard Industry," *Resource Recycling*, March/April 1986; "Around the World," *Resource Recycling*, July/August 1985; Chris Dupin, "The Wastepaper Boom: US Ports Love the Business," *Journal of Commerce*, March 28, 1986.

33. Aluminum Association, *Statistical Review for 1985;* European Glass Container Federation (Brussels), *The Glass Gazette*, Issues 1–12; U.N. Food and Agriculture Organization, *Waste Paper Data, 1982–84* (Rome: 1985); historical recovery rates in Chandler, *Materials Recycling.*

34. OECD, *Household Waste;* Chandler, *Materials Recycling.*

35. Judy Roumpf, "The Plight of Plastics Recycling," *Resource Recycling*, November/December 1984; Sigrid Huston, "PET Plastics Recycling: Ryder Conference '85," *Resource Recycling*, May/June 1985; PWMI, *Plastic Waste in Japan;* "State Watch," *Resource Recycling*, May/June 1985.

36. "Interview with Neil Seldman: New Visions of Waste Disposal," *RE:SOURCES* (Environmental Task Force, Washington, D.C.), Summer 1986; Tony Abatanti, *Fiber Market News*, private communication, November 3, 1986.

37. Chuck Papke, "Recycling Municipal Refuse, Sludge and Industrial Waste: Biocycle's West Coast Workshop," *Resource Recycling*, March/April 1985.

38. "County Profits From Recycling," *Resource Recycling*, July/August 1983; Lenis Burns, refuse collection division, Montgomery County, Md., private communication, October 2, 1986; OECD, *Waste Paper Recovery* (Paris: 1979).

39. PWMI, *Plastic Waste in Japan.*

40. Michael J. Ducey, "Waste-to-Energy Incineration Plants May Cut Future Wastepaper Supplies," *Pulp & Paper*, March 1985.

41. Milgram quoted in Charles Papke, "Plastics Recycling As a Business," *Resource Recycling*, September/October 1986.

42. PWMI, *Plastic Waste in Japan;* "Around the World," *Resource Recycling*, November/December 1985.

43. "Portland Metropolitan Area Solid Waste Reduction Program," Metropolitan Service District, Portland, Ore., April 22, 1986.

44. The states are Connecticut, Delaware, Iowa, Maine, Massachusetts, Michigan, New York, Oregon, and Vermont; Karen Diegmueller, "Buried in Garbage," *Insight*, January 27, 1986.

45. Jonathan Puth, recycling analyst, private communication, August 12, 1986; "Container Deposit News," *Resource Recycling*, July/August 1983; Puth, "Take Back That Trash."

46. I. Boustead and K. Lidgren, eds., *Problems in Packaging: The Environmental Issue* (New York: John Wiley & Sons, 1984); "Around the World," *Resource Recycling*, January/February 1985; "Deposit Law News," *Resource Recycling*, January/February 1985; Tore Planke, "Recycling: A Challenge, Not a Threat," *Beverage World*, June 1985; Derek Stephenson, "Ontario Unveils New Soft Drink Container Law," *Resource Recycling*, September/October 1985.

47. Stephenson, "Ontario Unveils New Soft Drink Container Law."

48. Steve Rypins and Charles Papke, "Reverse Vending Machine Update," *Resource Recycling*, January/February 1986.

49. "Reverse Vending Machines for Beverage Containers Installed," *Beverage World International*, October/November 1985; Tomra Systems, informational brochures, Asker, Norway, 1986; Rypins and Papke, "Reverse Vending Machine Update."

50. Guenther Lubisch, "All Glass Bottles Are Returnable," *Glass Gazette* (Brussels), November 1984; "Around the World," *Resource Recycling*, November/December 1984; Wolfgang Helm and Gerd Roeles, German waste analysts, private communications, May 22, 1986; "The 1985 Results," *Glass Gazette*, October 1986; "Around the World," *Resource Recycling*, May/June 1986.

51. OECD, "The Recycling of Beverage Containers in Switzerland," in *The State of the Environment* (Paris: 1985); OECD, *Household Waste*.

52. Aluminum Association, *Statistical Review for 1985;* "Reynolds Aluminum Will Close Its New Jersey Recycling Centers," *New York Times*, May 20, 1984; Community Environmental Council, *Solid Waste Management Plan of Berkeley*.

53. Sandra Johnson Cointreau et al., *Recycling from Municipal Refuse: A State-of-the-Art Review and Annotated Bibliography* (Washington, D.C.: World Bank, 1984).

54. Ibid.

55. Ibid.; "Around the Country," *Resource Recycling*, January/February 1986.

56. Joyce Purnick, "Testing a Plan for Recycling of City Trash," *New York Times*, July 16, 1985; "Community Recycling Update," *Resource Recycling*, January/February 1985; Richard Hertzberg, "Perspective on Recycling: New Jersey Steps Out Again," *Resource Recycling*, January/February 1985.

57. Lorie Parker, Waste Reduction Manager, Oregon Department of Environmental Quality, Portland, Ore., private communica-

tion, June 13, 1986; Oregon Senate Bill 405, 62nd Oregon Legislative Assembly.

58. Hertzberg, "Perspective on Recycling"; New Jersey Departments of Energy and Environmental Protection, "Statewide Survey of Recycling Programs," Newark, N.J., May 1985.

59. New Jersey, "Statewide Survey"; Dawn Schauer, "Innovative Methods Move Recyclables to Market," *Biocycle* (Emmaus, Pa.), May/June 1986.

60. Papke, "Recycling Municipal Refuse"; Derek Stephenson, "Recycling in Canada: Commitment to Recycling," *Resource Recycling*, January/February 1986.

61. Richard Keller, "Purchases of Recycled Paper: An Important Tool for Market Development," *Resource Recycling*, July/August 1983.

62. Ibid.; Clifford Case and Richard Keller, "Buying Recycled Paper: The Story Continues," *Resource Recycling*, July/August 1985.

63. "Recycling Equipment Tax Credits/Waivers," *Resource Recycling*, July/August 1986.

64. Neil Seldman and Jon Huls, *Waste to Wealth: A Business Guide for Community Recycling Enterprises* (Washington, D.C.: Institute for Local Self Reliance, 1985); Community Environmental Council, *Solid Waste Management Plan of Berkeley;* "Will Today's Soft Drink Bottle Become Tomorrow's Carpet," *Waste Age*, March 1986.

65. Bureau of the Census, *Statistical Abstract of the United States 1986* (Washington, D.C.: U.S. Department of Commerce, 1985); Peter M. Emerson et al., "Wasting the National Forests: Selling Federal Timber Below Cost," The Wilderness Society, Washington, D.C., September 1984.

66. H. Richard Heede et al., "The Hidden Costs of Energy," Center for Renewable Resources (now called Fund for Renewable Energy and the Environment), Washington D.C., October 1985; Sandra Postel, *Conserving*

Water: The Untapped Alternative, Worldwatch Paper 67 (Washington, D.C.: Worldwatch Institute, September 1985); Letcher and Sheil, "Source Separation and Citizen Recycling."

67. Letcher and Sheil, "Source Separation and Citizen Recycling."

68. See various chapters in Boustead and Lidgren, *Problems in Packaging.*

69. Papke, "Plastics Recycling"; Sheil quoted in Hertzberg, "Perspective on Recycling"; Roumpf, "The Plight of Plastics Recycling."

70. Diegmueller, "Buried in Garbage"; Jerry Powell, "Plastic Beverage Cans: What's Ahead?" *Resource Recycling,* November/December 1985; Kevin Thompson, "New Plastic Coke Can Sparks Controversy," *Journal of Commerce,* February 12, 1986.

71. Eleanor Johnson Tracy, "Plastic That Won't Clutter the Countryside," *Fortune,* September 1, 1986; N.L. Uttley, Market Development Manager, Marlborough Biopolymers Ltd., Stockton-on-Tees, U.K., private communication, July 3, 1986.

72. "State Watch," *Resource Recycling,* May/June 1986; "State Watch," *Resource Recycling,* May/June 1985; Puth, "Take Back That Trash"; Puth, private communication; Planke, "Recycling: A Challenge, Not a Threat"; Boustead and Lidgren, *Problems in Packaging.*

73. Nancy VandenBerg, "Recycled Materials Procurement Part 1," *Resource Recycling,* September/October 1986.

74. Ibid.; Nancy VandenBerg, Council on the Environment, New York City, private communication, October 31, 1986.

75. VandenBerg, "Recycled Materials Procurement."

76. "New Jersey Senate Approves Mandatory Recycling," *Resource Recycling,* September/October 1986.

77. Donald F. Barrett and Robert W. Crandall, *Up From the Ashes: The Rise of the Steel Minimill in the United States* (Washington, D.C.: The Brookings Institution, 1986).

Chapter 7. Sustaining World Agriculture

1. Data on per capita and total grain production in Africa and Latin America from U.S. Department of Agriculture (USDA), Economic Research Service (ERS), *World Indices of Agricultural and Food Production 1950–85* (unpublished printout) (Washington, D.C.: 1986); figures for 1986 derived from USDA, ERS, *World Agriculture: Outlook and Situation Report,* Washington, D.C., June 1986.

2. USDA, ERS, *World Indices.*

3. Ibid.

4. Data for 1986 from USDA, ERS, *World Agriculture: Outlook and Situation Report;* all other years from USDA, ERS, *World Indices.*

5. USDA, ERS, *World Indices.*

6. Ibid.

7. Soil loss information based on data from USDA, *The Soil and Water Resources Conservation Act: 1980 Appraisal, Part II* (Washington, D.C.: 1980), and wind erosion data from USDA, Soil Conservation Service, and Iowa State University Statistical Laboratory, *Basic Statistics: 1977 National Resources Inventory,* Statistical Bulletin No. 686 (Washington, D.C.: 1982).

8. For more information on the Food Security Act of 1985, see R. Neil Sampson, "A Landmark for Soil Conservation," *American Land Forum Magazine,* Spring 1986; Tim T. Phipps, "The Farm Bill, Resources and Environmental Quality," *Resources,* Winter 1986.

9. USDA, ERS, *World Indices.*

10. Population data and projections from Population Reference Bureau, *1986 World Population Data Sheet* (Washington, D.C.: 1986); world per capita grain area from USDA, ERS, *World Indices.*

11. Data for 1950–80 from W.R. Rangeley, "Irrigation and Drainage in the World," paper presented at the International Conference on Food and Water, Texas A&M University, College Station, May 26–30, 1986; irrigated area from 1980 to present is Worldwatch Institute estimate based on ibid.

12. Peter Beaumont, "Irrigated Agriculture and Ground-water Mining on the High Plains of Texas, USA," *Environmental Conservation*, Summer 1985.

13. Australia's irrigated area from Rangeley, "Irrigation and Drainage."

14. U.S. irrigated area from USDA, *Farm and Ranch Irrigation Survey-1984* (Washington, D.C.: 1986), and from John Hostetler, Agricultural Economist, USDA, ERS, private communication, May 29, 1986.

15. Club du Sahel quote from Asit K. Biswas, "Evaluating Irrigation's Impact: Guidelines for Project Monitoring," *Ceres*, July/August 1985.

16. Gordon Sloggett and Clifford Dickason, *Ground-Water Mining in the United States* (Washington, D.C.: USDA, 1986); for additional discussion of groundwater depletion in Texas high plains see Beaumont, "Irrigated Agriculture on the High Plains of Texas."

17. For aquifer depletion in China, see David Fraser, "Water Crisis Threatens to Dry Up China's Future," *New Straits Times*, May 8, 1986; for Tamil Nadu, see Sandra Postel, "Managing Freshwater Supplies," in Lester R. Brown et al., *State of the World-1985* (New York: W.W. Norton & Co., 1985); for Arizona, see Sloggett and Dickason, *Ground-Water Mining*.

18. Hall quoted in Janet Raloff, "Surviving Salt," *Science News*, November 17, 1984.

19. Information on competing uses of water in the Sun Belt states from Ewan MacAskill, "Colorado Cities Thirsting for Wilderness Water," *Washington Post*, October 15, 1986, from Marshall Ingwerson, "Use Begins to Shift From Farmland to Cities," *Christian Science Monitor*, August 26, 1985, and from "Mystery Farmland Buyer Turns Out to be Thirsty Denver Suburb," *U.S. Water News*, June 1986; Fraser, "Water Crisis Threatens China's Future"; Celestine Bohlen, "New Economics Shrinks Soviet Irrigation Plans," *Washington Post*, March 5, 1986; Mike Nicol, "South Africa Reaching Limit of Resources," *World Environment Report*, June 12, 1985.

20. Phillip Michlin, Western Michigan University, Kalamazoo, Mich., private communication, December 15, 1986.

21. For Soviet irrigation reducing electricity generation by 30–40 percent, see Thane Gustafson, "Transforming Soviet Agriculture: Brezhnev's Gamble on Land Improvement," *Public Policy*, Summer 1977.

22. Norman K. Whittlesey et al., *Energy Tradeoffs and Economic Feasibility of Irrigation Development in the Pacific Northwest*, Bulletin 896, College of Agriculture Research Center, Washington State University, Pullman, Wash., 1981; see also Gordon Sloggett, *Energy and U.S. Agriculture: Irrigation Pumping, 1974–83* (Washington, D.C.: USDA, 1985).

23. World fertilizer use from United Nations Food and Agriculture Organization (FAO), *Fertilizer Yearbooks* (Rome: various years); world grain area and grain production from USDA, ERS, *World Indices*.

24. FAO, *Fertilizer Yearbooks*.

25. U.S. fertilizer use from USDA, Statistical Reporting Service, *Commercial Fertilizers* (Washington, D.C.: 1985); 1986 figure is a Worldwatch Institute estimate based on information from Paul Andrilenas, USDA, Washington, D.C., private communication, August 1986.

26. Fertilizer use in China from Anthony M. Tang and Bruce Stone, *Food Production in the People's Republic of China* (Washington, D.C.: International Food Policy Research Institute, May 1980), and from Bruce Stone,

"Chinese Fertilizer Application in the 1980s and 1990s: Issues of Growth, Balance, Allocation, Efficiency, and Response," in U.S. Congress, Joint Economic Committee, *China's Economy in the Eighties* (Washington, D.C.: U.S. Government Printing Office, forthcoming).

27. Stone, "Chinese Fertilizer Application."

28. Elliot Berg, "Fertilizer Subsidies" (draft), World Bank, Washington, D.C., December 1985.

29. Ibid.

30. Unless otherwise indicated, data on energy use (oil equivalent) in agriculture throughout this chapter are Worldwatch Institute estimates based on the amount of oil embodied in the manufacture and maintenance of farm machinery and inputs such as fertilizers and pesticides, and the amount of energy needed to run tractors and irrigation pumps. Since no global data exist for pesticide use, their use and that of all other non-listed uses were assumed to be 20 percent of the total energy for all listed categories. Energy used in the manufacture of fertilizer and fabrication of farm machinery based on David Pimentel, *Handbook of Energy Utilization in Agriculture* (Boca Raton, Fla.: CRC Press, 1980); energy consumed by tractors based on USDA, *Agricultural Statistics* (Washington, D.C.: U.S. Government Printing Office, various years); energy for irrigation pumping based on Sloggett, *Energy and U.S. Agriculture: Irrigation Pumping, 1974–83;* total world fertilizer consumption and tractor fleet from FAO, *Production Yearbooks* (Rome: various years); world irrigated area from Rangeley, "Irrigation and Drainage" and from W.R. Rangeley, "Irrigation—Current Trends and A Future Perspective," World Bank Seminar, February 1983.

31. Growth of pump irrigation in India from World Bank, India Division, *Situation and Prospects of the Indian Economy—A Medium Term Perspective* (Washington, D.C.: April 1984); Government of India, Departments of State and Agriculture, *Economic Surveys* (New Delhi: various years); Rip Landes, USDA, Foreign Agriculture Service, Washington, D.C., private communication, October 4, 1986; pump irrigation data for China from Frances Tuan, USDA, Foreign Agriculture Service, Washington, D.C., private communication, October 2, 1986.

32. USDA, *Agricultural Statistics.*

33. Ibid.

34. Average grain yield per hectare in 1986 based on USDA, Foreign Agricultural Service, *Foreign Agriculture Circular—Grains,* FG 6–86, June 1986.

35. USDA, ERS, *World Indices.*

36. USDA, ERS, *China: Situation and Outlook Report* (Washington, D.C.: 1986).

37. Per capita grain production in Africa from USDA, ERS, *World Indices;* Edward V.K. Jaycox, "Africa: Development Challenges and the World Bank's Response," lecture delivered at Woodrow Wilson International Center for Scholars, The Smithsonian Institution, Washington, D.C., August 6, 1985.

38. Carryover stocks in 1976 derived from USDA, Foreign Agricultural Service, *Foreign Agriculture Circular: Grains,* Washington, D.C., various issues.

39. Shlomo Reutlinger, "Food Security and Poverty in LDCs," *Finance and Development,* December 1985.

40. Ibid.

41. Ibid.

42. USDA, ERS, *World Indices.*

43. John Kifner, "The Egyptian Economy Has No Place To Turn," *New York Times,* July 6, 1986.

44. USDA, ERS, *World Indices.*

45. Ibid.

46. Ibid.

47. Sampson, "A Landmark for Soil Conservation"; Phipps, "The Farm Bill, Resources and Environmental Quality."

48. Sloggett and Dickason, *Ground-Water Mining*.

49. Reductions in the number of tons of grain produced in states where groundwater mining may force the conversion of irrigated to dryland farming is a Worldwatch Institute estimate based on Sloggett and Dickason, *Ground-Water Mining in the United States*, and on both irrigated and dryland yield data for several crops in 11 affected states from Pimentel, *Handbook of Energy Utilization in Agriculture*.

50. Debora Mackenzie, "Ethiopia: Countdown to Disaster," *New Scientist*, November 1, 1984; Haiti's food production data from USDA, ERS, *World Indices*.

Chapter 8. Raising Agricultural Productivity

1. Data on adoption of high-yielding varieties from Dana G. Dalrymple, *Development and Spread of High-Yielding Rice Varieties in Developing Countries* (Washington, D.C.: U.S. Agency for International Development, 1986), and from Dana G. Dalrymple, *Development and Spread of High-Yielding Wheat Varieties in Developing Countries* (Washington, D.C.: U.S. Agency for International Development, 1986); regional grain area data from U.S. Department of Agriculture (USDA), Economic Research Service (ERS), *World Indices of Agricultural and Food Production 1950–85* (unpublished printout) (Washington, D.C.: 1986).

2. Population data based on estimates of agriculturally active populations from United Nations Food and Agriculture Organization, *1984 Production Yearbook* (Rome: 1985).

3. Population projections from Population Reference Bureau, *1985 World Population Data Sheet* (Washington, D.C.: 1985); grain-yield projections by Worldwatch Institute, based on world grain utilization data from

USDA, Foreign Agricultural Service, *Foreign Agriculture Circular — Grains*, FG-9–86, Washington, D.C., August 1986.

4. USDA, ERS, *World Indices*.

5. World Bank, *China: Agriculture to the Year 2000* (Washington, D.C.: 1985).

6. Ibid.; Bruce Stone, "Chinese Fertilizer Application in the 1980s and 1990s: Issues of Growth, Balance, Allocation, Efficiency, and Response," in U.S. Congress, Joint Economic Committee, *China's Economy in the Eighties* (Washington, D.C.: U.S. Government Printing Office, forthcoming).

7. Organisation for Economic Co-operation and Development, *The State of the Environment 1985* (Paris: 1985).

8. Rodale quoted in Charles A. Francis and Richard R. Harwood, *Enough Food: Achieving Food Security Through Regenerative Agriculture* (Emmaus, Pa.: Rodale Institute, 1985).

9. Robert Rodale, "Internal Resources and External Inputs — The Two Sources of All Production Needs," in Rodale Institute, *Regenerative Farming Systems* (Emmaus, Pa.: 1985).

10. D.F. Bezdicek et al., "Influence of Organic Nitrogen on Soil Nitrogen, Nodulation, Nitrogen Fixation, and Yield of Soybeans," *Soil Science Society of America Proceedings* (Madison, Wisc.), March-April 1974; D.F. Bezdicek, "Biotechnology and Farming Systems: On-Farm Applications and Consequences," in Institute for Alternative Agriculture, *Biotechnology and Agriculture: Implications for Sustainability* (Greenbelt, Md.: 1986); D.F. Bezdicek, Washington State University, Pullman, private communication, August 6, 1986.

11. For a review of regenerative practices, see Francis and Harwood, *Enough Food*, Rodale Institute, *Regenerative Farming Systems*, and Rodale Institute, *Proceedings of Workshop on Resource-Efficient Farming Methods for Tanzania* (Emmaus, Pa.: Rodale Press, 1983).

12. Dana G. Dalrymple, "The Development and Adoption of High-Yielding Varieties of Wheat and Rice in Developing Countries," *American Journal of Agricultural Economics,* December 1985.

13. Dalrymple, "High-Yielding Varieties"; Inter-American Development Bank, *Economic and Social Progess in Latin America: 1986 Report* (Washington, D.C.: 1986).

14. Consultative Group on International Agricultural Research (CGIAR), *1984 Annual Report* (Washington, D.C.: 1985); *News from the CGIAR* (Washington, D.C.), January/April 1986.

15. Dalrymple, "High-Yielding Varieties"; USDA, ERS, *World Indices;* Dunstan S.C. Spencer, "Agricultural Research: Lessons of the Past, Strategies for the Future," in Robert J. Berg and Jennifer Seymour Whittaker, eds., *Strategies for African Development* (Berkeley: University of California Press, 1986).

16. CGIAR, *1984 Annual Report.*

17. International Development Research Center, *The Fragile Web: The International Agricultural Research System* (Ottawa: 1983); CGIAR, *1984 Annual Report.*

18. Donald L. Plucknett and Nigel J.H. Smith, "Sustaining Agricultural Yields," *BioScience,* January 1986.

19. International Rice Research Institute (IRRI), *IRRI Highlights 1985: Accomplishments and Challenges* (Manila, Philippines: 1986).

20. Ibid.; CGIAR, *Summary of International Agriculture Research Centers: A Study of Achievements and Potential* (Washington, D.C.: 1985).

21. International Institute of Tropical Agriculture (IITA), *IITA Annual Report and Research Highlights 1985* (Ibadan, Nigeria: 1986); "Mycorrhizae: Can Africa Benefit?" *International Livestock Center for Africa Newsletter* (Addis Ababa, Ethiopia), July 1986; IRRI, *Highlights 1985.*

22. J.G. Hawkes, *Plant Genetic Resources: The Impact of the International Agricultural Research Centers* (Washington, D.C.: World Bank, 1985).

23. Debora MacKenzie, "Ethiopia: Famine amid Genetic Plenty," *New Scientist,* August 8, 1985; Jonathan B. Tucker, "Amaranth: The Once and Future Crop," *BioScience,* January 1986.

24. Gary Paul Nabhan, *Gathering the Desert* (Tucson: University of Arizona Press, 1985).

25. Michael Philips, "Rodale Research Center Holds Premier Amaranth Collection," *Diversity,* Number 9, 1986; William Liebhardt and Charles S. Kauffman, Rodale Research Center, Kutztown, Pa., private communications, March 26, 1986; Wes Jackson, *New Roots for Agriculture* (San Francisco: Friends of the Earth, 1980).

26. Quoted in Sterling Wortman and Ralph W. Cummings, Jr., *To Feed This World* (Baltimore, Md.: The Johns Hopkins University Press, 1978).

27. W.C. Liebhardt et al., "Research Needs for the Development of Resource Efficient Technologies," in Rodale Institute, *Regenerative Farming Systems.*

28. Peter R. Jennings, "The Amplification of Agricultural Production," *Scientific American,* September 1976.

29. Ibid.

30. Gerald G. Marten, "Traditional Agriculture and Agricultural Research in Southeast Asia," in Gerald G. Marten, ed., *Traditional Agriculture in Southeast Asia* (Boulder, Colo.: Westview Press, 1986).

31. Traditional acacia-based systems described in National Research Council, Board on Science and Technology for International Development, *Environmental Change in the West African Sahel* (Washington, D.C.: National Academy Press, 1983).

32. Ibid.

33. Michael McGahuey, *Impact of Forestry Initiatives in the Sahel* (Washington, D.C.: Chemonics, 1986).

34. Sedogo's research discussed in Christian Pieri, "Food Crop Fertilization and Soil Fertility: The IRAT Experience," in Herbert W. Ohm and Joseph G. Nagy, eds., *Appropriate Technologies for Farmers in Semi-Arid West Africa* (West Lafayette, Ind.: Purdue University International Programs in Agriculture, 1985).

35. Shifting cultivation is described in D.B. Grigg, *The Agricultural Systems of the World* (New York: Cambridge University Press, 1974).

36. Current research in alley cropping is described in IITA, *Annual Report 1985,* and in IITA, *Alley Cropping: A Stable Alternative to Shifting Cultivation* (Ibadan, Nigeria: 1984).

37. Spencer, "Agricultural Research."

38. U.S. Congress, Office of Technology Assessment (OTA), *Technology, Public Policy, and the Changing Structure of American Agriculture* (Washington, D.C.: U.S. Government Printing Office, 1986).

39. For overviews of the environmental implications of biotechnologies, see Jack Doyle, "Biotechnology Research and Agricultural Stability," *Issues in Science and Technology,* Fall 1985, and Jack Doyle, *Altered Harvest* (New York: Viking Penguin Inc., 1985).

40. OTA, *Changing Structure of American Agriculture.*

41. Marjorie Sun, "Engineering Crops to Resist Weed Killers," *Science,* March 21, 1986.

42. Data on conservation tillage in the United States from *No-Till Farmer,* March 1986; African conservation tillage research described in IITA, *Tasks for the Eighties: A Long-Range Plan* (Ibadan, Nigeria: 1981), and in IITA, *IITA Annual Report 1984* (Ibadan, Nigeria: 1985).

43. Frederick H. Buttel et al., "Genetic Engineering and the Restructuring of Agricultural Research," *The Rural Sociologist,* Vol. 3, No. 3, 1983; for the history of public agricultural research in the United States, see

Yujiro Hayami and Vernon W. Ruttan, *Agricultural Development* (Baltimore, Md.: The Johns Hopkins University Press, 1985).

44. Estimate of USDA-supported biotechnology research from U.S. General Accounting Office, *Biotechnology: The U.S. Department of Agriculture's Biotechnology Research Efforts* (Washington, D.C.: 1985); Monsanto investment from Frederick Buttel, "Biotechnology and Alternative Agriculture: An Overview of the Major Issues and Concerns," in Institute for Alternative Agriculture, *Biotechnology and Agriculture.*

45. These and other challenges facing the international research centers are discussed in Frederick H. Buttel and Randolph Barker, "Emerging Agricultural Technologies, Public Policy, and Implications for Third World Agriculture: The Case of Biotechnology," *American Journal of Agricultural Economics,* December 1985, and in F.H. Buttel et al., "The IARCs and the Development and Application of Biotechnologies in Developing Countries," in IRRI, *Biotechnology in International Agricultural Research* (Manila: 1985).

46. W.G. Padolina, "Strategies to Develop Biotechnology in the Philippines," in IRRI, *Biotechnology in International Agricultural Research.*

47. CGIAR, *1984 Annual Report.*

48. *News from the CGIAR* (Washington, D.C.), May/August 1986.

49. Randolph Barker, "Biotechnology and Farming Systems: An International Perspective," in Institute for Alternative Agriculture, *Biotechnology and Agriculture;* The Rockefeller Foundation, *The President's Review and Annual Report 1983* (New York: 1983); Kathleen Teltsch, "Rockefeller Unit Doubles Its Third-World Aid," *New York Times,* May 4, 1986; The Rockefeller Foundation, "The Rockefeller Foundation in the Developing World," New York, May 1986.

50. Robert Barker, "The Changed World of Research Opportunities," in Martin Gibbs

and Carla Carlson, eds., *Crop Productivity — Research Imperatives Revisited,* conference at Boyne Highlands Inn, Boyne, Mich., October 13–18, 1985, and at Airlie House, Va., December 11–13, 1985.

51. *News from the CGIAR*, May/August 1986.

52. For several perspectives on farming systems research, see Joyce Lewinger Moock, ed., *Understanding Africa's Rural Households and Farming Systems* (Boulder, Colo.: Westview Press, 1986); potential for farmer-scientist collaboration described in Marten, "Agricultural Research in Southeast Asia."

53. Paul Richards, *Indigenous Agricultural Revolution* (London: Hutchinson & Co., Ltd., 1985).

Chapter 9. Stabilizing Chemical Cycles

1. G. Tyler Miller, Jr., *Living in the Environment: Concepts, Problems, and Alternatives* (Belmont, Calif.: Wadsworth Publishing Company, Inc., 1975).

2. A.M. Solomon et al., "The Global Cycle of Carbon," R.M. Rotty and C.D. Masters, "Carbon Dioxide from Fossil Fuel Combustion: Trends, Resources, and Technological Implications," and R.A. Houghton et al., "Carbon Dioxide Exchange Between the Atmosphere and Terrestrial Ecosystems," in John R. Trabalka et al., *Atmospheric Carbon Dioxide and the Global Carbon Cycle* (Washington, D.C.: U.S. Government Printing Office, 1985).

3. G.M. Woodwell et al., "Global Deforestation: Contribution to Atmospheric Carbon Dioxide," *Science,* December 9, 1983; range from Solomon et al., "The Global Cycle of Carbon."

4. Roger Revelle, "Carbon Dioxide and World Climate," *Scientific American,* August 1982; Roger Revelle, "The Oceans and the Carbon Dioxide Problem," *Oceans,* Summer 1983; preindustrial concentration from Eric

W. Wolff and David A. Peel, "The Record of Global Pollution in Polar Snow and Ice," *Nature,* February 14, 1985.

5. Revelle, "Carbon Dioxide and World Climate"; Carbon Dioxide Assessment Committee, National Research Council (NRC), *Changing Climate* (Washington, D.C.: National Academy Press, 1983); Stephen Seidel and Dale Keyes, *Can We Delay a Greenhouse Warming?* (Washington, D.C.: U.S. Environmental Protection Agency (EPA), 1983).

6. Ice Age comparison from National Aeronautics and Space Administration (NASA), Goddard Space Flight Center, "Potential Climatic Impacts of Increasing Atmospheric CO_2 With Emphasis on Water Availability and Hydrology in the United States," prepared for U.S. Environmental Protection Agency, Washington, D.C., 1984.

7. NRC, *Global Change in the Geosphere-Biosphere* (Washington, D.C.: National Academy Press, 1986).

8. D.H. Ehhalt, "Methane in the Global Atmosphere," *Environment,* December 1985; estimates of warming from Gordon J. MacDonald, "Climate Change and Acid Rain," The MITRE Corporation, McLean, Va., December 1985, and from V. Ramanathan et al., "Trace Gas Trends and their Potential Role in Climate Change," *Journal of Geophysical Research,* June 20, 1985.

9. Global estimates from P.J. Crutzen and M.O. Andreae, "Atmospheric Chemistry," in T.F. Malone and J.G. Roederer, eds., *Global Change* (Cambridge: Cambridge University Press, 1985); U.S. figures from EPA, *National Air Pollutant Emission Estimates, 1940–1984* (Research Triangle Park, N.C.: 1986).

10. MacDonald, "Climate Change and Acid Rain"; Ramanathan et al., "Trace Gas Trends."

11. Crutzen and Andreae, "Atmospheric Chemistry."

12. Walter W. Heck et al., "A Reassessment of Crop Loss from Ozone," *Environmen-*

tal Science & Technology, Vol. 17, No. 12, 1983; Environmental Resources Limited, *Acid Rain: A Review of the Phenomenon in the EEC and Europe* (London: Graham & Trotman Ltd., 1983).

13. Jack G. Calvert et al., "Chemical Mechanisms of Acid Generation in the Troposphere," *Nature*, September 5, 1985; Ellis B. Cowling, "Acid Precipitation in Historical Perspective," *Environmental Science & Technology*, Vol. 16, No. 2, 1982.

14. A.H. Johnson et al., "Spatial and Temporal Patterns of Lead Accumulation in the Forest Floor in the Northeastern United States," *Journal of Environmental Quality*, Vol. 11, No. 4, 1982; James N. Galloway et al., "Trace Metals in Atmospheric Deposition: A Review and Assessment," *Atmospheric Environment*, Vol. 16, No. 7, 1982.

15. NRC, *Causes and Effects of Changes in Stratospheric Ozone: Update 1983* (Washington, D.C.: National Academy Press, 1984).

16. Ibid.; Peter H. Sand, "The Vienna Convention is Adopted," *Environment*, June 1985; recent production increase from Chemical Manufacturers Association, "Production and Release of Chlorofluorocarbons 11 and 12," Washington, D.C., October 1985.

17. NASA, "Knowledge of the Upper Atmosphere," draft, January 1986; EPA, "Analysis of Strategies for Protecting the Ozone Layer," prepared for Working Group Meeting, Geneva, Switzerland, January 1985.

18. NASA, "Present State of Knowledge of the Upper Atmosphere"; Paul Brodeur, "Annals of Chemistry," *The New Yorker*, June 9, 1986.

19. Ramanathan et al., "Trace Gas Trends"; "An Assessment of the Role of Carbon Dioxide and of other Greenhouse Gases in Climate Variations and Associated Impacts," statement from conference cosponsored by United Nations Environment Programme, World Meteorological Organization, and International Council of Scientific Unions, Villach, Austria, October 1985.

20. Miller, *Living in the Environment*; NRC, *Testing for Effects of Chemicals on Ecosystems* (Washington, D.C.: National Academy Press, 1981); David Pimentel and Clive A. Edwards, "Pesticides and Ecosystems," *BioScience*, July/August 1982.

21. NRC, *Testing for Effects of Chemicals*; Robert M. Garrels et al., *Chemical Cycles and the Global Environment: Assessing Human Influences* (Los Altos, Calif.: William Kaufmann, Inc., 1975); Arthur J. Vander, *Nutrition, Stress, and Toxic Chemicals* (Ann Arbor: University of Michigan Press, 1981); Lawrie Mott and Martha Broad, "Pesticides in Food: What the Public Needs to Know," Natural Resources Defense Council, Inc., Washington, D.C., March 1984.

22. For a comprehensive review of climate issues, see NRC, *Changing Climate*.

23. Michael E. Schlesinger and John F.B. Mitchell, "Model Projections of the Equilibrium Climatic Response to Increased Carbon Dioxide," in Michael C. MacCracken and Frederick M. Luther, eds., *The Potential Climatic Effects of Increasing Carbon Dioxide* (Washington, D.C.: U.S. Department of Energy, 1985).

24. S. Manabe and R.T. Wetherald, "Reduction in Summer Soil Wetness Induced by an Increase in Atmospheric Carbon Dioxide," *Science*, May 2, 1986; "The Role of Greenhouse Gases in Climate Variations," statement from Villach conference.

25. Dean Abrahamson, "Responses to Greenhouse Gas Induced Climate Change," testimony before the U.S. Senate, Committee on Environment and Public Works, Subcommittee on Toxic Substances and Environmental Oversight, Hearings, Washington, D.C., December 10, 1985; rule of thumb cited by Loyd Stone, Department of Agronomy, Kansas State University, Manhattan, private communication, June 1986.

26. Revelle, "Carbon Dioxide and World Climate"; William W. Kellogg and Robert Schware, "Society, Science and Climate Change," *Foreign Affairs,* Summer 1982.

27. Dean Abrahamson and Peter Ciborowski, "North American Agriculture and the Greenhouse Problem," Hubert H. Humphrey Institute of Public Affairs, University of Minnesota, Minneapolis, April 1983; Kellogg and Schware, "Society, Science and Climate Change."

28. M. Barth and J. Titus, eds., *Greenhouse Effect and Sea Level Rise: A Challenge for This Generation* (New York: Van Nostrand Reinhold Co., 1984); "The Role of Greenhouse Gases in Climate Variations," statement from Villach conference; Erik Eckholm, "Significant Rise in Sea Level Now Seems Certain," *New York Times,* February 18, 1986.

29. Sylvan H. Wittwer, "Carbon Dioxide and Climate Change: An Agricultural Perspective," *Journal of Soil and Water Conservation,* May/June 1980; Sylvan H. Wittwer, "Rising Atmospheric CO_2 and Crop Productivity," *Hortscience,* October 1983.

30. Paul E. Waggoner, "Agriculture and a Climate Changed by More Carbon Dioxide," in NRC, *Changing Climate;* Sylvan H. Wittwer, "Carbon Dioxide Levels in the Biosphere: Effects on Plant Productivity," *CRC Critical Reviews in Plant Sciences,* Vol. 2, Issue 3, 1985.

31. Irrigation figures from W.R. Rangeley, "Irrigation and Drainage in the World," paper presented at the International Conference on Food and Water, Texas A&M University, College Station, May 26–30, 1985.

32. Roger R. Revelle and Paul E. Waggoner, "Effects of a Carbon Dioxide-Induced Climatic Change on Water Supplies in the Western United States," in NRC, *Changing Climate.*

33. Trend in Lower Colorado from U.S. Department of Agriculture, *Agricultural Statistics 1983* (Washington, D.C.: U.S. Government Printing Office, 1983), and from Bureau of the Census, "1985 Census of Agriculture," U.S. Department of Commerce, Washington, D.C., 1984; present overconsumption in Lower Colorado from U.S. Geological Survey, *National Water Summary 1983—Hydrologic Events and Issues* (Washington, D.C.: U.S. Government Printing Office, 1984); irrigated area calculation assumes an annual consumptive demand of 5,500 cubic meters per hectare, which is 55 percent of the average per hectare withdrawals for irrigation estimated in Revelle and Waggoner, "Effects of a Carbon Dioxide-Induced Climatic Change"; existing irrigated area from ibid.

34. Global calculation based on average investment needs for new large-scale irrigation projects in the Third World of $5,000 per hectare, from Rangeley, "Irrigation and Drainage."

35. Cost estimate from John A. Laurmann, "Strategic Issues and the CO_2 Environmental Problem," in W. Bach et al., eds., *Carbon Dioxide: Current Views and Developments in Energy/Climate Research* (Dordrecht, Netherlands: D. Reidel Publishing Co., 1983).

36. William W. Kellogg, "The Socio-Economic Response: Human Factors in Environmental Change," paper presented at the annual meeting of the American Association for the Advancement of Science, Los Angeles, Calif., May 26–31, 1985.

37. Der Bundesminister Für Ernährung, Landwirtschaft, und Forsten, "Neuartige Waldschäden in der Bundesrepublik Deutschland," Bonn, West Germany, October 1983; Federal Ministry of Food, Agriculture, and Forestry, "1984 Forest Damage Survey," Bonn, West Germany, October 1984.

38. *Allgemeine Forst Zeitschrift,* Munich, West Germany, No. 46, 1985 and No. 41, 1986; G.H.M. Krause et al., "Forest Decline in Europe: Possible Causes and Etiology," paper presented at the International Symposium on Acid Precipitation, Ontario, Canada,

September 1985; see also Susan Tifft, "Requiem for the Forest," *Time* (international edition), September 16, 1985.

39. Krause et al., "Forest Decline in Europe"; Yugoslavia figures from *Allgemeine Forst Zeitschrift*, No. 41, 1986.

40. Dieter Deumling, Wissen, West Germany, private communication, March 1986; "Swiss Forests are Depleted Further by Pollution," *New York Times*, December 9, 1985; *Allgemeine Forst Zeitschrift*, No. 41, 1986.

41. Arthur H. Johnson and Thomas G. Siccama, "Acid Deposition and Forest Decline," *Environmental Science & Technology*, Vol. 17, No. 7, 1983; Raymond M. Sheffield et al., "Pine Growth Reductions in the Southeast," Southeastern Forest Experiment Station, Asheville, N.C., November 1985.

42. Arthur H. Johnson, "Assessing the Effects of Acid Rain on Forests of the Eastern U.S.," testimony before the U.S. Senate, Committee on Environment and Public Works, Hearings, February 7, 1984.

43. Sandra Postel, *Air Pollution, Acid Rain, and the Future of Forests*, Worldwatch Paper 58 (Washington, D.C.: Worldwatch Institute, March 1984).

44. Nico van Breeman, "Acidification and Decline of Central European Forests," *Nature*, May 2, 1985; Tomas Paces, "Sources of Acidification in Central Europe Estimated from Elemental Budgets in Small Basins," *Nature*, May 2, 1985.

45. Paces, "Sources of Acidification in Central Europe."

46. C.S. Holling, "Resilience of Ecosystems: Local Surprise and Global Change," in Malone and Roederer, *Global Change;* see also F.H. Bormann, "Air Pollution and Forests: An Ecosystem Perspective," *BioScience*, July/August 1985.

47. Andrew Csepel, "Czechs and the Ecological Balance," *New Scientist*, September 27, 1984; H.J. Ewers et al., "Zur Monetarisierung der Waldschäden in der Bundesrepublik Deutschland," paper presented at Symposium on Costs of Environmental Pollution, Bonn, West Germany, September 12–13, 1985.

48. Peter B. Reich and Robert G. Amundson, "Ambient Levels of Ozone Reduce Net Photosynthesis in Tree and Crop Species," *Science*, November 1, 1985.

49. Federal Ministry of Food, Agriculture, and Forestry, "1985 Forest Damage Survey," Bonn, West Germany, October 1985; Dieter Deumling, Wissen, West Germany, private communication, October 1985.

50. Michael Castleman, "Toxics and Male Infertility," *Sierra*, March/April 1985.

51. U.S. Congress, Office of Technology Assessment (OTA), *Acid Rain and Transported Air Pollutants: Implications for Public Policy* (Washington, D.C.: U.S. Government Printing Office, 1984); NRC, *Epidemiology and Air Pollution* (Washington, D.C.: National Academy Press, 1985).

52. Brazil figures from NRC, *Epidemiology and Air Pollution;* Dianwu Zhao and Bozen Sun, "Air Pollution and Acid Rain in China," *Ambio*, Vol. 15, No. 1, 1986; Shanghai reference from Michael Weisskopf, "Shanghai's Curse: Too Many Fight for Too Little," *Washington Post*, January 6, 1985.

53. Vander, *Nutrition, Stress, and Toxic Chemicals;* Organisation for Economic Co-operation and Development (OECD), *State of the Environment* (Paris: 1985).

54. Joel Schwartz et al., *Costs and Benefits of Reducing Lead in Gasoline: Final Regulatory Impact Analysis* (Washington, D.C.: U.S. Government Printing Office, 1985); figure on U.S. children from NRC, *Epidemiology and Air Pollution;* see also Richard Rabin, "Lead Poisoning: Silent Epidemic," *Science for the People*, July/August 1985.

55. Don L. Johnson and Quincy Dadisman, "Acid Helps Mercury Contaminate Lakes," *Milwaukee Sentinel*, October 2, 1985; Eugeniusz Pudlis, "Poland: Heavy Metals

Pose Serious Health Problems," *Ambio,* Vol. 11, No. 1, 1982.

56. Tri-Academy Committee on Acid Deposition, *Acid Deposition: Effects on Geochemical Cycling and Biological Availability of Trace Elements* (Washington, D.C.: National Academy Press, 1985); Thomas H. Maugh II, "Acid Rain's Effects on People Assessed," *Science,* December 21, 1984; OTA, *Acid Rain and Transported Air Pollutants.*

57. Magda Havas et al., "Red Herrings in Acid Rain Research," *Environmental Science & Technology,* Vol. 18, No. 6, 1984; Bernhard Ulrich, "Dangers for the Forest Ecosystem Due to Acid Precipitation," translated for EPA by Literature Research Company, Annandale, Va., undated.

58. Daniel P. Perl, "Relationship of Aluminum to Alzheimer's Disease," *Environmental Health Perspectives,* Vol. 63, 1985, pp. 149–153; Daniel P. Perl et al., "Intraneuronal Aluminum Accumulation in Amyotrophic Lateral Sclerosis and Parkinsonism-Dementia of Guam," *Science,* September 10, 1982.

59. Perl, "Relationship of Aluminum to Alzheimer's Disease."

60. "The Quest for Chemical Safety," *International Register of Potentially Toxic Chemicals Bulletin* (UNEP, Geneva, Switzerland), May 1985; Michael Shodell, "Risky Business," *Science '85,* October 1985; Philip M. Boffey, "After Years of Cancer Alarms, Progress Amid the Mistakes," *New York Times,* March 20, 1984.

61. William U. Chandler, *Banishing Tobacco,* Worldwatch Paper 68 (Washington, D.C.: Worldwatch Institute, January 1986); Arthur J. Vander, University of Michigan Medical School, Ann Arbor, private communication, April 1986.

62. NRC, *Toxicity Testing* (Washington, D.C.: National Academy Press, 1984).

63. Ibid.

64. Charles Benbrook, Executive Director, Board on Agriculture, National Academy of Sciences, Washington, D.C., private communication, May 1986; see Philip Shabecoff, "Senate Votes Tougher Pesticide Law," *New York Times,* October 7, 1986.

65. Ian C.T. Nisbet and Nathan J. Karch, *Chemical Hazards to Human Reproduction* (Park Ridge, N.J.: Noyes Data Corporation, 1983).

66. Janet Raloff, "Dioxin: Is Everyone Contaminated?" *Science News,* July 13, 1985.

67. Thomas H. Umbreit et al., "Bioavailability of Dioxin in Soil from a 2,4,5-T Manufacturing Site," *Science,* April 25, 1986; Susan Okie, "Dioxin May Weaken Ability to Fight Disease," *Washington Post,* April 18, 1986; Janet Raloff, "Infant Dioxin Exposures Reported High," *Science News,* April 26, 1986.

68. Ralph C. Dougherty et al., "Sperm Density and Toxic Substances: A Potential Key to Environmental Health Hazards," in J.D. McKinney, *Environmental Health Chemistry —The Chemistry of Environmental Agents as Potential Human Hazards* (Ann Arbor, Mich.: Ann Arbor Science Publishers, Inc., 1980).

69. Vander, *Nutrition, Stress, and Toxic Chemicals.*

70. Roger Lewin, "Parkinson's Disease: An Environmental Cause?" *Science,* July 19, 1985; for a fascinating sketch of how the link was discovered, see J. William Langston, "The Case of the Tainted Heroin," *The Sciences,* January/February 1985.

71. Emissions rates based on data from Ralph Rotty, Institute for Energy Analysis, Oak Ridge Associated Universities, Oak Ridge, Tenn., private communication, May 1986.

72. Eike Röhling and Jochen Mohnfeld, "Energy Policy and the Energy Economy in FR Germany," *Energy Policy,* December 1985.

73. Sand, "Vienna Convention is Adopted"; EPA, "Strategies for Protecting Ozone Layer"; Cass Peterson, "Chlorofluorocarbon Group Supports Production Curbs," *Washington Post,* September 17, 1986; status of negotiations from EPA,

"Stratospheric Ozone Protection Plan," *Federal Register*, January 10, 1986.

74. World Resources Institute (WRI), World Bank, and United Nations Development Programme, "Tropical Forests: A Call for Action," WRI, Washington, D.C., June 1985.

75. Schwartz et al., *Costs and Benefits of Reducing Lead in Gasoline;* Warren Brown, "End Nears for Leaded Gasoline—And Bargain Fuel Prices," *Washington Post*, December 29, 1985; Robert McDonald, "European Ministers Set Timetable for Auto Emission Standards," *World Environment Report*, April 17, 1985.

76. NRC, *Toxicity Testing.*

77. J. Clarence Davies, "Coping with Toxic Substances," *Issues in Science and Technology*, Winter 1985.

78. R.L. Frisbie and P.L. Adkisson, "IPM: Definitions and Current Status in U.S. Agriculture," in Marjorie A. Hoy and Donald C. Herzog, *Biological Control in Agricultural IPM Systems* (Orlando, Fla.: Academic Press, Inc., 1985).

Chapter 10. Designing Sustainable Economies

1. Adam Smith, *The Wealth of Nations* (Chicago: University of Chicago Press, 1976).

2. See Paul A. Samuelson and William D. Nordhaus, *Economics* (New York: McGraw-Hill, Inc., 1948) for the classic introduction to economics. For discussion of sustainable economics, see Hazel Henderson, "Ecologists Versus Economists," *Harvard Business Review*, July/August 1973, and Herman E. Daly, ed., *Toward a Steady-State Economy* (San Francisco: W.H. Freeman and Company, 1973).

3. See, for example, The Ecology Party, "Manifesto for a Sustainable Society," adopted at the third annual conference of the Ecology Party held in Sheffield, England, on September 25–26, 1976, and amended at Birmingham, England, September 1978.

4. Lung-Fai Wong, *Agricultural Productivity in the Socialist Countries* (Boulder, Colo.: Westview Press, Inc., 1986).

5. Ibid.; U.S. Department of Agriculture (USDA), Economic Research Service (ERS), *World Indices of Agricultural and Food Production, 1950–85* (unpublished printout) (Washington, D.C.: 1986). These statements hold whether productivity is measured in physical or economic terms.

6. István Láng, Secretary General, Hungarian Academy of Sciences, Budapest, Hungary, private communication, May 7, 1986.

7. István Láng, *Bioresources* (Budapest: Hungarian Academy of Sciences, 1982).

8. Stanislaw Gomulka, *Growth, Innovation and Reform in Eastern Europe* (Madison: University of Wisconsin Press, 1986); USDA, ERS, *Eastern Europe: Outlook and Situation Report*, RS-85-7 (Washington, D.C.: June 1985).

9. World Bank, *World Development Report 1986* (New York: Oxford University Press, 1986).

10. Wong, *Agricultural Productivity in Socialist Countries.*

11. Ibid.; Charles Cobb et al., *Economic Indicators of the Farm Sector* (Washington, D.C.: USDA, 1986); USDA, ERS, *USSR: Situation and Outlook Report* RS-86-3 (Washington, D.C.: May 1986).

12. Grain output figure compiled from USDA, ERS, *World Indices;* World Bank, *World Development Report 1986.*

13. D. Gale Johnson et al., *Agricultural Policy and Trade, A Report to the Trilateral Commission: 29* (New York: New York University Press, 1985); Keith Schneider, "Cost of Farm Loss Might Be Double Original Estimate," *New York Times*, July 22, 1986.

14. Johnson et al., *Agricultural Policy and Trade;* see also World Bank, *World Development Report 1986.*

15. William U. Chandler, *Energy Productivity: Key to Environmental Protection and Economic Progress*, Worldwatch Paper 63 (Washington, D.C.: Worldwatch Institute, January 1985).

16. József Bognár, Director, Institute of World Economics, Budapest, Hungary, private communication, May 9, 1986.

17. See, for example, János Kornai, *Contradictions and Dilemmas* (Cambridge, Mass.: The MIT Press, 1986).

18. Gábor Hoványi, Budapest, Hungary, private communication, May 12, 1986, and letter to the author, August 4, 1986; Chandler, *Energy Productivity*. See also Bela Balassa, *Reforming the New Economic Mechanism in Hungary*, World Bank Staff Working Paper No. 534 (Washington, D.C.: World Bank, 1982).

19. Chandler, *Energy Productivity;* data on steel production technology from International Iron and Steel Institute, Brussels, Belgium, private communication, June 1986.

20. International Iron and Steel Institute, private communication.

21. Romania, for instance, has a low equity ratio, but fuel and power shortages, as well as other constraints, have recently led to many hardships in that country.

22. William U. Chandler, *Investing in Children*, Worldwatch Paper 64 (Washington, D.C.: June 1985); William U. Chandler, *Banishing Tobacco*, Worldwatch Paper 68 (Washington, D.C.: Worldwatch Institute, January 1986).

23. Organisation for Economic Co-operation and Development (OECD), *OECD Economic Outlook* (Paris: 1985); David Lane, *Soviet Economy and Society* (New York: New York University Press, 1985).

24. Marshall I. Goldman, *The Spoils of Progress: Environmental Pollution in the Soviet Union* (Cambridge, Mass.: The MIT Press, 1972); N.H. Highton and M.J. Chadwick, "The Effects of Changing Patterns of Energy Use on Sulfur Emissions and Depositions in Europe," *Ambio*, Vol. 11, No. 6, 1982; OECD, *OECD Environmental Data, Compendium, 1985* (Paris: 1985).

25. Goldman, *The Spoils of Progress.*

26. Ibid.

27. Marshall I. Goldman, "Foreword," in Boris Komarov, *The Destruction of Nature in the Soviet Union* (Armonk, N.Y.: M.E. Sharpe Inc., 1980); Philip R. Pryde, "The 'Decade of the Environment' in the USSR," *Science*, April 15, 1983.

28. Stanley J. Kabala, "The Hidden Costs of Development," *Environment*, November 1985; Andrzej Kassenberg and Czesawa Rolewicz, *Przestrzenna Diagnoza Ochrony Srodowiska W Polsce* (Warsaw: Panstwowe Wydawnictwo Ekonomiczne, 1985), as described by Andrzej Kassenberg, Warsaw, Poland, private communication, May 17, 1986; Anita Bialic, Kraków, Poland, private communication, May 21, 1986; Elzbieta Bukowy, staff scientist, Environmental Pollution Abatement Center, Katowice, Poland, private communication, May 22, 1986; Zdzislaw Kaczmarek, Scientific Secretary, Polish Academy of Sciences, private communication, May 20, 1986.

29. Vaclav Smil, *The Bad Earth: Environmental Degradation in China* (Armonk, N.Y.: M.E. Sharpe Inc., 1984); Liu Dizhong, "Tree Target for 1986 Planted in Six Months," *China Daily*, July 9, 1986.

30. World Resources Institute/International Institute for Environment and Development, *World Resources 1986* (New York: Basic Books, 1986); Ed A. Hewett, *Energy, Economics, and Foreign Policy in the Soviet Union* (Washington D.C.: Brookings Institution, 1984); U.S. Department of Energy (DOE), Energy Information Administration (EIA), *Monthly Energy Review* (Washington, D.C.: January 1986); Paul Marer, *Dollar GNPs of the USSR and Eastern Europe* (Baltimore, Md.: The Johns Hopkins University Press, 1985); Central Statistical Board of the USSR, *The*

USSR in Figures for 1984 (Moscow: Fininsy i Statistika Publishers, 1985).

31. Elizabeth I. Perry and Christine Wong, eds., *The Political Economy of Reform in Post-Mao China* (Cambridge, Mass.: Harvard University Press, 1985).

32. "Economic Growth and Rural Development," *Beijing Review*, March 10, 1986; USDA, ERS, *China: Outlook and Situation Report*, RS-85–8 (Washington, D.C.: July 1985); James P. Sterba, "China's Change," *Wall Street Journal*, June 16, 1986.

33. USDA, ERS, *China: Outlook and Situation Report;* Perry and Wong, *Reform in Post-Mao China.*

34. "Minding Latin America's Business," *The Economist*, April 12, 1986; Mary M. Shirley, *Managing State-Owned Enterprises*, World Bank Staff Working Paper No. 577 (Washington, D.C.: World Bank, 1983); "Cruzado Enthroned," *The Economist*, March 8, 1986.

35. World Bank, *Brazil: Economic Memorandum* (Washington, D.C.: 1984).

36. U.S. Department of Commerce, International Trade Administration, "Investing in Mexico," Overseas Business Reports, Washington, D.C., December 1985; Youssef M. Ibrahim, "Nation in Jeopardy," *Wall Street Journal*, October 9, 1985.

37. Chandler, *Investing in Children;* Lester R. Brown and Edward C. Wolf, *Reversing Africa's Decline*, Worldwatch Paper 65 (Washington, D.C.: Worldwatch Institute, June 1985).

38. Jeffrey Bartholet, "Egypt Faces Harsh Cuts in Government Subsidies," *Washington Post*, June 26, 1986; Sadiq Ahmed et al., *Macroeconomic Effects of Efficiency Pricing in the Public Sector in Egypt*, World Bank Staff Working Paper No. 726 (Washington, D.C.: World Bank, 1985).

39. Organization of African Unity meeting reported on in African Development Bank and U.N. Economic Commission for Africa, "Economic Report on Africa 1986," Abidjan, Ivory Coast, and Addis Ababa, Ethiopia, March 1986.

40. Ibid.

41. Ibid.

42. U.S. Department of Commerce, International Trade Administration, "Doing Business in India," Overseas Business Reports, Washington, D.C., September 1985.

43. Sheetal Shankar, "A Decontrol Success Story," *Economic and Political Weekly*, June 1, 1985; Government of India, Ministry of Finance, Economic Division, *Economic Survey 1985–86* (Delhi: Controller of Publications, 1986).

44. "Death Watch At Synfuels Corporation," *Energy Daily*, December 20, 1985.

45. Johnson et al., *Agricultural Policy and Trade;* Schneider, "Cost of Farm Loss."

46. Marshall I. Goldman, *USSR in Crisis: The Failure of an Economic System* (New York: W.W. Norton & Co., 1983); Albert R. Karr, "Reagan Plan to Subsidize Wheat Sales to Soviets Will Cost U.S. $52 Million," *Wall Street Journal*, August 5, 1986.

47. "Privatization: Everybody's Doing It, Differently," *The Economist*, December 21, 1985; British Petroleum Company (BPC), *BP Statistical Review of World Energy* (London: 1985); DOE, EIA, *International Energy Annual 1984* (Washington, D.C.: 1985); DOE, EIA, *Monthly Energy Review.*

48. "Privatization: Everybody's Doing It, Differently," *The Economist;* BPC, *BP Statistical Review of World Energy;* DOE, EIA, *International Energy Annual 1984;* DOE, EIA, *Monthly Energy Review.*

49. "Privatization: Everybody's Doing It, Differently," *The Economist;* U.S. Department of the Interior, Bureau of Mines, *Minerals Yearbook, 1981, Volume 1* (Washington, D.C.: U.S. Government Printing Office, 1982).

50. Kornai, *Contradictions and Dilemmas.*

Chapter 11. Charting a Sustainable Course

1. Edward O. Wilson, "The Current State of Biological Diversity," presented at the Na-

tional Forum on Biodiversity, Smithsonian Institution and National Academy of Sciences, Washington, D.C., September 21, 1986.

2. Jonathan Leonard, "Grand Tour Through the Amazon Gasworks," *Harvard Magazine*, November-December 1985.

3. Harvey Brooks, "The Typology of Surprises in Technology, Institutions, and Development," in William C. Clark and T.E. Munn, eds., *The Sustainable Development of the Biosphere* (Old Tappan, N.J.: Prentice-Hall Publishing Co., forthcoming).

4. For a thorough description of the Global Change program, see T.F. Malone and J.G. Roederer, eds., *Global Change* (Cambridge: Cambridge University Press, 1985); M. Mitchell Waldrop, "An Inquiry into the State of the Earth," *Science*, October 5, 1984; David Dickson, "ICSU Gives Green Light to Global Change Study," *Science*, October 3, 1986.

5. Thomas F. Malone, testimony before the U.S. House of Representatives, Committee on Science and Technology, Subcommittee on Science, Research, and Technology, Washington, D.C., February 26, 1986.

6. Robert C. Cowen, "NASA Urges Intense Earth Surveillance," *Christian Science Monitor*, June 30, 1986; M. Mitchell Waldrop, "Washington Embraces Global Earth Sciences," *Science*, September 5, 1986.

7. For a discussion of current uncertainties surrounding carbon emissions, see Jill Jäger, "Floating New Evidence in the CO_2 Debate," *Environment*, September 1986; for an early effort to estimate carbon emissions due to deforestation, see G.M. Woodwell et al., "Global Deforestation: Contribution to Atmospheric Carbon Dioxide," *Science*, December 9, 1983; for the role of the oceans, see Andrew Crane and Peter Liss, "Carbon Dioxide, Climate, and the Sea," *New Scientist*, November 21, 1985.

8. National Science Foundation, "National Ozone Expedition Statement," press release, Washington, D.C., October 20, 1986.

9. Stefi Weisburd, "One Ozone Hole Returns, Another is Found," *Science News*, October 4, 1986.

10. Fred Pearce, "Unravelling a Century of Acid Pollution," *New Scientist*, September 25, 1986; results of the most recent U.S. soil survey from U.S. Department of Agriculture, Soil Conservation Service, "Preliminary 1982 National Resources Inventory" (unpublished printout), Washington, D.C., April 1984.

11. Wilson, "Current State of Biological Diversity."

12. Estimated cost of Global Change program from Dickson, "ICSU Gives Green Light"; effort needed for complete inventory of biological diversity from Edward O. Wilson, "The Biological Diversity Crisis: A Challenge to Science," *Issues in Science and Technology*, Fall 1985; technologies and analytic techniques described in more detail by Malone, testimony, Subcommittee on Science, Research, and Technology.

13. Peter Didisheim, legislative aide to Representative George E. Brown, Jr., Washington, D.C., private communication, November 3, 1986.

14. Gerard Piel, "Natural Philosophy in the Constitution," *Science*, September 5, 1986; Fred Hiatt, "6,500 College Scientists Take Anti-SDI Pledge," *Washington Post*, May 14, 1986; Barbara Carton, "In Growing Protest, Scientists Vow to Shun SDI Research Funds," *Washington Post*, October 15, 1986.

15. The World Bank, *Annual Report 1986* (Washington, D.C.: 1986); Hobart Rowen, "World Bank May Nearly Double Loans for Third World by 1990," *Washington Post*, September 22, 1986.

16. Burton I. Edelson, "Mission to Planet Earth," *Science*, January 25, 1985.

17. The evolution of China's population policy and the origins of the one-child program are discussed in H. Yuan Tien, *China:*

Demographic Billionaire, Population Bulletin, Vol. 38, No. 2 (Washington, D.C.: Population Reference Bureau, 1983).

18. Adebayo Adedeji, "Environmental Management in the Context of the Present African Economic Crisis," testimony before the World Commission on Environment and Development, Harare, Zimbabwe, September 18, 1986.

19. Current population data from Population Reference Bureau, *1986 World Population Data Sheet* (Washington, D.C.: 1986).

20. For data on fertility declines, see World Bank, *World Development Report 1985* (New York: Oxford University Press, 1985).

21. United Nations, Department of International Economic and Social Affairs, *Population Policy Briefs: The Current Situation in Developing Countries, 1985* (New York: 1986).

22. Hobart Rowen, "Birth Rate Accelerating in Africa," *Washington Post,* September 3, 1986.

23. Glenn Frankel, "In Zimbabwe, Birth Control Works," *Washington Post,* July 14, 1986.

24. "Family Planning," *Gazeta Mercantil,* June 16, 1986; for information on Mexico's initiatives, see Patrick Coleman, "The Power of Popular Music," *People* (London), Vol. 13, No. 2, 1986, "Spreading Soap Opera," *People,* Vol. 13, No. 2, 1986, and "Marketing Brings Results," *People,* Vol. 13, No. 2, 1986.

25. Robin Toner, "U.S. Withholds U.N. Population Funds," *New York Times,* August 28, 1986.

26. Ibid.

27. Atmospheric composition from "Atmosphere," in Encyclopedia Britannica, Inc., *Encyclopedia Britannica,* Volume 2 (Chicago: 1976), and James Lovelock, *Gaia: A New Look at Life on Earth* (New York: Oxford University Press, 1979).

28. Woodwell et al., "Global Deforestation"; Stephen Schneider and Randi Londer,

The Coevolution of Climate and Life (San Francisco: Sierra Club Books, 1984).

29. Maritta Koch-Weser, World Bank, Washington, D.C., private communication, November 4, 1986.

30. Erik Eckholm, *Planting for the Future: Forestry for Human Needs,* Worldwatch Paper 26 (Washington, D.C.: Worldwatch Institute, February 1979).

31. China's reforestation objectives are discussed in Vaclav Smil, *The Bad Earth* (Armonk, N.Y.: M.E. Sharpe, Inc., 1984).

32. Robert Ross, U.S. Forest Service, Washington, D.C., private communication, October 2, 1986; Francis Urban and Thomas Vollrath, *Patterns and Trends in World Agricultural Land Use* (Washington, D.C.: U.S. Government Printing Office, 1984).

33. Ward Sinclair, "USDA Readies Steps to Combat Erosion," *Washington Post,* February 18, 1986; Ken Cook, "Pinch Me, I Must Be Dreaming!" *Journal of Soil and Water Conservation,* March/April 1986; Ward Sinclair, "Conservation Plan Falls Short of Goals," *Washington Post,* June 10, 1986.

34. Research on trace gases is described in Stefi Weisburd, "Greenhouse Gases En Masse Rival CO_2," *Science News,* May 18, 1985.

35. Worldwatch Institute estimate based on economic data from Herbert R. Block, *The Planetary Product in 1980: A Creative Pause?* (Washington, D.C.: U.S. Department of State, 1981), and from International Monetary Fund, *World Economic Outlook* (Washington, D.C.: May 1986), and on primary energy consumption data from British Petroleum Company, *BP Statistical Review of World Energy* (London: 1986).

36. Warren Brown, "Fuel Standards Eased on '87, '88 Model Cars," *Washington Post,* October 3, 1986.

37. John McCaughey, "Long-Running Appliance Standards Battle is Settled," *Energy Daily,* August 15, 1986; Elizabeth

Tucker, "Appliance Efficiency Measure Urged," *Washington Post,* August 26, 1986; "Appliance Standards Ready," *Energy Daily,* October 20, 1986.

38. Elizabeth Tucker, "Energy-Standard Veto: No One Won, Groups Say," *Washington Post,* November 5, 1986.

39. "Improved Stoves Save Fuel," *Development Forum,* October 1986.

40. Philip H. Abelson, "Electric Power from the North," *Science,* June 28, 1985.

41. Han Baocheng, "The Benefits of the Three Gorges Project," *Beijing Review,* July 28, 1986.

42. Helen Gavaghan, "Time and Tide are Right for the Severn Barrage," *New Scientist,* July 17, 1986.

43. Ibid.

44. Eike Röhling and Jochen Mohnfeld, "Energy Policy and the Energy Economy in FR Germany," *Energy Policy,* December 1985; for non-nuclear alternatives in Germany, see Tony Catterall, "No Nukes, Says Bonn Party," *Energy Daily,* August 18, 1986; Thomas Land, "Sweden to Go Non-Nuclear," *Worldpaper,* January 1986; Michael Cross, "Nuclear Sweden's Final Meltdown," *New Scientist,* May 22, 1986.

45. Fred Pearce, "How to Stop the Greenhouse Effect," *New Scientist,* September 18, 1986; H.C. Cheng et al., *Effects of Energy Technology on Global CO_2 Emissions* (Washington, D.C.: U.S. Department of Energy, 1986).

46. Commission on Life Sciences, National Research Council, *Ecological Knowledge and Environmental Problem-Solving* (Washington, D.C.: National Academy Press, 1986).

47. Current data on China and India from Population Reference Bureau, *1986 World Population Data Sheet;* China's record increase in 1971 from Tien, *China: Demographic Billionaire.*

48. Ashok Rudra, "Technology Choice in Agriculture in India Over the Last Three Decades," presented at conference on Macro-Policies and Their Relationship to Appropriate Technology, Overseas Development Council and Appropriate Technology International, Washington, D.C., January 23, 1986.

49. Gerald O. Barney, Global Studies Center, Arlington, Va., private communication, October 31, 1986.

50. Population Reference Bureau, *1986 World Population Data Sheet.*

51. Celia Curtis, "Birth Control Vaccine Unveiled," *People* (London), Vol. 13, No. 2, 1986; Walter Sullivan, "Scientists Developing A New Drug That Blocks and Halts Pregnancy," *New York Times,* October 13, 1986; for a discussion of other promising contraceptive methods, see Linda E. Atkinson et al., "The Next Contraceptive Revolution," *Family Planning Perspectives,* January/February 1986.

52. Trends in contraceptive research and development are discussed in Linda E. Atkinson et al., "Worldwide Trends in Funding for Contraceptive Research and Evaluation," *Family Planning Perspectives,* September/October 1985.

53. Coal reserve data from British Petroleum Company, *BP Statistical Review.*

54. Data on tropical forest resources from U.S. Office of Technology Assessment, *Technologies to Sustain Tropical Forest Resources* (Washington, D.C.: U.S. Government Printing Office, 1984).

55. Cass Peterson, "Chlorofluorocarbon Group Supports Production Curbs," *Washington Post,* September 17, 1986; Stefi Weisburd, "Hope for International Ozone Accords," *Science News,* September 27, 1986.

56. Rushworth M. Kidder, "Barbara Tuchman," *Christian Science Monitor,* October 7, 1986.

Index